JESUS
IN AMERICA

JESUS
IN AMERICA

PERSONAL SAVIOR,

CULTURAL HERO,

NATIONAL OBSESSION

RICHARD WIGHTMAN FOX

HarperOne
An Imprint of HarperCollinsPublishers

JESUS IN AMERICA: *Personal Savior, Cultural Hero, National Obsession.* Copyright © 2004 by Richard Wightman Fox. All rights reserved. Printed in the United States of America. No part of this book may be used or reproduced in any manner whatsoever without written permission except in the case of brief quotations embodied in critical articles and reviews. For information address HarperCollins Publishers, Inc., 10 East 53rd Street, New York, NY 10022.

HarperCollins books may be purchased for educational, business, or sales promotional use. For information please e-mail the Special Markets Department at SPsales@harpercollins.com.

HarperCollins website: http://www.harpercollins.com
HarperCollins®, ✦®, and HarperOne™
are trademarks of HarperCollins Publishers.

FIRST HARPERCOLLINS PAPERBACK EDITION
PUBLISHED IN 2005

Designed by Joseph Rutt

Library of Congress Cataloging-in-Publication Data
Fox, Richard Wightman
Jesus in America : personal savior, cultural hero, national obsession /
Richard Wightman Fox. — 1st ed.
p. cm.
Includes bibliographical references and index.
ISBN 0–06–062874–x
1. Jesus Christ—History of doctrines—Modern period, 1500– 2. Theology, Doctrinal—United States—History—Modern period, 1500– 3. Jesus Christ—Cult—United States—History. 4. United States—Church history. I. Title.
BT198.F69   2003
232'.0973—dc22   2003056945

14 15 16 RRD(H) 10 9 8 7 6 5 4 3

In memory of my father
Matthew Bernard Fox
(1916–1998)

CONTENTS

JESUS
IN AMERICA

INTRODUCTION
THE FRUIT OF THY WOMB

I

My experience of Jesus begins with my father. An Irish-American Catholic television producer who moved my family from the East Coast to Los Angeles in 1953, Ben Fox was a man of prayer. And he wanted me to pray. Some of my earliest memories place me on the front seat of our woody station wagon, my legs bent under me, palm trees passing on either side as we rolled along, my father beaming over at me as I correctly put together a string of mysterious phrases. The rhythm of the syllables and the sound of the words made a comforting music. "Glory be to the Father, and to the Son, and to the Holy Ghost. As it was in the beginning, is now, and ever shall be, world without end. Amen." I had little idea what it meant, but I figured it made sense to the parents and the priests and the nuns. What mattered was that once the phrases were linked together right, the prayer felt beautiful and held the Father and the Son close together inside of it. Like my father and me in the car when his big smile traveled across the front seat from him to me and then back to him.

God was the father of Jesus, but there was that other human father, Joseph. He was a strangely uninvolved sort of father. I wondered if he was away at work all the time, the way my father was. And then there was the miraculous mother of Jesus. More moments in the car with my father as his deep voice intoned the Hail Mary, and I repeated it word for word. The mysteries of this prayer were physical and feminine. "Hail Mary, full of grace, the Lord is with Thee, Blessed art thou amongst women, and blessed is the fruit of thy womb, Jesus." Was Mary's womb named "Jesus"? What was a womb, anyway? I understood that Jesus was the plum or apricot of his mother's body. He was a delicious baby, bathed in his mother's nectar. I imagined Mary as quiet and warm like my mother, with a beautiful smile like hers. There in the car, my father's voice carried the Hail Mary and the Glory Be as sweet opportunities to know and feel. Not everything could be understood. The two prayers seemed right just as they were, not comprehensible but not confusing either. They tied Jesus together with his Father and his Blessed Mother, and they tied all three of them together with everyone else who ever prayed the same prayers. We were all humming along on the road of prayer.

Sunday Mass was all about prayer too. At St. Martin of Tours in Brentwood I saw my blustery man-of-the-world father brought to his knees, bowing his head during the holiest part of the Mass, the Canon. The priest intoned the Agnus Dei, repeating three times in Latin the words "Lamb of God, who takes away the sins of the world, have mercy on us." Then he reached the phrase "Domine, non sum dignus, ut intres sub tectum meum; sed tantum dic verbo, et sanabitur anima mea" ("Lord, I am not worthy that Thou shouldst come under my roof; but only say the word, and my soul will be healed"). I sat on the wooden pew and watched my father beating his breast three times. I watched as he worshiped Jesus and accepted what Jesus was offering: a chance to admit weakness and to hope for strength. My mother stayed home, since she was brought up Episcopalian, not Catholic. She always took my brother and me to our Catholic church when my father was away. She would sit in the pew watching and listening, not kneeling and beating her breast like the Catholics. Whenever the organ played during communion she would close her eyes to hear better. She always wished for more music. She could never get why Catholics did not want to sing as much as Episcopalians did.

When the time came to celebrate my First Communion, my father gave me a child's prayer book called *Pray Always*. Measuring four inches by two and a half inches, the little black leatherette book fit my hands perfectly. I was happy my father had given me this book full of holy pictures and words, just as I was glad later when he gave me an illustrated missal on my confirmation. He inscribed them both with fond words etched in his jagged handwriting. A pearl-colored crucifix was nestling in the inside cover of *Pray Always* with a one-inch-high gold-metal Jesus languishing on it. On the opposite page was printed a "Prayer before a Crucifix" whose words felt important and a little scary: "With deep affection and grief of soul I ponder within myself and mentally contemplate Thy five most precious wounds; having before my eyes that which David spake in prophecy: 'They pierced My hands and My feet; they have numbered all My bones.'" I knew that the five precious wounds were the ones Jesus had received during his Passion, when he was pierced in his feet, his hands, his side.

To be a child in the Catholic Church was to be aware of the suffering body. Father Murray, the pastor at St. Martin's, talked about martyred saints in his sermons, how they were beaten and bloodied for Christ's sake. They stood all the pain because they could talk straight to God in the middle of it. They would get a resurrected body in heaven, said Father Murray, but as I listened in the pew I was still thinking about their physical pain. If you followed Jesus, your body was going to be affected. I was not given Bible verses to memorize like Protestant children, I was not given hymns to sing, but the responses that I committed to memory from my blue paperback Baltimore Catechism, first published in 1891 and revised in 1941, taught me that agony accompanied glory: "Why did God make us? To show forth His goodness and to share with us

His everlasting happiness in heaven." "What were the chief sufferings of Christ? His bitter agony of soul, His bloody sweat, His cruel scourging, His crowning with thorns, His crucifixion, and His death on the cross."

I could see him suffering, in huge relief, on the life-size wooden crucifix attached to the wall behind the altar. During the hours for confession on late Saturday afternoons, the California sunshine would stream through a certain stained-glass window, casting a rich red light exactly on the wound in Christ's side. His head drooped; in death he looked more sorrowful than extinguished. When I looked at his face in that afternoon light, I would think of the part of the Salve Regina that goes, "To thee do we cry, poor banished children of Eve, to thee do we send up our sighs, mourning and weeping in this valley of tears." I felt sad looking at him, but the sadness had admiration and hope mixed into it.

The fourteen Stations of the Cross illustrated the story of Christ's suffering in even greater detail. Painted on the sides and back walls of St. Martin's, the Stations depicted his last hours. "Jesus is Condemned to Die" was the first Station, and "Jesus is laid in the tomb" was the last. They told the story of his suffering as the Roman soldiers pushed and prodded him up the path to Calvary. Simon of Cyrene helped him carry the cross, Veronica wiped his face, he said goodbye to his mother, and he met the women of Jerusalem. The ninth Station was the one that drew me in: "Jesus Falls the Third Time." Those five words mesmerized me. They rang with a stark finality that made me queasy. Did Jesus actually know it was the last time he would fall? Or was he too dizzy and disoriented to know what was happening? What a terrible kind of suffering! Maybe Jesus suffered less on the cross because at least by then he knew he had reached the end of his human road (see fig. 9).

The Stations and the crucifix instructed us that the human road was challenging for everyone. The sacraments and the prayers gave us support. So did the teachings of the church. I was let out of public elementary school early every Wednesday for catechism class at church. I was probably about ten when Father Murray came to the class and announced that anyone who received communion every first Friday over nine consecutive months would get to see Jesus before dying. My father's son, I was the only kid in the class who decided this was too rich a prize to pass up. True, getting up in time to make seven o'clock Mass on the proper Friday nine months in a row was an ordeal. But I had my mother, willing to drive me to church early. I succeeded in making eight straight first Fridays, but then forgot all about the ninth. What a shock when I realized, too late for Mass, what day it was. I felt horrible. The next day I went to the sacristy to ask Father Murray what I should do. "Just take communion next month," he answered, "and it'll be fine." For a moment I was elated, but even before reaching home I knew Father Murray had to be wrong. He should have taken the hard line: nine more months of trudging to early-morning communion. His casual answer led me to question the whole scheme. If I was going to be granted the sight of Jesus before I died, I knew it was going to be Christ's doing, not mine.

One Saturday afternoon a few years later, I was sitting alone at the back of the church after going to confession. Having done my penance of Hail Marys and Our Fathers, I was looking straight ahead at the crucifix, then looking sideways to the ninth Station of the Cross: Jesus Falls the Third Time. I suppose I was trying to pray, but mostly I was just looking at Jesus. Without warning two insights entered my mind, one on top of the other. I felt them rushing into my head and took them as real experiences of illumination. The first was direct: religion might be a completely human creation, God could be an invention of our minds, and Jesus could be a wonderful wise man, nothing more. All the practices and structures of faith, the prayers, the statues, the breast-beating, the windows, seemed human. The second insight amounted to a judgment on the first: the initial insight was too neat and too stark. It presumed knowledge about something we could not know. It arbitrarily limited the real to the visible or provable. And it took the mystery out of life. Human beings did invent religions, I told myself, but they did not invent God. They set up religions as a way of experiencing and re-experiencing their feeling that a God who lay beyond all human reckoning was somehow present in their midst. Jesus was a unique person with a double identity: a man whose teachings could be studied, and the mysterious emissary of an incomprehensibly grand divine power. Jesus was irresistibly elusive: available to be known yet always beyond knowing.

My father had given me a double gift. He wanted me to pray and he wanted me to think. Questions were welcome, a sign of God's benevolence in creating the human mind. My early experience ensured that there would be questions aplenty. My mother sat home while I prayed at Mass, or else she sat quietly in the pew because my father was away. She loved Jesus too, and met him in the lines of her favorite hymns from childhood—hymns like Charles Wesley's rousing Easter creation "Christ the Lord Is Risen Today." She sang it as a child in the choir at her Episcopal church. It is a cascade of "Alleluias" along with fine poetry such as "Lives again our glorious King / Where, O death, is now thy sting? / Once He died our souls to save / Where thy victory, O grave?" My mother never tried to teach me anything about religion, but she taught me anyway. She devoted herself to others. The paths to Jesus are many.

So are the paths to God. My best friend growing up in Los Angeles was Jewish. I met Ken Adashek when I was ten. We played Little League baseball together, went to the movies, sat in the same classrooms. In late December we would compare Hanukkah presents and Christmas presents. I thought he was lucky to have eight nights of gifts, and he thought I was lucky to get a huge bonanza on a single morning. He was not envious of my Christmas tree, though he did wonder why his next-door neighbors, also Jewish, got to have a tree when his family did not. It never occurred to me for a moment that Ken would be better off being a Christian, any more than that my mother should be a Catholic. I loved watching Ken's family light their menorah candles and hearing them recite some Hebrew prayers together. It brought to mind all the centuries when Ken's European ancestors lit candles and spoke those same words. His Reform synagogue was directly across Sunset Boulevard from St. Martin of Tours Church. When he had his confirmation I sat in the congregation and listened in proud amazement as he spoke to the assembly in Hebrew. If only Catholics could have a confirmation ritual like that, I said to myself. Ken would come to my church and I would recite a Latin prayer in front of the congregation, and afterward we would celebrate by getting our gloves and playing catch while I told him what the Latin meant.

I look back in wonder and appreciation at my father's linkage of Catholic conviction with urgent inquiry. One day in his old age he was riding in a Santa Monica city bus when he overheard the driver talking about Jesus. The driver was engaged in discussion with an ebullient woman sitting over to his right. Her hand was resting on the shopping bags piled up beside her. My father got up to join in. The woman put the bags on the floor so he could sit down. Before long they were the last three people on the bus. The driver pulled the bus over to the side of the street and they remained there for half an hour exchanging views on whether the resurrection was a fact or only a story. My father kept digging for the argument that would persuade the other two it was a fact. One part of him wanted to seal the victory; the other part wanted to listen to what they had to say. He reveled in the conversation as much as the conclusion. He called me up to tell me what had happened.

II

It is April 21, 2000, Good Friday. Christians around the world are commemorating the crucifixion of their Son of God, a Jewish healer and teacher from Nazareth who ran afoul of the Roman authorities in Palestine about 1,970 years ago. The crucifixion of Jesus, all scholars are agreed, is a demonstrable historical fact. Christians claim to know, by faith, much more about Jesus, starting with his resurrection on Easter. But we can all know, by studying history, that Jesus was crucified. The historical evidence is much clearer about that than it is about such matters as his birthplace (many biblical scholars doubt the historicity of the Bethlehem story and believe he was born in Nazareth) or his trial before Pilate (many scholars believe that scene to be fictional in whole or in part).

I am walking along in the Via Crucis (Way of the Cross) procession in the Colonia neighborhood in Oxnard, California. For thirty years the Chicano Catholics of Colonia, whose settlement there precedes U.S. statehood (1850), have performed this Good Friday reenactment. A bearded, barefoot Jesus in a long white robe and a crown of thorns drags his cross slowly down Juanita Avenue. Roman soldiers right on his heels are whipping his red-stained back. His eyes are cast down. Hundreds of the faithful, including a throng of children, press tightly behind the soldiers. Residents stand on balconies, and shoppers clog sidewalks in front of Lupita's Panadería and García's Discoteca y Video (see fig. 4).

Three times Jesus falls under the weight of the cross. When the procession reaches the plateau on the grassy field behind Nuestra Señora de Guadalupe Church, the Roman soldiers lay Jesus and the two thieves on their crosses, then hoist them upright (see fig. 5). Small children sitting behind a rope one hundred feet away scoot under it for a better view. Many minutes pass before the soldiers lift a sponge on a stick to Christ's lips (the gospels say the sponge was filled with vinegar). Many more minutes pass before they put a microphone on the end of the same stick so we can all hear Jesus say, "Dios mío, Dios mío, ¿porqué me has desamparado?" ("My God, my God, why have you abandoned me?") and "Padre, en tus manos encomiendo mi espíritu" ("Father, into your hands I commend my spirit"). Four- and five-year-old children sit transfixed as Jesus expires. The soldiers take down the body, and Mary, with a microphone concealed in her bright blue robe, sobs into it. Her wailing unsettles the crowd for another quarter of an hour.

Finally a soldier slings Jesus over his shoulder and takes him away as the crowd disperses. This soldier and his comrades are now out of character, chatting with friends and family as they depart the scene. No one is paying any attention to Jesus, the only one left in character. He is a limp rag of flesh bouncing on the soldier's shoulder as he is carried to the sacristy. In the church hundreds of people have already assembled for a communion service. Padre Eusebio Elizondo reminds everyone that in the original, first-century Via Crucis, death was not the end for Jesus. He rose again on the third day, and his body is present in ours when we eat the bread of life and believe in him.

The next day I am in the audience at the modern glistening Crystal Cathedral, where the Garden Grove Community Church is putting on a pageant called "The Glory of Easter." This professional production features equity actors in the main roles. Tickets cost fifteen to thirty dollars, a fair price given the elaborate special effects, live camels and horses, and scores of period costumes for the extras drawn from the congregation. The Reverend Robert Schuller launched this church in a drive-in theatre in 1955, and even today there is an "in-car worship center" adjoining the massive glass-walled cathedral—a Philip Johnson creation of 1980 that resembles an especially sleek New York City skyscraper. The little vehicles patrolling the parking area have "Traffic Ministry" painted on their sides. Schuller has mastered the upbeat message of self-development and mental peace through Christian belief, the liberal doctrine made famous in the twentieth century by Norman Vincent Peale.

Schuller has also mastered television preaching. His weekly "Hour of Power" contested the airwave dominance of conservative televangelism in the 1980s and 1990s. In a 2001 telecast Schuller said that Philippians 4:13 expressed the main idea of his ministry: "I can do all things through Christ which strengtheneth me." He called that verse a "scientifically provable" statement. "You are a creature designed by God to have positive expectations for your future."

People who succeed, he told his sun-drenched audience, have a
sense of direction, a passion, and a drive. Jesus will gladly grant
you those things. Some televangelists mocked Schuller's straightforward empowerment message, but no one could doubt either his
success or the impact of can-do thinking on many twentieth-century
evangelists, including some of the most conservative.[1]

The Crystal Cathedral seats almost three thousand, and at the
start of "The Glory of Easter" the Reverend Schuller's recorded voice
tells the full house that what we are about to see is the staging of "an
historical truth, the way it really happened." What we actually see is
a play composed by an author who had to choose among four gospel
accounts that tell the story of the Passion of Jesus with different, and
sometimes contradictory, details. "The Glory of Easter" contains a
brief crucifixion scene—ten seconds at most, as a curtain is lifted to
reveal an actor playing Christ on the cross—but the resurrection
scene goes on for many minutes. White-robed women wearing angel
wings shoot forth from the rafters, suspended by wires, and perform
a synchronized, midair ballet. Triumphant music and a laser-light
show announce that Jesus has risen.

The Oxnard and Garden Grove Passion pageants try to represent the fundamental truth about Jesus. The Catholic one centers on
the crucified body of Christ; the Protestant one, on the miracle-
working savior and resurrected Lord. Christian viewers will disagree about how successfully the pageants communicate gospel
truths. Many will find the Via Crucis performance interminable,
maudlin, and so fixated on Christ's flesh that it forgets his eternal
spirit. Many will find "The Glory of Easter" glib, passionless, and
dominated by state-of-the-art effects that eclipse Christ's simple humanity. But everyone, Christian and non-Christian alike, will agree
that the performances are cultural events as well as religious ones.
They are cultural in being artistic, but in a deeper sense they are
cultural in displaying some basic rituals of American life. They give
us a glimpse of what many Americans believe and how they act
out their beliefs. They show how certain sacred traditions brought

to the Americas from Europe centuries ago have been adapted to contemporary life. Whether Jesus is the eternal Son of God or only a great first-century Palestinian Jewish wise man, there is no doubt about his prominence as an American cultural figure over the last four centuries. For most American Christians today, Jesus is still "true God and true man," as the church decreed at Chalcedon in the year 451 of the Common Era. The actual Jesus was such a true man that he was embodied culturally as well as biologically in first-century Galilee. He was always Jesus of *Nazareth* in his own lifetime, always a practicing Jew from Galilee. Only after death did his Jewish and Gentile followers come to know him as Jesus, the "Christ" (meaning "messiah," or "anointed one"). Only much later did he completely lose his character as a Palestinian Jew and become firmly established in cultural terms as a trans-historical, divine member of the Trinity.[2]

Neither Jesus of Nazareth nor Paul of Tarsus, the great builder of early Christianity, could have guessed it, but as the centuries crept along, each successive evangelized society would embody Jesus differently. Christians of later epochs would have to swallow the hard truth that even if Jesus Christ remained always "the same yesterday, and today, and for ever," as Paul's Epistle to the Hebrews (13:8) put it, he had entered history as a cultural figure whose shape and meaning shifted. He would be perpetually reborn in one culture after another. Whether he was in fact God (as most Christians believe), a lesser but still divine being (as some Christians believe), or a wise human being inspired by God (as some Christians and many non-Christians believe), he was indisputably a man walking the earth in the first century. His incarnation guaranteed that each later culture would grasp him anew, for each would have a different view of what it meant to be human. Jesus had to be reborn if he was going to inspire or even make sense to people in every era.

Of course the broad features of Christ's identity were passed along from one culture to another. At different times greater or

lesser weight was assigned to his roles as divine king, sacrificial redeemer, holy child, apocalyptic prophet, miracle worker and healer,
wisdom teacher, social critic and reformer, luminous personality.
Jesus assumed regional and national shapes as those perennial features of his identity were adapted to local conditions. In nineteenth-
century America, for example, urban and rural working-class
Catholics, Baptists, and Methodists all appealed to Jesus for support as they sought leverage against mostly Anglo American cultural, political, and economic establishments. They made Jesus a
democrat, a man of the people, a crucified carpenter. They did not
stop regarding him as "Lord" and "King." Those patriarchal labels
were vital supports for Baptist and Methodist men as they eased
women out of the few positions of authority they had managed to
obtain during the hectic early-nineteenth-century years of evangelical expansion. Hierarchical labels for Jesus were also important
supports for the episcopal hierarchies (i.e., bishops) of the Catholics, Episcopalians, and Methodists. Jesus was reborn again and
again in nineteenth-century America, as one group after another
construed his divinity or his humanity in novel ways.[3]

In retrospect we might imagine that Jesus helped unite nineteenth-
century Catholic and Protestant Americans. When they jointly encountered Native Americans or Asian immigrants, he probably
did. But as they confronted each other in the nineteenth and even
twentieth centuries, Catholics and Protestants used Christ mainly
to emphasize their differences. Each group tried to protect him
from contamination by the other. Occasionally ethnic and religious
animosity turned violent—the burning of Catholic convents or
churches, assaults on Protestant neighborhoods—but in the main
the war was ideological. Pitched cultural battles were fought over
many issues, including the right way to represent and worship
Christ. Catholics took heart from the image of Jesus as the physically abused, suffering servant, a depiction the Irish had already
nurtured under English oppression. It was a portrayal guaranteed
to alienate, if not disgust, most Protestants, who regarded it as me-

dieval and idolatrous. Each group got to savor the conviction that it was being faithful to the original Jesus of the gospels.[4]

Protestants, especially northern, educated, liberal ones, held Jesus up as the ultimate individualist, the model of the self-made man. Catholics and many other Protestants praised him as the consummate family man. Catholics, naturally, kept him tied to his Holy Family of origin, an only son and a celibate adult. Protestants gave him siblings and imagined he might have been married. Jesus could be pushed in either direction, autonomous individual or family pillar. The solitary divine-human person promoted the relentless northern Protestant assault upon any customary practice that got in the way of personal development or social progress. Modernizing Americans liberalized Jesus into a God of pure "love" who had nothing but scorn for inherited "law," a radical critic of all "Pharisees" who preferred old-fashioned constraints to boundless freedom. Meanwhile, the Catholics' Holy Family member and the Protestants' personal savior could stand for the importance of tradition. With Jesus as their hero Americans could have their cake of old-time values and devour it too. They could get divine sanction for making all things new while believing that they honored their most precious inheritance of all, Christ himself. They could see themselves as a chosen people—the ancient Hebrew notion adopted in the seventeenth century by the Puritans—but a people chosen now for free-spirited development as individuals. Jesus, the chosen Son, provided vital underpinning for this *novus ordo seclorum* (new order of the ages): a nation of individuals embarked on an open-ended journey of territorial expansion, economic innovation, and social experimentation. As a symbolic figure, Jesus could offer moral support for that journey while also raising moral objections. Protestant and Catholic Americans could never have remade their nation in the nineteenth century without trusting Jesus to propel them forward while steering them away from sin.

The overall national infatuation with Jesus has been deepened by an array of subcultural traditions of allegiance to him. African

Americans, Latino Americans, Asian Americans, Irish Americans, Italian Americans, Anglo Americans, Native Americans, and many others have developed their identities in relation to Christ. Within each group he helps to link the past and present. Individual immigrants can choose to worship him in ways familiar to them from the Old World or select new ones that stand for and help speed their adaptation to America. Today many Latino Catholics are combining old and new by relying on Catholic rituals when marking important life events and attending evangelical or Pentecostal Protestant services when seeking emotionally potent encounters with Christ. Hispanic Protestantism takes over from the Catholic tradition a far more corporeal Jesus than most American Protestants recognize. This physical Jesus fits naturally with the hands-on healing practices of much Protestant revivalism and Pentecostalism.[5]

The African American tie to Jesus is the most historically complex of all the ethnically differentiated faiths in him. While it stemmed originally from a forced adjustment to the white world, it ended up exerting a major impact on the southern white Protestant culture to which blacks had been forced to adapt. Early on Jesus emerged for some African American slaves as the figure who bridged the African past and the American present. By the early nineteenth century, slaves had become Christians in large numbers. African convictions about the living presence of the dead and the reality of the unseen world made Jesus a powerful presence in dreams as well as wakeful states. Thanks to his paradoxical place as Lord and servant of both highborn and low, Jesus came to stand in African American religion for the mysterious agency through which, against all appearances, the last would ultimately—and even now, in faith—be made first. The last had a forceful cultural impact on the first. White Protestantism immediately understood the religious power of the black spiritual. African American creations such as "Steal Away to Jesus" or "Balm in Gilead" spoke of distinctively black yearnings for temporal as well as spiritual freedom and consolation. But whites could appropriate those spirituals as pleas for Jesus to free them from bondage to sin. "If you can't preach like Peter," declares the final verse of "Balm in Gilead," "if you can't pray like Paul, just tell the love of Jesus, and say He died for all."[6]

III

Over the nineteenth and twentieth centuries the United States became a modern, industrial society while remaining vigorously religious. At the start of the twenty-first century the United States was by far the most religious of advanced industrial societies. In 2003 eight in ten adult Americans said they were Christians (about half saying they were Protestant, about one-fourth saying they were Catholic). Four in ten Americans said they were "born again" or evangelical Christians. Four in ten also said they attended religious services every week—a figure roughly double that of most of the industrialized West. Surveys in the 1970s and 1980s showed that a colossal 70 percent of adult Americans said they believed Jesus was God or the Son of God, not just the founder of a great religion like Muhammad or the Buddha. Roughly the same proportion was certain Christ was resurrected from the dead. Half of all Americans— 60 percent of the Protestants and 40 percent of the Catholics— reported that they had "tried to encourage someone to believe in Jesus Christ or to accept Him as his or her Savior."[7]

One study in 2001 suggested that the Christian percentage of the adult American population fell in the 1990s, from 86 percent in 1990 to 77 percent in 2001. The Christian percentage was down not because other religions were attracting former Christians, but because the unchurched segment of the adult population was up. (Because of overall population growth, the *number* of American Christians rose over the decade of the 1990s—by eight million— even as their *proportion* declined.) Those adult Americans claiming no religion at all have almost doubled as a proportion of the population. Most of these new secularists are former (at least nominal) Christians, and like their forebears in earlier centuries, they may continue to feel an ethical or cultural attachment to Jesus. Sociologists Michael Hout and Claude Fisher note that many people who have stopped calling themselves Christians have not surrendered their Christian beliefs. They simply hold those beliefs less passionately or dogmatically than many practicing Christians do.[8]

The non-Christian part of the population has grown too, but not significantly enough to affect overall American attachment to Jesus. Jews have actually dropped in absolute numbers since 1990 (from 3.1 million adults to 2.8 million) and are now 1.3 percent of the adult population. Muslims, Buddhists, and Hindus have all at least doubled their numbers since 1990. There are now well over a million Muslim Americans, a million Buddhist Americans, and almost a million Hindus. But Muslim, Buddhist, and Hindu citizens still total less than 2 percent of the population.[9]

Even if Jesus is losing a small percentage of his religious disciples in America at the start of the twenty-first century, he is certainly an omnipresent symbol of religious, ethical, and philosophical seeking. He is so pervasive culturally that some representations of him have no apparent religious reference at all. Over the last generation, for example, his crucifix has taken on a secular life of its own as a hip fashion statement. But the commercialization of the cross—and of Jesus himself in secular as well as Christian music—may still carry with it a moral or spiritual yearning that marks it as religious. It is hard to separate religious from secular piety where Jesus is concerned. Amy Grant's 1991 album "Heart in Motion," which features the blockbuster romantic hit "That's What Love Is For," ends with "Hope Set High": try as you might "to see the light" on your own, you find out that "anything good" in life comes "from Jesus." Amy Grant identifies herself as a "religious" artist, one who happens also to sing secular songs. A more complete intermingling of the secular and the religious is revealed in the free-floating cultural status of "Amazing Grace." Is it a secular song or a religious hymn? Written in the late eighteenth century by the English pastor Joseph Newton, a former captain of a slave ship, it is frequently sung today at public events that are not explicitly Christian but are explicitly reflective, meditative, or celebratory. It has evolved into an "American" anthem affirming the whole local or national community's relation to God, or to a broadly spiritual if not religious "Judeo-Christian" tradition. Perhaps the hymn works in that secularized context because it never mentions Jesus but does feature some recognizably Jesus language (the blind see, the lost are found).[10]

Over two-thirds of the adults in one of the most modernized and industrialized countries in the world believe that a first-century Palestinian Jewish teacher and healer was and is the incarnation of God. Even if many of these people merely endorse the divinity of Christ when a pollster prods them to think about it, this percentage is about twice as large as the figure in most of the industrial West. This is a striking instance of American uniqueness. Why do so many Americans remain persuaded that Jesus is divine? Part of the explanation is that Christian churches have long since entered the deep fabric of American social life. They are community centers and charitable organizations as well as places of worship. People still believe in Jesus because they wish to belong to the assemblies that preach and celebrate him. Belief follows, without being wholly determined by, social placement and aspiration. In Europe, where the churches have tended to stick to charity work and to religious rites narrowly defined, leaving community-building and social fellowship aside, rates of churchgoing and membership—and of belief in Christ—are substantially lower.[11]

Churchgoers may like the social benefits of religion yet still practice their faith primarily because they believe in God. Their piety is not only a function of inherited habit, lifestyle choice, or social calculation. In the face of the mysteries and joys and reversals of their lives, many people seek the answers, comforts, and provocations that religion can provide. Where else can they go to express a spectrum of deep feelings about love, peace, sin, loss, and justice? Where else are they to look for help confronting the ultimate dilemmas of existence, or for maintaining emotional bonds with their ancestors? Where else can they assemble regularly to marvel at the wonders and bemoan the betrayals of everyday life? Jesus, for most Americans, is the God-man who offers forgiveness, succor, and hope. In the classic dialectic of Christian religious experience, he makes them feel better by loving them and he makes them feel worse by reminding them of their failure to love him and their neighbors.

Yet even when faith is deeply spiritual it is also cultural, the product of a group's history. Most Americans have their religious experiences with Jesus because for historical reasons it is he, not Buddha or Muhammad, who is recognized as the appointed messenger of divine wisdom—and in the classic Christian vision, as the mediator who reopened the channels of supernatural grace. Most American Christians believe Christ to be a transcendent and unchanging divine person. But human beings seeking to know such a resplendent person are forced to rely on culturally available forms of knowing. Naturally, those sanctioned means of knowing change with time. Recognizing that knowledge of Jesus is culturally shaped does not compromise his divinity. Suppose there is a God who wishes to make contact with individuals through their religious experiences. That God would have no choice but to work with the cultural forms that people can recognize as religious experiences. And those forms evolve historically. Today God does not communicate with Americans through omens or dreams or thunderbolts or bodily possession or the visions of saintly children as often as he did in earlier centuries. God communicates in modes that are culturally prominent in our day, such as silent prayer, or speaking in tongues, or physical and mental healing, or contemplating nature beside a mountain brook. These cultural forms change very slowly, and forms that have fallen into disuse are sometimes revived in later eras. In the United States today many people become or remain believing Christians because they wish to keep having the kinds of Bible-based religious experiences they imagine their ancestors had. They join churches to have a social life, but not just any social life. They choose a community either because it has preserved religious customs they cherish from the past or because it proclaims values they have embraced as adults. One reason why the Church of Jesus Christ of Latter-day Saints (the Mormons) is expanding so dramatically is that many former Catholics and Protestants see it as the most fully committed to "family values" of any American religion.[12]

IV

The name of Jesus, Emerson said in 1838, "is not so much written as ploughed into the history of this world." For almost two millennia Jesus has been ploughed and reploughed into Western thought, worship, and consciousness. Every generation has inherited all earlier conceptions and practices about Jesus and then added more of its own. That puts me in a challenging position as the author of this book. No single volume can offer full coverage of what millions of believers and nonbelievers, even in a single geographical area, have said, written, and felt about Jesus. Far more will have to be left out than included. The writer of John's Gospel said it well at the end of his labors: "And there are also many other things which Jesus did, the which, if they should be written every one, I suppose that even the world itself could not contain the books that should be written. Amen." Amen indeed. The only way to begin to do justice to American experiences of Jesus is to acknowledge at the outset that the topic can only be pointed at, not covered. In fact, the more you look at it, the bigger it gets. "Jesus in America" includes all the theology, preaching, worship, literature, art, music, plays, films, architecture, letters, and diaries devoted to him, along with countless cultural practices from Christmas pageants and municipal crèches to public prayers at the start of high school football games. The Library of Congress owns 17,239 books about Jesus and 7,719 more about God. A good number of them were published overseas, but many of those circulated widely in the American colonies and the United States.[13]

But all that is only the beginning. My subject is not just the history of images of Jesus, ideas about Jesus, and customs concerning Jesus. It is the history of American experiences of Jesus. Think of the American yearning for Jesus over the last four centuries as a din of sung and spoken language, thought, and feeling. Christians have expressed their craving to be close to Christ in a chorus of praise and petition that has peaked on the Sabbath but been audible too outside the boundaries of formal worship. Then consider the hundreds and thousands of people in America who have been praying silently to Jesus at every instant of the last four hundred years, in a chorus of pleading and thanksgiving that has never dimmed. If believers are right that their Lord and savior is hearing every word of this, imagine Christ's powers of attention. For Jesus there can be no respite. A God who hears everything, patiently and sympathetically, must take listening as a form of sustenance. I think it was Thomas Aquinas who mused that heaven would be a paradise of constant conversation with multiple partners at once. Easy for a contemplative Dominican monk to say, a man with all the silence he could desire. But that state of constant conversation may be what it is like for a divine Jesus, especially if those believers are right who claim that Christ speaks to them as well as listens.

What I can hope to do in my book is to keep my ear open to that collective cry for Christ while throwing some light on the basic historical patterns and particularities of Americans' devotion to Jesus. I want to document the diversity of American experiences of Christ across time—not every one of them, but a fair sample. I want to examine the intersection between Christ's multiple identities and certain historical events and trends—not all of them, but some of the most important ones. I want to analyze how Jesus crossed and helped reconstitute the very blurry line between the "religious" and the "secular" in American history. Most of all, I want to think about the relation between faith and culture without presuming that faith is simply the product of culture. I do not know whether believers are right about Jesus' being a divine Comforter who sends them his spirit. I do think that their belief in him makes perfect sense, and I know that their belief has profoundly shaped American and world history.

I restrict myself to American experiences of Jesus despite the distortion imposed by that choice. The seventeenth-century North American encounter between Indians and the European Christ took place in the larger context of Caribbean and South American meetings with European cultures. The Puritans and other colonial residents of the future United States were of course literally English, since there was not yet a United States. But Puritanism, fundamental to the formation of American national mythologies and to Protestant American piety in the eighteenth and nineteenth centuries, was an English as well as American religious movement. The evangelical revival of the eighteenth century was trans-Atlantic, not American. Nineteenth-century American Christians read John Keats and Ernst Renan and Mrs. Humphrey Ward on Jesus alongside Ralph Waldo Emerson and Charles Sheldon. The logic behind my choice of "America"—the United States and its colonial antecedents, with a nod to seventeenth-century New France, of which Protestant New Englanders were acutely conscious—is that in America the cultural incarnation of Jesus eventually took on some discrete meanings and forms. Again and again Jesus has helped Americans understand themselves as distinctively American—sometimes, ironically, by lending support to those who thought the truest "American" perspective was a cosmopolitan, trans-national one. The great Jewish scholar Joseph Klausner wrote in 1925 that Jesus of Nazareth was such a radical critic of national loyalties that he questioned even the Jewish nation, without which the Jewish religion that Jesus loved was bound to languish. Christ's allegiance was to God, and to the purification of each individual's engagement with God, whatever the cost might be to a stable social peace or a secure national identity. In the nineteenth and twentieth centuries most Americans tried to combine Christ's concern for personal purity with a decidedly un-Christlike embrace of the nation. Some Christians, aware of the contradiction, tried to adapt their Americanism to their Christianity by redefining patriotism as a trans-national faith in liberty, democracy, or modernization.[14]

I was tempted to limit this book to the post-revolutionary United States, permitting a more detailed treatment of the last two centuries. I decided that some coverage of the colonial period was indispensable for grasping what happened to Jesus in America in the nineteenth century. Essential contours of American devotion to Christ were "ploughed" into American culture well before the Revolution. Later developments cannot be understood apart from what preachers and thinkers such as George Whitefield and Jonathan Edwards and Benjamin Franklin said and did about Jesus in the eighteenth century. What they did and said, in turn, can be understood only in relation to what Catholics as well as Protestants were doing and saying in early-seventeenth-century New France, New Spain, and New England. It is crucial to start with the Catholic and Protestant Christs of the seventeenth century to show that Catholicism was a major force in America from the beginning, despite the small percentage of Catholics in the population before the 1840s. Protestants saw their own settlement in America from the seventeenth century forward as a brake upon Catholic influence in the New World. Indeed, they hoped eventually to liberate Indians from the "popish" errors to which they had already been exposed.

Yet in the end I have given more attention to Protestants than to Catholics. If this book were a history of American religions, I would say more about Catholicism and other non-Protestant religions. But in my view a book on Jesus in America has to lean to the Protestants. Over the course of American history Protestants did much more innovating in their conceptions and experiences of Jesus.

Protestants have recurrently voiced a double aspiration: to restore Jesus to his original purity—corrupted as much by their fellow Protestants as by Catholics—and to remake society in the image of his "Kingdom." On the whole Catholics have been satisfied that they already have complete access to the real Jesus. True, like Protestants they have experienced revivals of piety. But they have felt little desire to purify their cultural incarnations of him—save in the Vatican II period of the late twentieth century. Compared to Calvinistic Protestants, they have also been generally skeptical about remaking society, despite often seeing Jesus as a broadly "pro-life" advocate of social justice for the poor and mistreated. The Protestant drive to get closer to Jesus fuels a perennial quest to reimagine him so that he can be fully himself and fully usable in the struggle to transform society. I certainly am not implying that Protestant versions of Jesus are more significant religiously than Catholic ones. In America there have simply been more Protestant versions, just as there have always (in English-speaking America) been more Protestants than Catholics. Today Roman Catholics are the single largest American denomination, but Protestants still outnumber them by more than two to one. In earlier times Protestants were even more dominant.[15]

V

This book is for believers and nonbelievers alike. It is not a book about whether one should believe in Jesus, but about how Americans have believed in and portrayed him. Those who know a living Christ by faith share some important ground with those who do not. Both groups must agree that Jesus has had a historical trajectory within culture, even if (as most believers hold) he is also a divine being who transcends culture. "There is nothing in history," Emerson said in the 1840s, "to parallel the influence of Jesus Christ." Emerson was astonished at the staying power of a divine

Jesus in "these learned and practical nations of modern Europe and America." He predicted that a thousand years hence people would have a hard time believing that nineteenth-century "physicians, metaphysicians, mathematicians, critics, and merchants" had taken seriously the idea that a "poor Jewish boy" had been the incarnation of "the Triune God." Whatever our descendents may think a thousand years hence, we can be sure that a vast majority of Americans in 2004 give Jesus their credence and their love. For most believers he is a personal savior, for most nonbelievers he is a philosophical and ethical sage, and for all Americans he is an immediately recognizable cultural symbol. Jesus continues to help a huge population of Americans make sense of their deepest hopes, fears, cravings, and transgressions.[16]

In all likelihood Jesus is permanently layered into the American cultural soil. Yet given how much he has changed in the last four hundred years of his American incarnations, he will surely evolve substantially in response to social and religious developments we cannot foresee. Old depictions of Jesus will resurface, and new ones will emerge. His identity is elastic. There is no single Jesus, in America or anywhere else. He can lead crusades like a warrior and he can turn the other cheek. He can thrash about in the temple and cup a blind person's face in his hands. He can withdraw into the desert like John the Baptist and he can gather the little children. He can call for fulfilling the law, then for destroying it. He can linger with his mother and tell his disciples to leave their families behind. He can warn that the end-time is near and sketch the outlines of a new society. Americans will try their best to make him a predictable source of comfort, but he will remain unpredictable. New prophets will rise up to remind their countrymen that Jesus delivers condemnation along with solace, and many Americans will try to follow his injunction to lose their lives so as to find them.

As long as Americans take Jesus as their personal savior or cultural hero, some of them will carry their devotion to the point of obsession. Some will take him to be the sole answer to life's conundrums or the single valid path to salvation, and a segment of those believers will view alternative faiths with alarm. Some non-Christians will respond obsessively themselves, fearing the fanaticism that they detect either on or just below the surface of Christian conviction. They are right that Christianity, like all religions (including atheism), attracts some people who are adamant about the sins of others and impressed with their own purity. But even those Christians who worry more about the beam in their own eye rather than the splinter in their neighbor's eye will strike some nonbelievers as overwrought, if not compulsive. Jesus preached permanent revolution in the self. For a follower of Christ there can be no end to the self-scrutiny, and no end to the discovery of self-love masquerading as holiness. If Jesus keeps his lofty station as a prime American cultural hero in centuries to come, it will be for two reasons: because so many Christians find him useful as a means of congratulating themselves, and because so many find him indispensable as a critic of their self-congratulation.

For any foreseeable future, a large majority of Americans will continue praising Christ. They will find ingenious new ways to do as "Balm in Gilead" suggests: "just tell the love of Jesus." At the Iowa State Fair in 1999, champion butter sculptor Norma "Duffy" Lyon took a ton of butter and produced a rendition of the Last Supper. She had been sculpting butter for forty years, and was famous across the Midwest for her "butter cow." She chose the Last Supper to mark her seventieth birthday as well as her forty years of sculpting. It took her two weeks of work. The newspaper reported that "twelve disciples, with their robes, long hair and beards, appear in deep thought as their eyes look toward Jesus Christ." Mrs. Lyon, a mother of nine and grandmother of twenty-three, showed she was a biblical interpreter as well as a sculptor. According to the newspaper she "created the disciples in more relaxed positions than people might expect. Lyon, a lay minister at St. Patrick Catholic Church in Toledo, notes that in at least three references in the Bible, the disciples were 'reclining' during the Last Supper. She also said some people might disagree with the youthful look of the butter disciples, but she said most of the real ones were younger than Jesus." Lines of appreciative fairgoers stretched around the Agriculture Building to relish what Duffy Lyon had wrought "with the most common of breakfast spreads."[17]

The history of Jesus in America begins in childhood, as almost all Americans, Christian and non-Christian, encounter the figure of Christ in one fashion or another. Christian children encounter him in family rituals, church lessons, and public performances, such as the Via Crucis procession on Good Friday. Non-Christians meet him in public exhibits—municipal crèches, Christmas carols at malls, Christmas advertising in stores—and in family or schoolyard conversations. Christians take these observances as part of the natural American order of things, so much so that they have trouble noticing the pain and confusion Jesus has caused for many Jewish American children over the last two centuries. How could Jesus be a problem for anyone, Christians may ask, since he stands only for love, sacrifice, and peace? In practice, in America as in Europe, Christ has also stood for brutal intolerance and callous discrimination. It is difficult enough for children to cope with the milder forms of social exclusion that adults in a cultural minority group have learned to take for granted. Jewish children must still sometimes hear Jews denigrated or threatened as "Christ-killers." No wonder Jewish groups have mobilized opposition to such twentieth-century American films as D. W. Griffith's *Intolerance* (1916), Cecil B. DeMille's *King of Kings* (1927), and Norman Jewison's *Jesus Christ Superstar* (1973). And no wonder many Jews and non-Jews expressed dismay in 2004 at Mel Gibson's depiction of heinous Jewish leaders and a maniacal Jewish crowd in *The Passion of the Christ*. These age-old stereotypes pass unquestioned from film to film.[18]

American children of all backgrounds position themselves in the world by finding out who they are in relation to Christ, the single most important American cultural hero and religious figure. There has been no single history of Jesus in America because there have been so many different ways to experience him, secular as well as religious. My two kids heard a good deal about Jesus when they were little, since three of their grandparents were avid churchgoers and two were active proselytizers. Their mother and I were then holiday worshipers who regarded Jesus with awe and affection. When my kids were in first and second grade in Hamden, Connecticut, they would take the schoolbus home every day. Hamden was a very Catholic town. On Tuesday afternoons, the bus driver would drop off most of the children at the Catholic church for catechism before taking my kids and a handful of others home. One Tuesday my six-year-old and seven-year-old ran off the bus and up the front steps. "Dad," said the six-year-old, "are we Jewish?" "No," I said, "but Jesus was." The question was enchanting, and we all laughed as I tried to explain my answer. I realized I was doing with them, a quarter-century later, what my Catholic father had done with me in the front seat of the station wagon: passing along some knowledge of Jesus. I called my father up to tell him what had happened.

ONE

THE NAME OF JESUS CHRIST HAS BEEN SPOKEN

I

Jesus of Nazareth came into the world around the year 4 BCE, and word of him reached what Europeans called the "New World" fifteen hundred years later. But how did Jesus enter that world, and what kind of Jesus was he? He arrived in the minds, prayer books, and Bibles, on the crosses, holy cards, and rosaries, of European traders, explorers, and adventurers at the end of the fifteenth century. Spanish Catholic missionaries and settlers took him into Florida, New Mexico, and other parts of the Americas in the sixteenth century. In the early seventeenth century, French Catholics and English Protestants brought him to their settlements along the St. Lawrence River and the Atlantic seaboard. If we limit our attention to these Europeans, we immediately note the gap between Catholic and Protestant Christs. The Catholic Jesus was visible, material, and portable. Packed wooden ships carried sculptures, paintings, and crucifixes in their holds, along with other necessities. Jesus was represented in those religious objects and embodied physically in the mystery of the Holy Eucharist. Images showed him embedded in his Holy Family—Mary and Joseph—and surrounded by the saints (see figs. 1–3). He was the fleshy, wounded, bleeding, suffering Son of God whose sacrificial life was the model for each Christian's pilgrimage through the human vale of tears.

The early New England Protestants, like the Calvinists on the Continent, were in full rebellion against this Catholic love of "externals"—all the trinkets and visible symbols of faith. For them Jesus was present mainly in the Word read and preached, not in the sacrament shared. They banished images of Jesus not to downplay his importance but to respect his divinity. They kept him under his transcendent Father's wing, safe from idolatrous manipulation by human admirers. Like the Catholics, these Protestants centered their theology upon his redemptive sacrifice and his union with the Father and Holy Ghost in the Trinity. They felt his invisible spirit blow through their inmost hearts but were dismayed at the Catholic contemplation of his body and horrified at the Catholic consumption of his flesh. They thought Catholics were too complacent about their natural, unaided ability to imitate Christ's virtue, too liable to reduce faith to the pursuit of good works. Catholics, meanwhile, thought the Protestants had lost direct historic touch with Jesus by breaking the line of apostolic succession in the church he founded. By elevating the Bible over church tradition and the individual conscience over ecclesiastical authority, they had severed contact with the incarnate Christ. For all the Protestants' talk about finding Jesus in their hearts, they diminished his humanity by neglecting his pierced body. Spiritualizing him to safeguard his purity, they gave up the daily bread of his succor.[1]

The Catholic-Protestant split in theology and piety has remained the central fault line in American incarnations of Jesus ever since the seventeenth century. Yet the basic divergence between seventeenth-century Catholics and New England Puritans did not prevent them from finding common ground on some of Christ's cultural meanings. If we focus on the two groups' interactions with

Native Americans, some intriguing convergences come into view. Spanish and French Catholics and English Protestants all saw Christ as a gift they could bestow upon the Indians. All of the Europeans thought Jesus stood for and effected salvation from sin. The Catholics took him, in addition, as an agent of deliverance from a primitive social outlook. In their view he was both the incarnate God who transcended culture—who lifted faithful human beings into a placeless eternity of souls—and an agent of cultural progress. Jesus helped Catholics and Protestants alike to justify their American overtures. Both groups could see their American adventures as part of God's plan to liberate native souls from the devil's chains. Catholics went further and identified Jesus explicitly with the campaign to alter Indian social behavior. Yet it is an error to view the early American Jesus as primarily a servant of European imperial expansion. Surely many statesmen, explorers, and even clergymen would happily have confined him to that role. But Jesus was not so easily contained. As a symbol of everlasting love he occasionally offered resistance to the barbarities committed by Europeans in their practice of civilization. Christians in America as in Europe sometimes rose up to challenge worldliness, exploitation, and cruelty.

In their meetings with the Indians, the Europeans all settled on two basic identities for Jesus. He was the healer and the martyr. The Catholics in New Spain and New France added a third identity: the civilizer who combated dissolute habits. He taught the Indians to see those habits as offenses against God. Puritans resisted this civilizing use of Jesus. It made Jesus too cultural, too instrumental, too easy and undemanding a gift. Catholics gave Jesus away in their Eucharist with too few strings attached. He had to be held in reserve until Indians could actually read and experience his Word. But the Puritans joined the Catholics in preaching Christ's healing powers and his selfless martyrdom. Christ allowed Europeans and Indians alike to greet their own earthly end with equanimity. For the Catholics a select cohort of gifted souls could move

beyond the usual achievement of Christian virtue to a direct imitation of Jesus, in which they could anticipate a suffering, perhaps
even a martyrdom, like his.

Newly arrived Europeans wanted things from Native Americans, and the Indians they met wanted things from them. Europeans wanted to know where the furs, gold, and silver were. They
wanted land and food. They wanted knowledge of topography and
waterways. Indians wanted iron goods and weapons, clothes and
tobacco, barrels of peas and beans, and novel objects of all kinds,
including brass crosses and porcelain rosary beads. Sometimes
both parties wanted the same things, like land, although Europeans
and Indians had very different conceptions of what it meant to
"own" land. The biggest difference between the two sides may
have been that only the Europeans had something they urgently
wished the Indians to want: their religion. The Europeans wanted
Jesus ultimately to be everyone's exclusive savior. For some of
them Jesus was the inspiration and justification for their entire en-
terprise, the symbolic junction of their worldly and otherworldly
commitments. These pious newcomers wanted Indians to know
him and love him because they could not imagine living or dying
without him. They believed that his ultimate sacrifice on the cross
had changed human history, reopened the gates of heaven, and allowed men and women to transcend sinful passion and consecrate
themselves to God's service.

II

As soon as they got to their new world, Europeans made public
displays of their loyalty to Jesus for their own as well as the Indians' benefit. Juan Ponce de León picked Easter Sunday, the day
commemorating Christ's resurrection, as the proper moment for
the first official Spanish landing on the well-populated "island" of
Florida in 1513. Spanish reconnaissance and conquest from Colum-

bus on was announced as Christian outreach. Europeans were always frank about material goals as well as spiritual ones. They did not speak of God to hide their commercial and strategic purposes, but to put them in the right perspective. Eternal gains were paramount, and earthly gains were desirable and perfectly proper. Explorers and colonizers departed from Europe with ringing proclamations about bringing true religion to the heathen, "to see how," as Columbus put it in 1492, "their conversion to the Holy Faith might be undertaken." Yet religious goals were so tied up with worldly ones that Jesus could be depicted as Lord of earthly domains as well as eternal souls. When the Jesuits first disembarked in Canada in 1611, "a solemn Thanksgiving was enjoined," according to one of their early historians. "The figure of Christ, covered with a canopy, was carried about with the greatest possible ceremony, and he came auspiciously into the possession, so to speak, of the happy land."[2]

But thoughts of Jesus and his kingdom accompanied European voyagers in a personal way too. They often bore the trials of their journeys and labors by contrasting them to the far greater agony of Christ's sacrifice. The shipwrecked Spanish adventurer Cabeza de Vaca trudged for eight years (1528–1536) from Florida to Mexico, and reported on his return to Spain that his only consolation during the ordeal was "to think about the Passion of our Redeemer Jesus Christ, and the blood he shed for me, and to consider how much greater had been the torment that he suffered from the thorns." After her death in Quebec in 1651, Ursuline Marie de St. Joseph was hailed by her Mother Superior, Marie de l'Incarnation, for spending her final five years in New France living "only by faith and crosses." Sometimes Marie de St. Joseph had such "vivid impressions of the sufferings of Jesus Christ," her Mother Superior recalled, that she suffered "almost continual pains and weaknesses" in body and soul. She embraced the words of St. Paul, "I am crucified with Jesus Christ," and clung to her life of frigid deprivation in Canada because "it made her like her Bridegroom [Jesus]," a "victim

of suffering love." The sacrificial Jesus she modeled to her Algonquin and Huron pupils at the female seminary (she spoke the languages of both peoples), and to the adult Indians (male and female)
whom she counseled, had little in common with the triumphal
Christ proclaimed by Jesuit Pierre Biard after his arrival in Canada
in 1611: "We have taken possession of these regions in the name of
the Church of God, establishing here the royal throne of our Savior
and Monarch, Jesus Christ."[3]

Native Americans added their own understandings of Jesus to
the cultural mix from the moment they first learned of him from the
explorers or missionaries. It was a time of social emergency for
them because "the first Spanish sneeze," as Stephen Greenblatt
puts it, had propelled "millions of invisible bullets." The initial intersection between European and American peoples was a demographic disaster for the Indians. They had no protection against the
measles, smallpox, or influenza to which Europeans had often developed resistance. The religious paradox is stark: the Europeans
supplied both the diseases and the divine healer and redeemer who
helped some unknown number of Indians make sense of their
calamity. According to European observers, some Native Americans believed that their own shamans or gods could not account for
or reverse the tide of affliction. Naturally the Indians were interested in knowing more about the Europeans' Christ, a "savior"
who appeared to have the power to protect the Europeans from
falling ill. Inhabiting a world full of invisible spirits, they had no
reason to doubt his existence or his power. What they debated was
whether he could save them from disease as he had saved the Europeans, and whether the Europeans would allow him to if he
could.[4]

Europeans believed that Indians were seeking out Christian
stories and rituals to tap whatever power they might contain. If
they were right—if the Native Americans were not just being polite
but were on the lookout for any and all spiritual agencies that
meshed with their beliefs—then the Indians may have exerted a

substantial impact on the kind of Jesus the missionaries ended up preaching. Spanish Franciscans in New Mexico and Florida, French Jesuits along the St. Lawrence, and English Puritans in New England all had to simplify Christian truths if they were to make contact with Indians, or for that matter with ordinary Christians of their own faiths (the most undisciplined of whom consistently struck them as *less* spiritually promising than the Indians they met). The Jesus many Indians seem to have been most interested in was the Jesus who cured people of sickness and saved people from death, not the one who stressed obedience to the Father's commandments, love of enemies, repentance for sin, or the imminence of the coming Kingdom. Missionaries here as elsewhere adjusted their teachings to the interests of their audiences. Even the Jesuits in Canada and the Puritans in New England, who scoffed at the Spanish Franciscans' mass baptisms, tailored the gospel to the urgent Indian desire for cures.[5]

When the Jesuits began evangelizing the Hurons in the seventeenth century, the Indians engaged in a lively disagreement about the benignity or malignity of Jesus. But as the deaths from illness mounted, the Hurons became increasingly Christian (and pro-French). The Iroquois then attacked them more systematically, causing them to appeal all the more to Jesus for deliverance. In his report of 1650, Father Paul Ragueneau was forthright about the sad dynamics of this cultural crossing. Upon his arrival in the 1630s, he wrote, the Hurons lacked Christ but were rich in fisheries, hunting grounds, and trade with allied peoples. But "since the faith has entered their hearts and they have adored the Cross of Jesus Christ, he has given them, as their lot, a very heavy section of that Cross, leaving them prey to miseries, torments, and cruel deaths." They were now "a people wiped off the face of the earth," consoled only by the knowledge that "having died Christian, they have entered into the heritage of true children of God. Flagellat Deus omnem filium quem recipit." ("The Lord scourgeth every son whom he receiveth"—from Paul's letter to the Hebrews 12:6.)[6]

The unlucky Cabeza de Vaca and his three fellow wanderers trekking through the Southeast in the 1520s introduced thousands of Indians to Christ long before they had seen a clergyman. This was a century before Father Ragueneau canoed up the St. Lawrence to preach to the Hurons, and many decades before Spanish Franciscan missions appeared in Florida or New Mexico. None of Cabeza de Vaca's ragtag party was either a priest or a doctor, but, according to his account, one set of Indians after another begged the Spaniards to treat their sick. He claimed to have healed them repeatedly by making the sign of the cross over them (saying "In the name of the Father, and of the Son, and of the Holy Spirit" while outlining the shape of a cross with the motion of his hand). Word of the cures, he said, moved faster than he did. Encountering the Avavares Indians for the first time, he learned that "they already had news of us and about how we were curing and about the wonders that our Lord was working through us." The Avavares did not wait for one-on-one healing. They approached *en masse*, "placing their hands on our faces and bodies, and afterward they passed their hands over their own faces and bodies." The next day "they brought us the sick people they had, begging us to make the sign of the cross over them." In another place the welcoming stampede was so chaotic that some, "trying to arrive more quickly than others to touch us . . . crowded us so much that they nearly could have killed us."[7]

Cabeza de Vaca's party also met plenty of wariness and hostility along the way. Some Indians, he reported, were cautious because they feared Spanish slave roundups (kidnappings having begun in the Caribbean with Columbus's first trip, and on the mainland with Ponce de León's landing). Others were angry because of the epidemics the Europeans had caused. Cabeza de Vaca noted that one group of Indians contracted "a stomach ailment . . . from which half of them died. And they thought that we were the ones who had killed them." Another group, which lost eight men during Cabeza de Vaca's stay, "held it for certain that we were killing them by simply desiring it." Knowing their own prior state of health, they had correctly inferred European responsibility without having any more inkling of the disease process than the Spaniards had.[8]

Some of the Indians apparently wished to eliminate the visitors before they "desired" any more Indians into the grave, while others sought access to whatever healing power the Europeans were able or willing to bestow. A nonviolent reaction to the Europeans, no less than a violent one, reaffirmed the integrity of Native American beliefs. If Cabeza de Vaca understood the Indians correctly in believing they had elevated him to high station as a miracle-worker, the Indians were incorporating the Christian symbols and rites that fit into their own prior outlook. They encouraged Cabeza de Vaca to present them with those Christian meanings that they could most easily understand and that best met their needs and preconceptions. They made him a shaman who had a mysterious access to the world of spirits and a power to ward off illness or evil. Healing was the mutually agreed upon point of spiritual contact long before missionaries arrived with their Bibles and breviaries. It fit the bill because it relied the least on verbal communication (impossible given the linguistic gap) and because it was the area of greatest urgency. If Cabeza de Vaca was right about Indians' responses to him, Christ and his cross made an immediate entrance into Indian cultures because Jesus offered his aid at a time of social and medical disaster.

Cabeza de Vaca may have imagined his new vocation as a shaman, or invented it out of his store of memories after returning to Spain. It stands to reason that he would want to depict himself, upon his return to Europe, as a heroic agent of the faith, not a lucky survivor of an inept expedition. But it makes equal sense to suppose that he would have built up that image as a survival mechanism while on his torturous American journey and tried to impose it on the Indians he met. Playing the part of the divine healer may have protected him while also confirming in his own eyes the sense of cultural superiority he had brought with him from Spain. Becoming a renowned Christlike healer (he even raised one Indian from apparent death) allowed him to believe all the more in the power of the Christian God to vanquish the "devils" he thought the Indians cherished. At the very least, Cabeza de Vaca's story, along with later references to it, reveals how desperately some Europeans wished to see themselves as disciples of a healing Jesus and a sacrificial Jesus, not just a warrior Jesus who civilized by compulsion or violence. Their expansionist venture into their New World made more sense to them if it was a story not of dispossession but of selfless Good Samaritans offering assistance and thereby extending the sway of God's peaceful Kingdom.[9]

In the 1540s Hernando de Soto's expeditionary force traversed some of the same terrain crossed by Cabeza de Vaca a decade earlier. His men were startled to come upon Indian villages *not* on Cabeza de Vaca's path in which the dwellings were topped by crosses. Garcilaso de la Vega, one of the chroniclers of the expedition, wrote that "there was scarcely a house that did not have one. It was supposed that these Indians had heard of the good works and miracles" of Cabeza de Vaca; "the fame of those wonders" passed "from person to person and from country to country." The Indians "had heard it said that all the benefits those Christians had conferred in curing the sick was by making the sign of the cross over them," and "it gave rise to their observance of placing it over their houses, in the belief that it would also save them from all evil and danger, as it had cured the sick."[10]

Assuming the accuracy of Garcilaso de la Vega's report about the crosses on rooftops (his narrative has been accused of fictionalization in other respects), neither he nor any of De Soto's soldiers or friars had any way of knowing why the Indians used them, or whether there was any connection between the crosses and Cabeza de Vaca's earlier trip. Crosses had been employed decoratively and spiritually by a variety of peoples, including Mesoamericans, beginning with the Egyptians. And it was plainly in the self-interest of Indians confronted by an armed Spanish convoy to confirm any explanation the visitors might have preferred about the provenance of the crosses. Yet for all we know word of the cross and its powers had indeed spread beyond Cabeza de Vaca's route and the Indians were taking advantage of whatever magical properties it possessed. What Garcilaso de la Vega's account establishes beyond any doubt is how passionately the Spanish and other Europeans wanted to see their mission in the Americas as beneficent, not predatory. If the resident Americans had adopted the cross in response to Cabeza de Vaca's wonder-working, then the spirit of the Christian God was surely blowing across the continent.

While Cabeza de Vaca was effecting or affecting his cures near the Gulf of Mexico, French explorer Jacques Cartier reported having a similar experience along the St. Lawrence River. He became a virtual lay priest on his second trip up the St. Lawrence, in 1535. On his arrival at Hochelaga (today's Montreal), he gave the Iroquois headman "a cross and a crucifix," which he had him kiss before putting it around his neck. Then "the girls and women of the village, some of whom had children in their arms, crowded about us, rubbing our faces, arms, and other parts of the upper portions of our bodies which they could touch, weeping for joy at the sight of us." Cartier was made to sit on a special mat in the center of the village, whereupon a stream of "sick persons, some blind, others with but one eye, others lame or impotent" were brought forward "in order that he might lay his hands upon them, so that one would have thought Christ had come down to earth to heal them." Cartier proceeded to read the opening of John's Gospel (in French, a language the Indians could not fathom), and presented gifts of hatchets and knives to the men, beads to the women, and tin Lamb of God images to the children. (He refused to accept the Indians' reciprocal gifts of "fish, soups, beans, bread, and other dishes" because, lacking salt, they "were not to our taste.") Cartier's penultimate act before departing for France was to build a thirty-five-foot cross (five feet higher than the one he had left on his first voyage in 1534). His final act was to kidnap five adult Iroquois to take back to France, along with the five children he had already received as a gift.[11]

Europeans in North America had been erecting large crosses and passing out small ones ever since Columbus first hit the Bahamas. For Europeans and Indians alike, the crosses were symbols of political as well as religious import. Cartier's thirty-footer, planted at the Gaspé harbor in 1534, featured, just below the crossbar, "a shield with three fleurs-de-lys in relief" and a sign proclaiming LONG LIVE THE KING OF FRANCE. Indians fishing in the harbor assembled to watch the dedication of the cross. Cartier and his men put on an instructional performance to model the proper reverence. They knelt down with hands clasped, "worshipping it before them; and made signs to them, looking up and pointing towards heaven, that by means of this we had our redemption, at which they showed many marks of admiration, at the same time turning and looking at the cross." Moments later, the apparent admiration turned into ambivalence at best when the Native American "captain" pulled his canoe alongside Cartier's ship, "making the sign of the cross with two of his fingers" and pointing "to the land all around about, as if he wished to say that all this region belonged to him, and that we ought not to have set up this cross without his permission." Cartier dismissed that reaction because the French were claiming possession on the basis of an authority far loftier than the king of France. The triumphant Jesus beloved of explorers and heads of state supplied a legitimacy that trumped mere earthly distinction.[12]

In the seventeenth-century America of the Spanish, French, English, and Indians, the cross of Jesus conveyed a range of overlapping meanings. Placed around a neck or atop a roof, it healed or protected. Planted on a prominent spot of land, it staked a national claim. When a boatload of English Virginians (hence non-Puritans) sacked a French fortification at St. Sauveur in 1613, Father Biard reported that they "tore down our crosses, raising another to show they had taken possession of the country, and were the masters thereof. This cross had carved upon it the name of the King of Great Britain." A publicly erected cross had expressed ownership since Columbus's first voyage a century earlier. "In all the places, islands, and lands that he entered," according to his logbook, Columbus left a cross behind. He put them up (with the help of impressed Indian labor) as a sign "that Your Highnesses [Ferdinand and Isabella] claim the land as your own, and chiefly as a sign of Jesus Christ Our Lord and in honor of Christianity."[13]

Calling Jesus the "chief" signification of the cross—implying some secondary meaning too—exhibited the ideological instability at the heart of the Spanish imperial venture and of the broader European colonial juggernaut. Explorers such as Columbus said that the cross was primarily religious while acting as if it were primarily political. This discrepancy left a large opening for missionaries who had plans of their own for the peoples of the New World. Historians often take the early clergy as the obedient handmaidens of the conquering men in armor—either bad cops themselves, whipping the Indians (literally) into submission, or good cops who put sanctimonious camouflage over a seedy and perhaps genocidal history of expropriation. Such an assumption buys its very legitimate condemnation of European atrocities at too high a historical cost. By focusing on the undeniable contribution that religion made to Western arrogance and brutality, this viewpoint misses the complexity of the religious impulse and the special place of the clergy in their own cultures. They had a distinctive role in the European invasion and the Indian responses to it. Priests and ministers were not satisfied to let explorers, statesmen, or Native Americans shape Christianity in any way they pleased. The Franciscans and Jesuits were strong-willed advocates of what they considered *true* Christianity. The drama of the missionaries' spiritual vocation in the Americas is that however purely they might apprehend the sufferings of their crucified Lord and the glories of the heavenly paradise opened up by his sacrifice, they were still the faithful servants of European political powers (and of particular Indian peoples allied

to those powers). They could never escape their national identities
or their nation's political interests. Nor could they overcome their
own sense of cultural superiority over the Indians. But we have to
take note of the sacrificial as well as the self-righteous character of
their quest to bring saving knowledge of Christ to the thousands of
heathen who they feared would die without it. We have to confront
the spiritual depth as well as the cultural condescension contained
in the missionaries' faith that, as one Jesuit put it, "Jésus est le Dieu
des sauvages, aussi bien que le nostre" ("Jesus is the savages' God
as well as our own").[14]

III

Mention the 1620s to modern-day Americans and they are apt to
recall grade-school pageants with Pilgrim hats and shiny black
shoes with oversized buckles. They might be surprised to learn that
while a few hundred Pilgrims were worshiping Christ in Plymouth, thousands of Native Americans were attending Mass and
receiving communion in New Mexico and Florida. It is easy to forget the substantial Florida mission system put in place by Spanish
Franciscans in the seventeenth century. Although the missions
stretched from St. Augustine in Florida to present-day South Carolina, and from Gainesville west to Apalachee (Tallahassee), they
eroded after 1675 and, unlike the eighteenth-century California
missions, left no architectural trace. The Christian Indian and mes-
tizo presence in New Mexico has been more or less continuous
since the start of the seventeenth century. The Spanish moved north
into what we now call New Mexico in 1598, establishing Santa Fe
("Holy Faith") a decade later. Franciscans packed crosses, oil-
painted images, and statuary into their wagons, along with food
staples and medicine, farming and building tools, and extra sack-
cloth for new robes. By the 1620s they had erected scores of
churches with the aid of Indian labor. (Women built the walls; men

did the rest.) At their peak in the seventeenth century, about fifty Franciscans (there were about seventy in Florida) were engaged in "the conversion and pacification," as the missionary Fray Alonso de Benavides put it in 1630, of dozens of Indian communities. The friars and other Spaniards were expelled during the Pueblo Revolt of 1680 (twenty-one of the thirty-three Franciscans and almost four hundred of the twenty-nine hundred Spanish colonists having been killed in the uprising), but they returned to their evangelical and civilizing labors in the mid-1690s.[15]

Alonso de Benavides made the grueling fifteen-hundred-mile journey from Mexico City to Santa Fe in 1625, and reported in his 1630 *Memorial* to King Philip IV that one "nation" (group) of Pueblo Indians after another had accepted the faith. Baptisms took place *en masse*, but not without active consent. These were not coerced conversions of the sort earlier practiced in New Spain upon the Nahuatl-speaking peoples of the former Aztec empire—conversions condemned by Dominican priest Bartolomé de las Casas in his famous tract *In Defense of the Indians* (1552). Las Casas did not mind mass baptism itself. He objected only to "violent" imposition of the faith. Christ's teaching was the norm to follow, said Las Casas: "Men must not be forced to listen to the gospel." He pointed out that Jesus rebuked his disciples James and John (in Luke 9:54) for proposing "fire from heaven" as proper punishment for a Samaritan town that refused to receive Christ. Missionaries should let the image of Jesus "shine forth in our conduct. . . . We must not have more diligent concern for the salvation of men than Christ himself, who shed his precious blood for them." Yet Las Casas was no relativist. If the Indians chose to reject the faith after hearing it preached, "it is not our fault." They would bear full responsibility for their exclusion from "the sheepfold of Christ, . . . the place outside of which there is no salvation."[16]

Alonso de Benavides detailed a long string of successes in New Mexico for the Las Casas pacification strategy, including the baptisms of all six thousand souls in the fourteen pueblos of the Piro

people, the baptisms of most of the ten thousand people in the fourteen pueblos of the Tompiros, and the "conversion" (the step prior
to baptism) of all ten thousand Zunis in their eleven pueblos. These
rounded figures are plainly estimates, but they establish that the
Franciscans were persuading some Indian leaders to endorse some
Christian rituals on behalf of their peoples. When a group of friars
arrived in the Humana Nation for a prearranged group baptism,
there were ten thousand people waiting for them in a field. "Do you
ask for baptism with all your hearts?" Father Salas yelled. "With a
great shout, they all raised their arms, got up on their feet, and asked
for holy baptism. . . . Mothers who had their babies at their breast . . .
took their babies' arms and stretched them upward, asking at the
same time in loud voices for holy baptism for these children."[17]

According to Alonso de Benavides, the priests remained a few
days to preach and teach the Indians the Pater Noster (Our Father),
the Ave Maria (Hail Mary), and Salve Regina (Hail Holy Queen). As
they prepared to leave, the Indian "captain" protested, saying, "We
cannot yet do anything with God. . . . We have a lot of sick people:
heal us before you go." The friars agreed and set up a curative ritual
that ran from three in the afternoon until ten the next morning. The
sick formed a continuous line that passed between two priests, who
recited Latin prayers without interruption. "Blind people, lame
people, people afflicted with dropsy—everyone [was] cured of his
afflictions." The healing atmosphere was so thick that "even the soldiers accompanying the priests were able to work wonders." Like
Cabeza de Vaca, the Franciscan friars gladly put on the mantle that
Alonso de Benavides claimed was urged upon them by the Indians—that of Christ the healer—and joined the Indians in acting out
a communal passage from affliction to restoration.[18]

Amerindians could band together in certain rituals with priests
such as Alonso de Benavides and adventurers such as Cabeza de
Vaca because they all took the world as an enchanted place, filled
with mysterious portents and fabulous happenings. The seventeenth-
century New Mexico Franciscans may have shared more cultural

ground in this respect with the Pueblo Indians than they did with the contemporaneous Jesuits of New France or Puritans of New England. The Franciscans stood much closer to the Jesuits than to the Puritans. The Jesuits perpetually mocked Native American "superstitions" while retaining a good many of their own. The New England Calvinists were the most inclined to restrict miracles to happenings engineered directly by God, although many of them also gave credence to some extra-biblical powers and omens. While the Puritans often made room for the occult, they generally tried to shield the supernatural from contamination by the merely magical. The Franciscans, by contrast, shared with the Pueblo Indians a worldview steeped in magic.

In his *Memorial* of 1630, Alonso de Benavides supplied many examples of wonder-working. When certain members of the Picuris Nation tried to kill a priest, they failed because "he became invisible." On another occasion, "an old Indian sorceress" in the Taos Nation was gathering firewood with some Christian Indian women and tried to talk them out of their new devotion to monogamy. "The sky was clear and serene, but a bolt from the blue struck that infernal instrument of the devil right in the middle of those good Christian women." Her demise naturally convinced "everyone who had been secretly living in sin" to get married right away. Historian Ramón Gutiérrez, relying on Elsie Parsons's twentieth-century anthropological study of *Pueblo Indian Religion* (1939), doubts Alonso de Benavides's account. He speculates that "the Indians interpreted the event differently. For them, persons struck by the germinative force of lightning immediately became cloud spirits, thus confirming that what the [sorceress] woman said was morally true."[19]

The most famous miracles reported by Alonso de Benavides were the appearances of a Spanish mystic, Mother María de Agreda, in Pueblo country between 1620 and 1623. The Indians who had seen and spoken to her in their own language said that although "the lady in blue" resembled the Spanish nun pictured in one of the Franciscans' paintings, she was much younger, "a slip of a girl and beautiful." Upon his return to Spain, Alonso de Benavides visited Mother María and satisfied himself that she had indeed traveled repeatedly by spiritual means to New Mexico. The friars' fabulous stories had meaning for Spaniards and Indians alike, because they pointed beyond themselves to an invisible world of wonders. Historians writing about missionaries often claim that Europeans played on the natives' credulity to get conversions. David Weber writes, for instance, that "Franciscans often sought to dazzle natives with showy vestments, music, paintings, statuary of sacred images, and ceremonies." But the friars were dazzled themselves by what the Nicene Creed called "visibilium omnium et invisibilium," "all things visible and invisible."[20]

The seventeenth-century Spanish preference for voluntary rather than forced conversions—a pacification strategy operating, of course, in the larger coercive context of Spanish rule—put a premium on the friars' diplomatic skill and graphic preaching. In his *Memorial* to the king, Alonso de Benavides gave a striking example of both. As an initial overture to the nomadic "Apaches" (Navajos) in 1629, Fray Alonso sent twelve Christian Tewas to a Navajo encampment. For good luck, they departed on September 17, the eve of the celebration of the Stigmata of St. Francis, and they carried as offerings a rosary, a feather-tipped arrow (signifying peace), a pipeful of tobacco "ready to smoke," and a feather indicating that the pipe had already been smoked in Pueblo country. Duly impressed by the display, the Navajo captain, with the rosary around his neck, journeyed to the Tewa pueblo, where Alonso had mobilized "1,500" Tewas as a welcoming committee. At a candlelit meeting in the church, Alonso de Benavides explained to the captain that "the Creator, and Lord of all creation, had died on a cross to free us from eternal suffering." A painting on the altar helped illuminate the terror awaiting lost souls. "I told him that anyone who did not worship God, and who was not baptized, must be damned. And anyone so condemned would burn in hell in eternal suffering." The captain immediately declared his faith in the Christian God, and Alonso de

Benavides marked his conversion by hanging arrows from the altar. The Navajo leader wanted to be baptized forthwith, but the Spaniard told him that would have to wait. The Franciscan goal was not individual conquests, but the baptism of all "200,000" Navajos, and that could happen only when Franciscans had been invited to live among them. Spiritual growth depended upon carefully monitored religious practice. Progress toward heaven required advance toward civilization. A year later Alonso de Benavides was glad to report that "a priest of very great spirit" was "pursuing the conversion and pacification of these people."[21]

For the Franciscans of New Mexico, Christ healed people of disease and saved sinners from the hell to which Adam's misbehavior had consigned them. Christian preaching from the apostolic period onward had linked sin to bodily disease, both causally and metaphorically. Sin caused sickness, while bodily affliction supplied images for conveying the meaning of spiritual disarray. Louise Burkhart's study of Franciscan vernacular preaching in sixteenth-century Mexico shows how sin was systematically tied to illness for the Nahuatl speakers who were in steady decline from diseases introduced by the Spanish. "When Fray Francisco Jiménez arrived in a town," she writes, "he began by explaining to the inhabitants that he had come to give 'the medicines necessary for the health of souls to those who were spiritually ailing.'" God's grace was a medicine; Christ's sacraments were a treatment for "soul-sickness." The Indians had long believed that moral misdeeds could provoke physical disease, and when Franciscans connected sexual excess to dismal physical consequences, the Indians apparently nodded in agreement. The hard leap for the Nahuas was the notion of spiritual sickness as a state distinct from physical ailments. For the Spanish, becoming civilized meant coming to feel sinful about ungodly actions or thoughts apart from physical consequences, to apprehend sinfulness in general. It meant coming to know a certain divine healer and to recognize the debilitating condition that only he could heal.[22]

The seventeenth-century Pueblo Indians had just as much trouble as the Nahuas understanding the concept of sin. Yet without grasping the notion of sin, how was it possible to truly know or believe in Jesus, whose divine-human identity revolved entirely around his sacrifice to atone for human sin? Missionaries in all areas could finesse this problem by focusing on the power of Christ's physical healing and the heroism of his physical martyrdom. The Franciscans could finesse it further, since belief for the Spanish was formal and collective in structure. Religious experience and religious ritual were virtually identical for the Franciscan-taught Indians of New Mexico. The Native Americans of New France and New England, by contrast, were expected to exhibit an individually felt and articulated conviction about Christ the savior. Still, the Pueblo Christians made individual confessions, which required an enumeration of discrete sins. They were told to "study their sins," according to Alonso de Benavides. To help remember their misdeeds, they "recorded" them "on a series of knotted strings" which they brought along to the confessional. The Indians could understand the concept of breaking rules or taboos. They just had trouble grasping the idea that they offended Christ by disobeying his moral commands.[23]

It did not take the Pueblo Indians long to realize that the friars were strangely fixated on sexual sins, and they often submitted to the outward form of Christian marriage to placate the priests. According to the Franciscans, the seventeenth-century Indians rarely sought out the marriage sacrament on their own. Ramón Gutiérrez, in his imaginative reconstruction of seventeenth-century Pueblo Indian experiences of Jesus, has shown how the Franciscans brought Christ to bear on their campaign of sexual reform. Like the Jesuits in New France, they used Jesus as a tool for reforming behavior that struck them as animalistic. Christ was both civilizing means and spiritual end. The friars tried to root Jesus in the deepest recesses of Pueblo life, at the junction of spatial and temporal experience. The mission church was placed at the sacred center of the pueblo, the first major step in the assault on the Indians' ancestral religion. Within the church Christ was visualized on the cross and among his saints on the three-tiered *reredos,* a wooden, wall-mounted screen depicting a variety of holy personages as well as the Trinity (see figs. 2–3).

The events of Christ's earthly life were fixed on the annual calendar, while the Holy Sacrifice of the Mass regularly rehearsed the peak episode of that life: his Passion. The emotional intensity of the transubstantiation—the conversion of bread and wine into Christ's body and blood—was magnified by its spatial prominence on the high altar of the church. Special Christian celebrations were superimposed on Pueblo rituals, most notably around Christmastime. Good Friday observances joined prior Pueblo practices of flagellation and bloodletting to Christian ones. Jesus the bleeding Son of God made eminent religious sense to many of the Pueblo Indians, even as many of them resisted him for being a tool of European conquest. Gutiérrez puts his finger on the dense web of religious and political forces at the heart of interlocking European and Indian experiences of Jesus. From the Indians' standpoint, the friars' (and Christ's) extraordinary self-renunciation in choosing lifetime celibacy signified profound holiness, and the priests' rites of bodily mortification gave further evidence of their sanctity.

Some Indians were drawn to the conquerors, and to their Jesus, because of the disciplined piety modeled by Christ and followed by some of his priests. The governor of New Mexico himself participated in the self-mutilation during the Good Friday observance in 1598. He "cruelly scourged himself, mingling bitter tears with the blood flowing from his many wounds." In 1660 Fray Salvador de Guerra was so upset to see the Isleta Pueblo Indians performing a prohibited katsina dance that he took off his clothes, whipped himself, placed a crown of thorns on his head, and walked back and forth carrying a large cross. The dancing stopped immediately, and some of the tearful Indians asked the priest's forgiveness.

We cannot tell how many Indians moved from knowledge of Jesus as healer and martyr to full-fledged embrace of him as savior.

We do know that the Pueblos were divided about how to respond to Christ and how to respond to the European invasion. We can be sure that thousands of Indians participated in Christian rituals. Events such as the Via Crucis procession involved hundreds of marchers. In 1655 a reported six hundred Carac and Tajique penitents carried "large and small crosses on their shoulders" while an undetermined number of Hopis dressed as hermits in haircloth shirts and beat themselves with nail- and wire-studded whips. And we know that when thousands of Pueblo warriors revolted against the friars and against Spanish rule in 1680, they struck back at Christ too. Altars were desecrated, statues and paintings smashed, churches demolished—retaliation for two generations of Spanish confiscation and destruction of Pueblo religious objects and structures. Priests sometimes met their deaths at the hands of the very Indians whom they had "most favored" and whom they regarded as the "most intelligent." As they prepared to die, some allegedly told their killers of their joy to be leaving this world as martyrs for Christ.[24]

Before the revolt, the Franciscans believed that their spiritual goal—replacing the rule of the devil with the reign of Christ—was jeopardized as much by the Spanish as by the Indians. The Spaniards modeled avaricious dealing, casual sexual conduct, and worse. How did Satan operate in New Mexico? asked Alonso de Benavides. "One of his usual tricks" was to appeal to "the greed of our Spanish governor," who did not hesitate to kill even Christian Indians or sell them into slavery if it would increase his income or power. The chief obstacle to Christian conversions, according to some Franciscans, was the venality of their own countrymen. When the friars returned in the mid-1690s after fifteen years of exclusion, their main concern was rooting out the forbidden moral and religious practices to which the Indians had reverted in their absence. Fray Gerónimo Prieto tried to stamp out the circular stone structures where the Indians offered corn, green grass, or feathers in petitioning the spirits for rain or other favors. "When I knocked them down," he wrote, "the interpreter came to tell me that the people said that I should not have done so, that it was their custom, which they had always observed, and that the kingdom had revolted because this had been taken away from them, and that if it were to be taken away from them they would again rise in rebellion. To this I exhorted them that it was a deception of the devil, that the stones could give them nothing, that only God was the all powerful to whom they should appeal for help." Gerónimo Prieto tried both "kindness and threats," but to no avail. "I have torn them down various times, but each time they have again set them up." The Indians' error lay not in petitioning an unseen power for gifts, but in failing to petition the correct unseen power.[25]

Fray Francisco Corbera was an itinerant in the Zuni and Moqui Nations in 1692, enduring "the severe cold of winter . . . without sleeping under a roof." When he accepted an assignment to the Pueblo mission of San Ildefonso in 1694, he acknowledged the danger posed by rebellious Indians. But for him and his fellow friars "losing our lives" mattered little if it meant that "the souls of these poor people could not be lost." One effective means of bringing them to Christ was for the missionaries to live in poverty themselves. "They are very much influenced by the friendly treatment and love" of their ministers, and even more so by "personal abnegation." Francisco Corbera took heart from future prospects for the faith among the Indians but conceded that he could judge only by what they showed him. They might be deceiving him. As one of his colleagues put it, "As regards their inner thoughts, only God can know." But even if "everything goes wrong," Corbera wrote, "it will only be a benefit to us, as they would take our lives . . . and what greater gain could we achieve than to lose our lives for the salvation of souls?" He did not believe that the Pueblo Indians would rise again against the Spanish, however, for in his estimation the Pueblos' main enemy was the Apaches, from whom the Spanish had often protected them. Francisco Corbera's prognostications proved wrong. A year later he received the unanticipated but welcomed benefit of dying for Christ. In June 1696, in the last act of

Pueblo resistance against the Spanish, Native American warriors killed Corbera and four other friars by torching his church, in which he and other Spaniards had taken refuge. His martyrdom became a symbol of heroic sacrifice in the Spanish community, just as the Indian warriors' attack became a legendary act of courage in Pueblo memory. For the Europeans the deaths in the church magnified the image of Jesus as martyr and supplied renewed impetus for Christian colonization in the eighteenth century.[26]

IV

When Parisian historian Mark Lescarbot announced in 1610 that "le nom de Jesus-Christ est annoncé ès terres d'outre mer" ("the name of Jesus Christ has been spoken in the lands beyond the sea"), he meant that Christ had finally been preached correctly—that is, not in the Spanish manner. True, the Spanish had brought "some light of the Christian religion" to the New World, but their efforts were compromised by "cruelty and avarice." At the French colony of Port Royal (in today's Nova Scotia), by contrast, "la parole immuable de notre Sauveur Jesus-Christ" ("the unchangeable word of our Savior Jesus Christ") had been spoken and heard. He proudly reported that the Native American Micmac leader Membertou, along with twenty of his family, had just been baptized by Father Fléché, the secular French priest at Port Royal. Yet the Jesuit Pierre Biard, who arrived in New France the following year, promptly challenged the Membertou clan's conversion. He tested Membertou's family and found that they had no grasp of "the common creed, the Lord's Prayer, the commandments of God, the sacraments," and other doctrines "totalement nécessaire" to the making of a Christian. They could not remember their baptismal names and kept messing up when they tried to make the sign of the cross. Biard believed that his Jesuits would bring more rigor to the missionary field. In his view, Lescarbot's critique of the Spaniards did not go far enough. It was not just their "avarice and greed" that needed correcting, but their practice of mass baptisms. The North American battle to purify Christianity of magical or worldly corruptions began not when Pilgrims and Puritans arrived in New England in the 1620s and 1630s, but when French Jesuits arrived in New France in 1611.[27]

The Jesuits, like the New England Puritans, were slow in making baptisms because they thought true faith depended upon the individual believer's consciousness of Christ's saving power. Having that kind of consciousness depended, in turn, on being civilized. The Puritans objected to the Catholics' explicit use of Jesus as a civilizing agent, but they too wished the Indians to learn civilized habits. On the other hand, Jesuits and Puritans were clear about the limits of civilization: it was not an end in itself, only a preparation for a life dedicated to the sacrificial love of Christ. The Jesuits were so convinced of the necessary-but-not-sufficient character of civility that they often regarded their own deeply ingrained civilized behavior as a spiritual threat. Many of them saw their careers in New France as a way of combating European ease and complacency. Sharing the Indians' hardships much of the time, they effected a cultural crossover in which they taught civilized styles of thought and action to the Indians while partially renouncing such styles themselves. Each party needed a spiritual exchange with the other in order to fulfill its own proper imitation of Christ. The Jesuits needed the Indians' help in stripping their lives down to essentials, and the Indians needed the Jesuits' help in learning to think and act in accordance with Christ's commands (no polygamy or vengeance, for example) and with modern standards of rationality (no more taking dreams as portents or commands, and no more listening to "sorcerers").

The Jesuits had "to become savage with the savages," as Father Paul Le Jeune put it, if they were going to have any success at either civilizing the Indians or purifying themselves. To teach civilized habits, they needed to learn the local language, and that

demanded isolation from other Frenchmen. In 1634 Le Jeune joined
a six-month winter hunting expedition of the Montagnais. The
party barely escaped starvation, as he recalled in a long report for
his superiors and for potential French donors and recruits. He and
two dozen Indians were reduced to eating wood, bark, and old bits
of hide, which not even the famished dogs would touch. "A soul
very thirsty for the Son of God, I mean for suffering," he wrote,
"would find enough here to satisfy it." On Christmas Day there
was nothing to eat, a privation more easily borne, Le Jeune
thought, if one recalled the dire condition of the Holy Family "in
the stable at Bethlehem." The Montagnais rested in their tent cab-
ins, "wasted and thin, silent and very sad, like people who parted
with life regretfully." Le Jeune spent the day getting two prayers
translated and preparing a special Oratory. He placed a napkin on a
cabin pole and attached to it a crucifix, a reliquary (containing the
bones of a holy person), and an image from his breviary. Then he
called the Indians together to hear the prayers. The first one was a
petition to Jesus enmeshed in a doctrinal lesson and a call to faith:

> O Jesus, son of the All-powerful, you who took human
> flesh for us, who were born of a virgin for us, who died for
> us, who were resurrected and ascended into heaven for us,
> you have promised that if something is asked in your
> name, you will grant it. I beg you with all my heart to give
> food to these poor people, who wish to believe in you and
> to obey you. These people promise you entirely that if you
> help them they will believe perfectly in you, and that they
> will obey you with all their hearts. My Lord, hear my
> prayer; I offer you my life for these people, very glad to die
> that they may live and know you. Amen.[28]

The Montagnais interrupted him just before the end of the
prayer, when he expressed his readiness "to die." "Take back those
words," one said, "for we all love you, and do not wish you to die

for us." They thought he was actually going to kill himself. He tried to explain that he was not announcing a course of action, but affirming a conviction. Loving, in his calculus, had a logical connection to dying. As the Gospel of John expressed it, the greatest love ("agape" in the Greek) revealed itself in a willingness to lay down one's life for one's brother. Le Jeune was conveying a central Christian tenet, showing the Indians that religious faith involved a state of continuous mental exertion. One could list one's beliefs as a series of propositions, and distinguish them from the false beliefs of others through rational disputation. Faith revitalized itself by vanquishing objections mounted against it. The prayer also attempted to communicate Le Jeune's own special vocation, for the moment different from theirs. They needed to learn how to believe and what to believe; he needed to prepare to give his life out of love. Even being killed by Indians, he had written in 1633, was not to be feared, since dying at their hands would bring the deceased closer to "our good Master, put to death by those to whom he came to bring life." Le Jeune was fighting an uphill battle in teaching that death was a logical outlet for love or that belief was an exclusionary affair. One Montagnais tried to persuade him that pluralism of belief was superior to a single truth for all. He argued that "all nations had something especially their own. . . . Just as he [the Montagnais] believed us when we [the Jesuits] told him something, or when we showed him a picture, so likewise we ought to believe him when he told us something that was accepted by his people." To believe something meant accepting it as the honorable conviction of someone, either oneself or another.[29]

Half a decade later the Montagnais were still dubious about Le Jeune's contention that the Jesuits had to come to New France out of love for them. In 1639 Le Jeune reported again that they could not fathom what he and other Jesuits meant when they spoke of following Jesus by sacrificing themselves for others. Even the brightest ("les plus spirituels") of the Indians assumed there had to be some other motive for the priests' leaving France, putting up with privation, and giving the Indians so many "good things" without asking anything in return. Some concluded that the Jesuits intended the Indians' "ruin," a conclusion supported by the obvious fact (frequently attested to by the Jesuits) that since the arrival of the French the Montagnais had been far sicker than before, while the French had not been sick at all. Before the Europeans came, said one Indian in 1637, "only the old people died," but "now more young than old died." Le Jeune only made matters worse when he pointed out that the priests had come to Canada for benefits that would be experienced only after death. Hearing death mentioned again, even the most "fair-minded" of the Montagnais, including some of the Christian Indians, thought it all the more certain that the priests had come to kill them.[30]

Sometimes these Christian converts became so extravagant in their piety that the priests had to rein them in. The Jesuits were alarmed at the zeal displayed by Indian families settled into a Christian village at Sillery in the 1640s. These ardent believers begged for harsher penances. Father Buteux, a Sillery priest, gave an especially mournful man "a penance three times as severe as I would have given a Frenchman for the same offense," whereupon the sinner complained, "Is that all you assign for so great a sin? Make me endure something that will torment my body." Downriver at Tadoussac a priest was initially pleased when Ignace, a Christian Indian cured of an illness, reported that he had visited heaven, where he saw and spoke to Jesus. Jesus "showed me his hands and his feet, pierced by great nails, and then he said, . . . 'Ignace, what you have endured during your illness is nothing. It is I who suffered, while hanging on the cross for you, I who am your Creator and your King. When I send you any affliction—hunger, thirst, sickness, poverty—suffer it patiently for me, and in imitation of my example.'" The priest was not sure whether the vision was "veritable" or imagined, but he liked its initial effects: "The wicked were frightened and the good were consoled." Men, women, and children scourged themselves "in imitation of the holy Penitents of whom they had heard." But the contagion got out of hand as individuals tried to outdo one another in lashing themselves with a knotted cord. The priest "assured them of the pardon of their sins" and "warned them not to perform any other public penance without the advice of their Confessors." Civilized behavior was temperate behavior, and proper piety occupied a middle ground between self-satisfaction and self-laceration.[31]

The Tadoussac priest's endorsement of Ignace's vision for its practical fruits is noteworthy in light of the Jesuits' usual condemnation of the Indians' belief in the truth of their dreams. No other Native American habit or practice, apart from polygamy, seemed to the priests more uncivilized. "I make sport of their dreams," said Father Le Jeune in 1634. His dismissal mystified the Montagnais. "What do you believe then," they asked, "if you don't believe in your dreams?" When he replied that "I believe in him who has made all things, and who can do all things," they thought he was making no sense, since unlike them he was believing in something he had not "seen." "They have a faith in dreams that surpasses all credence," wrote Father Jean de Brébeuf of the Hurons. "If Christians were to act upon all their divine inspirations with as much care as our Savages carry out their dreams," he quipped, "they would no doubt very soon become great saints." Putting so much stock in dreams played havoc with a properly rational sense of cause and effect. Taking dreams as messages from the spirit world blurred the line, in the Jesuits' view, between the supernatural realm of God's spontaneous agency and the natural world he had created, a world that ordinarily operated according to observable and predictable laws. Like many Puritans, the Jesuits were determined to root out any popular belief in spirits that compromised the hegemony of the one God in three persons.[32]

That stance allowed them to leave room for God to modify the normal workings of cause and effect whenever he wished, a loophole that permitted much overlap in practice with the Indians' own dream-centered perspective. In effect the Jesuits were telling the

Indians that conversion to Christianity did not entail a total rejection of their traditional worldview. It required only the purifying of
it, seeing themselves as individual souls linked directly to a single
higher spirit, the triune God, who alone could redeem people from
their sinful state. The new conception was essential if Native Americans were to develop a correct sense of their true situation: sinners
deserving of perdition but offered rescue by a wonder-working
God. This God valued them just as he did the Europeans. They
were "souls redeemed at the same price as ours," said Father Julien
Perrault, by "him who has loved us all so much." Human worth
had nothing to do with cultural level. The Indians' value would not
increase when they became civilized. Only their knowledge of their
value would increase.[33]

The Jesuits' reports contained many examples of divine intervention in the natural world, acts of God that supplied a point of
contact and credibility with their Native American hosts. During a
dry summer spell, a Huron sorcerer blamed the lack of rain on the
cross planted in front of Father Brébeuf's door, an explanation the
priest thought ridiculous on the face of it. Yet when a group of
Huron youths put up another cross in order to shoot their arrows at
it, he reported that "our Lord did not permit them to hit it even
once." Brébeuf then repainted his own cross, placed "the body of
our Lord crucified" on it, and had the Indians "adore and kiss" it.
When this ritual was followed by rain and "a plentiful harvest," he
encouraged the Indians to believe (and may have believed himself)
that the cause of their good fortune was the penitent observance.
The sacrament of baptism also illustrated this fudging of the line
between the magical and the spiritual. While the priests usually
preached that "the life-giving waters of Holy Baptism principally
impart life to the soul, and not to the body," as Brébeuf put it, they
sometimes encouraged the Indians to believe that physical ills
could indeed be cured by it. When a woman baptized on her
deathbed recovered and "broadcast everywhere" that the baptism
had healed her, Brébeuf welcomed the publicity. "Indeed," he

noted, "she was virtually dead, but as soon as she was washed with the holy water she began to feel better." Jesus seeped into early American cultures as a miracle-worker who made sense to people all along the spectrum from magical to non-magical consciousness.[34]

Of course the Jesuits' reserving so much space for supernatural agency in the physical world left an opening for anti-Christian disputants on the Indian side. These opponents showed the priests that if disputational skill was a sign of civilization, then some Native Americans had advanced further than the French had expected. In an after-dinner speech Father Le Jeune told an assembly that his love for them had come from the God "who created the first man, from whom we have all descended." That made them all brothers, who "ought all to acknowledge the same Lord, . . . to believe in him, and obey his will." A "sorcerer" interrupted him to announce that he would believe in this God only if he could see him. Le Jeune countered that he could recite the names of those who had seen the Son of God on earth, and name all the countries those witnesses had visited. The sorcerer replied, "Your God has not come to our country, and that is why we do not believe in him." Le Jeune answered that there were two kinds of sight, spiritual and physical. What you see "with the eyes of the soul may be just as true as what you see with the eyes of the body." The sorcerer saw his opening. "I see nothing except with the eyes of the body, save in sleeping, and you do not approve our dreams. . . . You don't know what you're talking about. Learn to talk and we'll listen to you." Le Jeune was being arbitrary, the Indian was saying, ruling out or approving spiritual perception when it pleased him, not to mention making an illogical leap from his own expressed motivation for coming to Quebec to the claim that the Jesus he had brought with him was the universal God. A universal savior would logically have revealed himself to *all* peoples, not *some* peoples.[35]

The vigor of the sorcerer's response as reported by Le Jeune suggests that some Jesuits may have wondered if the line between savagery and civility was blurrier than their letters home could admit. Le Jeune believed that the Montagnais were at Aristotle's "survival" stage of development, prior to the next two stages of "civilization" and "contemplation." They were so continuously chasing after their food that they did not have the leisure to cultivate logically defensible beliefs about anything, much less belief in a Jesus brought to them from Europe. They were so hungry so much of the time that one Indian told him his favorite Christian prayer was "Mirinan oukachigakhi nimitchiminan" ("Give us today our food, give us something to eat"). Yet he was also convinced of their intelligence and generosity, as in the ease and eagerness with which they simplified their language in order to communicate with him. The Hurons evangelized by Father Brébeuf were far more settled and agricultural than the Montagnais, and hence in the Jesuit view readier for civilized practices. Brébeuf came close at times to seeing them as virtual Christians already, on account of their extraordinary hospitality toward all strangers. "I think I have read, in the lives of the Fathers," he wrote, "that a pagan army was converted on seeing the charity and hospitality of a Christian town, the inhabitants of which vied with each other in caressing and feasting the strangers—judging well that those must profess the true religion and worship the true God, the common Father of all, who had hearts so benign and who did so much good to all sorts of persons, without distinction." This was a nation that "our Lord" appeared to have "predisposed" to "the fire of his graces."[36]

Still, the Indians were in the dark night of ignorance even for Brébeuf, and he prayed it would please God "to illumine them." From a doctrinal standpoint the civilizing process had to begin with the fact that "their souls, which are immortal," were destined to eternal placement in either heaven or hell, and that they had "the choice, during life," to go whichever way they wished after death. The red-hot tortures of hell seemed to have registered with many Indians, who quickly got the point that it was better not to burn. "A good old man responded," wrote Brébeuf, that "whoever wants to go into the fires of hell is welcome to do so; as for me, I wish to go to heaven." But some of the old men remained obstinate, appealing for support to the "all-purpose refuge" of their belief that "their country is not like ours, that they have another God, another paradise, in a word, other customs." Hence the Jesuits centered their conversion campaign on the young.[37]

Targeting children made good sense if the goal was to remake secular habits as well as religious beliefs. And children's consciousness lent itself to the rudimentary language skills of the priests. With Indian children as well as the few French children living with the Jesuits in Canada, the priests could civilize through a combination of carrots and sticks—prizes of food or trinkets for good responses at catechism, whippings for misbehavior of all sorts. Yet using the rod on Indian children required getting them away from their parents, who thought the French treatment of children was barbaric. When a group of Indians visiting a ship on the St. Lawrence observed the French about to mete out a whipping to a French cabin boy (for having hit an Indian on the head with his drumstick), one of the Indian adults stood in the way and asked to be whipped in his stead. Indians complained about the French hitting their children, while the Jesuits found fault with Indian men for hitting their wives, though they felt there was nothing they could do to stop it. In the case of children, the Jesuits repeatedly pleaded for French donations to support boarding schools in Quebec in which proper discipline could be enforced without shocking the tender sensibilities of Indian parents.

It was the Huron girls (Brébeuf thought) who showed a special interest in Jesus. He reported in 1636 that the priests went from dwelling to dwelling teaching all the young children, baptized or not, the sign of the cross, the Our Father, the Hail Mary, the Apostle's Creed, the Ten Commandments, and the Prayer to the Guardian Angel, all in their own language. The younger kids would then teach the older ones. Girls returning from the forest would intercept a priest and "begin to recite what they know. What a consolation to hear these districts resound with the name of Jesus, where the devil has been, so to speak, adored and recognized as God for so many centuries." Two decades later the Huron Christian community was made up mostly of women. "I can say with truth," wrote Father François Le Mercier in 1654, "that among savages as in the rest of the world, they are the devout sex." Yet the Jesuits' letters are full of heroic stories of male as well as female piety, among children as well as adults. Most of the children simply learned their prayers by rote, but Father Le Jeune took special pride in one precocious boy who went beyond memorized truths. "You say it's necessary to believe in order to go to heaven," Le Jeune said to a young Montagnais boy. "Do you believe?" "Yes, I believe, I do my best to believe," the boy answered. "What do you believe?" "I believe in the Father, in the Son, and in the Holy Ghost; I believe that the Son was made man in the womb of a virgin named Mary." "Is the Virgin God?" After thinking a moment, the child replied, "No, she is not God, because you say that there is only one God."[38]

Systematic catechizing was directed at the children, but the Jesuits were always eager to bring the behavior of adults into line with Christ's prescriptions. The marital bond enjoined by Christ was as unknown to the eastern woodland tribes as it was to the Pueblo Indians. All the missionaries, Catholic and Protestant, bemoaned "the liberty with which," as Brébeuf put it, Indian men "change their wives at pleasure." Father Perrault on the island of Cape Breton noted that the locals paid no attention to the indissolubility of marriage, and he hoped to change their "polygamous" ways by linking sexual continence to the worship of Christ. Jesus modeled bodily discipline, giving his body up for "torture," then offering it in perpetuity in the Eucharist "en viandes" ("as food"). As Father Perrault saw it, in a perfect circle of causation, Jesus presented his own flesh each day for the "sole purpose" of helping us to glorify him for the sacrifice on Calvary that had made his flesh available to us in the first place. The elegance of Perrault's formulation shows that while his time among the Indians of Cape Breton may have done little to change the customs of the island, it certainly helped him articulate his own Christological vision.[39]

The same goes for the Jesuits' efforts to persuade Native Americans to follow Christ's love-commandment in their dealings with one another. In 1637 Father Le Jeune managed to persuade a Huron war party to forgo the "filthy custom" of enjoying a pre-battle feast in which they were served by "completely nude" women. But he had a harder time convincing them to Christianize their approach to war. He saddled them with a set of fine distinctions. The right to kill their Iroquois enemies depended upon loving them too. He would offer God's benediction for their campaign only if they gave the Iroquois every opportunity to observe an earlier peace agreement. The Hurons had to give God a fair chance to make the Iroquois honorable. The leaders of the war party promised to obey these strictures, got the priest's blessing, but then reverted to old habits. Once among the Iroquois they exhibited an "intolerable pride" and committed "countless insolences," such as proclaiming themselves magically protected (perhaps partly because of the Jesuit blessing), and were promptly smitten by the enemy. "God greatly humiliated them, for their Captains and some others were put to death." In 1639 a joint Huron-Algonquin war party captured over a hundred Iroquois, who were distributed among the Huron villages for torture. The Jesuits were on record in opposition to these ritual killings, especially to the eating of enemy flesh, and they did their best to baptize the Iroquois victims before their deaths. But the Hurons, concluding that these baptisms fortified their victims, "resolved no longer to allow us to baptize these poor unfortunates, reckoning it a misfortune to their country when those whom they torment shriek not at all, or very little."[40]

A decade later Brébeuf was himself tortured to death by the Iroquois, who had overrun a Huron encampment. According to the later report of some escaped Huron prisoners, his attackers were assisted by Huron infidels acquainted with Christianity. They transformed the torture into a considered anti-Christian statement.

In addition to applying the usual necklace of red-hot hatchets and belt of burning bark, they cut off his tongue and lips to prevent him from uttering the name of Jesus. As they stripped "the flesh from his legs, thighs, and arms, to the very bone, and then put it to roast before his eyes, in order to eat it," they derided him by saying, "You see plainly that we treat you as a friend, since we shall be the cause of your eternal happiness. Thank us, then, for these good offices which we render you, for the more you suffer the more your God will reward you." This flesh-stripping, according to Jesuit Christophe Regnaut, was common in Huron tortures of the Iroquois as well as Iroquois tortures of the Hurons. What was novel in Brébeuf's case was the "kettle full of boiling water . . . poured over his body three times, in derision of Holy Baptism." Each of the three ablutions was accompanied by the words "Go to Heaven, for you are well baptized."[41]

Of all the Jesuits in New France Brébeuf may have been the best equipped to grasp that his own ritual torture in 1649 was the result not of savagery but of a different system of cultural practices, a system even in this extreme instance adapting itself to novel European beliefs. For over a decade Brébeuf had tried to counter the widespread impression that the Hurons lived like beasts. Granted, they were not "perfectly civilized" like the Japanese and Chinese. But assembled in villages of three hundred or four hundred households, and supporting themselves year-round by agriculture, they did have a "political and civil life." Bringing Jesus to them was therefore a problem of *translating* as much as *civilizing*. The challenge was to give the Hurons access to the meanings of Christian stories and symbols—meanings hidden from them by differences of language as well as experience. "The parables and the more familiar discourses of Jesus Christ are inexplicable to them," wrote Jérôme Lalemant, Brébeuf's colleague among the Hurons, in 1640. "They are unfamiliar with salt, leaven, castle, pearl, prison, mustard seed, casks of wine, lamp, candlestick, torch; they have no idea of Kingdoms, Kings, and their majesty; not even of shepherds, flocks, and a sheep-fold." Brébeuf found it impossible even to convey the sense of the sign of the cross to the Hurons in their own language. In 1636 he asked his superior, Paul Le Jeune, for permission to retranslate it. Instead of "in the name of the Father, and of the Son, and of the Holy Ghost," he suggested "in the name of our Father, and of his Son, and of their Holy Ghost." That form was required by their language, in which all personal nouns were preceded by possessives:

> Certainly it seems that the three persons of the most Holy Trinity would be sufficiently expressed in this way, the third being indeed the Holy Spirit of the first and second; the second, Son of the first; and the first, our Father, in the phrase of the Apostle [in Ephesians 3 and in the Lord's Prayer]. . . . Would this usage be acceptable until the Huron language is enriched, or the mind of the Hurons opened to other languages? We will do nothing without advice.[42]

For the Jesuits of New France as for the Franciscans of New Mexico, bringing Jesus to the Indians meant living in their villages and instructing them in his gospel. "A missionary does no great good to the savages unless he lives with them," Father Jacques Gravier wrote from the Mississippi River in 1700. The Indians needed monitoring: practicing the faith meant literally *practicing* it, rehearsing it. Heathen habits would dissolve when overwhelmed by repeated acts of Christian worship and virtue. This Catholic sense that the faith could be learned by the doing of it rested on the assumption that after Adam's fall human beings, however weakened in apprehension or resolve, had retained a "natural" inclination to know and serve God. That universal human potential gave Catholic missionary work a special urgency. Since even uncivilized peoples had enormous untapped spiritual capacity, missionaries could have a dramatic impact upon their eternal fate. Bringing Jesus to them could turn them away from sin, leading them to choose obedience to

God's commandments. Franciscans and Jesuits felt that countless souls depended on them for deliverance. Believing that God had selected them for this weighty calling, they could submit with equanimity to final torments of the sort endured by Brébeuf.[43]

Where the French Jesuits differed from the Spanish friars was in their reticence about adult baptism. They baptized only those Indian adults who were dying or who had come to a well-articulated conviction about Christ as their savior and themselves as sinners in need of his redemption. But baptism was only the outward sign of an inward grace, as Father Pierre Biard pointed out in 1612. Indians who responded to the gospel of Jesus with "true repentance," who wished to "incorporate themselves with our Savior, Jesus Christ," would be saved even without baptism. The reverse was also true. Any baptized Christian might die in sin and be damned in perpetuity. In the Jesuits' eyes the heroes of the faith were not those who were baptized, but those who had caught the gospel spark, baptized or not. Joseph Chiwatenhwa, a Huron from the village of Ossossane, was baptized only when seriously ill. According to Father François Mercier, he had long "passed for a Christian among his own people," having never gambled, smoked, used charms for luck, had more than one wife, or "indulged in diabolical feasts." After recovering from his illness he made the final surrender "to reason and to the Holy Ghost" by "ridiculing his dreams" and meditating on the "Holy Commandments." He took to praying for forty-five minutes at a stretch, "all the time on his knees, which is a very difficult position for a savage." For Father Mercier, Chiwatenhwa was a shining light of French civility, but more important he had received from God the gift of "a holy tenderness of heart." After his baptism he went on to preach "Jesus Christ boldly and on all occasions" until captured by the Iroquois and martyred for the faith in 1640.[44]

The Jesuits knew that French-style civility was no end in itself. Like Joseph Chiwatenhwa, a young, unnamed Algonquin man went far beyond moral uprightness in voicing an obedience that in Father Le Jeune's estimation transcended human cultural identity altogether. "Some of my people cast upon me the reproach that I am becoming a Frenchman, that I am leaving my own nation," the nineteen-year-old told him in 1639. "I answer them that I am neither Frenchman nor savage, but that I wish to be a child of God. All the French, including their Captain, could not save my soul; it is not in them that I believe, but in him who has made them themselves." Le Jeune added that "he expressed all this to us better in his own language than I can report in ours." Of course the young Algonquin was not transcending culture, but catching the universalizing thrust of the culture of Jesus, putting on "the new man," as Paul said in Colossians 3:10–11, "where there is neither Greek nor Jew" but "Christ is all, and in all."[45]

TWO

I WAS A
CHRISTLESS CREATURE

I

The Calvinists of New England shared the Jesuits' wariness about precipitous conversions and pushed it even further. Puritan minister John Eliot, the famous "Apostle to the Indians," was frequently pestered by English critics who wondered why he had not made more Indian Christians. After all, English colonization had been launched with the usual European promise to make "the poore Natives," in John Cotton's public advice to the departing John Winthrop in 1630, "partakers of your precious faith." The English settlers, Cotton explained, would get temporal benefits by partaking of the Indians' land, while the Indians would reap spiritual gains. Since Jesus had sacrificed himself for all people, he was the natives' precious Lord too: "Winne them to the love of Christ for whom Christ died." But Puritan evangelizing of the Indians did not begin until Eliot went to work in 1646, and even then only a few ministers paid the natives any mind. Those who did, including Thomas Shepard, grew tired of the naysayers back in London, who had more "spleene than judgement." They were oblivious to "the vast distance of Natives from common civility, almost humanity itselfe." Only "a spirit of life from God (not in mans power)" could "put flesh and sinewes unto these dry bones; if we would force them to baptisme (as the Spaniarts do about Cusco, Peru, and Mexico, having learnt them a short answer or two to some Popish questions) or if we would hire them to it by giving them coates and shirts, to allure them to it . . . we could have gathered many hundreds, yea thousands it may be by this time, into the name of Churches; but we have not learnt as yet that art of coyning Christians, or putting Christs name and Image upon copper mettle."[1]

The Puritans did not like hearing whisperings from London that they were evangelical slackers, but in response they chastised themselves for not doing more. John Winthrop had beat his breast on the subject in 1629, before leaving England. "It is a scandale to our religion," he wrote, "that we shewe not as muche zeale in seekinge the conversion of the heathen as the Papistes doe." The Catholics sent out "their most able men," while Protestants "sende onely suche as we can best spare, or are a burden to us." Best men or worst, there was no way Puritans in America could compete with Catholics in making converts. Their clergymen did not and could not live among the Indians, since each of the ministers had a congregation of his own to shepherd. They could not baptize Indian children whose parents were heathen. (The Jesuits supplied French godparents to take their place.) They could not pass out hundreds of crosses, pictures, and rosaries as tokens and reminders of faith. They thought having true knowledge of Jesus required reading the Bible oneself, and they knew Indian literacy was years or decades away.[2]

But the main reason they could not compete was that they did not want to. The Puritan "communion of the saints" amounted to a restricted covenant. Full church membership was extended not to the many who professed belief in God but to the few who gave evidence of pure lives and saving experiences of faith. This exclusivity did not just make it hard for Indians to become full-fledged Christians. It made it hard for Englishmen. When the Reverend

Richard Mather (father of Increase and grandfather of Cotton) tried to gather a new church in Dorchester in 1636, the magistrates and other ministers at first turned him down. With a single exception the members of his group had failed to persuade the assembled officials that their faith was genuine. They had talked about Christ's importance to them, about how he had reformed their lives, and about the dreams he had induced in them. The problem, as Governor John Winthrop summed up their "errors," was that "they had never truly closed with Christ (or rather Christ with them) but had made use of him only to help the imperfection of their sanctification and duties, and not made him their sanctification, wisdom, etc.; they expected to believe by some power of their own and not only and wholly from Christ."[3]

Catholics and Puritans were equally passionate about their devotion to Jesus—so passionate that each group found the other's veneration of him dangerously deficient. Puritans thought Catholics took devotion away from Jesus when they prayed to the Virgin Mary or the saints. Catholics thought Puritans took devotion away from Jesus when they banned images of him. Yet these public differences of opinion obscure a much deeper gap between them on what it meant to believe in Christ. Although the Puritans had their own disagreements, they all agreed that human beings, created in the image of God, had been deeply damaged by Adam's rebellion. His sin had so disordered their natural minds and appetites that they needed God's intervention even for their proper knowledge of him, not to speak of their salvation. Natural reason was not wholly warped or antithetical to faith, but it was a much less helpful resource than Catholics supposed. And it misled people into imagining that they could know or approach God through their own well-intentioned efforts. God could be met only in the saving gospel of Christ revealed in the Bible, which each believer needed to read directly. People got guidance from their ministers in grasping the meanings of Scripture, but they had to understand it, not just nod their heads. And they had to do more than understand.

They had to pray for God's saving action in their hearts. Becoming a member of a Christian congregation meant not wishing for a life-changing spiritual experience of Jesus, but having one.

True Christians knew that their own efforts to save themselves were unavailing. Even their own desire to be close to Christ was double-edged, since it made them exaggerate their own power to move toward him. They had to surrender this illusion of effective power residing in themselves. If their self-surrender was pure enough, if they truly put their faith in Jesus, God could choose to "justify" them (consider them righteous) and "sanctify" them (flood them with the Holy Spirit). The initiative was his. The sign of sanctification (an ongoing process of purification, unlike the sudden, one-time justification) would be a calm and joyful ardor in loving God and neighbor. Yet even sanctification, the visible sign of grace that accompanied the invisible justification, was no proof that a person was headed to heaven. God was the all-sovereign Lord of creation, not some tribal deity whose judgments human beings could decode or control. True, he had made a covenant with humanity, promising salvation for those who believed in Jesus. But he alone could determine ultimately whether a believer's faith was authentic (and of course, given his time-transcending omniscience, he already knew what that final judgment would be). Puritans had to learn to live with uncertainty, or rather with the certainty that if they felt for a moment free of sin or bound for paradise, they were quite likely deluding themselves. One could never fully know one's own heart. God was the only reader of that hidden book.[4]

Few Catholics or Protestants knew exactly how their styles and conceptions of Jesus differed. But they were quick to disparage one another's faiths, which often stood in for national allegiances. English revulsion at alleged Jesuit schemes to "rere in all parts of the world" the "kingdom of Antichrist," as John Winthrop put it in 1629, were so well broadcast that Indians heard about it from other Indians. The Hurons, for example, heard from Indian travelers that the English "on the seacoast toward the south" considered the Jesuits "people who would doom and ruin the world." When Charles Meiaskwat, a Montagnais Christian, visited an English settlement in Maine, he got an immediate lesson in Protestant-Catholic animosities. Knowing nothing of the Englishmen's religion (and in any case, according to Jesuit Bartélemy Vimont, unable to distinguish visually between the English and the French), he innocently displayed his rosary beads. One of the Englishmen was disgusted at the sight. "It is the Devil who invented what you're holding," he said. The quick-witted Charles retorted that, on the contrary, the devil was putting those very words in the Englishman's mouth. Charles upped the ante by informing his antagonist that "you despise the Son of God and his Mother." The Englishman stood his ground. Pointing to an old rag in the dirt, he said, "What you're holding [the rosary] is worth no more than that." But Charles delivered the coup de grâce, in Vimont's version of the duel. "Believe this," he announced. "God sees and hears you. Know certainly that you will burn in hell, since you despise what God has made and commanded."[5]

Despite the substantial Catholic-Protestant divergence on how to follow Christ, and on the legitimacy of visualizing him, they still shared much theological ground. That overlap permitted them, in their encounter with Native Americans, to concentrate on the same healer and martyr roles for Jesus. Those identities were rooted in the Europeans' common Trinitarian theology: Jesus was fully man and fully God, and he had died to ransom humanity from Adam's sin. The Catholics could also preach Jesus as a civilizer, thanks to their idea that church membership in principle included entire populations, not just a justified and sanctified elect. In theory Puritans preached to whole populations too, since all residents were supposed to attend Sabbath meetings. But only full members had access to the communion table. For Catholics the Holy Eucharist— Christ's actual body—was available to anyone who had learned enough of Jesus to be baptized. The phrase "give us this day our daily bread" had a different meaning for Catholics than for Protestants, since Catholics often took the Eucharist itself to be their daily spiritual sustenance. From the Jesuit viewpoint, the Indians' taking Christ into their body permitted them to make further progress in civility while sparking a few extraordinary souls to pass through civility to true holiness.

The paradox of the Puritans' approach to the Indians is that while they barred Jesus himself from serving as an instrument of the civilizing process, they did employ biblical instruction in general—and hence Jesus the Word of God—as a tool of cultural improvement. Jesus entered the civilizing mission through the back door as one teacher among many from the Hebrew and Christian Scriptures. The Puritans actually brought as much religion to the civilizing task as the Franciscans in New Mexico did. They just reversed the polarities of religion and civility. They made religiously driven civility the dominant dimension, while the Franciscans made civilly mandated religious ritual paramount. Both groups saw religion—the Bible for the Protestants, the church for the Catholics—as the main bulwark of moral order. The Jesuits did too, but they added an additional wrinkle, letting spirituality float free of or conflict with civility. These highly educated men could see the wilderness, and the savage, as a means of grace for the overcivilized. They honored education nearly as much as the Puritans, and labored to get Indian children to school. But they did not see reading as a precondition for informed faith. The Puritans were truly the people of the Word. Jean de Brébeuf might toil over the right translation of the sign of the cross, but John Eliot took on the whole Bible. His translation into the Massachusett language was published in 1663, the first Bible printed in America in *any* language. For the Puritans biblical knowledge was civilizing even if it led to no conversions, and they thought it would certainly lead to a few.

When the Puritan missionaries John Eliot in Natick (a village founded in 1651 as a gathering point for "praying Indians") or Thomas Mayhew, Jr., on Martha's Vineyard mentioned that Jesus was a healer, they discovered what Franciscans, Jesuits, and even adventurers such as Cabeza de Vaca had earlier reported. Indians started listening in earnest. When Eliot's Indian proselytes delivered their own oral confessions, they sounded just like English confessors, except for their constant harping on sickness and death. Jesus the healer made special sense to them since they feared succumbing to the diseases that had already decimated their communities. The plague of 1616–1618 (brought by European traders who preceded the Pilgrims and Puritans, and responsible for making Plymouth look invitingly vacant in 1620) and the smallpox of 1633 may have wiped out 90 percent of the Massachusett population. John Eliot and Thomas Mayhew, like the Franciscans and Jesuits, were preaching to Native Americans still reeling from terrible human losses and new European practices. Belief in Jesus was one cultural innovation that bore directly on illness and death. Some small cohort of Native Americans in early seventeenth-century New England—those who did not mind being accused by their fellow Indians of forsaking their ancestors out of love of the English— came to Jesus because he cured.

II

The martyrdom of Christ did not figure as a personal life-model for Puritan clerics as it did for Franciscans and Jesuits. Even the idea of Christ as a model played itself out differently. For Puritans the whole notion of imitating Jesus was suspect, since it implied to them an idolatrous belief in one's natural power to conquer sin, to live purely, as he did. Yet Puritans like Cotton Mather (along with later Protestant evangelicals) loved the medieval writer Thomas à Kempis, and endorsed his idea of the *Imitatio Christi* if it meant "meditat[ing] on the Lord JESUS CHRIST, and his wondrous love to miserable sinners, in dying a cursed and bitter death for our sin." That kind of imitation allowed for extolling the virtues of Jesus while remembering the gulf that separated him from all human striving. "It has been a Satanic Stratagem," said Mather, "to press the Imitation of Christ, with an intent thereby, to draw off the minds of men from faith in the satisfaction and propitiation, of Christ. . . . There are incommunicable perfections of the Lord Jesus Christ, wherein a Christian may not propose to imitate Him." For their part, of course, Roman Catholics considered the Puritans too pessimistic about human nature after the Fall. Yes, Adam's sin had undermined people's attainment of virtue, but their potential for it survived. They still possessed the natural capacity to pursue Christ's example, though following him would surely entail suffering rather than ease.[6]

The Puritans' favorite phrase, "walking in the ways of the Lord" (Deut. 5:33), implied the kind of imitation of Jesus that they endorsed. They tried to copy his utter obedience to the sovereign Father. Catholic imitation of Jesus put the emphasis on intentions and outcomes—the self-sacrificing pursuit of good works—while the Puritan stress lay on the rigorous self-abasement preceding any good works that sanctified Christians might also do. Martyrdom did figure centrally in Puritan preaching, since it was built into their Trinitarian scheme of redemption through Christ's sacrifice. And Puritans, like Catholics, told stories of martyred heroes. When the Puritans wished to convey the awe-inspiring power of God in the New World, they could not relate countless Indian baptisms, as the Jesuits and Franciscans did, but they could tell the story of Wequash Cook, who "suffered Martyrdome for Christ."

Wequash was a Pequot warrior who began with a low opinion of both Englishmen ("silly, weake men") and their God ("a Musketto God, or a God like unto a flye"). That was before he found out in battle that "one English man by the help of his God" and his firearms could "slay and put to flight an hundred Indians." But this God of power and might evolved into the Prince of Peace as Wequash, living among the English in Connecticut, learned to put revenge behind him. "If any did smite him on the one cheeke, he would rather turne the other, than offend them." He also conquered his other "dearest sinne"—lust—"by putting away all his wives, saving the first, to whom he had most right." He capped his newly civilized life of monogamy and peacemaking by preaching to other Indians "like that poore woman of Samaria [in John 4], proclaiming Christ, and telling them what a treasure he had found, . . . warning them with all faithfulnesse to flee from the wrath to come, by breaking off their sinnes and wickednesse." In the midst of his preaching Wequash took sick—perhaps poisoned by Indian opponents (as the English alleged), thus qualifying him as a venerable martyr.[7]

Some of the Indians evangelized by Jesuits in Quebec lay on their deathbeds and gloried in the eternal life that surely awaited them. By contrast, Wequash lay on his deathbed near Saybrook and contemplated his worthlessness. Roger Williams, who had met and instructed him three years earlier, came to his bedside. "Me much pray to Jesus Christ," Wequash said to him. The solemn Williams was not impressed. "I told him so did many English, French, and Dutch, who had never turned to God, nor loved Him." Wequash gave the start of an adequate Puritan response to that rebuff. "Me so big naughty heart, me heart all one stone!" Beginning with a low opinion of the English God, he had ended with a low opinion of himself. But in Williams's judgment Wequash had gotten only to the verge of spiritual justification. He had not yet felt the inrushing of the Holy Spirit. He had not learned to express "love to Christ" or to feel the tranquil assurance of Christ's mercy. Jesus had only judged him, convicted him of sin. Williams did take Wequash's piety as a sign of future spiritual progress among Native Americans. That progress would finally silence the English critics who looked at America and wondered, in light of "the boast of the Jesuits" and the "wonderfull conversions of the Spaniards," "what have the English done in those parts, what hopes of the Indians receiving the knowledge of Christ?"[8]

Several Indians evangelized by Eliot made public confessions of faith in which they supplied the one reason why the English had some reason to hope: sickness and death had led the Indians to Jesus as an antidote. Of course Eliot had tried to teach them that Christ healed the soul, not the body. But he confused matters by also teaching that "if we are loth to part with sin, God will chastise us with sickness, poverty, and other worldly crosses, to call us to repentance." The Indians naturally concluded that if God could damage their bodies, then he or his divine Son could repair them too, something they may have thought any deity of consequence could do. Totherswamp, one of the most articulate Christian Indians, confessed that he had initially resisted praying to God because he had "many friends who loved me, and I loved them, and they cared not for praying to God, and therefore I did not. But I thought in my heart that if my friends should die, and I live, I then would pray to God; soon after, God so wrought, that they did almost all die, few of them left; and then my heart feared, and I thought, that now I will pray unto God. . . . Yet at first I did not think of God, and eternal life, but only that the English should love me, and I loved them. But after I came to see what sin was, . . . and then I saw all my sins, lust, gaming, etc . . . I can do no righteousness, but Christ hath done it for me; this I beleeve, and therefore I do hope for pardon." Waban, in whose wigwam Eliot had done his first preaching in 1646, also confessed that for years he had not truly listened. It was only "after the great sickness" that "I considered what the English do, and had some desire to do as they do." He also considered what Christ could do: "He can heale us both soul and body."[9]

Monequassun, another of Eliot's converts, began his confession with a recitation of Bible passages, as befitted one who had "desired to learn to reade Gods Word" and "did much pray to God that he would teach me to reade." He had wondered "how should I, my wife, and child be cloathed, if I spend my time in learning to read." But that turned out to be the least of his worries. For "God laid upon me more trouble, by sickness and death; and then I much prayed to God for life, for we were all sick, and then God would not hear me, to give us life; but first one of my children died, and after that my wife; then I was in great sorrow, because I thought God would not hear me, and I thought it was because I would not follow him, therefore he hears not me; then I found this sin in my heart, that I was angry at the punishment of God. But afterward I considered I was a poor sinner, I have nothing, nor child, nor wife, I deserve that God should take away all mercies from me." Eliot closed the session of Indian confessions by reading aloud the statement of Nookau, who summed up what had drawn so many of his peers to the gospel. "Before I prayed I was sick, I thought I should die; at which I was much troubled, and knew not what to do; then I thought, if there be a God above, and he give life again, then I shall beleeve there is a God above, and God did give me life; and after that I took up praying to God."[10]

Monequassun's confession included his remorse over undue attachment to his "long hair," a sin he had "prayed God to pardon." His ultimate realization "that it is a shame for a man to wear long hair, and that there was no such custom in the churches," shows how tightly the English tied civility to religion, while keeping Jesus-worship and civility apart. When "divers sachems and other principal men amongst the Indians" assembled at Concord in 1646 to request a grant of land for a town of their own, the English drew up a list of two dozen rules the Indian residents would have to obey. The Indians accepted bans on "powwowing (cures effected by witches or sorcerers in league with the devil)," murder, fighting, lying, stealing, adultery, fornication, buggery, wife-beating, having "any more but one wife," "greasing themselves," and disguising themselves or "howling" during "their mournings." They agreed that an Indian could no longer "pick lice [out of hair], as formerly, and eat them," "play at their former games," or "come into any Englishman's house except he first knock." They promised to "observe the Lord's day," pray to God "both before and after meat," and resist "the wiles of Satan." And of course they swore to "wear their hair comely, as the English do." Fines ranged from five shillings for uncomely hair to twenty shillings for profaning the

Lord's day or beating one's wife. Adultery, murder, and buggery meant death.[11]

John Eliot's account of the origin of his Indian evangelizing reveals further complexities in the Puritan "civil religion." When he began talking to the Indians, he spoke only of "the law of God" in order "to convince, bridle, restrain, and civilize them, and also to humble them," as Moses had done in giving the law to his own "rude company." The Indians at first found their own customs perfectly satisfactory, "and despised what I said." Only later did some of them "come into the English fashions, and live after their manner." According to Eliot some small group of Native Americans *asked* to become civilized, and even criticized the English (as Winthrop and others had long been doing) for having neglected their evangelization. Eliot told them that becoming like the English would mean laboring in a double vineyard, spiritual and temporal: to "know, serve, and pray unto God," and to "work in building, planting, clothing." Still, only a few Indians, such as those at Noonanetum, evinced any interest in changing their ways. Those at Dorchester Mill, among others, remained indifferent to the offer. And other Indians showed their displeasure by scoffing at anyone sidling up to the English. One "sober Indian" who went "up into the country" with two of his sons talked openly of "God and Jesus Christ," only to find his sons mocked by the locals. They called one of them "Jehovah," the other "Jesus Christ."[12]

III

It is easy to miss the character of Eliot's religious civility by reducing it to a reformation of indecorous habits, a civilizing work-discipline (a version of Max Weber's rational asceticism, in which Puritans kept careful accounts of their worldly and spiritual lives), or a pious repression of earthy instinct (a version of the old saw that the straight-laced Puritans had no fun). Eliot's civilizing process was all prelude to the hoped-for spiritual outcome: Jesus would actually enter the Indians' hearts. In anticipation of that outcome Eliot taught piety as well as civility. Like his fellow ministers, he distinguished himself from the Catholics by holding Christ in reserve. Jesus had his own agenda and could not be approached casually. But Eliot prepared the way for Christ's coming by showing Indians how to confess and how to weep over their sins. Weeping, like confessing, was an outward sign of readiness for Jesus.

Wampoowa, for example, was hauled before Eliot's regular assembly of Indians and Englishmen for wife-beating (at this gathering even the governor was present). When asked what his wife had done to provoke his "passion," he surprised everyone by blaming himself entirely. Realizing the gravity of his sin, but knowing too that "God was ready to pardon it in Christ," Wampoowa "turned his face to the wall, and wept, though with modest endeavor to hide it; and such was the modest, penitent, and melting behavior of the man, that it much affected all to see it in a barbarian, and all did forgive him." When Waban gave his public confession of faith before the magistrates, his delivery was so stammering that some of the dignitaries doubted his testimony. But one of the English observers quickly attested to his sincerity by noting that "he spake these expressions with tears." And when Eliot reproved his own Indian servant for drinking too much "sack" while on a journey, the man immediately "humbled himself with confession of his sin and tears." Eliot still called him before the assembly for more penitence, where he duly "did confess his sin with many tears."[13]

The weeping reported by Eliot in response to his preaching and chastisement was so general that Thomas Shepard saw it as a sign of "some conquering power of Christ Jesus stirring" among the Indians. According to Shepard, Eliot was understating the torrent of tears. When Eliot's servant was weeping before the assembly "there were so many [tears] as that the dry place of the wigwam where he stood was bedirtied with them, pouring them out so abundantly. Indians are well known not to be much subject to tears; no, not when they come to feel the sorest torture, or are solemnly brought forth to die." On this occasion "the word" of God was directly responsible for the weeping, and "what it will end in at last the Lord best knows." Perhaps it was linked, thought Shepard, to the gathering in of "the eastern Jews" in Turkey, which recently had been reported by millennialists ever on the lookout for signs of the endtimes. Following the Book of Daniel, they believed that the conversion of the Jews would presage the Second Coming of Christ.[14]

At the very least, in Shepard's estimation, the wave of Indian weeping announced a new birth of religious civility among them. They seemed to Shepard to be readying themselves for an eventual heart-encounter with Christ by learning an essential Christian practice. Individuals had genuine religious experience, the Puritans thought, as they confronted God one-on-one, without Catholic-style clerical mediation. How could solitary worshipers know if they had truly heard and felt the Word of God, rather than concocting some pious amalgam of their own, and how could their fellow Christians be sure their faith was authentic? By witnessing visible signs of their change of heart—above all, copious tears. Having ruled out sacramental formalism or priestly office or penitential whipping and scourging as routes to real contact with God, evangelical Protestants had no choice but to rely on emotional exhibits. They depended upon periodic bursts of communally observed sentiment to satisfy themselves, temporarily, that they were truly bound to Jesus. In place of the Catholics' bloody processions and bleeding Jesus, the Puritans relied on a bodily fluid compatible with English civility: the stream of tears disclosing a contrite heart.

The Puritan civilizing campaign was a call to Englishness containing an ultimate call to Christ, yet it did not entail a clean sweep of Indian customs. Eliot disliked powwowing as much as anyone, but he respected the powwows' (i.e., medicine men's) knowledge of traditional healing even as he condemned what he deemed their devil worship. As long as the powwows stuck to effecting "recovery from sickness" through the use of "roots, and such other things which God hath made for that purpose," powwowing was not only "no sin," but a positive good. Likewise, Thomas Shepard was tolerant of Indian dreams, since they might contain actual communications from God. "I attribute little to dreams," he said of his own life. "Yet God may speak to such [as the Indians] by them" even if he does not use dreams to speak "to those who have a more sure word to direct and warn them." English customs and habits of mind were not imposed on Indians *en bloc.* The Puritans could not share church membership with non-literate peoples, so one might have expected them to impose a more uniform blanket of English customs on them. Probably the English desisted because apart from Eliot and a few others, they did not regard Native Americans as an important part of New England's future—or any part at all.[15]

The Indians in Puritan America who sought out John Eliot's preaching because they wished "to come into the English fashions, and live after their manner," set in motion a long-term civilizing process that may ironically have helped to preserve Native American identities. Jesus the healer, martyr, and (in Catholic America) civilizer gave Native Americans at least some measure of protection against cultural extinction. As James Axtell has pointed out, the Christian faith provided a crucial cover of legitimacy, allowing Indians to maintain their most precious cultural possession of all— their basic identity as members of always evolving Indian peoples. The English and later the American authorities, cultural and political, may have thought assimilation was complete when Indians voiced interest in following Jesus. Meanwhile, some of those Native Americans who became Christian (as a majority of Indians are today) managed to preserve consciousness of themselves as Indian, not just Christian. Had Native Americans uniformly resisted English culture and religion, English pressure might have forced a complete surrender of Indian identities.[16]

John Eliot taught his Indian pupils to remember the old Calvinist formula that Christ was priest, prophet, and king. In their interconnected experiences of Christ, however, Native Americans and

Europeans focused on his roles as healer and martyr, and among the Catholics on his role as civilizer. Theological and experienced meanings were always multiple and always interlocking. The Indians in New France who thought crucifixes were white men's "war sticks" were expressing one truth about the civilizing Jesus. The Indians in New France who, like the Sagamore Chkoudun, "wore the sign of the Cross upon his bosom, which he also had his servants wear," and who had "a great Cross erected in the public place of his village," often expressed another. Open-ended meanings for Jesus were guaranteed by his unusually capacious and mysterious identity as God and man. Perhaps a few Indians were drawn to him for the same reason that some Europeans were: he seemed to transcend any one culture—indeed, to call single-culture loyalty into question. In any event, to judge by Jesuit and Puritan reports about them, Native Americans occasionally joined Europeans in spirited inquiry about the meanings of Jesus. Christological discussion was an arena for displaying logical talent as well as proper faith. Jesus saved, but he also provoked thought. Missionaries loved reporting their debates with Indians because those conversations reflected well on Indian intelligence as much as missionary diligence. And they showed that both parties had caught the spirit of Jesus of Nazareth, who liked to ask intricate, disarming questions of his own.[17]

"Seeing we see not God with our eyes," one man asked Eliot, "if a man dream that he seeth God, doth his soule then see him?" "I see why I must feare Hell, and do so every day," noted a second. "But why must I feare God?" A third queried, "Why doth God make good men sick?" Others wondered: "Where was Christ borne [after the resurrection]? Where is he now? How may we lay hold on him, and where, he being absent?" One woman sought clarification about "whether . . . I praie, when I speak nothing, if my heart goes with that which my husband praieth," while a man needed to know "whether a husband should praie, if he still continue in passion against his wife, though not so much as he was." One dialectically tormented inquirer asked an especially complex question that brought European civility and theology into a head-on collision. "Suppose a man, before he knew God, hath had two wives, the first barren and childless, the second fruitful and bearing him many sweet children. Which of these two wives is he to put away? If he put away the first, who hath no children, then he puts away her whom God and religion undoubtedly bind him unto, there being no other defect but want of children. If he put away the other, then he must cast off all his children, with her also, as illegitimate, whom he so exceedingly loves." The question was raised, Thomas Shepard wrote, because "this is a case now among them, and they are very fearful to do any thing cross to God's will and mind herein." Eliot and Shepard were both stumped, and told the Indians that this was another of the "many difficult questions propounded by them, which we have been unwilling to engage ourselves in any answer unto, until we have the concurrence of others with us."[18]

Much as the Reverends John Eliot and Thomas Shepard, like Fathers Paul Le Jeune and Jean de Brébeuf, enjoyed their dialogues with Indians, we have to remember that these were very one-sided conversations. The Jesuits and Puritans may not have made fun of Indian beliefs the way Cabeza de Vaca did, but they did not enter into open-ended discussion about them either. Their civilizing and evangelizing mission, for all its complexities, still imposed one culture's vision of what it meant to be cultured. Europeans sometimes summoned Jesus as a critic of European colonial excesses. But they always tethered him in the end to the campaign for European control, even when a Shepard, a Brébeuf, a Marie de St. Joseph, or a nameless nineteen-year-old Algonquin took him as the model for their own departures from civilization, their quests for purity of heart.

IV

The beliefs that seventeenth-century New Englanders, Puritan or non-Puritan, held about Jesus may seem instantly recognizable to us, since many twenty-first-century Christians espouse the same doctrinal positions. In some cases today's believers cherish traditional doctrines about Jesus *because* they are so old. But seventeenth-century belief, Puritan as well as Catholic, took place in a much more enchanted world than ours. In that era a much higher proportion of Christians took for granted the existence of an invisible and dangerous realm of spirits—the most important of whom was Satan—and the reality of witches, charms, signs, portents, and other occult phenomena. Historian David Hall has shown that established clergy and leading citizens such as Samuel Sewall joined rank-and-file farmers in seeking spiritual meaning not just in the Bible but in the "wonders" of the natural world—earthquakes, thunder, births of "monsters," and other momentous occurrences.[19]

The Bible itself, of course, was full of such natural wonders. But in the Bible as in everyday experience, the natural was never *just* natural. Every single event carried meaning in God's overall plot. God alone knew the full sense of that plot, but its broad outline— creation, fall, and redemption—gave each person's life its basic framework. Nothing was arbitrary. Everything could be read, however dimly. Some things were terrifyingly ominous, like a slice of the moon temporarily shaded by the earth. Others were reassuring, like a preacher whose voice so sparkled with the Spirit that listeners felt the Word of God pierce their hearts. Seventeenth-century men and women, educated and uneducated, inhabited a world in which visible and invisible forces collaborated or collided to produce life-transforming or life-threatening moments. The prospect of salvation through Christ was a double deliverance, from the daily dangers of earthly existence and from the eternal torments of hell.

Inevitably, some believers wandered from the universal interest in wonder-lore toward a superstitious reliance on magic. The rigors of everyday life were anxiety-inducing enough. But Calvinist orthodoxy made Puritans all the more anxious, since they were continuously reminded of their unworthiness and forever deprived of final assurance about their fate. Among Puritans Jesus was sometimes grasped in much the same way that some Indians may have taken him: as a potent wonder-worker whose aid could be summoned by magical incantation. In *The Danger of Taking God's Name in Vain,* Puritan minister Samuel Willard claimed that the devil had "taught men to use the name of God, or of Christ, or of some notable Sentence that is recorded in God's Word (which is also his name), either for the keeping of Devils out of places, or for the Curing of these or those Maladies that men labour of." In his view this was "an horrible abusing of the Name of god to such purposes as serve egregiously to the Establishing of the Devils Kingdom in the hearts of men." Increase Mather (father of Cotton Mather) also condemned the "use of any of the sacred Names or Titles belonging to the Glorious God, or to his Son Jesus Christ, as Charms." In his *Essay for the Recording of Illustrious Providences* he noted that some people were actually invoking Latin phrases, in imitation of medieval Catholic practice, as remedies for physical ailments. He reported that "In Nomine Patris, et Spiritus Sanctis, Preserve thy Servant" was being recited as a cure for toothache.[20]

This popular use of Jesus made some of the clergy redouble their efforts by the 1690s to protect Christian doctrine—and Christ himself—from contamination by superstition. Jesus worked wonders, they stressed, but not in response to ritual manipulation by human beings. His immanence in the world was on his own terms, always a function of his sovereignty and transcendence. Official insistence on an orthodox Trinitarian Christology was thus partly a strategy for disciplining the people. They had to be constantly reminded that Jesus could not be summoned to keep danger at bay or to ensure health or prosperity. Sermons year after year repeated the central gospel doctrine from Matthew: the rain falls alike on the just and the unjust; the sun rises on the evil as well as the good. The human propensity to use Jesus as a protection against misfortune made the Puritans all the more adamant about the need for an established church. It was the only way to protect Jesus and his Word from succumbing to self-serving and weak-kneed worshipers who thought they could make Christ their talisman.

From a twenty-first-century point of view it may seem paradoxical, but the theologically orthodox clergy were helping to spread a modern outlook by emphasizing the utterly transcendent (as well as immanent) sovereignty of God and Christ. Of course they were not setting out consciously to modernize or secularize their culture. They were trying to preach the gospel and preserve a proper relation to the divine. But in guarding Jesus against small-minded human scheming, they were helping to purify the world of all autonomous, midlevel supernatural forces. The Father, Son, and Holy Spirit were to be the only legitimate supernatural forces, though they might employ angels to do messenger service and Satan and his minions might still occasionally rouse themselves for rearguard evildoing. The people in the pews had to be made to see that the all-powerful Trinity of divine persons kept their own counsel and acted only upon their own initiative. Proper preparation for spiritual conversion would follow: one readied oneself to receive the unmerited gift of saving grace—though the Puritans held that the state of preparation required a prior unmerited gift.

Meanwhile, stressing the sovereignty of God rid the secular world of extraneous spiritual underbrush and set human beings on a path of understanding ordinary earthly processes through rational, cause-and-effect investigation. God in Christ and in Holy Spirit might break into that world from time to time, but only when it suited the divine purpose. The daily responsibility of human creatures was to respect God's sovereignty, confess their sins, plead for mercy, and otherwise mind their own business by interpreting the world as a web of human habits and natural forces. Clearing the everyday world of mysterious and uncontrollable spirits prepared the way for eighteenth- and nineteenth-century Christians to take one of two paths: to reaffirm the miraculous, autonomous powers of the remaining, legitimate invisible forces (the Father, the Son, and the Holy Spirit), or to give up invisible forces altogether and reinvent Jesus as a uniquely virtuous man of the world himself.

V

The Puritans surely spent more time worrying about the half-heartedness or superstitiousness of their own people's interest in Jesus than they did about Catholicism. Catholic practices posed no threat at all within the English colonies. Only a few Catholics had taken up residence in Maryland. Lord Baltimore, a Catholic convert, founded the colony in 1634, but the Catholic Church had no special recognition there. Protestants were on the first ships to arrive, and others were recruited to build up the settlers' ranks. The Catholics struggled gamely to establish an outpost for the faith in the mostly hostile colonial atmosphere. Within a month of arrival, Jesuit Andrew White, one of two missionaries in the initial group, directed his fellow settlers to carve "a great cross out of a tree." After "reciting humbly on our knees, with feelings of profound emotion, the Litany of the Holy Cross," they erected it "as a trophy to Christ our Saviour." But the Glorious Revolution in England in 1688 led to the appointment in Maryland of a royal governor and the establishment of the Anglican Church. Catholics amounted to no more than 10 percent of the colony's population of about thirty-five thousand in 1700.[21]

From the Puritan vantage point the Quakers and Baptists were a different story. Though their memberships were tiny in the seventeenth century—there were four Baptist churches in America in 1660, all in Rhode Island, where the first Quaker Yearly Meeting was held the following year—they made the Puritans very nervous. The Puritans had embraced dissent from the Church of England, but they could justify that stance only by containing the idea of dissent within narrow bounds. They were not separatists like the Pilgrims of Plymouth Colony. They were reformers still wedded to the old principle of a single true church for everyone. They thought there could be no legitimate dissent from their own dissent. Otherwise there would be an endless tide of new churches and erroneous doctrines. But their attack upon the worldliness and complacency of the Church of England gave heart to Baptists and Quakers in the Old World and the New. Baptists, Quakers, and Puritans all wished to praise and protect the living Jesus and to intensify the believer's apprehension of what Cotton Mather called his "incommunicable perfections." Their disputes were vitriolic because they all felt so attached to the original Jesus and the living Jesus. Each group was vigilant about shielding Jesus from centuries of ecclesiastical corruption.

Most Baptists shared the Calvinist theology of the Puritans, including their convictions about Jesus. Jesus was the divine Son sacrificed by the Father to effect the redemption of some unknown cohort of specially chosen saints. Efforts to earn one's salvation through good works availed nothing, although those selected for paradise by God's eternal fiat would likely be among those who performed godly acts in this life. The seventeenth-century Puritans did take "sanctification" (a post-conversion life of good works) as evidence of "justification" (the reception of Christ's saving grace). But the pursuit of good works could never curry God's favor. Of course people actively responded to God's gifts. But Puritans, like other Calvinists, howled at the "Arminian" assumption that human beings, through their own efforts, could contribute anything substantial to their own salvation. Any such concession to human powers was a direct affront to God, a dismantling of his sovereign power.[22]

Some "General" Baptists in England and America took an Arminian stance, in which God's offer of salvation became more or less universal, and people could decide on their own whether to accept it or not. But even the "Particular" (Calvinist) Baptists posed a threat to the Puritan holy commonwealth. Their dissent might appear in retrospect to be of minor moment, since their numbers were so small and their main issue was the apparently narrow one of restricting the sacrament of baptism to adults and performing it by full immersion. But their convictions on baptism amounted to a severe indictment of the Puritans for not protecting the immediate link between each believer and Jesus. As Harvard College President Henry Dunster (a defector to the Baptists) put it 1654, baptizing infants meant "forcibly depriv[ing] spiritual babes . . . of their due consolation from Christ." The Puritan argument that a child was tied to Christ through the mediation of a parent, who represented "the public person" of the child, seemed to Dunster empty and formalistic. "There is no further person but Christ for us to stand in," he said. One could only be "engrafted into Christ by personal faith, . . . not by parental."[23]

Dunster's position posed a dramatic challenge because it stripped the Puritans' *collective* mission of its place in the history of redemption. God in Christ, from the Baptist viewpoint, was joined directly to individual adult souls. There was no need for the Puritans' established civil-religious order, in which "visible saints" (those who could attest publicly to their conversion experience) and their baptized children stood as a corporate witness to and providential agent of God's plan. Of course the Puritan experience of Jesus was individual and personal too, but individual connections to God were layered into a set of concentric circles: family, church/town, commonwealth. Wider circles of authority were part of God's plan, a means of protecting the whole group of believers from the vagaries of individual opinion. Left to themselves, people easily fell into errors about Jesus and their relationship to him. Baptists gave the people more credit. In their view the greater danger came from fancy-talking college-bred clergymen, who strangled spiritual ardor with their sanctimonious disquisitions.

The Particular Baptists eased access to church membership and recruited popular preachers and lay exhorters who turned up the emotional volume of worship. But they were as orthodox as the Puritans on predestination, the Trinity, and Christ's atonement. Like the Puritans, they knew that being church members did not mean they either merited salvation or could be counted ultimately among the elect. They were personally tied to Jesus, but he did not do their bidding. They remained sinners begging his forgiveness. Their theological orthodoxy did not stop them, any more than it stopped the Puritans, from slipping into the very human craving for some sign of election. Today we think of the church as a place where people get to feel they are bound for heaven. Puritans and Baptists made it the place where people were cautioned against taking their passionate embrace of Jesus as evidence that they were headed for glorious union with him.[24]

The Baptists were a major conundrum for the Puritan leadership in the seventeenth century, but the Quakers were a scourge. They went much further than the Baptists in reconceiving Christian faith as well as practice. They did not just modify baptism; they got rid of water baptism altogether. They did not just call for more enthusiasm in church; they overturned Calvinist theology and mocked Puritan ceremonies. They did not just drown the fine distinctions of Puritan scholars in a bath of emotionalism; they rejected the unanswerable authority of Scripture itself. For the Quakers Jesus was a living force in the believer's heart, an "inner Light" or "seed of God." He was not to be found in any one book. He could not be contained or adequately represented in writing. For the Puritans, a disciplined people of the inherited and unchangeable Word, this was utter and irredeemable madness. The Good Book was the only protection believers—and Jesus—had against the silly extravagances of self-appointed prophets, sages, and enthusiasts.

The Puritans did not bother to try to civilize the Quakers, who in the 1650s were as alien and dangerous to Puritans as Communists were to many Americans in the 1950s. They silenced them, banished them, and in four notorious cases gave them the gift of martyrdom, while imagining that they were defending Christ against insidious attack. English farmer Marmaduke Stephenson was plowing his Yorkshire plot in 1655 when the "Word of the Lord came to me in a still small Voice . . . saying to me, in the Secret of my Heart and Conscience, 'I have Ordained Thee a prophet unto the Nations.'" When he heard that the Massachusetts authorities had enacted the death penalty for any Quaker arrested for a third time, he heard the Word of the Lord telling him to "go thither." He joined William Robinson on the Boston scaffold. The Quakers naturally took those two executions in 1659, and those of Mary Dyer in 1660 and William Leddra in 1661, as reenactments of Christ's Passion, with the Puritans standing in for the Romans. "Herein I rejoyce," wrote Robinson in prison as he waited to die, "that the Lord is with me, the Ancient of Days, the Life of the Suffering Seed, for which I am freely given up."[25]

Throughout American history radicals challenging religious and even secular establishments have appealed to Jesus for support. Of course the tradition of claiming devotion to the anti-establishment Jesus, who had tangled with secular (Roman) as well as religious (Jewish) authorities, is much older than that. The earliest Christian martyrs of the Roman empire believed they were taking up the cross of Christ. From their start in the seventeenth century up to the present, the Quakers have put special weight on their close ties to Jesus. The seventeenth-century Quakers would risk everything for him, including their lives. And they would strive to be filled with his spirit in this life, rather than waiting for a possible redemption in a life to come. The Puritans, they thought, were keeping Jesus too distant. They were needlessly sequestering the Lord's Word, as the Quaker James Nayler put it, "above the stars." They had lost touch with the transformed life of holiness that Christ had made possible for his saints. They had forsaken Christ's own teaching that God was fully present as an inner light in each of his followers. The Quakers maintained a belief in sin, and believed that Christ's sacrifice had effected the salvation of humankind. But they held that human beings had much greater access to the perfection of Christ in this life than the Puritans could imagine. Shocked and disgusted, the Puritans accused the Quakers of claiming divinity for themselves. The Quakers responded, as George Fox did from prison in 1655: he was not himself "the Son of God," he said, but "the Father and the Son was all in me, and we are one."[26]

Here the Quakers were actually taking a standard Puritan belief—the sanctification and joy that infused the Christian life at its holiest—and pushing it to the limit. In retrospect we can see that they were much closer to Puritan convictions than they or the Puritans could possibly grasp. But by detaching the doctrine of sanctification from the tensely balanced Puritan framework of justification-sanctification, they invited an especially virulent anathematizing from the Puritan leadership. Much as later Marxists seized upon the liberal dream of progress and said, "The point is to change the world, not to just talk about changing it," the Quakers accused the Puritans of giving lip service to holiness rather than seizing it. The bitterness each group felt for the other was in direct proportion to the huge terrain they shared.

Puritans looked like dead formalists and stern legalists (as well as heinous executioners) to Quakers and Baptists, whose emotional enthusiasm, in their own minds, was an urgent corrective to the Puritans' spiritual torpor. But we cannot take the Quakers' and Baptists' understandably anti-establishment view at face value. Generations of American writers have endorsed their view, seeing the Puritans as officious moralists bent on burning, whipping, or banishing their opponents. Even the Puritans' main twentieth-century interpreter and defender, Perry Miller, so emphasized their high-powered intellects and abstruse doctrines (to show that their theology was no mere afterthought to their moralism) that the popular image of the Puritans as highfalutin hairsplitters and judgmental absolutists persists to this day.

Puritans, wrote Miller, "showed no mercy to the spiritually lame and the intellectually halt; everybody had to advance at the double-quick under full pack." The Puritans even, supposedly, de-emphasized Jesus. "They went as far as mortals could go in removing intermediaries between God and man; the church, the priest, the magical sacraments, the saints and the Virgin; they even minimized the role of the Savior in their glorification of the sovereignty of the Father." Much of Miller's two-volume *New England Mind* proceeds to undercut that judgment, showing how essential Christ was to the Puritans' covenant theology and prayer life. But Miller's work contributed forcefully to the presumption that it was later evangelicals who put Jesus at the center of American Protestant piety. Nineteenth-century American Methodists and Baptists did indeed become fixated on "accepting Jesus as one's personal savior," the formula that has become a virtual American Protestant mantra. But an emotional, Christ-centered piety marked the faith of the seventeenth-century Puritans, as well as that of the separatists they loved to hate, the Quakers and Baptists.[27]

Perry Miller himself quotes a story told by Thomas Hooker, a leading Puritan minister, regarding the believer's intimate tie to Christ. (Following the apostle Paul, the Puritans always said "Christ," or "Christ Jesus," or "Lord Jesus," almost never the familiar "Jesus" commonly used by Quakers.) It was a parable about two sick women. The first "desires the Physitian, to bee healed by him, the other desires him not so much to be healed, but shee is desirous to be married to him. So it is with the soule that is carried in a kinde of love and affection to godlinesse, hee would not have Christ onely to heale him, but he would be married to Christ." This marital imagery was mainstream among the New England Puritans, as it had long been among European Catholics and Protestants. Thomas Shepard ended one of his sermons at his Cambridge meetinghouse by officiating at a mock marriage ceremony between Christ and each of the members of his congregation. The New England clergy did not stop at evoking the marital tie to Jesus. They supplied reproductive and erotic metaphors as well. "Have you a strong and hearty desire to meet him in the bed of loves?" asked John Cotton in 1651. "Lord make my Love and thee its Object meet," intoned poet and minister Edward Taylor in a 1713 meditation on the Song of Songs 5:10, "And me in folds of Such Love raptures keep." His 1708 meditation on John 6:53 made the new birth like the first birth in its reproductive concreteness. "The Soule's the Womb. Christ is the Spermadote [giver of seed] / And Saving Grace the seed cast thereinto."[28]

Once we get over our shock at Puritan officialdom's use of such language (it turns out it was the Victorians, not the Puritans, who were the prudes), we realize that they were not endorsing sensuality in general. Like the ancient Hebrew authors of the Song of Songs, they were seeking a language to convey the intense passion of the union with the Lord. The Puritans were analogizing in two directions at once. At its peak the spiritual love between Christ and Christian was so ecstatic that it was like the physical embrace between two human lovers. And at its best the earthly love between spouses was so ecstatically spiritual that it was like the union with Christ. Here the Puritans were breaking with the Catholic tradition, which tended to restrict the heights of spiritual achievement to those monks and nuns who left the "world" behind. For the Puritans, ordinary believers could now aspire to inhabit those heights. Spousal relationships, meanwhile, could be seen as divinely sanctioned. Bound together in love, a couple was armed for the battle against sin. Their family and those of their neighbors formed a moral foundation for the commonwealth.

The Puritans' intimate relationship with Jesus was of course not a bond between equals. (Puritan marriage was a bond between spiritual, though not social, equals.) The passion in this love came in part from the surprise of it. "Man marry God? God be a Match for Mud?" asked Edward Taylor in 1687. "I am to Christ more base, than to a King a Mite—And shall I be his spouse? How good is this? It is too good to be declar'de to thee. But not too good to be believe'de by mee." He continued:

Yet to this Wonder, this is found in mee,
I am not onely base but backward Clay,
When Christ doth Wooe: and till his Spirit bee
His Spokes man to Compell me I deny.
I am so base and Froward to him, Hee
Appears as Wonders Wonder, wedding mee.
Seing, Dear Lord, its thus, thy Spirit take
And send they Spokes man, to my Soul, I pray.
Thy Saving Grace my Wedden Garment make:
Thy Spouses Frame into my Soul Convay.
I then shall be thy Bride Espousd by thee
And thou my Bridesgroom Deare Espousde shalt bee.[29]

VI

For all their mystical outpourings about the pleasures of union with Christ and with one's spouse, the Puritans knew that either union was hard to achieve. There were two obstacles. First, too much love of one's spouse could actually get in the way of love of the Lord. Second, however much one might desire a full embrace of Christ, one was always at risk of losing him by luxuriating in the feeling that he had been found. Thomas Shepard, one of the big three in the immigrant generation of New England ministers (along with John Cotton and Thomas Hooker), was especially articulate about these obstacles. His personal agitation about them gives us a clear window on one of the main dynamics of Puritan piety: the relentless scouring of one's heart for evidence of self-aggrandizement, hypocrisy, or pride. The Puritans' overriding sense of human sinfulness might seem at first glance to be just the same as the sin-consciousness of later American evangelicalism. But later evangelicals often reduced sin to the breaking of moral rules. They often dropped the Puritans' conviction that sin was a perennial affliction, manifested sooner or later in every person's self-serving ruses. The

devil worked most shrewdly, they thought, in getting people to believe they were holy.

From the start the Reverend Shepard's life was a parade of personal disasters. His mother died when he was four, his father died
when he was ten, and his stepmother neglected him. He recollected
in his *Autobiography*, written in 1639 when he was thirty-four years
old, that it was "God who took me up, who loved me" when "I could
take no care for myself." The stringent Puritan version of Christianity won him over when he was a student at Cambridge, rescuing him
from the "bowling, loose company" with whom he "lived in unnat-
ural uncleanesses not to be named and in speculative wantonness
and filthiness with all sorts of persons which pleased my eye." Just as
the Puritan focus on the power of sin helped him understand his
youthful experience, so the Puritan sense of the majesty of God answered his childhood craving for a reliable caregiver. Meanwhile,
Puritan devotion to the Christ whom God had made "wisdom, and
righteousness, and sanctification, and redemption" (1 Cor. 1:30) offered Shepard the "free justification" celebrated by Reformed Protestants. This was Christ direct from Palestine, unbesmirched by
tradition, Christ "with a naked hand, even naked Christ." Shepard
chose to become one of Paul's "fools" for Christ, one of those who
confounded the "wise" of the world whose knowledge was of "en-
ticing words" but not of the "Spirit" (1 Cor. 1:27, 2:4). "Weak in every
way," Shepard reflected, he had still been selected to become "a poor
means of scattering the knowledge of Christ."[30]

Weak in every way. That self-assessment by Shepard is crucial
for grasping the persuasiveness of the Puritan path to many New
Englanders of the seventeenth century. Not just threatened by a
dark wilderness, not just uprooted from their familiar haunts in
Essex or Northumberland, not just tempted by "bowling, loose
company," Shepard claimed to be limited in his human substance.
A stark awareness of his boundaries led him, first, to faith in a living, triune God who offered escape from his limits, but second, to a
cautionary approach to that escape. Wanting it was no guarantee of

having it. Wanting it might be a function of having been taught to want it. Shepard understood that the Christian worldview might make sense to him only because he was brought up that way. He asked "whether if I had been educated up among the Papists I should not have been as verily persuaded that Popery is the truth." At times of darkness, throughout his life, he felt he might be deluding himself about Christ's being God and the Scriptures' being true. But then he would be flooded with the knowledge that those very moments of averting his eyes from God were occasions used by God to make his free grace all the more resplendent. Shepard knew from experience that his periods of despair were overcome through no conscious machinations of his own. He concluded that the times of depression must be the times when Christ loved him the most by sending his comforter, the Holy Spirit.[31]

For Shepard the Trinity was a doctrine to be experienced as much as believed in. The three persons of the Godhead amounted to a great chain of divine being and acting. As he expressed it in his *Journal*, the Father was his ever-present caretaker and chastiser. He might be an invisible sovereign, but his guiding hand or punishing judgment lay so close at hand that no step or breath was taken without his direct superintendence. Close by, but also removed: with Adam's sin a moral divide separated the Father and his children. God bridged that distance by sending his Son. "Jesus Christ [was] near me, next unto me—next unto me because he comes in as mediator between God and my soul." Christ resembled "a midman . . . in a pit," who "holds both him below and him abovemost." Without Christ there would be no way out of "the chasm sin made." The final step of the Trinitarian experience was the realization that "Christ was most near to me by his word and the voice of that." Just as Christ stood "between God and me that were distant," so "the word [came] between Christ and me." By sending his spirit in the Word, the Son crossed the final expanse that Shepard could not traverse himself. Faith was the always spasmodic movement of believers toward the Word that was always on its way to them. In a sense Christ was the Word sent by the Father and the Holy Spirit was the Word sent by the Son, but the spatial layout of a divine chain of communication pointing toward humanity was metaphorical. In reality all three persons of the Trinity acted in concert. Differentiating their functions was a way of clarifying the activity they undertook together. They collaborated in transmitting a Word that justified and sanctified.[32]

Shepard believed that his actual experience of Father, Son, and Holy Spirit made his belief true, not an invented convenience. But he also learned, time and again, about the danger of resting in that knowledge. Feelings of union with Christ blended imperceptibly into feelings of self-love, including undue joy in his family. He might think he was devoting himself to Christ when he was only delighting in his human ties. The Father knew how to punish such spiritual sloth. In Shepard's case, God took away children and wives, one after another. When his second wife, Joanna (Thomas Hooker's daughter), died after childbirth, Shepard was desolate:

> This affliction was very heavy to me, for in it the Lord
> seemed to withdraw his tender care for me and mine which
> he graciously manifested by my dear wife; also refused to
> hear prayer when I did think he would have harkened and
> let me see his beauty in the land of the living in restoring
> her to health again; also in taking her away in the prime of
> her life when she might have lived to have glorified the
> Lord long.

What made this loss so "very great" was Joanna's "incomparable meekness of spirit, toward myself especially." She managed the family finances, gauged "the evils of men," "loved God's people dearly," and "loved God's word exceedingly."

> The night before she died she had about six hours unquiet
> sleep, but that so cooled and settled her head that when she

knew none else so as to speak to them, yet she knew Jesus
Christ and could speak to him, and therefore as soon as she
awakened out of sleep she brake out into a most heavenly,
heartbreaking prayer after Christ, her dear redeemer, for
the spirit of life, and so continued praying until the last
hour of her death—Lord, though I unworthy; Lord, one
word, one word, etc.—and so gave up the ghost. Thus God
hath visited and scourged me for my sins and sought to
wean me from this world. . . . I saw that if I had profited by
former afflictions of this nature I should not have had this
scourge. But I am the Lord's, and he may do with me what
he will. He did teach me to prize a little grace gained by a
cross as a sufficient recompense for all outward losses. But
this loss was very great.[33]

The losses were so devastating that they made sense to him
only as God's reprimanding him for having loved his own flesh
and blood too much. Unbeknownst to him, his earthly affections
had chewed away at his bond with Christ. When his first wife was
"in sore extremities four days" after giving birth, it was not only
because of the "unskillful midwife." It was because he had grown
"secretly proud and full of sensuality, delighting my soul in my
dear wife more than in my God." The grim lesson was that "the
Lord by this affliction of my wife learnt me to desire to fear him
more and to keep his dread in my heart." In practice love of spouse
and love of God did not fit seamlessly together. He had aspired to
union with Christ as "Lord and Savior and Husband," but that
union was eroded by his unwitting descent into the pleasures of
merely human fondness.[34]

It is nearly impossible today for American Christians, evangelical or not, to imagine a Christian faith in which love of family gets
in the way of love of God. Nineteenth- and twentieth-century
evangelicals gave up Shepard's zero-sum conception because the
family had become an object of cultic worship in its own right.

Sentimentalizing the family became such a strong current in American culture, north and south, that Christ appeared more and more often for American Protestants as the infant Jesus whom Catholics had been worshiping in Europe for centuries. In nineteenth-century America, Christmas—formerly a rowdy secular revel—emerged as a religious holiday to rival Easter. The baby Jesus could now be extolled (the Protestants endeavored to keep Mary out of the spotlight) and the American family could be apotheosized in a rich layering of religious and secular celebration. Whatever the degree of their religious commitment, Christians could express their familial ties by recounting the tale of the wandering threesome in Bethlehem. The more spiritually minded could relish the irony of God's becoming human in the vulnerable body of an infant. That was one more proof that "God hath chosen the weak things of the world to confound the things which are mighty" (1 Cor. 1:27).

Shepard's Puritan version of God's justice made his sovereignty seem punitive and even malicious to many later evangelical Protestants. How could God be so jealous of the love human beings had for one another? But many later evangelicals had just as much trouble with Shepard's and other Puritans' view of the conversion experience. Nineteenth- and twentieth-century evangelicals tended to make the believer's embrace of Jesus a matter of choice. Evangelicalism turned Arminian: Do you accept Christ as your personal savior or not? For Shepard all the good will in the world availed not at all, since the will—the choosing faculty—was so heavily tainted with self-seeking. He had been tempted by many seductive errors, he wrote in his *Autobiography*, but never by Arminianism, "my own experience so sensibly [tangibly] confuting the freedom of will." Jesus answered the deepest human strivings, but he was "foolishness" to "the Greeks" (1 Cor. 1:23), an answer that lay beyond any rational accounting. Anyone who chose to follow Christ had to suspect that the choice was laced with covert motives, from the search for social standing to the quest for psychic relief. Shepard's experience of wrenching loss, along with his admitted craving for mental assurance and public recognition, told him that the love of Christ promised special suffering too.[35]

VII

The Puritans' Trinitarian experience was deeply personal, as they felt the power of God in the protection or punishment offered by the Father, the redemption accomplished by the Son, and the electric presence of the Spirit in the transmission of the Word. The roles overlapped, but seeing God as three distinct persons gave the Puritans a rich field of symbols and metaphors for expressing their sorrows, fears, and yearnings. Christians since the earliest days of the church had spoken this language in their daily rituals. Speaking of the Lord, of Christ, and of Spirit allowed Puritans (and other seventeenth-century Christians, including Catholics and Anglicans) to seed the whole world with God's intentions and power. It allowed them to see all of life as a cosmic drama, "God's great plot," as Shepard said. It was a story in which God took the three divine roles and in which every human being was invited to take the stage in a supporting part.[36]

As Puritans spoke of God's doings, they tacitly expressed a division of divine labor. The "Lord" (the Father) was the chief protector, whether of an individual (like the young, orphaned Thomas Shepard) or of a whole people (like the New Englanders endangered by Pequot Indians in 1637). When Pequots killed a dozen English people at Saybrook and Wethersfield, the violence was perpetrated (said Shepard) by Sassacus, their chief sachem, who "sucked the blood" of the English and "found it so sweet." When a few days later seventy armed Englishmen massacred three or four hundred Pequot men, women, and children inside a fort—"cooped up there for the divine slaughter," said Shepard—it was "the Lord" who "utterly consumed the whole company except four or five girls they took prisoners." Seeking security in what they considered a devil-infested wilderness, the Puritans relied upon a vengeful Father to wield the sword in their defense.[37]

Christ, meanwhile, offered salvation to God's elect, a company that Puritans such as Shepard and John Eliot believed would surely include some of those Indians willing to trade their heathen habits for properly penitent self-control. Jesus could transform individuals into saints just as he could bring harmony to warring communities. It was he who delivered peace within Puritan ranks when they were beset by doctrinal dissent. The Antinomian Controversy, sparked in part by Anne Hutchinson's public attacks on ministers such as Shepard, was resolved in his estimation by "the grace and power of Christ." In the summer of 1637, when the Father was avenging himself upon the Pequots, "a most wonderful presence of Christ's spirit" reigned at a special synod in Cambridge. The assembled church elders proclaimed Hutchinson's errors and "convinced and ashamed . . . the defenders of them."[38]

The Antinomian Controversy boiled down to a bitter dispute about how the Holy Spirit, the third divine person, was to be experienced, and how Christ should be conceived in relation to the Spirit. Anne Hutchinson, mother of eleven children and daughter of a Puritan minister, decided she was called to lead weekly religious discussions for women in her home. Her meetings were so popular that they expanded to include men as well, and Hutchinson developed a devoted following. All of this was fine with the other ministers, since Puritans in England had encouraged women to launch home prayer and discussion sessions. Things turned sour only when Hutchinson began attacking the ministers (excepting John Cotton, her favorite) for heterodoxy: they were preaching a gospel of "works," she said, by emphasizing the preparation a believer could undertake prior to receiving God's grace. Had this been all she claimed, there might have been room for compromise. But she went on to assert that she spoke with an authority derived not from the reading of Scripture alone, but (as she put it during her examination by the General Court in November 1637) "by an immediate revelation," "by the voice of his own spirit to my soul." This adumbration of the Quaker doctrine that would bedevil Massachusetts Bay a generation later was too much for John Winthrop, Thomas Shepard, and other officials, who saw to it that Mrs. Hutchinson was excommunicated and exiled to Rhode Island.[39]

The silencing of Anne Hutchinson was certainly the striking down of an obstreperous woman by a male establishment, as many recent writers have noted. John Winthrop's labeling her an "American Jezebel" ensured that many late-twentieth-century students of the controversy would conclude she was silenced *because* she was a woman. In fact she was chastised because she was making religious claims based on a special, post-biblical revelation. Any man making such claims would have been targeted for censure too, although spared the added insult that he had dishonored his sex. In turning on Hutchinson, Shepard and his colleagues were protecting their own authority. The reading of the Bible took precedence over individual experiences of the Spirit. True, reading the Bible was the responsibility of individual believers, but it had to be overseen by educated ministers who had mastered its intricacies. Christ's Word was revealed once and for all in Scripture, a fortress of unchanging truth in need of protection against believers impressed with their own interpretive flair. Anne Hutchinson thought she dwelled in the same historical dispensation as Abraham, who heard the voice of God directly. She was close to asserting that the Holy Spirit had taken up residence in her soul. Shepard and his colleagues responded, in effect, that his only residence was in the Trinity. Scripture resided, for its own protection, in a church run by sanctioned ministers trained in biblical interpretation.[40]

Shepard and his peers were walking a thin line, encouraging believers to meet Christ in unmediated fashion, but warning them against seeking individual inspiration. The Holy Spirit had a distinct part to play in God's plot, but it was not to short-circuit the Bible or preempt the ministers who unfolded its truths. The Holy Spirit was the succor Christ offered to believers as they trod the treacherous path toward him. Respecting the authority of Christ required second-guessing one's own adequacy as his disciple. Yet along the way unexpected joy erupted in one's heart. That divine spark was the unmistakable presence of the Spirit. Justification was by Christ, and the "assurance of it," as Shepard wrote, was by "sanctification, being enabled thereto by the spirit."[41]

Shepard's own church members in Cambridge learned to speak this complicated Trinitarian language, and they performed their experience of it publicly during their "confessions." These recitations of their inner spiritual conversions were a condition for full church membership. In his notebook Shepard recorded what his congregants said, and sixty-eight of those confessions from the 1630s and 1640s have come down to us. They are rich time capsules of Trinitarian experience. They show us how rank-and-file Puritans saw Jesus in relation to the Father and the Holy Ghost. In addition, they disclose the skill with which church members internalized and then publicly reproduced the ideas Shepard had been preaching to them. They took Christ as the indispensable mediator between themselves and God. He was their "personal savior," as evangelical Protestants have said ever since, but the Puritans' inflection of that phrase was very different from today's evangelical usage. They liked to imagine him as the believer's "spouse," but he remained impersonal as much as personal. He was not pictured as a friend always at one's side, or as a companion to confide in. Nor did the Puritan Holy Spirit inhabit the believer's heart. The Antinomian Controversy had put an end to talk of indwelling Spirit. The Spirit had to pass through the channel of Scripture.

Yet to judge by their confessions, Shepard's faithful breathed an atmosphere so suffused with Scripture that the air itself was charged with the Holy Spirit. Whatever might befall them, they could pluck multiple verses of Hebrew Scriptures or New Testament out of the air. Each confession follows a curve of experience, and advances are made along the curve as biblical passages are brought to mind. The believers report an early state of separation

from the Lord and show how the Lord intervened to bring them toward Christ. They arrive at some degree of assurance that they
have "closed" with him, only to be left wondering at the end
whether it is the real thing. Shepard had instructed them well. He
had made sure they saw their faith as a seesaw ride: nearer my God
to thee, farther my God from thee, nearer once again. The confessions are about seeking and finding and losing track of what has
been found. They show that in practice there was as much distance
between believer and Christ as there was between believer and the
Lord (the Father). And just as much proximity. The Lord oversaw
every moment of every day, making note of every thought, every
pain and joy. The Lord was actually more likely to impinge upon a
believer's daily life than Jesus was. Christ was always present as a
glowing beacon of wisdom and redemption, but in their sin human
beings often failed to notice him. They could not help noticing the
Lord, because he was immediately upset when they succumbed to
temptation (which was often) or wavered by putting self ahead of
God (which was almost always). They wished to avoid sin because
they feared his wrath, but even more than that, they "mourn[ed]
for sin as it grieved God." He was so close to them, however distant
they might feel him to be, that their measly human sins could hurt
him.[42]

"I was a Christless creature," said Elizabeth Cutter in her
confession in the 1640s. She had realized her forlorn state after
"hearing from foolish virgins"—the five virgins in the gospel who
waited for the bridegroom but neglected to keep oil for their lamps.
When the bridegroom suddenly arrived at midnight, they could
not see well enough to go out and meet him. By the time they had
found oil, it was too late, leading Jesus to conclude, "Watch therefore, for ye know neither the day nor the hour wherein the Son of
man cometh" (Matt. 25:13). Goodwife Cutter was initially immobi-
lized by her discovery. She did not "seek nor call God Father nor
think Christ shed his blood for me." But then she had the insight reported by many of the confessors. They were completely unworthy

sinners, but that was exactly the group Christ came to save. Then verse after verse tripped off her tongue: "Christ came to save sinners" (1 Tim. 1:15), "Christ came not to save righteous but sinners" (Matt. 9:13), "and to find lost and broken hearted" (Luke 4:18). She followed that litany with the single verse that turns up most frequently in the congregants' confessions: "Come to me, weary," her (or Shepard's) shorthand for Matthew 11:28, "Come unto me, all ye that labour and are heavy laden, and I will give you rest."[43]

These Puritan seekers were plainly in need of rest from the rigors of self-examination. The paradoxical Puritan path held out the promise of rest and deliverance while ensuring that God alone would provide them, and in his own good time. Human efforts to shore up the self or achieve tranquility were bound to fail. Even Christ's assurance danced in front of the believers' eyes, but dissipated when they tried to grab hold of it. Mary Sparrowhawk's confession, like many others, exhibits the up-and-down trajectory of the experience of faith. Asked by Shepard at the end of the confession "whether she had assurance, . . . she said no, but some hope."

And she saw her own emptiness and Christ's fullness, and such a suitableness between Christ and me, and chapter 7 [John 7:37]—if any thirst, let him come to me and drink. And hearing Lord called to any, she thought she was one of those any, and seeing nothing would satisfy her but the Lord, and nothing in heaven or earth she desired nothing like him, she thought the Lord called her to himself.[44]

The logic of her experience resembles Shepard's as related in his *Autobiography*. Puritan believers recognize their sinfulness and their inability to climb out of the chasm on their own. Then they realize that Christ has special love for losers like them. Suddenly their lives feel charged with new purpose and passion, as if they are in love. Their minister monitors the new engagement, making sure it does not get ahead of itself. The new human lover has to learn to keep waiting, oil and lamp in hand, for the bridegroom to appear. It could be any day now.

Except for the renegade Quakers and a few other dissenters, all of the Christians on the North American continent in the seventeenth century—the Puritans and Baptists in New England, the Anglicans in Virginia, the Catholics in Maryland, New France, and New Mexico—took Jesus as the divine Son of God, sole redeemer of humankind. That theological conviction was all but universal. But its universality was tied to its abstractness and its capaciousness. On the ground, in their actual religious experience, Catholics and Protestants, Europeans and Indians, and individuals within each group felt the divine Sonship of Jesus in multiple ways. In the European-Indian encounter, Jesus was healer, martyr, and civilizer. For Catholics and Anglicans he was the sacrificial lamb consumed in the Eucharist and the prime model for human imitation. For Puritan ministers and their fellow-Calvinist Baptists, he was the bridegroom to be met whenever he chose to arrive. The persuasive power of the Puritan vision of the encounter with Christ is demonstrated by the zeal with which Roger Williams, no Puritan on matters of church and state, promoted it. In his view Catholics, like Quakers, were unaware of the depth of their sins, holding instead a "high lofty Conceit of their Perfection." The Quakers were worse, since they renounced Christ's divinity altogether, making him merely a "Type and Figure, a pattern and Example how Christians ought to walk." The true goal of the Christian was to know "experimentally [experientially] what true and saving grace is," and to grasp that "the Blood which he shed upon the Cross at Jerusalem was a sufficient price and Satisfaction unto God for the sins of the whole world."[45]

Thomas Shepard's faithful showed in their confessions how well they had learned to verbalize this evangelical Protestant faith. The experiential heart of Puritanism was the paradox that doubt was compatible with assurance. Doubt was not only possible, but mandated: you had to doubt your faithfulness because of the overwhelming power of your own sin. Yet Christ loved you even in your doubt. The paradox was that letting go of the idea of ultimate assurance in this life freed a person to leave the final result to Christ, and thus arrive at adequate assurance. "Still I am doubting," said Robert Holmes at the end of his confession, "but I know I shall know if I follow on, and if he damn me, he shall do it in his own way." While waiting with their oil in one hand and their lamp in the other, Shepard's confessors could celebrate what Cotton Mather called the "incommunicable perfections" of Christ. Barbara Cutter enumerated a string of them, drawing on one Bible verse after another:

> And hearing the excellency of person of Christ, . . . Lord much affected her heart with it, as first was it full of beauty and glory, 1 John, full of grace [John 1:14], that grace was poured out on his lips, Psalms [45:2]. His heart was full of love and pity [Isa. 63:9], mind full of wisdom [Rev. 17:9?].

The litany of Christ's excellencies naturally prompted more doubts about herself, as her somewhat obscure concluding words make clear. The "Lord did leave saints doubting [so] as to remove lightness and frothiness," and "to cause [them to look] for fresh evidence, and by this means kept them from falling. Lord made these suitable to Lord and to draw my heart nearer to himself. And so answered all doubts from Christ. I saw somewhat more, and this day in forenoon." Doubt as a component of true assurance: Puritanism reveled in paradoxes like this one. But the doubt concerned the believer's capacities and flaws, not God's existence or authority. The practice of self-doubt encouraged by Shepard and other Puritan ministers reaffirmed God's sovereignty. God alone knew a person's heart or a person's fate.[46]

THREE

BRIMFUL OF A SWEET FEELING WITHIN

I

In John's Gospel (3:1–21) the Pharisee Nicodemus goes one evening to see Jesus in secret. He hails him as "a teacher come from God," and Jesus rewards him with a teaching: "Verily, verily, I say unto thee, except a man be born again, he cannot see the kingdom of God." Nicodemus scratches his head. "How can a man be born when he is old? Can he enter the second time into his mother's womb, and be born?" Jesus tries to explain. "Verily, verily, I say unto thee, except a man be born of water and of the Spirit, he cannot enter into the kingdom of God. That which is born of the flesh is flesh; and that which is born of the Spirit is spirit. Marvel not that I said unto thee, Ye must be born again. The wind bloweth where it listeth, and thou hearest the sound thereof, but canst not tell whence it cometh, and whither it goeth; so is every one that is born of the Spirit." Nicodemus is more confused than before. "How can these things be?" he wonders.

Nicodemus sounds innocent enough, but the gospel Jesus is exasperated by what he takes as willful ignorance. He barrages this educated but clueless "master of Israel" with an emphatic nine-verse monologue about God's plan of redemption for the world. Halfway through it he utters the lines of John 3:16 that American evangelical Protestants have long prized above all other biblical verses: "For God so loved the world, that he gave his only begotten Son, that whosoever believeth in him should not perish, but have everlasting life." John's Gospel does not say whether this tight linkage between believing in Jesus and living forever changed Nicodemus's own heart. John has this "ruler of the Jews" becoming a follower of Jesus (he defends Jesus against doubting Pharisees [7:51] and supplies the "myrrh and aloes" applied to Jesus' body after the crucifixion [19:39]), but gives no details about Nicodemus's belief in him. Whatever the impact of Jesus' words on John's Nicodemus, there is no doubt about their effect on generations of American evangelicals, stretching back to the "awakenings" of the 1730s. For many millions of these Christians it has summed up their faith, and described how they felt when they were reborn. They were so swept up in the invisible stirrings of the Holy Spirit that their own hearts gusted like the wind. "Born of the Spirit," they felt transformed by a surging power that came from Christ and somehow *was* Christ. Whereas Catholics had for centuries been taking "the body of Christ" into their own bodies when they received the Eucharist, born-again Protestants took the Spirit into their "hearts," a place in their bodies that was not just physical but mysteriously spiritual too. The "heart" was a metaphor that stood for intensity of feeling and obedient opening to Christ's overture.

As more and more eighteenth-century American Protestants embraced the born-again version of "believing in Jesus," Christ himself was reborn in American culture. His cultural status and meaning were bound to shift when masses of Protestants embarked upon a passionate, "personal" relationship with him. Mystical and pietistic longings for Jesus have a long history in Christianity, and some eighteenth-century immigrants to America—especially to Pennsylvania—drew on those traditions. Moravians, Mennonites, Amish, and Hutterites took for granted a personal intimacy with Christ. They tended to separate themselves from mainstream American culture in order to keep that intimacy pure. Many Germans in Lutheran and Reformed churches also brought pietistic practices to Pennsylvania in the eighteenth century. The novel development of the 1700s was the spread of personally intense piety among Protestants whose church traditions were largely non-pietistic, including Presbyterians such as Gilbert Tennent in New Jersey and Samuel Davies in Virginia.

As the eighteenth century progressed, more and more American Protestants of all ethnic backgrounds took Christ's scolding of Nicodemus, along with his repeated censure of other Pharisees, as a call to dispense with their own educated "masters." Like many of their fellow Protestants in England, Wales, and Scotland, they cast their lot with a revivalist faith in which access to Jesus was unmediated ("immediate"). The upshot of this passionate piety was to minimize the importance of sharp boundaries between Father, Son, and Holy Spirit, and to allow "Jesus" to function as an umbrella term for all three. Where Shepard categorized Christ as "mediator between God and my soul," "mid-man in the pit," revivalists appealed to him as the all-purpose provider of divine largesse. To a degree this shift was rhetorical, a matter of stylistic change rather than doctrinal departure. Nearly all revivalists were firm defenders of the Trinity. But revivalism had the overall effect of putting felt experience ahead of creedal precision. More precisely, the Trinity was less often felt as an experience, and more often taken as a propositional creed. Jesus could now be experienced as a person in his own right, not just as a person in relation to two other persons. The Father slipped increasingly into the shadows and the Holy Ghost into a derivative position as the emanation of the Son's spirit. Born-again believers did not reject the Father or Holy Ghost. They simply dwelt on the living power of "Jesus." His atoning function within the Godhead took a backseat to his indwelling function within the believer's reborn heart.

In the Puritan practice of the faith, the Son had been the Father's obvious subordinate, even if theologically the Son, Father, and Holy Ghost were three equally essential "persons" in one eternal Being. Thomas Shepard felt closer to the Father on a day-to-day basis than he did to Jesus. It was the Father who chastised him and nurtured him, the Father who afflicted him and rescued him from adversity. When Mary Rowlandson, a minister's wife in Lancaster, Massachusetts, was taken prisoner by Indians for three months in 1676, she drew solace not from the New Testament but from the Old. One of her Indian captors offered her a Bible, and she turned immediately to Deuteronomy 28 and 30 to read about God's promise of mercy. She then scoured the Hebrew Scriptures for passages that helped her see her own afflictions as a microcosm of those suffered by the ancient Israelites. She was sustained by verses that asserted the unknowability of God's decrees and the justice of her own punishment. "For my thoughts are not your thoughts, neither are your ways my ways, saith the Lord," she read in Isaiah 55:8. She took comfort from asserting her own unworthiness. However severe her trial, she knew that God had punished her "less than I deserved." Her memoir makes only two New Testament references (out of dozens of scriptural quotations), and neither refers to Jesus. In the first (from Luke 15) she likens herself to "the poor Prodigal [Son]," confessing that like him she had "sinned against heaven, and in thy sight." In the second (Heb. 12:6) she cites a line from Paul that might as well be from the Hebrew Scripture: "For whom the Lord loveth he chasteneth, and scourgeth every son whom he receiveth."[1]

Of course until the Revolution of the 1770s and 1780s Protestant American revivalism was British revivalism. But it was British in more than a political sense. The spread of the born-again experience was common to the British Isles as well as the mainland American colonies. And on both sides of the Atlantic revivalist religion came in Calvinist and anti-Calvinist forms. Calvinists stressed the inability of believers to contribute in any significant way to their salvation, or to their born-again experience, while anti-Calvinists emphasized the importance of the believer's act of free will in choosing God's grace. The three greatest innovators of the mid-eighteenth century came from England: the Calvinist George Whitefield and the anti-Calvinist brothers John and Charles Wesley. The greatest American-born theologian of the eighteenth (or any) century, the Calvinist Jonathan Edwards, influenced believers on both sides of the Atlantic. Like most Massachusetts ministers he spurned "enthusiasm" and disparaged what he called the "will-worship" of revivalists like the Wesleys. But he also knew from his own observation in Northampton that many emotionally exuberant rebirths were genuine. His discriminating defense of the "awakenings" gave legitimacy to revivalism everywhere.

Whitefield was the most celebrated evangelist of the eighteenth-century American colonies because he spent so much time traversing them and firing up outdoor throngs of five or ten thousand at a time. He made fifteen crossings of the Atlantic between 1740 and 1770, spending the equivalent of two years of his life at sea. But John Wesley, only briefly in America as a missionary in Georgia in the 1730s, reaped the ultimate harvest from the soil sown by his Calvinist counterpart. Wesley's Arminian Methodism took root in America during the revolutionary years and then began its phenomenal sweep across the new United States in the last decade of the century. The Methodists brought the born-again experience to an ever-larger proportion of American Protestants. During the nineteenth century more and more Baptists and Presbyterians, principal heirs to the Calvinist tradition, scrambled to match the Methodists' momentum by broaching Arminianism themselves. In the new republic denominational success depended on the upbeat Arminian message that each individual was empowered to leave sin behind.

In the 1830s the Presbyterian Charles Grandison Finney conducted huge outdoor revivals like those of Whitefield a century before, but he scrapped Whitefield's doctrine of double predestination (the idea that some are destined from all eternity to go to heaven, others to hell). Already by Finney's time born-again religion was assuming its modern, post-Calvinist shape. Arminian in outlook, it was methodically organized to reap an abundant harvest of converts. The only difference between Finney's carefully choreographed revivals and those of Baptist preacher Billy Graham in the mid-twentieth century was Graham's access to radio and television. The main current of evangelicalism had left Calvinism behind: Jesus saved, and he saved everyone who decided to believe in him and kept his commandments. The God of Shepard and Edwards had jealously guarded the knowledge of any individual's eternal fate. Only *some* of those who proclaimed their faith in him would be gathered to him in the end. In a post-revolutionary America in which individuals believed they deserved what they had worked for, Calvinism was bound to seem nonsensical.

In retrospect we can see that the born-again version of belief in Jesus, Arminian or Calvinist, was far better suited than the laborious Puritan conversion to the social realities of an exploding and migratory population. In 1700 there were about 250 thousand Europeans and Africans in the mainland British colonies, up from about fifty thousand in 1650. By 1770 the colonial population had reached almost two million. Around four hundred thousand, or 20 percent of the population, were African slaves, 150 thousand of them in Virginia alone. A quarter million Germans had arrived by 1770, a number equivalent to the entire colonial population of 1700. By 1800 there were five million Americans, almost one million in Virginia (a figure more than twice as large as the population of any of the next three largest states, Pennsylvania, New York, and Massachusetts). Estimates of the Indian population north of the Rio Grande during the colonial period range from two million to seven million, but very few natives in the British colonies had responded to Christian preaching. The dominant Protestant denominations devoted fewer resources, proportionally, to evangelizing the Indians than smaller groups did, such as the Moravians in Pennsylvania.[2]

Since the American population grew twenty times over between 1700 and 1800, the overall numbers of both revivalist and non-revivalist Christians were bound to grow larger. But over the course of the century the revivalists increased their rate of growth in spectacular fashion. By the end of the century their rate of increase was mounting, partly because by then enslaved as well as free African Americans were turning *en masse* to Christianity and to the born-again experience. A distinctive African American Jesus began to emerge, a heavenly redeemer who was also, like Moses, the liberator of an oppressed people. In the nineteenth century he would become the central fixture of black American culture that he remains today. But revivalist religion made eminent sense to masses of European Americans too. The Puritans' system of supervised conversions could be attempted only in settled communities of those who could read Scripture and enjoy or endure intricate clerical ruminations on biblical texts. Revivalism could take people wherever it found them, in whatever state of education, social status, or geographical dispersal. The Puritan Jesus was lodged in a transcendently stable and hierarchical Father-Son relation. The revivalist Jesus blew like an invisible wind, while planting himself securely in each believer's heart. This Jesus was as mobile and energetic as the American populace.

Orthodox Calvinists read John 3:16 and stressed the first clause: God so loved the world that he gave his only begotten Son. Jesus was a Son surrendered by a Father, whose love could be measured by that very act of sacrifice. The primary focus was on the Father's majesty, magnified beyond measure by his bold and caring initiative. He loved his fallen creatures so much that he willingly endured the immeasurable grief of a parent witnessing, and indeed initiating, the suffering of his own child. Of course God knew he would get his Son back in the end. But orthodox believers were still stunned by God's "condescension," as Jonathan Edwards put it, his willingness to subject his Son to the rigors of mortal life in general and to the agonies of betrayal and crucifixion in particular. Of

course in the orthodox view human beings remained fallen creatures after the incarnation. But by offering the life of his Son, God
had set in motion a plan of redemption that would bring at least
some of them—those chosen according to his eternal hidden de-
cree—to a final reunion with him.

Revivalists switched the emphasis to the second clause of John
3:16: believe in Jesus and you will not perish but be saved. Do what
it takes to save yourself: take Jesus as your personal savior. The
availability of Jesus diverted attention from the Father's magnani-
mous act. For a seventeenth-century Calvinist like Thomas
Shepard, the atonement was the *Father's* sacrifice as well as the
Son's. It was he who gave Jesus up. Jesus was essential to the drama
because of his selfless participation in a quasi-legal transaction.
He was the Father's means of canceling a debt. Someone had to pay
for Adam's rebellion, and Jesus alone, thanks to his divinity, was
equipped to erase a sin so heinous that it had infected every single
human being throughout the history of the world. Eighteenth-
century revivalists did not deny that Jesus was obedient, or that his
sacrifice forgave a massive debt. Many of them were just tired of
the old legal framework. It now seemed lifeless, incapable of moving people to vigorous, personally felt faith. Audiences glazed over
when they heard it preached. Their sinfulness was obvious to them,
but so was their capacity for strong emotion and a transformed life.
The revivalists harped on Christ's limitless power to pour his Holy
Spirit into the hearts of the faithful.

The ever-available Jesus of the born-again experience was not
and is not distinctively American. But he has had distinctive staying
power in American culture. There are many other potent Jesuses in
American culture too, and the overall American devotion to Christ
is a function of all the varied Catholic, Protestant, Eastern Orthodox, and secular ways of worshiping and praising him. But nowa-
days no single way of "walking with Jesus," as evangelicals like to
put it, can compare for breadth of appeal with that of the revivalists
who preached the rebirth of John 3:16. It was the all-inviting Wes-

leyan version of rebirth that became the most dominant of all. Wesley's Methodists believed that God's saving grace really was free. It was free for Calvinists like Shepard in the seventeenth century and Edwards in the eighteenth only in the sense that God was free to bestow it on, or deny it to, whomever he pleased. The Methodists thought that God wished everyone to have it, and that everyone who sought it faithfully could count on receiving it. This was the spiritual scheme that made the most sense to masses of white and black American Protestants in the new republic. As believers were reborn in the Spirit, Jesus himself rose up in their hearts and was figuratively resurrected anew. They rose together to a new life beyond sin, beyond death. "Plenteous grace with Thee is found, Grace to cover all my sin" wrote Charles Wesley in the last verse of his classic 1740 hymn "Jesus, Lover of My Soul," one of the most beloved hymns in American Protestant history.

> *Let the healing streams abound;*
> *Make and keep me pure within.*
> *Thou of life the fountain art,*
> *Freely let me take of Thee;*
> *Spring Thou up within my heart,*
> *Rise to all eternity.*

II

Unbelievers, skeptics, and nominal Christians increased their numbers in eighteenth-century America alongside the evangelical Christians, Anglicans, Lutherans, and Quakers. Educated Americans in the eighteenth century were as liable to turn toward secular Enlightenment as they were to Christian belief. They were most likely of all not to choose one or the other, but to try to bridge the two.

Their desire to articulate a rationally compelling Christianity was nothing new. The largely Arminian Church of England, which grew in favor in the northern as well as southern colonies in the late seventeenth and early eighteenth centuries, went the furthest toward embracing what John Locke called "the reasonableness of Christianity." For most Anglicans reason was a source of knowledge about God, fully congruent with but independent of God's revelation in the Bible. Calvinists could not abide that kind of creeping rationalism, and volubly denounced it. But the revivalist outpourings beginning in the 1730s persuaded even many Calvinists sympathetic to them, such as Jonathan Edwards, to reemphasize the essential place of rationality in the life of faith. Educated anti-Calvinists, such as Edwards's nemesis Charles Chauncy of Boston's First Church, put even more weight on secular learning as a protection against revivalistic "enthusiasm." People's beliefs in eighteenth-century America, as in every other place and time, evolved as they took up intellectual arms against ideas or habits they considered dangerous. The remarkable thing about the American story, from the seventeenth century on, is the continuing appeal of Jesus to people of every position and disposition, from the most orthodox to the most anti-clerical.

While the revivalist evangelicals put new emphasis on the name and approachability of Jesus (without explicitly doubting the Trinity), many advocates of rational Christianity dispensed with the Trinity altogether. It seemed to them a metaphysical abstraction, a medieval mystery with no present purpose and no biblical warrant. Why not set Jesus free from a logically absurd three-in-one Godhead? Christian rationalists could still take Jesus as divine even if he was not on the same level of divinity as the Father. He could be a special more-than-human being sent by God to redeem people by filling their hearts with love and modeling a life of purity and sinlessness. Taking Jesus off the high pedestal of the Godhead, they thought, would do more to protect the sovereignty of the Father— the Calvinists' original goal—than attachment to the irrational view that three persons could magically merge into one Being. Of course the Trinity could have come to seem irrational only when sinfulness had ceased being experienced as such a deep warping of the natural will that there was no reversing it without a monumental and gratuitous intervention: the sacrifice of one divine person by another. For secular and Christian rationalists (and for Arminian evangelicals) sinfulness was now a condition to be climbed out of by disciplined moral endeavor. God's grace remained indispensable for the Christian rationalists and Arminians, but human beings had the natural power to collaborate with it (as Roman Catholics had contended for centuries).

The Unitarian alternative to Trinitarianism gathered force in educated circles in eighteenth-century Anglo America (though the Unitarian denomination developed only in the nineteenth century). And it helped convince a small group of enlightened gentlemen to go even further toward secularizing Christ. If Jesus was not part of the Trinity, why see him as divine at all? Why not let him be a merely human wise man like Socrates, one whose ideas were far and away the most valuable of all time? For men such as Benjamin Franklin and Thomas Jefferson, who regarded human reason as the greatest gift of God, calling Jesus human rather than divine was hardly a slight. They rejected his divinity in order to accentuate his genius as a philosopher and teacher. The case of Benjamin Franklin—worldly *bon vivant*, scientific-minded inventor, and vanguard theorist of the modern self—is emblematic of the persistent power Christ has exerted upon many modern American Christians who have left the practice of religion behind. Franklin, this most apparently secular of eighteenth-century Americans, did not abandon Jesus or God. In fact, his secularity was defined in part by his continuing belief in them.

Twentieth-century historians of American culture often used Franklin and Jonathan Edwards as twin poles of eighteenth-century American consciousness. Franklin was depicted as the exemplar of modernity and scientific reason, Edwards as the representative of a superstitious past. Franklin became the heroic precursor of a liberal-minded cosmopolitanism. "The Calvinism in which he was bred left not the slightest trace upon him," wrote Vernon Louis Parrington in 1927. "He was a free man who went his own way with imperturbable good will and unbiased intelligence." Franklin (born January 17, 1706) was poised at the fountainhead of a secular stream flowing toward modern humanism, while his near age-mate Edwards (born October 5, 1703) was left to tend the embers of a dying Puritanism. Edwards, said Parrington, "was the unconscious victim of a decadent ideal and a petty environment." His life was "a spiritual tragedy enacted within the narrow walls of a minister's study." His was "the greatest mind of New England," but his cloistered devotion made him "an anachronism in a world that bred Benjamin Franklin."[3]

This winner-takes-all approach to cultural history misses the fact that for all Franklin's humanizing of Jesus and his distrust of orthodox religion, his secularity was decisively marked by his Calvinist inheritance. He was certainly unique in his time for his arresting mix of humor, practicality, self-dramatization, and self-deprecation. But those very traits, which have made him seem secular to later generations, are actually clues to his typically eighteenth-century style of secularity. Modernists did not invent the ironic sensibility. The ancient Jews knew all about it, and the Calvinists got it ultimately from them. Franklin secularized the ironic mentality that his childhood Calvinism had imbued in him. Thinking about Jesus and about God allowed him to articulate a secular faith that preserved essential elements of the Calvinist worldview. Praising Jesus and believing in God were not extraneous holdovers from his childhood piety, but integral parts of his mature secular-religious outlook. The cultural history of Christ in America is as much the story of secularizers such as Franklin as it is the story of evangelizers such as Edwards or the Wesleys. Evangelicals and secularizers tried to rescue Jesus from each other's clutches. Each side felt virtuous when it was protecting Christ against the onslaught of the opposition.

"Imitate Jesus and Socrates," Franklin advised in the early

1780s in his *Autobiography*. That "precept" was the path to "humility," the last of thirteen virtues Franklin recommended to the young. At first his list had stopped at twelve, he joked, but a Quaker friend "kindly inform'd me that I was generally thought proud ... of which he convinc'd me by mentioning several Instances;—I determined endeavouring to cure myself if I could of this Vice or Folly among the rest, and I added *Humility* to my List. ... I cannot boast of much Success in acquiring the *Reality* of this Virtue; but I had a good deal with regard to the *Appearance* of it." As Socrates revealed the depth of his wisdom by doubting that he knew much, Franklin showed how humble he was by second-guessing his humility.[4]

A wry smile must have curled Franklin's lip as he wrote "imitate Jesus and Socrates." The apparently simple injunction contained a hidden assumption: that Jesus and Socrates modeled the same life of virtue, or at least two complementary visions of that life. What if imitating one hero got in the way of imitating the other? Jesus summoned his followers down a very different course than Socrates, even if both paths entailed a moral stringency so uncompromising that it led each leader to trial and martyrdom. It was one thing to heed the ancient Athenian, to seek purity and knowledge through relentless self-examination, and through the ever-wider exposure of ignorance and corruption in the world. It was another to repent one's sins, forgive one's enemies, and obey one's Father in heaven. But making Jesus a wise man like Socrates, rather than a sacrificial lamb, a healer, or an apocalyptic prophet, made him serviceable to Americans keen on enlightenment as well as individual advancement. Imitating Jesus alongside Socrates would mean being tolerant and self-critical, standing up for one's own rationally defended principles—pressing them all the way to the death if necessary—while defending everyone else's right and obligation to do the same. And it would mean puncturing the pretensions of assorted phonies and self-aggrandizers, the Sophists and Pharisees of every age (including oneself). Franklin's "imitate Jesus and Socrates" was one opening salvo in the modern American quest for a Jesus whose teachings and example were useful to everyone, whatever their religious (or secular) beliefs.

Franklin probably regarded Socrates, the "humble Enquirer and Doubter," as a greater personal influence upon him than Jesus. He moved from the distant judgmental God of his Calvinist youth to the distant benevolent God of his adulthood without experiencing, or missing, the companionship of Christ. Jesus may have been a minor note in his childhood piety, dominated by the forbidding, sovereign Father, and Jesus was perhaps an equally minor note in his adult piety, in which the God of nature held the world lovingly in his grasp. Franklin was moved but bemused when George Whitefield, his longtime friend and publishing client, tried to lead him to Christ. "I do not despair of your seeing the reasonableness of Christianity," Whitefield wrote to him in 1740. "Apply to GOD; be willing to do the divine will, and you shall know it." A decade later Whitefield added that "as you have made a pretty considerable progress in the mysteries of electricity, I would now humbly recommend to your diligent unprejudiced pursuit and study the mystery of the new-birth. . . . One at whose bar we are shortly to appear, hath solemnly declared, that without it, 'we cannot enter the kingdom of heaven.' You will excuse this freedom. I must have *aliquid Christi* [something of Christ] in all my letters." In the *Autobiography* Franklin remembered that Whitefield "us'd indeed sometimes to pray for my Conversion, but never had the Satisfaction of believing that his Prayers were heard."[5]

Still, Franklin admired Jesus' moral and spiritual insight, as he wrote privately in 1753. "He prefer'd the Doers of the Word to the meer Hearers'; . . . the heretical but charitable Samaritan, to the uncharitable tho' orthodox Priest and sanctified Levite: and those who gave Food to the hungry, Drink to the Thirsty, Raiment to the Naked. . . &c. tho' they never heard of his Name, he declares shall in the last Day be accepted, when those who cry Lord, Lord; who value themselves on their Faith tho' great enough to perform Miracles but have neglected good Works shall be rejected . . . but now a days we have scarce a little Parson, that does not think it the Duty of every Man within his Reach to sit under his petty Ministrations, and that whoever omits them offends God. I wish to such more Humility." Franklin preferred ethical acts to pious pronouncements, yet he remained the good Calvinist in spite of himself, minimizing the effect that all of his Jesus-endorsed "good Works" might have on God's decision about his fate. This was no watchmaker God who set the world in motion and left it to run its course. No one "could deserve Heaven for the little Good they do on Earth. . . . For my own part, I have not the Vanity to think I deserve it, the Folly to expect it, nor the Ambition to desire it; but content myself in submitting to the Will and disposal of that God who made me."[6]

In this private communication, imitating Jesus diverged from the imitation of Socrates while still overlapping with it. It meant submitting to the will of the Creator, performing good deeds, and combating undue pride about one's excellence. It also meant turning against anachronistic practices in the realm of religion as well as business. To show how serious he was about revising merely human customs, however culturally sacred, Franklin took on nothing less than the Lord's Prayer. That reformist exercise, probably written in the late 1760s, was never published, a wise decision for a man who would have shrunk from the resulting outrage. Franklin thought the traditional language of the prayer had gotten in the way of its meaning. Rather than worshiping the old formula, turning the words themselves into little divinities, people should understand what they are saying while still feeling the beauty of it. Some of the prayer was too wordy ("Our Father, which are in Heaven"), Franklin thought. One word ("hallowed") was obsolete. Other terms, like "Name" and "Kingdom," were culturally specific to the ancient Jews and should be made relevant to eighteenth-century experience.

Tampering with sacred verse might seem the height of hubris, but Franklin draped himself in the mantle of humility. The old

"Give us this day our daily bread" should be scrapped because it suggested "Give us what is ours" and had "too little of the grateful Acknowledgment and Sense of Dependance that becomes Creatures who live on the daily Bounty of their Creator." And the earlier "Forgive us our debts as we forgive our debtors" implied "that we have already in and of ourselves the Grace of Forgiveness." His version stressed instead "our Dependance on God, the Fountain of Mercy, for any Share we may have of it, praying that he would communicate of it to us." These are utterly Calvinist sentiments. Franklin's whole revision amounted to a Calvinist appeal against galloping Arminianism. It ran as follows: "Heavenly Father, may all revere thee, and become thy dutiful Children and faithful Subjects; may thy Laws be obeyed on Earth as perfectly as they are in Heaven: Provide for us this Day as thou hast hitherto daily done: Forgive us our Trespasses, and enable us likewise to forgive those that offend us. Keep us out of Temptation, and deliver us from Evil." This reverent retranslation exposed a lingering taste for piety in a man usually remembered for sardonic wit. But Franklin's sensibility was ironic without being cynical. Today we tend to assume that irony is at odds with sincerity. For Franklin irony was a means of rescuing sincerity from sanctimony.[7]

Franklin refused any version of Christianity that promised him salvation. When the ever-ebullient Whitefield told him that "believing on JESUS," getting "a feeling possession of GOD in your heart," would give him an assurance of salvation, Franklin, as usual, smiled and held back. He was skeptical not about God but about the human capacity for genuine self-surrender. People preferred self-flattery and self-delusion. The idea that Jesus would offer him an assurance of salvation—even if assurance was understood in orthodox Calvinist fashion as something short of a guarantee—struck him as a threat to humility. His *Autobiography* shows that he preferred to see life as a groping for self-mastery in full knowledge that such a goal must remain chimerical. He liked the tension between his undeniable importance as God's creature and his relative insignificance in God's overall scheme. God had made him small and unequipped to master his own fate, but there was no need to be liberated by Jesus from the contingencies of life. The ever-distant but ever-present God was the mysterious master of everyone's fate, his control so absolute that it paradoxically allowed people to accept their lot unflinchingly. With God in charge there was no need to fret. Turning to Jesus for deliverance would take away the cosmic gap between Franklin's puniness and his Creator's majesty. He preferred to think of his fate as lying wholly in God's hands and beyond anyone's power to affect, even Christ's. Like Mary Rowlandson a century earlier, he got assurance, paradoxically, from his knowledge that God's decrees were unknowable.[8]

Typically, Franklin turned unworthiness into humility through humor. A month before his death in 1790 he wrote to Yale's president, the Reverend Ezra Stiles, who had asked his views on Jesus. He replied that "I have some Doubts as to his Divinity, tho' it is a question I do not dogmatize upon, having never studied it, and think it needless to busy myself with it now, when I expect soon an Opportunity of knowing the Truth with less Trouble. I see no harm, however, in its being believed, if that Belief has the good Consequence, as probably it has, of making his Doctrines more respected and better observed." The striking thing about Franklin, as about Tom Paine, Thomas Jefferson, and other enlightened American republicans of the late eighteenth century, is that they kept hailing his "doctrines" after giving up on the doctrines of the Trinity, the incarnation, and the resurrection. They split Jesus off from the church because they thought the church had perverted his simple truths. In Franklin's estimation, the greatest danger in the moral life was self-satisfaction, and the Christian church's Jesus promoted that vice by promising deliverance from sin. The Jesus who made sense to Franklin was the Jesus who resembled Socrates, the great critic of complacency. Needing no redemption from sin, Franklin needed no divine redeemer. He needed a Jesus freed from the church and reborn as a model of humility in the face of an inscrutable God.[9]

III

Naturally Jonathan Edwards, America's greatest ever Christian theologian, had a lot more to say about Jesus, and about God, than Benjamin Franklin did. Edwards wrote and preached constantly about Christ between the 1720s and his death, from a botched smallpox inoculation, in 1758. Franklin and Edwards actually shared a great deal of ground in their insistence on God's utter sovereignty and on the human propensity for self-absorption and self-delusion. But they diverged dramatically in their views of sin and, as a consequence, in their views of Christ and the church. The self-worship to which human beings succumbed, said Edwards, stemmed from the original sin that tainted all human endeavor since the beginning of time. True, Jesus offered a model of humility, as Franklin held. But for Edwards he set a vivid example of humility only because he had accepted a unique mission as sacrificial lamb. His humanity derived ultimately from his divinity, and his wisdom too flowed out of his redemptive role. Granted, the power of human sin often perverted the church, as Franklin contended. But for Edwards the church remained the place where Jesus was most truly protected as the living Word. A human institution, the church frequently sinned by turning Christ into a symbol that people used to covertly praise themselves instead of God. Yet the church could always be reformed with God's help. In the long run, Jesus was far safer there than in the culture at large.

To encounter Edwards's thinking about Christ (like the Puritans, Edwards rarely referred to "Jesus" unless that name was coupled with "Christ" or "Lord") is to witness a phenomenally talented mind at work. Son of a well-known New England minister and grandson of a famous one (Solomon Stoddard), Edwards managed to convert his inherited calling into a theological adventure. He could not help enjoying himself as he deployed armies of scriptural citations, syllogistic proofs, and rhetorical devices to defend Christian orthodoxy. For example, while other theologians debated whether the doctrine of the Trinity was fully revealed in Scripture, Edwards, bored by such a scholastic exercise, gleefully identified a second Trinity, an image of the first. Christ could be likened to an eternal Father, and humble believers to his Son, while the Holy Spirit resembled the "delight and love flowing out towards the church." During three decades of intellectual production, meanwhile, he stressed that Christian virtue had nothing to do with fancy thinking or lofty education. At its most vital, Christian belief displayed a humble appreciation for God's love and justice. It required literacy and reason, so that a person could read the Bible (and strive to read it with interpretive discrimination), but it entailed no esoteric attainment. Knowledge was necessary but not sufficient. The sufficiency in the life of faith was love.[10]

Edwards occupies a key role in the history of Jesus in America because he was an instigator and interpreter of what he called "the surprising work of God in the conversion of many hundred souls in Northampton" in 1734 and 1735. His series of ruminations on that revival, and the following one in the early 1740s, helped publicize the experience of "new birth" that so many American Protestants have sought out for nearly three centuries. Edwards was never a revivalist preacher in the thunderous, theatrical mode of a George Whitefield or a Gilbert Tennent, the Presbyterian evangelist in New Jersey. He did invite the indefatigable Whitefield to address his congregation in Northampton in 1740, and like the rest of the audience (according to Whitefield's diary), Edwards wept through the whole service. But he took a far bigger part than either Whitefield or Tennent in justifying the awakenings in the eyes of many skeptical clergy and lay people, then and since. He did so by arguing that despite their inevitable excesses, the revivals succeeded in bringing many people back to a proper relation to Christ. Edwards was a crucial force in *making* American Protestant piety evangelical and also a central figure in *clarifying* what it meant to be born again in the Spirit. It meant stepping out on a pilgrimage, to seek, with the gift of divine grace, a lifelong practice of humility, obedience, service, and joy.[11]

Like his Puritan forebears who bemoaned the routinized piety of
the Church of England, Edwards saw the proper relationship between Christ and the born-again believer as charged with passion.
But true piety also diverged from the emotional enthusiasm of many
awakened Christians. They often claimed that Christ had come to
them personally, chosen to forgive their sins especially. They loved
him because of what he had done for them, not because of who he
was in his own right. Genuine faith, said Edwards, had an impersonal element that protected it against all such prideful dwelling
on oneself. Here Edwards's orthodoxy overlapped with Franklin's
theistic skepticism: both men abhorred the self-congratulation of
many Christians. In his 1747 funeral sermon for his young protégé
David Brainerd, who had died of tuberculosis, Edwards praised the
missionary (to the Indians) for having rejected the enthusiasm of
"those whose first faith consists in believing that Christ died for
them in particular." Such Christians had decided to love God "because they supposed they were the objects of his love," not because
he was the sovereign Lord of all. They "rejoiced more in their own
supposed distinction from others, in honor and privileges and high
experiences, than in God's excellency and Christ's beauty." Brainerd had known that one's initial meeting with Jesus had nothing to
do with "any pleasant warm feeling in [one's] breast." If that was
what one was feeling, one was not worshiping the almighty God
but an idol of one's own sculpting.[12]

In an authentic conversion Christ remained remote even as he
sent his Holy Spirit. As Edwards put it in a private letter in 1751,
"the most intimate embrace" between Jesus and the Christian is
"kept from an indecent familiarity" by the believer's heightened
awareness of Christ's "infinite majesty." The paradox of knowing
Christ was that getting close to him meant accepting an initial separation from him, abasing oneself while accentuating the "efful-
gence of his glory." Jesus had to be honored as judge before he
could be embraced as friend, and his role as judge persisted after he
became one's tender companion. Judgment remained, but not fear

of judgment, since one now trusted God's righteousness implicitly. With the proper distance established, a sweet immersion in Christ's love could deepen. "His love has brought him into such a relation to us as our friend, our elder brother, our Lord, our head and spiritual husband, our Redeemer, and hath brought us into so strict an union with him that our souls are his beloved bride." This love is passionate in the same visceral way that human soul-love is passionate. Christ does not just change a person's heart; he shoots an arrow through it. "Christ and the true Christian have desires after each other," Edwards said in a famous 1735 sermon. He quoted the Song of Songs 3:1–2: "By night on my bed I sought him whom my soul loveth: I sought him, but I found him not. I will rise now, and go about the city in the streets and broad ways. I will seek him whom my soul loveth."[13]

IV

The emotional outpourings of the faithful during the Northampton revivals in the 1730s and 1740s included bodily as well as verbal and intellectual responses. Commentators then and since have taken sides on the legitimacy of such vocal and physical manifestations as shouting, trances, and shaking fits. Edwards staked out the middle ground, distinguishing himself from sticklers for propriety such as Boston preacher Charles Chauncy and defenders of spontaneity such as Connecticut's volatile James Davenport. Davenport's perfervid piety was far easier to dismiss than urbane calls for rectitude. This grandson of John Davenport (a celebrated founder of the New Haven colony in the 1630s) excelled in whipping his listeners into wild emotional release. He left women in particular "fainting and in hysterics," according to one critic. A bill of particulars drawn up against him by the General Assembly of Connecticut accused him (in Charles Chauncy's paraphrase) of "an indecent and affected imitation of the agony and passion of our blessed saviour." Imitating Christ was bad enough, but "by voice and gesture" he also dramatized "the surprise, horror, and amazement of persons suppos'd to be sentenced to eternal misery." Davenport burst his own balloon in 1742 when he led a group of supporters in a raucous dance around a burning pile of "worldly" books, wigs, and fancy clothes. He soon repented of all these transgressions, but he had given Charles Chauncy the smoking gun he needed to condemn the revivals' "enthusiastical spirit."[14]

The emphasis that historians have put on the eighteenth-century dispute over emotional extravagance versus self-restraint has obscured the deeper issue at stake. What Chauncy cared most deeply about was not refined behavior as such, but self-control as a sign of rational self-possession. Chauncy represented a gathering wave of enlightened Christians impressed by God's gift of human reason. With education and determination, people could know God and do good. Bodily manifestations were offensive because they symbolized a rejection of rational approaches to the divine. Edwards was no more inclined than Chauncy to favor emotional worship for its own sake. Nor was he any less impressed by the achievements of human reason and science, or any less committed to an educated ministry. They both believed that clergymen had to know ancient languages so they could protect Holy Scripture from the self-interested perversions of pious or impious Bible-wavers.

The problem Chauncy posed, from Edwards's standpoint, was not his love of reason but his downplaying of submission to God. He and others like him were pushing love of reason so far, Edwards sensed, that it was becoming a doctrine of self-sufficiency. Celebrating their natural powers was squeezing consciousness of divine majesty out of their lives. They were praising God's Fatherhood in the abstract but dispensing with it in daily experience. Believers were becoming "will-worshippers"—boosters of their own marvelous capacities—rather than God worshipers. The potential consequences for Christ were ominous. If God's sovereignty could slip out of human consciousness, so could true awareness of Christ's atoning sacrifice. It would not be forgotten entirely. People might retain it, for example, as a beautiful tale of heroic human aspiration. As Edwards wrote in 1734, "A person by mere nature may be liable to be affected with the story of Jesus Christ, and the sufferings he underwent, as well as by any other tragical story: he may be the more affected with it from the interest he conceives mankind to have in it: yea, he may be affected with it without believing it; as well as a man may be affected with what he reads in a romance, or sees acted in a stage play."[15]

Wishing to restore a general conviction of God's active rule over human life, Edwards looked everywhere for signs of it. He learned from direct observation during the revivals that God reminded human beings of his sovereignty by touching their bodies. For Chauncy bodily exhibits got in the way of searching for spiritual truth. They could be of no use to God in his dealings with human beings. God reached out to them through mind and soul, not body. Edwards saw no reason *a priori* to exclude the body as a possible slate for God's signature. He could imprint his Word upon it if he so chose. Of course not all bodily fits were divine inscriptions. Conversely, many saints were infused with the Holy Spirit without manifesting anything physically. True Christians understood that if God did touch their bodies, he was communicating his own transcendent glory, not bestowing any special virtue on them. He was using individual bodies to instruct a wider believing community, the whole "body of Christ."

Three individuals in Edwards's community were affected physically. One was the four-year-old Phebe Bartlett, who subjected herself to a steady regime of secret prayer, continual weeping, and "wreathing her body to and fro, like one in anguish of spirit." Little Phebe was beleaguered by doubts about her salvation, but she found assurance in realizing that Christ had come for sinners like her. That assurance did not mean she stopped crying. Asked by her mother one morning why she had wept long into the night, Phebe said it was because "I was thinking about God and Christ, and they loved me." Knowing the parents personally, and trusting their story, Edwards had no doubt that the Spirit had actually wrought a change in tiny Phebe's soul. Two other local children under the age of ten had also received "saving knowledge of Jesus Christ," and children in other communities had been saved too. Phebe was a spiritually precocious soul, not a juvenile freak.[16]

With Phebe Bartlett God had evidenced his sovereign power by prompting a little girl to prodigious feats of piety. In the case of Abigail Hutchinson, a sickly young woman who longed for union with Christ, God designated her eroding body as a public marker of his authority and mercy. Abigail's physical frame was not seized by fits. It simply wasted away. As her body gave out prior to her death, her soul rose to new heights of purity. Abigail saw her physical dissolution as an unsought gift from God. "She had great longings to die," Edwards wrote, "that she might be with Christ." At the same time, she "was like a little child," aglow with "a sense of the glory of God appearing in the trees, and growth of the fields, and other works of God's hands." Asked by her sister why she kept smiling all the time in spite of her affliction, she replied, "I am brimful of a sweet feeling within!" She realized that she was "quite willing to live, and quite willing to die, . . . perfectly easy, in a full submission to the will of God." Like the tubercular missionary David Brainerd, who slowly deteriorated in Edwards's own house a decade later, Abigail had overcome a selfish yearning for immediate union with Christ. Her spiritual challenge was to accept her bodily existence for as long a period as God chose. She gave her body to God, but also to her fellow townspeople. In her declining days, they kept coming by to ask if she "held her integrity still, whether she was not afraid of death." Finally so weak that she could not speak, she showed them by signs that she had no fear because she trusted God's plan for her.[17]

Abigail Hutchinson's reticent physical performance was more like the old lives of the saints than the eighteenth-century stories of wild eruptions and seizures. But it helped Edwards establish the legitimacy of his third case, a mature woman subject to fits of fainting and leaping about. Her behavior looked on the face of it like a plain instance of enthusiasm unleashed. In the context of Hutchinson's travails, it looked more traditional. The woman in question was Edwards's own wife, Sarah, although he concealed her identity in his published account. During the revival of the early 1740s she felt an especially ardent passion for God. Edwards stressed that the physical display had begun when "it was a very dead time through the land"; hence it was not the product of any "distemper catched from Mr. Whitefield or Mr. Tennent." Indeed, Sarah resembled Phebe Bartlett: she had experienced "great transports" of soul beginning at the age of five or six. Her current holiness differed only in degree, not kind, from her childhood faith. Now she was swimming "in the rays of Christ's love, like a little mote swimming in the beams of the sun, or streams of his light that come in at a window." Christ's love flooded down like "a constant stream of sweet light," and her soul streamed up in love to him, "so that there seemed to be a constant flowing and reflowing from heart to heart."

Sarah's husband reveled in natural metaphors for Christ's love in all of his preaching and writing. The entire world, natural as well as human, was saturated with the divine presence. Edwards could gush like a Romantic Wordsworth over the awe-inspiring grandeur of creation. It was Christ who bathed the cosmos in warm liquid sunshine. Being so sure of the beauty and sovereignty of God, Edwards approached the natural and human worlds as emanations of God's love. Those created domains in turn supplied a pool of metaphors for understanding the God who made the universe and the Son of God who made it shine. "Christ is the sun, and the word written and preached are the rays," he wrote when still in his teens. "As [when] the sun . . . rises, all things are thereby revived and awakened out of sleep and silence, so when Jesus Christ shines into the souls of men, they are revived out of their deep and dead sleep of sin."[18]

Sarah's "extraordinary views of divine things" produced, according to her husband, "very great effects on the body." Sometimes she sank "under the weight of divine discoveries" and was "de-prive[d] of all ability to stand or speak." Sometimes she was pos-sessed of "a kind of omnipotent joy" that caused her "to leap with all the might, with joy and mighty exultation of soul." What distin-guished Sarah's case from enthusiasm, however, was that she never suspected her close encounters with Christ had delivered her from sin. Unlike "the Wesleys and their followers, and some other high pretenders to spirituality in these days," Sarah knew that she could never be "perfectly free from sin." Her body-altering soul experi-ences with Christ were harbingers of a potential future blessedness, not a mark of present distinction. Indeed, at the very moments when she was most intensely illuminated by "the pure and holy light of God's glory," she also understood "how loathsome and pol-luted the soul is, soul and body and every act and word appearing like rottenness and corruption." Sarah had made that point herself in the written statement that her husband used as the basis for his account of her experiences. Christ, she wrote, had "appeared to me as a mighty Saviour, under the character of the Lion of the tribe of Judah, taking my heart, with all its corruptions, under his care, and putting it at his feet." But far from making her feel sinless, her sense of "the immediate presence and love of God"—a presence "so near, and so real, that I seemed scarcely conscious of anything else"—pro-voked "a deep abasement of soul, under a sense of my own unwor-thiness."[19]

It did not occur to Jonathan Edwards to conclude from the cases of Abigail and Sarah that women experienced Christ in a dis-tinctive manner. He was plainly worried, on the contrary, that read-ers would believe her experiences were the natural product of a "weakness of nerves" commonly associated with women. He con-ceded that in earlier years she had suffered from depression and had been "at times almost overborne with it." But her recent piety, he claimed, was wholly unrelated to that history. She had passed the previous three years "without one hour's melancholy or dark-ness." The "vapors" that continued to have "great effects on [her] body" were now spiritually rather than psychologically directed. God had put himself in charge of her body, with her energetic consent. He had in effect chosen her mortal frame as an especially receptive site for signaling his power and presence. He had not healed her of the vapors but had turned them to evangelical use. By publishing an eloquent account of her spiritual experience, Edwards promoted that divine use of her. God chose Sarah's adult female body for holy pedagogy just as he chose David Brainerd's adult male body or Phebe Bartlett's juvenile frame.[20]

Neither Abigail Hutchinson nor Sarah Edwards saw their physical or mental struggles as an imitation of Christ. Like their Puritan forebear Mary Rowlandson, they saw their travail as a gift and a test, not as an invitation to compare themselves to Jesus. Yet of course for them as for Jonathan Edwards the ultimate instance of God's use of the human body to proclaim his sovereignty was the incarnation of his own Son. The entire redemptive drama hinged upon the human life, death, and resurrection of the sacrificial lamb, the Second Adam, whose "deluge of love to sinners," as Edwards phrased it, put history back on course toward union between God and his saints. Edwards reveled in the paradox of the incarnate Son, wholly divine and wholly human. He loved the symmetry between the first Adam, through whom sin and death entered the world, and the second Adam (Christ), through whom sin and death were conquered. He marveled at the "diverse excellencies" of a lamb who defied all logic by doubling as the lion of Judah. Jesus alone could bring together "without contradiction" the "infinite highness" of God and the "lowness and littleness before God" that marked his human life. He was ineffably grand and perfectly humble. This distinguished him even from the Father and the Holy Ghost, neither of whom could be called humble since they "exist only in the divine nature." The gorgeous array of unexpected fusions in Christ's nature was not a reason to have faith in him. Loving the story was not the same as loving the person. The faithful received, in addition to the awe, a new "sense of the heart" or

"spiritual light" that allowed them to love him as savior while celebrating all the succulent delicacies of his nature.[21]

God was ingenious: What better way to signal the urgency of
human submission to the Father than to model such a surrender
within the Godhead itself? "Christ, as he was a divine person,"
Edwards preached, "was the absolute sovereign of heaven and
earth, but yet he was the most wonderful instance of submission to
God's sovereignty that ever was." He was the most marvelous case
because the divine self-submission was physical as well as spiritual, hence fully visible to human beings. Christ's contemporaries
had witnessed it, then preached the good news of it. Ironically,
Edwards noted, the utter humanity of Christ was most plainly revealed not in his bodily suffering, but in the mental torment that
accompanied it. Jesus was not a person with the mind of God and
the body of a man. He was a man in mind and body. True, he was
incapable of sinning since his will had not been corrupted by
Adam's fall. But he was completely human in every other respect—
"in all things . . . made like unto his brethren" (Heb. 2:17). Jesus was
so fully a "creature" in mind, said Edwards, that he could not recall
the "infinite glory and happiness" he had known when he was sitting at the right hand of the Father. He remembered only vaguely
that he had earlier inhabited an exalted plane of some sort. With the
mental as well as physical equipment of a man, he underwent a
psychic anguish at the end of his life that was far worse than his
physical pain. Indeed, he experienced more fear and trembling
than the many martyred saints who later accepted their final tortures with steely resignation.[22]

Edwards deduced the extreme mental pain of the crucifixion
from the unbearable agony Christ suffered in the Garden of Gethsemane. The agony was so intense, according to Luke 22:44, that
"his sweat was as it were great drops of blood falling down to the
ground." In his 1739 sermon on that verse, Edwards went back to
the Greek. In the original, the "great drops" were "lumps or clots."
Imagine the scene, Edwards told his congregation. It must have

been a cool evening for Christ's blood to be so "congealed and stiff-ened" that it fell not in drops but in clots. Imagine further the character of Christ's "inward distress and grief," so "violent" and "unspeakably extreme" that his blood was "pressed out through the pores of his skin" even on a cool night when a person would not be likely to sweat at all. The Garden scene was an essential preparation for the crucifixion because it enabled Jesus to register the horror of what he faced. "If Christ had not fully known what the dreadfulness of these sufferings was, before he took them upon him, his taking them upon him could not have been fully his own act as man; there could have been no explicit act of his will about that which he was ignorant of." Jesus had to act freely as a man if his obedience to the Father's will was to be complete. The Garden interlude gave Christ the chance to apprehend what the Father was asking of him as a man. And it gave the Father a chance to display his Son's submission. Jesus wavered when he asked God to "re-move this cup from me," but he quickly rallied by adding, "never-theless not my will, but thine, be done."[23]

The risk that God took in making a physical, hence visible and publicized, exhibit of his self-submission was that human wor-shipers would miss the lesson. They might make an idol of Christ's body rather than taking it as the efficacious vehicle and sign of God's redemptive plan. Edwards, like other Calvinists, was aghast at Catholic images of Jesus. "Images" were of the "imagination," hence frivolous and self-serving, not impersonally grounded in bib-lical revelation and rational analysis. The "papists" bedecked their churches with "beautiful and affecting" representations of Christ, and "the craft of the priests" even managed to make the images "move, and speak, and weep." Whether stationary and mute or mobile and emoting, the pictures were diversionary at best, de-structive of true piety at worst. Yet Catholics, said Edwards, merely made blatant a temptation to which many Protestants also suc-cumbed. Protestants filled their heads if not their eyes with images of "Christ hanging on the cross, and shedding his blood," and satisfied themselves that for that reason they knew Christ. Those mental representations were just as "external" to Christ's real person as the Catholics' icons were. "Ideas of outward appearances," Edwards wrote, "are not spiritual." As Thomas Shepard had pointed out a century earlier, "saving knowledge" of Christ did not resemble a visual sighting of him. Many people had seen the earthly Jesus in his own day without realizing who he was. The pious believers centuries later who claimed to see Christ "immediately as if here on earth" might be equally in the dark about who they were looking at. Beholding an image of him had no spiritual value in itself.[24]

V

Edwards thought American Christians had a special responsibility to deliver the church from "external" veneration of Christ. The New England revivals of the 1730s and 1740s appeared to be "the first fruits of that glorious day" when God "shall renew the world of mankind." The "old world" was where Christ had been "born literally" and made "the purchase of redemption." It was also where "the blood of the saints and martyrs" had been shed. It made sense to Edwards that as history moved closer to the millennial age—"those times of the peace and prosperity and glory of the church"—the new continent "that has not shed so much blood" would come into its own. The Old World had a special tie to Christ's human body, the New World to his resurrected body. America's charge was spiritual rebirth. Edwards loved the logical reversal: just as Europeans had given America its first birth, Americans would model for Europeans a second birth of the spirit. There was ample biblical warrant, Edwards noted, for such a historic turnabout. The Jews had given Christ his first birth, yet they would ultimately enter "the evangelical dispensation" through the ministration of Gentiles. Likewise the Europeans who had begotten the

Americans would be brought into the final days by their New World offspring.[25]

Edwards was well aware that the Americans who had been given their first birth by Europeans were not the original inhabitants of the continent. When he was installed in the frontier town (and Indian mission) of Stockbridge, Massachusetts, in the 1750s he lived beside and preached to Mohawks and Mahicans. But even in the Connecticut Valley in 1739, when he composed his sermon series on "a history of the work of redemption," he was thinking about the role the American Indians had played in the divine plan. They had suffered, in his view, the unfortunate fate of being the devil's playthings. Satan had had them to himself for a very long time, since America had come into "reach of the light of the gospel" only with European exploration.

Thankfully, said Edwards, the New World had become a place "full of Bibles, and full of at least the form of the worship of the true God and Jesus Christ." A few Indians were even showing "an inclination to be instructed in the Christian religion." The French, naturally, had been no help at all. As Edwards put it in a sermon to the Mohawks in 1751, the French "pretend to teach the Indians religion, but they won't teach 'em to read. They won't let 'em read the Word of God. They are afraid that if they should read the Scripture, they would know that their [the French's] ways are not agreeable to the Scripture." The English were scarcely faultless. They had ignored their responsibility to the Indians too, a "shameful neglect . . . by which the great God has undoubtedly been made very angry." Edwards invited the Mohawks "to come and enjoy the light of the Word of God, which is ten thousand times better than the light of the sun. There is such a thing as this light's shining into the heart, as it does into the hearts of all good men. And when it does so, it changes their hearts and makes 'em like to Jesus Christ. 'Tis as when you hold a glass out in the light of the sun, the glass will shine with a resemblance of the sun's brightness. Like a sweet and beautiful flower in the spring."[26]

Satan may have used America and its Indian communities as a base camp and safe haven, said Edwards, but the devil worked even more insidious mischief in the civilized world, where he spread "corrupt opinions" about Christ. In a 1739 sermon he enumerated the worst of the offenses. No sooner had the Reformation begun, with Luther's revolt in Germany, than the Anabaptists emerged. They falsely claimed, on the basis of Christ's injunction to be perfect, "even as your Father which is in heaven is perfect" (Matt. 5:48), that "there ought to be no civil authority." Hence "they refused to submit to magistrates, or any human laws." They were shortly followed by enthusiasts like the Quakers, who pretended "to be inspired with the Holy Ghost, as the prophets were." More threatening in America than the Quakers, Edwards thought, were the Socinians, Arians, and deists. All three rejected or restricted the divinity of Christ. Socinians (named after the seventeenth-century Italian Unitarian Faustus Socinus) "held that Christ was only a mere man." The Arians (after Arius, a fourth-century European heretic) granted that Christ was more than a man but held that he and the Holy Ghost "were but mere creatures"—God had created them, hence they were not coequal with him in the Godhead. The deists repudiated "the whole Christian religion." They accepted "the being of God" but denied "that Christ was the son of God, and say he was a mere cheat." Yet the Arminians were, in Edwards's eyes, the most dangerous of all. They were virtual Trojans inside the church gates. Many of them proclaimed their attachment to the Trinity and the divinity of Christ, but all the while they compromised his sovereignty. They revived the ancient Pelagian heresy, which minimized original sin and emphasized Christians' natural power to work toward their salvation. Not only had the Church of England become "almost universally" Arminian, but the stance had "greatly prevailed among the Dissenters" on both sides of the Atlantic.[27]

Edwards's survey of opinion on Christ in 1739 is a nice reminder that his own views on Jesus were hardly dominant in his own day, even in New England. They were much less so after his death in 1758. His lifelong attack on Arminianism, summed up in his treatises on *Freedom of the Will* (1754) and *Original Sin* (1758), fell on increasingly deaf ears. Rationalist deists and Arminian Christians (whether rationalists themselves or evangelicals such as the Methodists) could all agree on the ability of individuals to pursue the good and avoid sin if they put their minds and hearts to it. Even Edwards's most ardent disciples, his protégé Samuel Hopkins and other proponents of "New Divinity," labored to reconcile God's sovereignty with the belief that sinners possessed a natural capacity to stop sinning if they wished. Hopkins's cohort grasped that Edwards's version of free will was now systematically dismissed or misunderstood. He had preached that people were naturally free to sin or not sin, but given their inheritance from Adam they systematically preferred to sin—and kept right on sinning even as they beat their breasts and proclaimed their obedience to God.

For the New Divinity thinkers the main religious problem of the day was not skepticism about original sin, though there was plenty of that, but too much wrong-headed attachment to it. Their preoccupation with it was making too many Christians passive about seeking holiness. They were reconciled to their sinning; it was all they thought they were good for. Hopkins (along with Jonathan Edwards, Jr.) became an early advocate of the anti-slavery movement in part for this reason. One could chip away at one's own slavery to sin by attacking unfreedom everywhere. Sins such as slaveholding could be itemized and combated one by one. This redefinition of sin—seeing it as an array of discrete wrongful acts rather than a general condition against which natural resistance was futile—helped spark an era of broad social reform in America as well as Europe. Individuals and institutions (prisons, schools, insane asylums, poorhouses, hospitals) could all be improved. Slavery was an especially important target because two people could be delivered in each act of emancipation. The slaveholder could expunge his sin while slaves could attain the free civil status corresponding to the spiritual freedom they had already possessed in principle even under slavery. Jesus evolved considerably as a cultural figure as he intersected with these developments. On the one hand, his role as the sacrificial lamb who atoned for indelible human sin diminished, since sin was increasingly subject to human management and even eradication. On the other hand, Jesus stepped forward as a provocative preacher of individual and social progress and even perfection.[28]

If his insistence on original sin seemed anachronistic after his death, Edwards's support for intensely passionate Christian piety fell on increasingly receptive ears. Evangelicals (including John Wesley, who outlived his age-mate by thirty-three years) paraded his name in support of their campaign against "head" religion. Edwards's conviction that the "sense of the heart" was intellectual as well as emotional dropped from view. By the end of the eighteenth century his elegant Christological synthesis had been eclipsed by the various "corruptions" he had enumerated. His viewpoint remained significant as an alternative path available to later Christians dissatisfied with easygoing, companionate Christs. Edwards's paradoxical Jesus, like Shepard's savior, was distant yet approachable, a judge as well as a friend. He was the passionate bridegroom of those men and women who prostrated themselves, then rose to greet his warm light.

The single best image for conveying Edwards's view of Christ is the bridegroom choosing his bride—as long as we forget the male-female specification that our own gender-conscious era automatically imposes on that image. For orthodox Christianity the human soul had a rank, but no gender. The great chain of being went from animals to human beings to angels to God. The incarnate God-man, of course, had gender as well as rank. He had to be given a sex if he was to be fully human, so gender was to that extent of his essence. But maleness was a contingency of his placement in first-century Palestine, just as the maleness of the Father

was a contingency of ancient Hebrew culture. The biblically derived bride-bridegroom analogy made such good sense to Edwards
because it preserved hierarchy (the bridegroom was self-evidently
superior to the bride) while infusing the bond with a gender-
neutral passion of service and companionship. In the late eighteenth century, when hierarchy came under increasing religious as
well as political suspicion, the non-gendered marital metaphor
teetered on the brink of irrelevancy. More and more Christians
wanted their Christ configured in non-hierarchical fashion—an immediately available companion (even if still supernatural), not a
peremptory king, judge, or husband who meted out affection or
punishment as he pleased. The bridegroom-bride analogy had to
be dropped or revised.[29]

VI

The flexibility of the hierarchical bride-bridegroom analogy was
amply revealed in the late eighteenth century by the Shakers, a
small band of English enthusiasts who arrived in America in the
1770s. Originally known as "shaking Quakers" in England, they
founded a settlement near Albany, New York, and initially kept to
themselves. But in the 1780s the revolutionary authorities saw the
Shakers' sectarian withdrawal from the affairs of the world as a
sign of insufficient ardor for American independence. With their
leaders periodically jailed for "conspiracy," the Shakers deepened
their deviation from established social norms. They resembled
seventeenth-century Quakers in accentuating their differences from
other Christians, but they ultimately went much further than the
Quakers. They did not just welcome such physical extravagances in
worship as shaking, dancing, shouting, and falling down. The
Shakers took the extraordinary step of embracing celibacy, a means
of combating the sinfulness of the flesh and achieving sanctification
in this life.

Even more outrageous, from the standpoint of other Christians, was the Shakers' conviction that one of their founding leaders, "Mother" Ann Lee, was touched by divinity. An account published by a former Shaker in 1781 reported that Lee was said to have "the fullness of the God Head" within her. Some Shakers considered her "the Queen of heaven, Christ's wife." There is no direct evidence that Lee claimed this distinction for herself. But the belief in her special chosenness spread. In 1808 a Shaker group in Ohio published a *Testimony of Christ's Second Appearing,* arguing that Ann Lee herself embodied the returned Christ. She was an anointed one (the literal meaning of "Christ," or "Messiah") just as he had been. She represented the completion of the redemptive plan, which now mirrored the male-female structure of the created order. The Shakers made a shrewd use of the bride-bridegroom analogy: they kept the hierarchy but made it gender-equal. They gave Jesus an elevated female companion, then emphasized the equality of all other community members under the joint authority of Christ and of the "mother" who was "to be revered, believed, and obeyed."[30]

The political disloyalty attributed to the Shakers during the Revolution was also charged against the Methodists, thanks to their English roots and the unabashed Tory sentiments of Englishman John Wesley. But they began their stupendous American growth in the revolutionary era by bracketing politics and preaching a holiness to which everyone could aspire. They declared war on Calvinist predestination and made sanctification a goal people could pursue in the midst of their ordinary social lives. There was no need for a Shaker-style renunciation of sex and family. Americans north and south of all political views (along with many in the substantial minority that did not care one way or the other about the Revolution) found the Methodists' populism and supernaturalism appealing. No one was too common, too poor, or too black to be approached by a Methodist preacher or lay person and offered a chance at salvation and even sinlessness—with sin redefined as discrete acts of wrongdoing, not a state of concealed and corrosive self-aggrandizement. Circuit-riding Methodists explicitly patterned themselves on Jesus as they wandered the back roads of America and relied for sustenance on the largesse of their converts. The itinerants commanded devotion because they sacrificed themselves so completely to the cause of bringing Christ to everyone. They were the eighteenth-century Protestant American equivalent to the seventeenth-century Jesuits trudging through the Canadian woods.[31]

The Methodists wished every single person to become a self-reliant individual by choosing Jesus as savior. Religion in this Arminian framework was a kind of self-empowerment. But it is a mistake to see Methodism as an endorsement of individualism and leave it at that. The Methodist call was to join a community of believers who helped each other overcome the selfish excesses of individualism. Like the Calvinist evangelicalism of the American Baptists, whose ranks also mushroomed in the late eighteenth and nineteenth centuries, Methodism preached God's infinite love for every person. That gave every individual an immeasurable worth. But a lofty view of the dignity of each person, and of each person's potential for sanctity, was not equivalent to valuing individual exploits above community welfare or stability. The validation of individual experience could prompt people to stand against social mores, but they usually did so hand-in-hand with their fellow religionists. They derived a new sense of their potency as individuals thanks to their participation in a new community. The figure of Jesus stood right at this intersection of individual and community. On the one hand, he symbolized the entire "body of Christ," within which individuals were nurtured. On the other hand, his reported impatience with Pharisees, money-changers, and even his own disciples for losing sight of spiritual purity showed individuals how to take institutions to task whenever they fell short of perfection.[32]

Evangelicalism was thus critical as well as supportive of individualism, and the individualism it heralded was often explicitly religious and not political at all. Methodists in particular saw religion as transcending politics. During the Revolutionary War, for example, Methodist preacher Benjamin Abbott took note of the general presumption in America that the Methodists were Tories. He granted that some were indeed Tories but quickly added that "for my part I never meddled in the politics of the day. My call was to preach salvation to sinners, to wage war against the works of the devil." He talked politics only when he once ventured from New Jersey into Pennsylvania and a group of Presbyterians insisted he preach in favor of the war. He apparently acceded, but he took more interest in teaching the well-behaved Germans in his audience how to fall down in pious fervor, and to realize that "it was the power of God making it happen."[33]

Abbott's memoir is full of revelations about the early Methodists' ways of thinking about and praising Jesus. Abbott was proud of his own rough-and-tumble background—"drinking, fighting, swearing, gambling" until he was forty years old—because it signaled his "primitive" approach to the gospel. The college-educated, he thought, were apt to miss the plain meaning of Scriptures. His account is alive with the visions, dreams, and portents of traditional folk religion, and with the singing, weeping, and falling down common to Calvinist and Arminian revivalism ever since the time of Abbott's birth in the 1730s. One nighttime service on the eastern shore of Maryland at the end of his career in 1794 was typical of many others in his narrative. "We had a proper shout," he reported, "one fell to the floor, and lay as if she were dead, and when she came to, she shouted and gave glory to God for her deliverance."[34]

During his own conversion experience in 1772, he "saw by faith" both Jesus and the Father ("the Ancient of Days"). Jesus extended his arms wide and told him, "I died for you." Then God said, "I freely forgive thee for [sic] what Christ has done." At that point Jesus approached him "as if with a cup in his hand, and he gave it to me, and I took it and drank thereof: it was like unto honey for sweetness." Abbott's sanctification followed a few years later, after the war had begun. He was slain "flat to the floor, and lay as one strangling in blood, while my wife and children stood weeping over me." He lay there half an hour, "and felt the power of God running through every part of my soul and body, like fire consuming the inward corruptions of fallen depraved nature." When he got up, he felt he "had got new eyes, for everything appeared new, and I felt a love for all the creatures that God had made, and an uninterrupted peace filled my breast. In three days God gave me a full assurance that he had sanctified me, soul and body." Methodism rescued Abbott from the doctrines of "unconditional election and reprobation" that had stained his Calvinist youth. It was "real heart religion." Methodists "had the pardoning love of God in their souls," and "knew their sins were forgiven." At one worship service after another Abbott "felt lost in the ocean of love: we had a powerful, melting, shouting time."[35]

Abbott's Methodism combined frequent experiences of deep religious feeling with direct knowledge about what those experiences meant. His faith did not accommodate any wavering. Piety and self-doubt were mutually exclusive. Religious experience was overwhelming emotionally and transparent intellectually. Abbott took as much pride in his debating victories as he did in his preaching. Traipsing through the middle colonies in the 1780s, he "tore up Calvinism with all my power," since it denied that one could be sinless. Again and again he took Presbyterian and Baptist listeners to task for objecting to his view of sanctification. One Presbyterian elder told him that anyone claiming to know "his sins were forgiven . . . ought to be burned, for he made himself as perfect as an angel in heaven. Nay, said he, I would help to burn such a man myself." Abbott snapped back that if the elder had never felt "Christ applied to the washing away of his sins, his religion was still no better than the devil's. This shut him up, and he went away silent, and afterward told his minister that he slept none that night."[36]

Abbott's favorite proof text was 1 John 3:9, which in his eyes plainly guaranteed the truth of the idea of sinlessness: "Whosoever is born of God doth not commit sin; . . . he cannot sin, because he is born of God." Naturally Abbott's favorite text to preach from was

"Ye must be born again." Calvinism was preventing people from reaping the full reward of the new birth. They were capable of becoming a good deal more like the sinless savior than the Calvinists allowed. Calvinism was also preventing people from seeing Jesus. At one of Abbott's stops a young woman "cried out, 'I see Moses and Elias,' repeating it many times over. I said, 'See Jesus!' She replied, 'He is coming!' And clasping her arms to her body, cried several times, 'I have got him! I have got him!' And sprang up, shouting praises to God for her soul's deliverance. I said, 'If you have got him, be sure to keep him close to your heart.' 'I will,' said she." "This," Abbott concluded, "is the religion of Jesus."[37]

The Methodists grew rapidly by inviting everyone into the church. John Wesley had found an ingenious middle ground between Puritan-style exclusivity and Anglican-style universalism: let anyone join, but monitor their behavior and enforce a strict discipline. Backsliding would be common, but so would the redoubling of many fallen-away members' efforts to avoid sin. Wesley was more afraid of leaving some souls out of the church, thus isolating them from the indwelling love of the Spirit, than of compromising the sovereignty of Christ. In the long run hypocritical believers using Jesus for self-flattery or social prestige could be rooted out of the church. Theologically the Methodists took up a position midway between the two traditionally democratic (i.e., plebian) Protestant American groups, the Baptists and the Quakers. All three minimized the importance of educated leaders. The Methodists shared the Baptists' veneration of the Bible and the Quakers' sense that personal holiness was attainable. Methodist eclecticism found the middle ground on Jesus too: like the Baptists they preserved his transcendence by keeping the Trinity and a once-and-for-all divine revelation in biblical times; like the Quakers they harped on the believer's capacity to embody holiness. Even institutionally the Methodists located the center, maintaining the hierarchy of the Wesleys' Anglican upbringing (leadership by bishops) while encouraging local lay initiative.

Lay initiative in the early years of Methodism included some stalwart women and African Americans, who often persevered in the face of other Methodists' opposition. The life of "Old Elizabeth," a Maryland slave born in 1766, shows how a charismatic Methodist woman's experience of Jesus was shaped by the resistance she encountered. Elizabeth's story, narrated when she was ninety-seven years old, begins with her new birth in 1778 at the age of twelve. Her conversion resembled Benjamin Abbott's: a sighting of Jesus "standing with His hand stretched out to receive me," saying "Peace, peace, come unto me," followed by a visit with the Father, who was surrounded by "millions of glorified spirits in white robes." But then a whispering voice challenged her to "call the people to repentance, for the day of the Lord was at hand." She realized this charge was a "heavy yoke," and "wept bitterly at the thought of what I should have to pass through." From that point on her misgivings warred with her sense of calling. She did not doubt God, but she second-guessed her strength and worthiness.[38]

Sold to a Presbyterian "for a term of years, as he did not think it right to hold slaves for life," she emerged a free woman in the mid-1790s and began to speak out in Methodist meetings. One day she opened the Bible at random (a common strategy of the day for those in search of divine advice) and her eye fell on this passage: "Gird up thy loins now like a man." She was taken aback at the instruction, and was told by "all that were accounted pious" to give up the idea. "It was hard for men to travel," they said, "and what would women do?" She "returned to the Lord, feeling that I was nothing, and knew nothing." Many years of struggle ensued, in which she chose silence over speech. It finally dawned on her that she had been "rejected by the elders and rulers, as Christ was rejected by the Jews before me." This insight allowed her to convert the disdain of the ministers she met into deeper spiritual passion. "The Lord showed me that it was His will I should be resigned to die any death that might be my lot, in carrying his message, and be entirely crucified to the world. . . . I knew nothing but Jesus Christ, and him crucified." Elizabeth traveled through Maryland and Virginia for the dangerous work of preaching to slaves, then carried the gospel to free blacks in Michigan for four years before returning to Philadelphia. Jesus had given her a life's commission, as he had Benjamin Abbott, but he had also rescued her from the perennial self-disparagement exacerbated by her many detractors.[39]

VII

In her travels Elizabeth received constant support "through the different states of the Union" from "many of the Quaker friends." Abbott's encounters with the Quakers had been occasions for dragdown debates over the sufficiency and finality of the scriptural Word. Elizabeth relied on the Quakers to offer aid that was not forthcoming from her fellow Methodists. It stood to reason that the Quakers would help, since from the seventeenth century they had embraced female "witnessing" in their own ranks. In addition, they had taken the mid-eighteenth-century lead in questioning the propriety of Christians owning slaves. Quaker writer John Woolman's two essays "On the Keeping of Negroes" (1754, 1762) judged "the Spirit of Christ" incompatible with depriving one's "fellow creatures of the sweetness of freedom." The "life of our blessed Saviour when on earth, as it is recorded by his followers," expressed "one uniform desire for the eternal and temporal good of mankind," a desire that "discovered itself [revealed itself] in all his actions."[40]

By the revolutionary era many Calvinists had seconded Woolman's call, and Methodists, as their numbers increased after independence, followed suit. Philadelphia physician Benjamin Rush, a signer of the Declaration of Independence in 1776 and a Presbyterian, followed Woolman in proclaiming (in 1773) that slavery could not be reconciled with "the sublime and perfect Religion of the Great Author of Christianity." Rush considered slavery so self-evidently contrary to the doctrine of natural rights that Jesus—

who Rush conceded never spoke about slavery one way or the other—could not possibly have tolerated it. "There is scarcely a parable or a sermon in the whole history of his life, but what contains the strongest arguments against slavery." By Rush's lights, every time Jesus condemned vice and praised virtue he was necessarily condemning slavery, since slavery was so obviously a vice. "Can it be believed that this divine Lawgiver . . . could approve of an Evil, which involved in it every thing that was destructive to the Happiness of Individuals and Society?" The next generation of anti-slavery writers would have to confront the basic question that Rush begged: how to cope with the historical development of culture, which permitted an institution like slavery to escape Christ's highly sensitive moral antennae and then emerge as an intolerable evil.[41]

In his *Autobiography*, written after the Revolution, Rush described how his religious faith had changed since his days as a Presbyterian medical student in Philadelphia in the 1760s. Even then he had "delighted in . . . hearing evangelical ministers of all denominations," an ecumenical opportunity that Philadelphia was uniquely equipped to provide. As historian Jon Butler has noted, in the eighteenth century Philadelphia and the larger Delaware Valley comprised the New World center of ethnic and religious pluralism: Anglicans, Presbyterians, Baptists, Quakers, German Lutherans and Reformed, and many smaller groups, including Jews. A vibrant African American community, slave and free, made possible the late-century Methodist congregations that ultimately produced the African Methodist Episcopal Church, founded by the gifted organizer and preacher Richard Allen in 1816. Christian religion took such a variety of forms that the old historians' query—did "religion" promote the Revolution or not?—is unanswerable as posed. "Religion" in general did not exist. Only religions did, and individual denominations were often split on the issue of independence from Britain. Backers of independence rarely invoked Jesus himself in support for their cause. They found the Hebrew Scriptures,

centered on the chosen people and the Providence of God, more
pertinent to the case at hand. Jesus himself entered the revolutionary era as an opponent of war and an opponent of slavery. After the
war he appeared frequently in sermons interpreting independence
as the dawn of a new millennium.[42]

During the Revolution Rush himself had let religion slide ("political life" had been "unfavourable to the divine life in my soul"),
but in the late 1780s he once again "felt a strong desire to partake
of the Lord's Supper." Since Calvinism no longer made sense to
him, he was confirmed in 1788 at St. Peter's (Anglican/Episcopal)
Church. His own experience of two distinct Christian traditions led
him to the insight that a proliferation of religious perspectives
could bear spiritual fruit for the community. Each school of thought
or denominational edifice appeared able to encompass only part of
the truth about God and Christ. "How few Sects honour Father,
Son, and Holy Ghost in Religion as they should do," he wrote in
1800. "The Socinians honour the Father only, the Catholics the
Saviour chiefly, and the Quakers the Holy Spirit above both! How
few include all the ends of our Saviour's death in their belief of the
Atonement. Each contends for one end only, while 6 or 7 other ends
are clearly revealed in the Scriptures." By 1811, two years before his
death, he was laying out a fully pluralist perspective, as sketched in
his commonplace book:

> It would seem as if one of the designs of Providence in per-
> mitting the existence of so many Sects of Christians was
> that each Sect might be a depository of some great truth of
> the Gospel, and that it might by that means be better pre-
> served. Thus to the Catholics and Moravians he has com-
> mitted the Godhead of the Saviour, hence they worship and
> pray to him; to the Episcopal, Presbyterian, and Baptist
> Church the decrees of God and partial redemption, or the
> salvation of the first fruits, which they ignorantly suppose
> to include all who shall be saved. To the Lutherans and

Methodists he has committed the doctrine of universal redemption, to the Quakers the Godhead and influences of
the Holy Spirit, to the Unitarians, the humanity of our
Saviour, or the doctrine of "God manifested in the flesh."
. . . Let the different Sects of Christians not only bear with
each other, but love each other for this kind display of
God's goodness whereby all the truths of their Religion are
so protected that none of them can ever become feeble or be
lost. When united they make a great whole, and that whole
is the salvation of all men.[43]

Rush's endorsement of diversity as a means to unity differed
from a related idea expressed by John Woolman as early as the 1720s:
all genuinely spiritual faiths, whatever their differences of form
might be, boiled down to the same fundamental truths. "The outward modes of worship are various," wrote Woolman, "but wherever men are true ministers of Jesus Christ it is from the operation of
his spirit upon their hearts." Rush pulled this capacious Quaker
idealism back toward orthodoxy by insisting that actual truths
were contained (and thereby preserved) in the external differences,
not just in the inward spirit. Yet he broke from orthodoxy by dis-
missing the idea that any one approach to Christ was normative.[44]

Rush's doctrinal pluralism was doomed in nineteenth-century
American culture because more and more Protestants found it simpler to follow Woolman's example and posit an underlying spirit
independent of all historically shifting forms. That way nothing essential would ever be lost. An inward spirit that trumped differences of outward form made eminent sense to many who found
Methodist heart-religion as unpalatable as they did Calvinist orthodoxy. The Methodist middle-of-the-road solution—freely available
grace joined to a traditional Trinity, a miracle-working Christ, and a
heightened consciousness of sinful behavior—seemed archaic to
Unitarians, Universalists, and many Congregationalists and Episcopalians.

Yet the Methodists, liberal Protestants, and secularists such as Benjamin Franklin, for all their undeniable differences, united in ways they could not perceive at the time. They all embraced a modern American cultural assumption that crossed secular and religious lines: individuals were now free to choose their fates, whether eternal or temporal. No believable God would deny them that freedom. The malleable figure of Jesus helped American Protestants of all stripes move into the modern era together. Whether they preferred him supernatural as did the Methodists or natural as did many liberals, they could agree that he made it possible for human beings to find new depths and passions within themselves.

Ralph Waldo Emerson reached that conclusion in the early nineteenth century in his continuous ruminations on Christ. But "Good Peter," an Oneida Indian, came to the same conclusion sometime between 1766 and 1808. We know this because one day he was asked on short notice to preach a sermon. Samuel Kirkland, Congregational minister to the Oneidas in those years, mentioned Peter's performance to his friend Timothy Dwight, who recorded the story in his *Travels in New-England and New-York*:

> While Mr. Kirkland was a missionary to the Oneidas, being unwell, he was unable to preach on the afternoon of a certain sabbath; and told Good Peter, one of the head men of the Oneidas, that he must address the congregation. Peter modestly and reluctantly consented. After a few words of introduction he began a discourse on the character of the Saviour. "What, my brethren, said he, are the views which you form of the character of Jesus? You will answer, perhaps, that he was a man of singular benevolence. You will tell me that he proved this to be his character by the nature of the miracles which he wrought. All these you will say were kind in the extreme. He created bread to feed thousands who were ready to perish. He raised to life the son of

a poor woman who was a widow, and to whom his labours were necessary for her support in old age. Are these then your only views of the Saviour? I tell you they are lame. When Jesus came into our world he threw his blanket around him but the God was within." This I had from Mr. Kirkland himself.[45]

We are separated from Good Peter's tantalizing comments by two centuries or more, and by two ministerial mediators, Kirkland and Dwight. We can only guess whether Peter, like Thomas Shepard's confessors, was repeating a message he had heard his minister preach, or was adapting Kirkland's teaching in an impromptu meditation of his own. Kirkland's delighted reaction suggests the latter possibility. If so, Peter may have been applying Luke 17:20–21: "The Kingdom of God cometh not with observation; the Kingdom of God is within you." Yes, Jesus performed miracles, making his power visible by "throwing his blanket around him" (i.e., not "around" his shoulders, but into the world about him). Yet those manifestations of his divinity led people to focus on the signs of it, not the source. He carried the power of God inside himself. Whatever the meaning of Peter's original words, Dwight's recording one version of them reveals a central fact about Jesus in America over the last four centuries: his name has been spoken continuously, earnestly, and hopefully by a vast and diversified body of interpreters.

FOUR

WHEN SHALL I SEE JESUS?

I

Benjamin Rush's reflection that the Revolution took him away from religion, while the post-revolutionary period brought him back to it, applied to his personal piety, not his public activity. The issue that preoccupied revolutionaries in America as in Europe—political liberty—could not be separated from the quest for religious liberty. Republicans in the new United States, as in revolutionary France, kept up the battle to rein in or destroy the power of established churches. State churches, in the republican view, assaulted liberty in two ways. First, as virtually all republicans argued, established churches brandished superstitious dogmas and mysteries that kept people in the dark about the rational capacities of their own minds. Second, as a few republicans such as Thomas Jefferson and especially James Madison contended, state churches interfered in the sacred, one-on-one encounter between the believer and God. Indeed *any* official support for religion threatened the integrity and intensity of the individual's bond with God. Government sponsorship necessarily trivialized faith by associating it with social conformity. Even the slightest state promotion of faith undermined religious freedom by taming its terrors, relieving individuals of the responsibility to meet their God in full fear and trembling.[1]

The great difference between the leading American revolutionaries and the leading French revolutionaries is that the Americans,
like Rush, so frequently returned to a personal faith in Jesus once the
revolutionary moment had passed. The most accomplished American
thinker of the day, Thomas Jefferson, found it both possible and necessary to venerate Jesus, though he took him as a man of wisdom
rather than a divine being. The Europeans could not keep Jesus even
to Jefferson's degree, because to them Christianity itself, not just the
established church, reeked of the Old Regime. "In France," wrote
Alexis de Tocqueville in 1835, "the spirit of religion and the spirit of
freedom" marched "in opposite directions," while in America "they
were intimately united." In Europe Christianity had attached itself to
"the powers of the earth." With those "now in decay," Christianity
was "buried under their ruins." New sects and denominations
were proliferating in the United States in the 1830s, but their disagreements did nothing to weaken the hold of Jesus on the population. Tocqueville remarked in 1840 that Christian religion in America
had "mingled with all the habits of the nation and all the feelings of
patriotism," becoming "an established and irresistible fact, which no
one undertakes either to attack or to defend." For Americans Christ
had become a flexible symbol of love, sacrifice, and idealism who
crossed lines of class, region, denomination, ethnicity, and belief itself.
"The perfection of Christ's moral character is a fact," wrote one Unitarian minister in 1845. "Almost all unbelievers admit the fact," giving Americans a "sacred ground common to all." Jesus was not only
perfect, he was the perfect democrat, the man and God of the people.[2]

Of course in a democratic atmosphere so suffused with Christ-
talk and Christ-worship, it made sense for a post-revolutionary
politician such as Jefferson (or, in the next generation, an iconoclastic writer and lecturer such as Emerson) to claim an alliance with
Jesus. He was at the heart of an entire cultural language in which
the Protestant population was fluent. (In 1800 there were only fifty
thousand Catholics and two thousand Jews in a population of five
million.) He was a currency one could spend, a type of credit one

could store up. Jefferson, Emerson, and many other critics of tradition wanted to show that one could stand against certain religious structures and habits of mind without falling into French-style atheism. Appealing to Jesus gave legitimacy to their anti-clerical liberalism. The gospel writers, who had depicted Jesus as a rebel against sclerotic religious authority, made it easy for a scientific rationalist such as Jefferson or a poetic rationalist such as Emerson to sidle up to Jesus. Those such as Jefferson and Emerson who wished to dissociate themselves from orthodox conceptions of divinity could proclaim, in effect, "Jesus made me do it."

For all of their many differences of temperament and historical placement, Jefferson and Emerson both took Jesus as the most eminent philosopher of the human condition. They arrived at this position independently, a sign of how pervasive and serviceable Jesus was in all corners of the early-nineteenth-century American cultural environment. In these early decades of the new American nation Jesus took root as sage of the enlightened and savior of the people. He reached a kind of critical mass as a cultural hero. For the rest of the century most individuals and groups would necessarily make sense of their lives and goals by defining themselves in relation to him. In the revolutionary generation Jefferson was typical of the most intellectually distinguished Americans in hailing Christ's wisdom. What he kept quiet about on the whole was his conviction that Jesus was human, not divine. Thomas Paine held the same position, and with no political career to protect, did so in print. But it is Jefferson who shows most clearly why anti-clerical Americans of his time remained so fond of Jesus. Christ the timeless philosopher was a reliable ally against reactionary clergy, many of whom remained committed to established religion in the states after the First Amendment banned establishment at the federal level in 1791. Jefferson wished ultimately to rescue Jesus from the churches, and that campaign helped him demonstrate, to himself and a small coterie of educated gentlemen, just how dispassionately rational a modern nineteenth-century American could be.

II

Benjamin Franklin had toyed with the Lord's Prayer, but Thomas Jefferson, ever the revolutionary, went to work on the gospels themselves. Ever the diplomat too, he kept his campaign of biblical recasting mostly to himself. Like Franklin he believed that no tradition was so sacred as to escape rational scrutiny and revision. But there the resemblance ends. In contrast to the draconian Jefferson, Franklin looks positively respectful of old-time piety. In reconstructing the Lord's Prayer he kept the whole of it, trying only to make its meanings clearer and closer to the Calvinist conviction that "there is no good in us." Jefferson plucked what he liked from the four gospels and shredded the rest. Private or not, his campaign to extract the "diamonds" of Christ's true words from the "dunghill" of theological invention that buried them is a stark exhibit of the Enlightened mind at work.

Jefferson's labor on the gospels began while he was a first-term president. His own religious views, or lack of them, had been a major issue in the election of 1800, and his Federalist antagonists had gone back on the attack in 1803. They were calling for war in the West over American access to New Orleans, and they linked Jefferson's alleged weakness as commander-in-chief to his supposed French-style religious infidelity. Had he not been attacking the clergy for years, and assaulting the tradition of tax-supported churches ever since he and Madison concocted the Virginia Statute on Religious Freedom? And, as the Reverend Clement Moore (later the author of "'Twas the Night Before Christmas") put it, had not Jefferson thumbed his nose at Scripture when he wondered "whether the blacks be really men, or only an intermediate grade between us and the brutes"? The Bible, said Moore, plainly showed that everyone descended from Adam. It did not help the president's case that in 1802 Thomas Paine had returned to the United States after many years in revolutionary France and received a grateful welcome at the White House. Paine was of course still celebrated as the silver-penned author of the republican manifesto *Common Sense*, one of the two sacred texts of 1776 (along with Jefferson's own Declaration of Independence). But Paine's recent *Age of Reason* (1794) had enraged much American as well as British opinion with its derisive putdown of Christianity.[3]

Common Sense had been perfectly in tune with the American times, but *The Age of Reason* was almost perfectly at odds with them. Paine chose a time of cultural revulsion against the French Reign of Terror to ridicule the Christianity that a new wave of believers took as protection against disorder. Paine laid out the Bible's inconsistencies and implausibilities with the same battering-ram glee he had earlier turned on the monarchy. The two targets, he contended, were interwoven in a single system of oppression: church and state in league against "the choicest gift of God to man, the GIFT OF REASON." Paine, along with Franklin and Jefferson, was a believer in God and in a future life. He opened *The Age of Reason* by proclaiming his intention to thwart the atheism spawned by the French Revolution. He wanted to decontaminate religion by replacing Christianity with "pure and simple deism," the sole faith equipped to revere "the power, wisdom, and benignity of the Deity," while resisting "the purpose of despotic governments." He said repeatedly that he had no quarrel with Jesus. Indeed, his "respect for the moral character of Christ" made him doubt whether Jesus had anything to do with devising the miracles and mysteries that made the Christian religion so obviously puerile and untruthful. "The God in whom we believe," he wrote, "is a God of moral truth, and not a God of mystery or obscurity. . . . Truth never invelops *itself* in mystery." Paine was a vehement rationalist, but he was not an opponent of religion. He was a militant de-Christianizer and a self-labeled friend of Jesus.[4]

Jefferson had no interest in pushing "Deism" as a religious alternative to the established churches, or in publicizing his reverence for Jesus. Like Madison he thought people's spiritual beliefs were between them and God, of no concern either to one's fellow citizens or to the state (whence came his and Madison's doctrine of "separation"). But like Paine he did want to protect Jesus from the churches' embrace, and as a politician seeking reelection he wished to make known that the Federalists were wrong in portraying him as anti-Christian. A perfect opportunity to establish his Christian credentials, but to do so in relative privacy, arose when Joseph Priestley, the renowned English scientist, republican, and Unitarian, sent him a copy of his new booklet *Socrates and Jesus Compared*. Jefferson immediately asked Priestley to expand the essay into a full comparison of Jesus with ancient Hebrew as well as Greek moralists. He had been thinking of doing the job himself, he added, ever since Benjamin Rush had asked him in the 1790s for a statement of his views on Christianity. Such a work would show that Jesus was "a master workman," whose "system of morality was the most benevolent and sublime probably that has been ever taught; and eminently more perfect than those of any of the antient philosophers." Jefferson agreed with Priestley that Jesus had made one especially glorious improvement on both the Greeks and the Hebrews: he harped on "the belief of a future state"—that is, life after death. Social order depended on that doctrine. Jesus understood that; Socrates did not.[5]

Jefferson let the well-connected Rush know about the exchange with Priestley and reported that his own views were "very different from that Anti-Christian system imputed to me. . . . To the corruptions of Christianity I am indeed opposed; but not to the genuine precepts of Jesus himself. I am a Christian, in the only sense in which he wished any one to be; sincerely attached to his doctrines, in preference to all others; ascribing to himself every human excellence, and believing he never claimed any other." Jefferson cautioned Rush against exposing his ideas to "the public," or to "the malignant perversions of those who make every word from me a text for new misrepresentations and calumnies." But the admonition left Rush at liberty to share Jefferson's acceptance of the "Christian" label with the appropriate private parties. The grapevine of circumspect gentlemen would spread the word that the president looked fondly on some sort of Christian belief.[6]

Enclosed in his letter to Rush, and in similar letters Jefferson sent to other friends at the time, was a "Syllabus"—a detailed outline of the sort of booklet he wished Priestley to produce. It would start with Pythagorus, Socrates, Epicurus, Cicero, Epictetus, Seneca, and Antoninus, and show that their thought was "really great" on the managing of one's own passions in order to attain "tranquility of mind." But all of them were "short and defective" on "our duties to others," failing to extend "the circle of benevolence" beyond "kindred and friends" to "neighbors and countrymen," much less to "the whole family of mankind." As for the ancient Hebrews, they rightly insisted on a "Deist" conception of God—a term that Jefferson used to mean monotheistic or unitary, as opposed to polytheistic or Trinitarian (he was not signing up for Paine's actual Deist religion). But the Hebrews had "degrading and injurious" ideas about God's attributes and failed, like the Greeks, to grasp that "other nations" were meant for inclusion in the circle of "peace, charity, and love."

With faulty predecessors like those, Jesus—"meek, benevolent, patient, firm, disinterested, and of the sublimest eloquence"—was poised for a historic victory. He faced an uphill battle, however, because "like Socrates and Epictetus, he wrote nothing himself." Worse, "he had not, like them, a Xenophon or an Arrian to write for him." He was stuck with "the most unlettered and ignorant of men," who put his teachings on paper only from memory, "and not till long after the transactions had passed." Only fragments of his own discourses survived in the general chaos of transmission, in which his doctrines were "mutilated" first by the gospel writers, then by succeeding generations of church authorities. Still, "notwithstanding these disadvantages, a system of morals is presented to us, which, if filled up in the true style and spirit of the rich fragments he left us, would be the most perfect and sublime that has ever been taught by man."

Christ's moral system was the most perfect for three reasons. First, it embraced "all mankind, gathering all into one family." It was universal, not parochial. Second, it "taught emphatically the doctrine of a future state"—a belief essential for promoting "moral conduct." And third, whereas the Greeks and Jews were interested only in right "actions," Jesus pushed through "into the heart of man; erected his tribunal in the region of his thoughts, and purified the waters at the fountain head." Wrongdoing began not with the act, but with the first thought that contemplated the act. Jefferson's rundown was hardly adequate as a summary of the Greeks, Hebrews, or Jesus as moralists. Socrates, for one, had more to say about "duties to others" than Jefferson supposed. But Jefferson's short Syllabus aspired only to get Priestley's prestigious pen behind the idea that Jesus answered a pressing American question. The United States was now a republican society, liberated more or less, in Jefferson's view, from corrupt clerical establishments. But that new freedom refocused rather than solved the problem of cultural authority. In the republican era, he believed, moral foundations had to rest upon individual white men, not corporate bodies. The moral formation of those citizens was more urgently necessary than ever before. True, every human being had a "moral sense" instilled by the Creator. But that sense was a potential faculty, not a guaranteed capacity. The moral vision of Jesus, disencumbered of all the supernatural balderdash that "caused good men to reject [it], and to view Jesus himself as an impostor," could spark people to develop their ethical talents.[7]

Jefferson's hopes for Priestley's breakthrough treatise were dashed when the old man died in early 1804. Benjamin Rush, meanwhile, had voiced displeasure at Jefferson's use of Jesus as a moral but not divinely appointed authority. He agreed that republicanism needed Christian underpinnings, and had indeed been pushing that view on Jefferson for many years. But unless the president made a place for Christ's divinity, making "his death as well as his life necessary for the restoration of mankind," Rush would not endorse Jefferson's venture. The Lord had to be taken whole, divine and human, or not at all. Even Priestley, who as a Unitarian humanized Jesus far more than the Trinitarian Rush, had chided the president for supposing that Jesus claimed no divine mission. That assertion by Jefferson was "an opinion that I do not remember ever to have heard before." Holding that position made it impossible to comprehend how "so many persons, hundreds in the first instance, and thousands presently after, [came] to believe that Jesus *did* pretend to a divine mission."[8]

Rush's rejection and Priestley's death took the wind out of Jefferson's pedagogical sails. He shelved the selection of gospel passages he had compiled for Priestley's use (a document Jefferson privately called "The Philosophy of Jesus"). He also set aside the dream of putting the Republic on the rock of Christ's purified wisdom. But he did not give up the goal of liberating the authentic Jesus, as he still protested in 1816, from those "who call *me* infidel and *themselves* Christians and teachers of the gospel, while they draw all their characteristic dogmas from what its Author never said nor saw." In retirement he returned to the gospels for a more systematic scissor-and-pasting than he had accomplished in "The Philosophy of Jesus." This time he obtained New Testaments in Greek, Latin, and French as well as English and created what he called a "narrative" of Christ's life and a record of his moral teachings. This time he told no one what he was doing. "The Life and Morals of Jesus of Nazareth," as he called his creation, was unknown even to his family, who discovered the eighty-two-page manuscript, neatly bound in red Morocco leather, upon his death in 1826.[9]

Jefferson's surgical strike on the gospels in 1819 or 1820 is a touching testament to an elderly man's undying faith in reason. He was at least seventy-five years old when he picked up his scissors and produced four columns of approved gospel text, moving left to right from Greek to Latin to French to English. The "Life and Morals of Jesus" cleansed the gospels of any passage that suggested Jesus believed himself divinely ordained. Jefferson pasted in the first part of Luke 2:40, for example ("And the child grew, and waxed strong in spirit, filled with wisdom"), but lopped off the last phrase ("and the grace of God was upon him"). He dropped all of Luke 2:49, in which the young Jesus chastises his parents for wondering why he was lingering in the temple. ("How is it that ye sought me? Wist ye not that I must be about my Father's business?") And he let Jesus tell off the sellers in the temple in John 2:16 ("Make not my Father's house an house of merchandise"), but did not let him utter his concluding thought in 2:19: "Destroy this temple, and in three days I will raise it up," a reference (according to the gospel writer) to "the temple of his body." And while he permitted Jesus to conclude from the camel going through the eye of the needle that "with men this is impossible, but with God all things are possible" (Matt. 19:26), he cut Jesus off before he could say, "Ye which have followed me, in the regeneration when the Son of man shall sit in the throne of his glory, ye also shall sit upon twelve thrones, judging the twelve tribes of Israel" (19:28). Needless to say, Jefferson's narrative concludes with the crucifixion, not the resurrection. The last verse elides the start of John 19:42 ("There laid they Jesus") with the end of Matthew 27:60 ("and . . . rolled a great stone to the door of the sepulchre, and departed").

Jefferson thus detached the wisdom of Jesus from the supernatural, apocalyptic, and eschatological frameworks adopted by the gospel writers, whom Jefferson repeatedly disparaged for such failings as "ignorance," "absurdity," "charlatanism," and "imposture." Occasionally, he conceded that Christ's own teaching was marred by ignorance. Priestley may have been right, Jefferson thought: Jesus considered himself divinely chosen. As Jefferson put it in a letter in 1820, "Elevated by the enthusiasm of a warm and pure heart, conscious of the high strains of an eloquence which had not been taught him, [Jesus] might readily mistake the coruscations of his own fine genius for inspirations of an higher order." Socrates had also been tempted to attribute his wisdom to a higher source, "a guardian daemon." But in neither case was outside inspiration a "reality." Jefferson concurred with Paine: Christ's belief in his own divine inspiration had to go because it misled people into worshiping an idol, praying for miracles rather than rolling up their sleeves and working for rationally chosen ends.[10]

But that concession jeopardized Jefferson's entire project of extracting, as he had put it to John Adams in 1813, "the very words only of Jesus" from the "misconceptions" of the "evangelists." If Jesus was a man of his times in believing himself divine, he could easily have been an eschatological prophet too. One delusion entailed another. If he thought he was divinely appointed, he could have seen himself as the fulfillment of various Old Testament prophecies. He could have thought he cured the blind and raised the dead, as many other healers also did—including, according to the gospel writers, his own disciples. Jefferson could not permit Jesus to inhabit his own pre-modern culture. He extracted a moral system from the gospels and he extracted Jesus from his world. He needed Christ to be a transcultural, universal figure, so he confidently removed the prophecies and the healings. For example, he scrapped Matthew 26:56 (where Jesus capped off the Gethsemane scene by saying that "all this was done, that the scriptures of the prophets might be fulfilled"). And while he let Jesus confound the Pharisees on the question of healing on the Sabbath (Luke 14:3, 5), he eliminated the actual healing of the man with dropsy (Luke 14:4) that sealed Christ's point. All these parings and scourings were designed to throw into relief the timelessness of the maxims and parables. "The Life and Morals" is a digest of Jesus' greatest hits, sayings such as "Inasmuch as ye have done it unto one of the least of these my brethren, ye have done it unto me" (Matt. 25:40), "For whosoever exalteth himself shall be abased; and he that humbleth himself shall be exalted" (Luke 14:11), and "There is nothing from without a man, that entering into him can defile him; but the things which come out of him, those are they that defile the man" (Mark 7:15).[11]

Since Jefferson offered no commentary on his selections, there is no way to know how he interpreted the two dozen parables and scores of maxims he chose to include. Likewise there is no way to be sure why he deleted many famous sayings, such as "Every kingdom divided against itself is brought to desolation; and every city or house divided against itself shall not stand" (the Matt. 12:25 reflection made famous by Lincoln in an 1858 speech), "Ye have the poor always with you; but me ye have not always" (Matt. 26:11), or "He that hath, to him shall be given; and he that hath not, from him shall be taken even that which he hath" (Mark 4:25). If he did treasure any particular verse, we can guess that this leading man of the Enlightenment cherished Matthew 5:14–16 above all the rest: "Ye are the light of the world. A city that is set on an hill cannot be hid. Neither do men light a candle, and put it under a bushel, but on a candlestick; and it giveth light unto all that are in the house. Let your light so shine before men, that they may see your good works, and glorify your Father, which is in heaven."

God was essential to Jefferson's scheme, as he was to Paine's, but a divinely chosen Jesus wrecked it. God's superintendence was the protection society needed against disorder: human beings could safely experiment with new social arrangements because God built balance into his natural order, an order that included the natural hearts of men. "The practice of morality being necessary for the well-being of society," he wrote privately in 1809, "[our Creator] has taken care to impress its precepts so indelibly on our hearts that they shall not be effaced by the subtleties of our brain." This was not heart-over-head doctrine, not a concession to "enthusiasm," but a declaration that heart and head worked together to stabilize the operation of reason in the world. Jesus was indispensable not as redeemer but as sage. He was the greatest teacher of all because he understood that the rational moral sense implanted by God in every person could prompt a revolution in human equality. Jefferson's God wanted people to renew the created world through rational action, and his prophets were men of wisdom like Jesus.[12]

In 1819 Jefferson wrote that he never went to bed "without an hour, or half hour's previous reading of something moral, whereon to ruminate in the intervals of sleep." "The Life and Morals" may have been one of his favorite bedtime texts. It would have been a double object of contemplation, disclosing the moral wisdom of Jesus and the rational handiwork of Jefferson. If his daily meditation included an expression of gratitude to his Creator, he thanked God for the gift of reason. He said as much in 1814 in response to one Miles King, a recently converted Methodist preacher. King had written him an eleven-page letter announcing that God had told him to plead with Jefferson to embrace "the christian System of Salvation . . . to seek untill you shall find Christ Jesus . . . for the place that Knows you now will Soon Know you no More for Ever! and do my friend and illustrious fellow citizen, timely consider, even now lay it close to your heart, that God! hath commanded all men every where to repent, because he hath appointed a day in the which he will Judge this world in Righteousness, by that man (God-man) whom he hath Ordained, Jesus Christ! whereof he hath given an assurance to all men in that he hath raised him up from the dead!"

Jefferson thanked King for his "kind intentions" toward his "future happiness." He told King they shared an ultimate faith in reason: it was only by appealing to his reason that King knew his mandate to proselytize Jefferson was "real" and not "imaginary." Reason was "the only oracle which god has given us to determine between what really comes from him, and the phantasms of a disordered or deluded imagination. When he means to make a personal revelation he carries conviction of its authenticity to the reason he has bestowed as the umpire of truth. You believe you have been favored with such a special communication. Your reason, not mine, is to judge of this: and if it shall be his pleasure to favor me with a like admonition, I shall obey it with the same fidelity with which I would obey his known will in all cases." In the final analysis, Jefferson said, people took "different roads . . . to that our last abode: but, following the guidance of a good conscience, let us be happy in the hope that, by these different paths, we shall all meet in the end—and that you and I may there meet and embrace is my earnest prayer."[13]

The great irony of "The Life and Morals of Jesus," Jefferson's secularization of the gospels, is that in the twentieth century it was lauded as evidence of Jefferson's firm commitment to religion and to Christ. His desire to save Jesus from the churches, and from Christ's own apparent misconception about his divinity, was transmuted into a desire to champion Christian values in the face of rampant secularism. Under its new title of "The Jefferson Bible," his "Life and Morals" was published in 1904 by none other than the U.S. government, so that the Congress could hand out free copies to its members. It has been in print ever since. Perhaps Jefferson had to be Christianized if he was to become worthy of iconic status in his own right, a subject fit for eternal sculpting on Mount Rushmore. The Deist Paine, meanwhile, no less religious than Jefferson in life, met a different fate. Having publicly sneered at the Christian church's Jesus, Paine was anathematized. A century after his death Teddy Roosevelt called him "that filthy little atheist." Jefferson the early-nineteenth-century infidel became Jefferson the sage of Monticello and a minor gospel-authoring evangelist in his own right.[14]

III

In a moment of ill-starred prognostication Jefferson once predicted that the religious future belonged to the Unitarians. Before his death he probably realized that Miles King and other Christians of the revivalist persuasion had proved him wrong. The Methodists and Baptists comprised a gathering wave of tidal proportions. Estimates of the numbers of new church members (and of the "adherents" who never joined officially) are very approximate. But there is no question about the big jump among the Methodists and Baptists. From their meager memberships in the late eighteenth century they raced to the head of the Protestant pack by the 1830s. In

1835 there were slightly over fifteen million Americans. About four million—one in four—were Baptist adherents (about five hundred thousand of them were members of Baptist churches). Roughly three million—one in five—were Methodist adherents (about seven hundred thousand of them members). The next biggest Protestant group was the Presbyterians, with about two million adherents (three hundred thousand members). At that time there were about eight hundred thousand American Catholics and fewer than two hundred thousand Unitarians.[15]

In antebellum America the rationalist celebrants of the wisdom of a merely human Jesus were outnumbered by many hundreds to one. The few outright detractors, who denied any significance for Jesus, remained silent, fearing social exclusion if not physical harm. The small Jewish community in New York City produced some articulate voices who tried to put Jesus in a larger perspective. They too often praised Christ for his unique wisdom. According to Mordechai Noah, a well-known Jewish writer and political figure, Jesus the preacher had "an eloquence such as no mortal has since possessed." Christians, said Noah, ought to do a better job of upholding everything he taught. Instead of trying to convert the Jews, they should remember that Christ tied his own Second Coming to the Jewish reclamation of Jerusalem. And instead of blaming Jews for the crucifixion, they should realize that the joint Jewish-Roman execution of Jesus was ultimately God's doing. Without the crucifixion, according to the Christian outlook, there could have been no salvation from sin.[16]

Jesus swept through American culture in the early nineteenth century as he had done in "awakened" communities in the early eighteenth, one trembling convert at a time. The contagion was now national in scope. The best way to get a sense of the breadth of the excitement is to listen to some personal accounts. Four of the five stories I have chosen are from young Americans whose new births followed aspects of the old Calvinist narratives of the seventeenth and eighteenth centuries: conviction of one's sins followed by regeneration through the promised but always surprising arrival of the Spirit. Several also indicate the new power of the Methodist paradigm, in which Jesus steps forward to offer himself to all who ask his help. "Regeneration" in the Methodist-leaning accounts comes much closer to the perfect holiness of "sanctification" than it could for the Calvinists, who continued to notice their distance from God even when they felt most wholly "justified." The fifth testament is from a Protestant convert to Catholicism, a reminder that there were hundreds of thousands of Catholics in the United States before the mass migration of Irish and German Catholics immigrants in the 1840s. The American Catholic Jesus of the early nineteenth century was already utterly different from the Jesus preached by reborn Protestants, and he became more distinctive still when tethered, as he was increasingly in the mid-nineteenth century, to Irish American and German American ethnicity.

One evening around 1805, when she was about fourteen, Zilpha Elaw, a free-born African American orphan living with Quaker parents in Pennsylvania, had a horrifying dream. It was "of the day of judgment, accompanied by its terrific thunders. I thought that the Angel Gabriel came and proclaimed that time should be no longer; and he said, 'Jehovah was about to judge the world, and execute judgment upon it.' I then exclaimed in my dream, 'Oh, Lord, what shall I do? I am unprepared to meet thee.'" She tried to run away in her dream, but could not. Then she awoke, doubly afraid when she realized the dream had occurred between first light and sunrise. In her part of the world, she explained, that meant the dream was "prophetically ominous, and would shortly come to pass." She began attending Methodist meetings, and though she "increased in knowledge daily," she "possessed no assurance of my acceptance before God." She begged him to forgive her sins—especially her loathsome habit of taking the Lord's name in vain.

As she was milking a cow one evening, she began singing a hymn she had learned at the Methodist meeting:

Oh, when shall I see Jesus, and dwell with him above;
And drink from flowing fountains, of everlasting love.
When shall I be delivered from this vain world of sin;
And, with my blessed Jesus, drink endless pleasures in?

She turned her head "and saw a tall figure approaching, who came and stood by me. He had long hair, which parted in the front and came down on his shoulders; he wore a long white robe down to the feet." It was "the Lord Jesus," who "stood with open arms and smiled upon me." As he came closer, "I felt that his very looks spoke, and said, 'Thy prayer is accepted, I own thy name.'" Elaw knew others would think the whole incident had been "a vision presented merely to the eye of my mind." But there was proof that she had not imagined the Lord's appearance: the cow "turned her head and looked round as I did; and when she saw, she bowed her knees and cowered down upon the ground." After seeing Jesus, Elaw was relieved once and for all of debilitating guilt and early-morning terror. "I claimed God as my Father, and his Son Jesus as my dear friend, who adhered to me more faithfully in goodness than a brother: and with my blessed Saviour, Redeemer, Intercessor, and Patron, I enjoyed a delightsome heavenly communion, such as the world has never conceived of." Elaw went on to become an itinerant preacher in the North and even the South (where she risked arrest or kidnapping and sale into slavery). In the 1840s she preached in England, there delivering, by her count, more than a thousand sermons to audiences discomfited not by her color but her sex.[17]

Unlike his age-mate Zilpha Elaw, Charles Grandison Finney (born in 1792) grew up with no religious formation. His father was one of the many New Englanders who had moved their families to central New York in the 1790s (in this case Oneida County). His parents were typical too in being unchurched. They and their neighbors immediately set up common schools, but congregation-building had to await the arrival of ministers. The preachers who passed through provided not gospel instruction but a good laugh. One gave entire sermons with his fingers jammed stiffly into the pages of his Bible. He was marking passages to read from, and the fingers would be slowly liberated, one at a time, as he read. This behavior was especially hilarious for an audience accustomed to large arm circles of gesticulation.

As a young lawyer in Adams, New York (Jefferson County), in the 1810s, Finney first took an interest in the Bible because so many old legal authorities referred to it. He began attending the Presbyterian church and was "mystified" by the "hyper-Calvinism" of the minister. But mulling over such alien notions as "repentance," "regeneration," and "sanctification" made him "restless." He soon realized that "if the soul was immortal I needed a great change in my inward state of mind to be prepared for happiness in heaven." The stakes were too high to drift along in worldly contentment. But the local Presbyterians seemed to him to be drifting along too, constantly berating themselves for their failings, and lamenting that their prayers for "a revival of religion" were not answered. They contradicted themselves by proclaiming their faith in Christ but then disregarding his words "Ask, and it shall be given you; seek, and ye shall find; knock, and it shall be opened unto you" (Matt. 7:7). If Finney was going to embrace Christianity, it was going to be with the firm assurance of receiving, finding, and having it opened. Finney's Presbyterianism was absorbing a heavy dose of Arminian empowerment.[18]

On October 10, 1821, at age twenty-nine, Finney gave himself to Christ. The night before, he had felt "as if I was about to die. I knew that if I did I should sink down to hell. I felt almost like screaming." But the next day he realized that "instead of having, or needing, any righteousness of my own to recommend me to God, I had to submit myself to the righteousness of God through Christ. Indeed the offer of Gospel salvation seemed to me to be an offer of something to be accepted, and that it was full and complete; and that all that was necessary on my part, was to get my own consent to give up my sins, and give myself to Christ." Dazzled by his insight, he went into the woods to tell God of his new dedication. "But lo! When I came to try, I was dumb; that is I had nothing to say to God; or at least I could say but a few words, and those without heart." He writhed in agony all afternoon, one minute feeling his trust in the Lord, the next fearing he had "lost all my conviction . . . and grieved the Holy Ghost entirely away."

As he descended to the village he felt an eerie calm in his heart. "What is this," he asked himself, "that I cannot scare up any sense of guilt in my soul, as great a sinner as I am?" He went to his office, took out his "bass viol," and began playing and singing "sacred music." Like Zilpha Elaw's singing in the cow stall, Finney's music prepared the way for a momentous encounter. "It seemed as if my heart was all liquid; and my feelings were in such a state that I could not hear my own voice in singing without causing my Sensibility to overflow." He entered a dark room that nevertheless "appeared to me as if it was perfectly light." And there, "as I went in and shut the door after me, it seemed as if I met the Lord Jesus Christ face to face." Much later it occurred to him that the meeting was "wholly a mental state." But at the time "I saw him as I would see any other man. . . . I fell down at his feet and poured out my soul to him. I wept aloud like a child, and . . . bathed his feet with my tears." His mind finally "became calm enough to break off from the interview" with Christ, but another person of the Trinity was waiting to approach him. "The Holy Spirit descended upon me in a manner that seemed to go through me, body and soul. I could feel the impression, like a wave of electricity, going through and through me. Indeed it seemed to come in waves, and waves of liquid love. . . . And yet it did not seem like water, but rather as the breath of God. I can recollect distinctly that it seemed to fan me, like immense wings; and it seemed to me, as these waves passed over me, that they literally moved my hair like a passing breeze." This "mighty baptism of the Holy Ghost," a divine wind blowing where it listeth, gave him just what he had known he needed: the

double "experience of justification, and so far as I could see, of present sanctification." Finney went on to lead major revivals throughout the North and in England and Scotland. He was a Presbyterian
evangelist who helped bring the spirit of the Methodists—ask and
you shall receive—into the old Reformed denominations.[19]

In 1822, less than a year after Finney entered the woods of Jefferson County, New York, sixteen-year-old Joseph Smith walked
into the woods of Ontario County, a hundred miles to the west. He
was seeking (as he wrote a decade later in his raw, untutored script)
"plates of gold upon which there was engravings" from "ancient
days and deposited by the commandments of God." Like Finney,
he had been poring over the Scriptures out of worry over the fate of
his "immortal soul." And like Finney he was shocked by the gap
between the professions of pious Christians and their actual performance. Finney was alarmed that they kept bemoaning their flaws
when Jesus had promised to give them whatever they asked. Smith
was disturbed that they could all read in the Bible that "God was
the same yesterday to day and for ever" (referring to Heb. 13:8,
which actually speaks of *Christ*) yet persist in bickering over the
right way to read his Word. The profusion of alternative Christian
visions in the 1820s struck him as a grave spiritual emergency.
God's remedy for the disintegrative din was to appoint a new
prophet with an authoritative message. Most New Yorkers thought
Smith was just one more discordant voice. His followers believed
he was God's instrument for putting an end to religious chaos.

Smith's born-again experience, like Elaw's and Finney's, came
as an explosive release from feelings of sinful inadequacy. He had
turned to God for help the churches could not render, and his plea
conducted him to John 3:16:

> I cried unto the Lord for mercy for there was none else to
> whom I could go and obtain mercy and the Lord heard my
> cry in the wilderness and . . . a piller of light above the
> brightness of the sun at noon day come down from above

and rested upon me and I was filled with the spirit of god and the Lord opened the heavens upon me and I saw the Lord and he spake unto me saying Joseph my son they sins are forgiven thee. Go thy way walk in my statutes and keep my commandments behold I am the Lord of glory I was crucifyed for the world that all those who believe on my name may have Eternal life.

His concurrent, stream-of-consciousness paraphrase of Psalm 104 shows how he had already begun to see himself not just as sinner, but as image of God. Smith's Mormon Church would subsequently take that classic Christian claim—humanity was made in the image of God—and push it further than Protestantism or even Roman Catholicism had chosen to do.

For I looked upon the sun the glorious luminary of the earth and also the moon rolling in their magesty through the heavens and also the stars shining in their courses and the earth also upon which I stood and the beasts of the field and the fowls of heaven and the fish of the waters and also man walking forth upon the face of the earth in magesty and in the strength of beauty whose power and intiligence in governing the things which are so exceding great and marvilous even in the likeness of him who created them and when I considered upon these things my heart exclaimed well hath the wise man said it is a fool that saith in his heart there is no God.[20]

This moment of regeneration was just the beginning of Smith's unique rebirth to the status of prophet. It was followed by multiple visits from an angel of the Lord, who alerted him to the gold plates buried in Ontario County. He set out to find them on September 22, 1822, but he was unsuccessful. He had failed, the angel told him, because he had succumbed to "the power of the advisary." Smith realized he had slid back: he had been tempted by the devil to become a treasure hunter who "saught the Plates to obtain richs," rather than having "an eye single to the glory of God." After accepting his chastisement, he renewed his search and finally succeeded in locating the plates on September 22, 1827. The problem of how to translate the markings—hieroglyphics that even "the Learned" in "Eastern Cittys" could not decipher—was solved when the Lord provided "spectacles for to read the book." Joseph translated the Book of Mormon himself, laying the textual foundation for a new and at last authoritative church, the Church of Jesus Christ of Latter-day Saints.

Published in 1830, the book recorded that Jesus had come to America after the resurrection and conducted a ministry among an ancient people called the Nephites. He reiterated many of the teachings and repeated some of the actions (like the Sermon on the Mount) familiar to readers of the New Testament. Smith thus grounded his movement in a new revelation that expanded on an old revelation. Protestants and Catholics shook their heads in dismay, since in their view revelation had ceased in the apostolic age. They also scoffed at the healing miracles claimed by Smith and some of his disciples—not an imitation of Christ but an instauration of Christ. Smith, meanwhile, who like Zilpha Elaw experienced the visual presence of Jesus along with saints and angels, had laid an original foundation for a new American religion. According to this religion's novel sacred text, Christ had graced the New World with a ministry like the one he had given the Old World. Jonathan Edwards's prediction that Jesus might be given a second birth in the New World had in Smith's vision long since been fulfilled. America had been launched on its divine errand many centuries before the arrival of the Puritans.[21]

When the condemned slave Nat Turner (whose rebel band had killed fifty-five white Virginians in August 1831) recounted his "confessions" in his jailhouse cell, he presented himself in the same double fashion as Joseph Smith: a born-again Christian and a prophetic leader. He was no more than three or four years old, he said, when people started whispering he "surely would be a prophet." For there were "certain marks on my head and breast" that showed he was "intended for some great purpose." And he set his Southampton County slave quarters abuzz when he spoke knowledgeably of things that had happened before his birth. As a young man he consecrated himself to fasting and prayer. One day as he was plowing, "the Spirit that spoke to the prophets in earlier days" spoke to him too: in a paraphrase of Luke 12:31 the Spirit announced that if he sought the kingdom of heaven "all things shall be added unto you." He reported this and subsequent revelations of the Spirit to his fellow servants, and they became his followers. They believed that his revelations were from God, not from any of the numerous lesser spirits who they also thought spoke to human beings. Turner made a point of distinguishing himself from the many pretenders who got influence over others "by means of conjuring and such like tricks," well-established methods that he always held in "contempt."

The visions proliferated, and grew threatening. Once he "saw white spirits and black spirits engaged in battle, and the sun was darkened—the thunder rolled in the Heaven, and blood flowed in streams. . . . I sought more than ever to obtain true holiness before the great day of judgment." Like Elaw, Finney, and Smith, he was aiming for more than regeneration and justification. He wanted the holiness spoken of by the Methodists, and sensed he was called, like Smith, to prophesy. "And from the first steps of righteousness until the last, was I made perfect, and the Holy Ghost was with me, and said, 'Behold me as I stand in the heavens'—and I looked and saw the forms of men in different attitudes—and there were lights in the sky to which the children of darkness gave other names than what they really were—for they were the lights of the Saviour's hands, stretched forth from east to west, even as they were extended on the cross on Calvary for the redemption of sinners." As he was laboring in the field and seeking the meaning of the vision, he "discovered drops of blood on the corn as though it was dew from heaven." Then, in a remarkable repetition of Joseph Smith's discovery of an alien language on the plates in the forest, Turner "found on the leaves in the woods hieroglyphic characters, and numbers." They made it clear to him that Christ's blood, after having been shed by him on earth, and rising with him to heaven "for the salvation of sinners," was now descending again "in the form of dew." The Savior was "about to lay down the yoke he had borne for the sins of men, and the great day of judgment was at hand." Turner went down to the river with his followers for the baptism previously denied to them in the church. Then the Spirit announced to him that the "Serpent was loosened," and that he must fight against it, "for the time was fast approaching when the first should be last and the last should be first." Like Smith, Turner saw himself as an American prophet of the latter day.[22]

In 1805, about the time Zilpha Elaw and her cow had their joint encounter with Jesus, thirty-year-old Elizabeth Seton met Jesus for the first time in the Holy Eucharist of the Roman Catholic Church. Seton was raised an Anglican in revolutionary New York City, and as a well-to-do matron helped found the Society for the Relief of Poor Widows with Small Children in 1797. She had five children of her own. In 1803, after her husband was stricken with tuberculosis, the family spent four months in Italy seeking a cure for the disease. Instead he got worse. Caring for him as he wasted away, Seton gained a new appreciation for the physical sufferings of Christ. Italian friends, meanwhile, introduced her to Roman Catholicism. When she returned to New York after her husband's death, she disregarded the protests of her family and chose a path of certain social exclusion by becoming a Catholic. Like Joseph Smith, she had found a seat of authority that rose above the vagaries of individual opinion or sectarian one-upmanship. "I will go peaceably and firmly to the Catholick Church for if Faith is so important to our salvation I will seek it where true Faith first began, seek it among those who received it from God himself."

Her conversion experience did not feature the sudden rush of Spirit described by the evangelical Protestants. Elaw, Finney, Smith, and Turner were all filled with the Spirit after a grueling preparation. They were delivered from guilt or fear or confusion. They all had visions in which they saw Jesus. Seton had no vision, no sudden transformation. Her conversion capped a period of painful indecision, but she did not use the Protestant language of feeling "convicted of sin." She joined the Catholic Church when she realized that she had already, without knowing it, come to feel Catholic. But her gradual conversion, like the Protestants' tumultuous ones, brought her closer to Jesus. Where they, following the third chapter of John's Gospel, imagined the closeness as a new infusion of "Spirit," she believed she was incorporating Jesus, literally taking him in physically as well as spiritually. His body came into hers in the Holy Eucharist. Having Jesus inside her provoked no altered mental state. She remained the same person she had been, a poor sinner trying to follow God's difficult commandments to love him and to love her neighbors. The Eucharist did not enter her heart; it filled her stomach. The objectivity of it was essential to her. It was a regenerative force, like the Protestants' Spirit, but not once and for all. She had to keep consuming it. It was more like a transfusion than a transmutation.

Seton went to communion as often as she could. For a time she was obsessive about it, sprinting from church to church on Sunday morning so that she could take communion several times. Ultimately she received the sacrament several times a week. "At last," she had written after making her First Communion, "God is mine and I am his." She imagined herself as a "poor poor dwelling" that was "all his own." She depicted Jesus as the eucharistic means by which God took over her body and soul. "It seemed to me my King had come to take his throne, . . . my defence and shield and strength and Salvation made mine for this World and the next. . . . [T]ruly I feel all the powers of my soul held fast by him who came with so much Majesty to take possession of this little poor Kingdom."

Seton's meeting with the divine warrior-protector freed her from the ordeal of having to fend for herself. "O happy bondage!" she wrote later. "Sweet servitude of love." Real freedom, ironically, meant submitting to greater power. Many evangelical Protestants believed that freedom flowed out of submission to God, but the Calvinists as well as the Methodists believed that their spirits had been reborn. Seton imagined no basic change in herself. She remained "the poor poor dwelling," but she had embraced a new dependency and found a new vocation. In 1809 Elizabeth Seton took her vows as a Sister of Charity of Saint Joseph and spent the last sixteen years of her life as a pioneer in parochial education. In 1975 she became the first United States–born saint of the Catholic Church.[23]

IV

The anti-Calvinist liberal Protestants of the early nineteenth century dissociated themselves from the Catholics' mystical apprehension of the body of Christ in the Eucharist and from the evangelical Protestants' transformational rebirth. Both groups, from the liberal point of view, made the mistake of deifying Jesus rather than the Father. The Boston-based Unitarians, who led the liberal Protestant movement beginning in the 1820s, are remembered above all for their anti-Calvinism—their rejection of human depravity as well as predestination. But in claiming to safeguard the sovereignty of the Father they showed how faithful they could be to one pillar of the Calvinist edifice. They were so dogged about protecting the Father's authority that any worship of Jesus as a coequal divine person seemed to them an affront to the Creator. It was a violation of the Second Commandment. They were exasperated that other Protestants could admonish Catholics for praying to the Virgin Mary—such prayer allegedly robbed Jesus of his full stature—and not notice their own idolatry in praying to Jesus. As William Ellery Channing asserted in his famous throw-down-the-gauntlet sermon on "Unitarian Christianity" (1819), putting Jesus in the Godhead "injures devotion" by "taking from the Father the supreme affection, which is his due, and transferring it to the Son." Love of God was all or nothing: to divert any of it from the Father was to worship idols.[24]

Unitarians thought making the Son the second person of the Trinity had another disastrous effect. It made Christians lose sight of the real greatness of Jesus, his perfect humanity. Catholic mysticism and Protestant evangelicalism shrouded Jesus in supernatural mystery. In fact he was a man like us: we could imitate and befriend him. He was also a man unlike us: God had chosen him for a special mission, and for special elevation. The Unitarians came up with a synthesis as strikingly original as that of the Methodists. Where the Methodists kept the depravity of human nature and offered a readily available divine Jesus to redeem it, the Unitarians kept the transcendent purity of the Father and articulated a fully human Jesus to bask in it. The Unitarians and Methodists thought they were operating at cross-purposes. The Trinitarian Methodists believed the Unitarians put too much stock in reason, not enough in the Bible. The Unitarians thought the Methodists were authoritarian in their church structure and superstitious in their supernaturalism. In retrospect we can see how their joint Arminianism—a new birth in the name of Christ was available to anyone who sought it—allowed them to collaborate on a historic reconfiguring of Jesus. He became the sweet companion—human for one group, divine for the other—whom people could call upon whenever they wished. In both cases the original bridging effort—depravity linked to the free choice of Jesus for the Methodists, the Father's divine otherness tied to the Son's human likeness for the Unitarians— broke down over time. By the late nineteenth century the Methodists were letting depravity drop away, and the Unitarians were losing contact with the Father.

The Unitarians centered their religious appeal upon the perfect humanity of Jesus, but like their founding father Channing, they tried to preserve an aura of divinity around him. They endorsed the old Arian position from the fourth century: although Jesus was a man, not God, he had been created by God from all eternity, and in his presently resurrected state, he was a mediating force between God and humanity. In the early nineteenth century only a handful of American Unitarians, such as James Freeman of King's Chapel in Boston, took the Socinian stance. That view considered Jesus nothing more than a human being, although one chosen by God for a divine mission ending in his death and resurrection. Certain liberal Congregationalists in the eighteenth century (notably the Boston preachers Charles Chauncy and Jonathan Mayhew) had already prepared the way for Unitarianism by moving away from the orthodox doctrines of the Trinity and the partial atonement (the Calvinist idea that only a portion of humanity would be saved). As the nineteenth century progressed, the humanity of Jesus resonated more and more throughout the mainstream Protestant churches, whether still officially Calvinist like the Congregationalists, Baptists, and Presbyterians, or Arminian like the Methodists and Disciples of Christ.[25]

A newly human Jesus made sense to the Unitarians and to many other liberals because they had come to a new sense of what it meant to be human. Being human meant cultivating the full potential of human reason as well as honoring the God of the Bible. Being human meant pursuing self-realization, finding personal independence within a set of communities, from the family and locality to the nation and world. Being human meant worshiping God with passionate love and obedience. Unitarians claimed to be more biblical than the Trinitarians, not less. Reason was not opposed to faith. The Bible was God's revelation, but it could be read accurately only by the light of reason. Holy Scripture was not a transcript of God's speech, but a human record of God's promptings. There was no way for God to communicate with his creatures apart from calling upon all their human capacities. As a human production, the Bible was full of paradoxes and outright contradictions.

Storytellers, prophets, and evangelists had striven mightily to convey God's meanings, and naturally they had left loose ends. The Protestant principle of *Sola Scriptura*—by the Bible alone—signified to the Unitarians that every believer was an interpreter and a translator, weighing the possible meanings of each passage and settling on the most reasonable one. Reason permitted serious students of the Bible to penetrate to the heart of God's revelation, to know the real truth of it. Anyone who denied the place of reason in reading the Bible was only a hair's breadth away from full-blown skepticism. Skeptics and Christian anti-rationalists were alike in making textual interpretation arbitrary, a matter either of intuitive feeling or authoritarian mandate.[26]

The New Testament, for the Unitarians, became a field of exciting new discoveries. They rubbed their eyes in wonder. Jesus too was human, a man bedazzled by the commanding authority of his Father in heaven. Unitarians were so smitten by their discovery of themselves and of Jesus as individual seekers in freely chosen obedience to the Father that they could not believe other Christians did not see the same picture. Trinitarians were willful blockheads. True, they were giving the masses what they wanted: "an object of worship like themselves," as Channing put it. The ordinary run of people liked their God to be "clothed in our form," rather than "a Father in heaven, a pure spirit, invisible and unapproachable, save by the reflecting and purified mind." Channing was not surprised at the anthropomorphic tendency of "the popular theology," but he was still "astonished that any man can read the New Testament, and avoid the conviction, that the Father alone is God." Of course there were some passages that might seem to imply Jesus was God. But they had to be discounted, given the huge preponderance of passages in which the Son plainly asserted his inferiority to God. Such discounting was a basic principle in the interpretation of any text, biblical or not. Trinitarians used the principle themselves when they sloughed off passages "in which human beings are called gods, and are said to be partakers of the divine nature, to know and possess all things, and to be filled with all God's fullness."[27]

For the Unitarians God was a "pure spirit," unlike Jesus, but Jesus nevertheless took on a purity in their eyes that made him strangely inhuman too. The Unitarians' Jesus, like Jefferson's, was a man without a culture, standing aloof from the contingencies of his time and place. Like many other nineteenth-century liberal Christians, the Unitarians were faced with a quandary: How could they make Jesus fully human while preserving his unmatched magnificence? Their solution was to elevate him above any specific history. "We are immediately struck with this peculiarity in the Author of Christianity," Channing wrote in 1821. "All other men are formed in a measure by the spirit of the age," but "we can discover in Jesus no impression of the period in which he lived." He was as free from "the modes of thinking, the hopes and expectations of [his] country, . . . and as exalted above them, as if he had lived in another world. . . . His character has in it nothing local or temporary. It can be explained by nothing around him. His history shows him to us a solitary being, living for purposes which none but himself comprehended, and enjoying not so much as the sympathy of a single mind." Channing was one Unitarian who still insisted on the veracity of the New Testament miracles, but he agreed that the biggest miracle of all was the emergence of Jesus himself from the inhospitable soil of a culturally primitive Palestine. The job of modern Christians was to lift Jesus beyond the uncomprehending stare of his own contemporaries.[28]

To Channing Jesus was inexplicable as a man of first-century Palestine because no one from that place and time could have articulated "a universal religion intended alike for Jew and Gentile, for all nations and climes." His character was no less original than his religion. Channing had read his Edwards: Jesus displayed "a union of excellences" never before found together. But Channing's version of Christ's logically impossible features of character comprised only human personality traits, not a harmonizing of divine and human components. He joined "an unparalleled dignity of character, a consciousness of greatness," with "a lowliness and unostentatious simplicity which had never before been thought consistent with greatness." He combined "an utter superiority to the world, to its pleasures and ordinary interests, with suavity of manners and freedom from austerity." He also blended "strong feeling and self-possession; an indignant sensibility to sin and compassion to the sinner; an intense devotion to his work, and calmness under opposition and ill success; a universal philanthropy, and a susceptibility of private attachments; the authority which became the Saviour of the world, and the tenderness and gratitude of a son." The last combination of elements came closest to an orthodox, Edwardsian formulation, but Channing left "the authority which became the Saviour of the world" vague enough to cover all possible points on the divine-human spectrum.[29]

For the highly educated Unitarians, the joining of apparently irreconcilable characteristics into a complex "moral harmony" represented the height of perfection in a human being. Like Edwards, Channing knew that no human being could ever attain Christ's level of perfection. Unlike Edwards, Channing saw no reason why people should not try. They folded the imitation of Christ into their love for him. They felt about him as they would feel about an older brother or father whom they relied upon as a model and who offered a perpetually and unconditionally warm embrace. Their Jesus, they believed, was universal in his appeal. He gave Americans a "sacred common . . . ground," as Unitarian missionary William Adam wrote in 1845, since "almost all unbelievers admit the fact" of Christ's perfect moral character. Believers went beyond admitting that fact to "rejoice in it and derive ever new supplies of moral strength from the contemplation of the deep and holy beauty which shines forth in the person and life of their Lord and Master."[30]

The Unitarians and many other liberals loved the "person" of Jesus so much because they cared so deeply about becoming full persons themselves. The most vehement complaint Unitarians had

about the Trinity was not that it was unbiblical or, as Jefferson complained, that it was logically absurd (how could "three" be "one"?).
Its worst feature was that it denied Jesus his full stature as a "person." The Trinitarians might claim to be giving Jesus true personhood as the second member of the Trinity, but for the Unitarians
that amounted to no personhood at all, since it imposed "two natures" on Jesus rather than one. "It is really a matter of astonish-
ment to us," wrote Unitarian minister Alvan Lamson in 1828, "that
any one who reflects at all on the subject, does not perceive the in-
superable difficulties which the hypothesis of two natures presents." Trinitarians were closet Quadritarians, for they turned Jesus
into two persons, one divine and one human. With the Father and
the Holy Spirit, that made four in all. Nothing was more self-
evident to early nineteenth-century liberals than that personality
was unitary, a single substance. Everyone knew that "a person is an
intelligent agent; he has one will and one consciousness; he has
perceptions and feelings, which he may properly call his own."
Personality was in its essence "simple" and "undivided," and it entailed "individuality," which "belonged to Jesus as truly and properly as it belongs to any other being." The Trinitarians divided
Jesus against himself. Whatever was true of "man" at his best (his
distinctive, seamless personality) must also, of necessity, be true of
Jesus. For the liberals "reason" and "love" came together in Jesus to
form the most exemplary human life. Jesus stood eternally for that
harmonious convergence.[31]

V

On October 10, 1826, three months after Jefferson's death, the
twenty-three-year-old Ralph Waldo Emerson received his license
to preach. The following June 24 he rose to address Nathaniel
Frothingham's congregation at First Church, Boston, on Paul's
theme "We Preach Christ Crucified" (from 1 Cor. 1:23). That sub-

ject, he said, might seem "morose" in an age accustomed to
"smooth and pleasant speculation on agreeable topics," a time
when everyone was exchanging "congratulations" on "the distinguished advancement of the age." But there was little chance that
pausing for a few "gloomy entertainments of the soul" would un-
duly burden anyone's mind after the Sunday service—"that danger," Emerson quipped, "departed with a former age." He could
safely conduct his audience "to the field of blood, to a ghastly and
atrocious spectacle, to the hill of Calvary and the passion of Christ."
That "grave and mournful theme" would deliver the needed reminder, in a culture attuned to "ease and hilarity," that "we are
baptized into suffering."

Emerson evoked the final sorrows of Jesus by depicting the torments of his body in relation to the clarity of his mind and the victory of his soul. Crowned with thorns and draped with a purple
robe, Jesus stumbled up "that disastrous mountain" with a serenity
untouched by the taunts of "Herod and his men of war." The arm
that had worked miracles "hung unnerved by his side," and the
tongue "which had spoken peace to the stormy sea, and life to the
dead, was dumb." His mind wandered from "the dizzy spectacle
around him" and fixed upon the future, "the weary centuries wherein his name is taken by unholy lips and his doctrine perverted to an
unhallowed use of power and pride." He grieved as he contemplated the "painful progress which the doctrine of the Resurrection
has yet to make through the superstition and sin of the world." But
then he beheld a saving remnant, "the faithful who in this latter
day shall consecrate themselves with pious self-devotion" to his
cause.

In Emerson's narration, time past became time present. Christ's
scourged body was still plodding up the path to Golgotha, but he
was fixing "his searching eye" upon Emerson's own congregation,
along with every other assembly of future believers. A single moment of history assumed eternal shape: the cause "in which he is
about to offer up his life . . . rests on you, my friends. . . . It invites

you . . . it implores you, to love yourselves as he has loved you, to take up your cross and be his faithful disciples, to make not vain the labour, the agony, and the death which he is finishing, but to show men at last how they may overcome the body in seeking the welfare of the soul." Christ's death was still unfolding; his life's meaning lay in the hands of each man and woman who, after his death, would swear allegiance to him. The influence of Jesus upon the world had already been inestimable for centuries, but it was paradoxically "but *beginning* to be felt." His gospel was always new, always a proclamation of good tidings for the living, not the dead.[32]

Emerson was training for the Unitarian ministry in 1827 (he was ordained at Second Church, Boston, in 1829), so it is no surprise that the Jesus of his "Christ Crucified" sermon was Unitarian in conception. Jesus was not "a portion of the Deity," but neither was he simply the "first of men." God had put him into the world "in the high capacity of Saviour of men," an elevated calling bestowed upon no other wise man. But this early sermon carried a strong hint of the Jesus Emerson would preach as a secular lecturer and essayist after he had resigned his pastorate in 1832. "We Preach Christ Crucified" was much more interested in the death of Jesus than in his resurrection. Emerson's Jesus was on his way to becoming a de-divinized wise man like Jefferson's, but he was more than a teacher of timeless maxims. He was a man of wisdom who dismantled Jefferson's wall of separation between divine and human (not the same as the wall separating church and state). Jefferson had wanted to protect the man Jesus from insinuations that he was divine. Emerson wanted to show that Jesus exuded humanity, paradoxically, because he knew that all men could partake of divinity by opening up the wonders that lay within. Over the next two decades, as Emerson became a popular lecturer and internationally renowned essayist, his wrestling with Jesus as personal lodestar and as American national obsession helped a whole generation of liberals find a post-Calvinist, and often post-religious, identity. His influence on American conceptions of Jesus may have been more profound than that of any other nineteenth-century American, religious or secular. His impact was direct and indirect: people read his essays and heard his lectures, but they also read and listened to other writers and speakers decisively shaped by Emerson's views.[33]

Emerson resigned his parish ministry on September 11, 1832, ostensibly because he no longer believed it appropriate for the church to commemorate the Last Supper with the rite of communion. Jesus, he believed, had not instituted such a ritual. It would make as much sense, he thought, for modern New Englanders to engage in ritual foot-washing. That practice was more clearly mandated by Jesus than the supper was, but both were irrelevant imports, Middle Eastern customs with no vitality in America. Yet Emerson's emerging objections to historic Christianity were much broader than this, as his journal entries began to make clear even before his "Lord's Supper" pre-resignation sermon of September 9, 1832. "I have sometimes thought that in order to be a good minister it was necessary to leave the ministry," he wrote in June. "The profession is antiquated. In an altered age, we worship in the dead forms of our forefathers. Were not a Socratic paganism better than an effete superannuated Christianity?" Franklin and Jefferson had said privately (and Paine publicly) that people were too busy worshiping Jesus to imitate his demanding kind of moral life. Emerson now said privately that people were too busy praising Jesus to imitate his search for the divine within. Adoring Jesus had gotten in the way of reaching for the fully human stature Jesus had achieved. "Is it not time to present this matter of Christianity exactly as it is," he wrote on August 10, 1834, "to take away all false reverence from Jesus, & not mistake the stream for the source? . . . God is in every man. God is in Jesus but let us not magnify any of the vehicles as we magnify the Infinite Law itself. We have defrauded him of his claim of love on all noble hearts by our superstitious mouth honor. We love Socrates but give Jesus the Unitarian Association."[34]

Emerson was just warming up. His journal entries grew white-hot as he got closer to his July 1838 appearance at the Harvard Divinity School, where he made some of his most radical thoughts public. "You can never come to any peace or power," he mused, "until you put your whole reliance in the moral constitution of man & not at all in a historical Christianity. The Belief in Christianity that now prevails is the Unbelief of men. They will have Christ for a lord & not for a brother. Christ preaches the greatness of Man but we hear only the greatness of Christ." His public remarks in July to the six graduates of the Divinity School and their teachers were almost equally vehement. Jesus was "the only soul in history who has appreciated the worth of a man." "Historical Christianity" had enmeshed Jesus in a cult of personality. That error "corrupts all attempts to communicate religion," Emerson told the graduates. The church had not taught "the doctrine of the soul, but an exaggeration of the personal. . . . [The church] dwells, with noxious exaggeration[,] about the *person* of Jesus. The soul knows no persons. It invites every man to expand to the full circle of the universe, and will have no preferences but those of spontaneous love." The goal of the spiritual life was to escape devotion to externalities, such as the Jesus icon, and experience the eruptive presence of a force so massive, so eternal, and so unpredictable, that it could best be called an "impersonal" law or principle. That law could transform one's own "person," and was thus "personal" as well as "impersonal." The paradox was that finding one's fully personal soul meant reaching the level of impersonality, hence losing "persons" altogether.[35]

In his journals at the time, and in his renowned essays of the 1840s, Emerson spelled out his opposition to the Christian infatuation with personality. It led people to clamor after individual immortality, whereas Jesus never "utter[ed] one syllable about the naked immortality of the soul, never spoke of simple duration." Here Emerson inverted Jefferson, who praised Jesus for dwelling on "the future state" more than the Greeks, Romans, or Jews did.

Emerson lauded Jesus for realizing more clearly than the Greeks did that the eternal was not coming later, but was already here. To grasp at personal immortality was to miss the whole point of Christ's preaching. His call was not to a final resting place in eternity, but to the eternal that was ever present in our midst. "The only way," he wrote in 1839, that "Jesus or [any] other holy person helps us is this, that as we advance without reference to persons on a new, unknown, sublime path, we at each new ascent verify the experiences of Jesus & such souls as have obeyed God before. We take up into our proper life at that moment his act & word & do not copy Jesus but really are Jesus, just as Jesus in that moment of his life was us. Say rather, it was neither him nor us, but a man at this & at that time saw the truth & was transformed into its likeness."[36]

Emerson was hitting the Massachusetts Unitarian clergy where it hurt the most. They had put all their chips on Christ's personality when they turned against Trinitarian orthodoxy, against the idea that the one God was made up of three Persons. Giving Jesus a perfect personality was their way of keeping him quasi-divine as they demoted him from the Godhead. But to call Jesus the most perfect human being failed an elementary empirical test, as Emerson told his friend Elizabeth Palmer Peabody in 1835. "Perfect in the sense of complete man [Jesus] seems not to me to be, but a very exclusive and partial development of the moral element. . . . [H]is life is one original pure beam of truth but a perfect man should exhibit all the traits of humanity & should expressly recognize the intellectual nature. Socrates I call a complete universal man fulfilling all the conditions of man's existence. Sublime as he is I compare him not as an ethical teacher to Christ, but his life is more humane." Emerson believed the Unitarians were trapped in the same pit that their supposed enemies, the Calvinists, had carved out. The Calvinists' other main opponents, the revivalist Methodists, were stuck there too. They all thought the religious life was about venerating someone else rather than seizing the chance God had given them and becoming someone new. As for the mass worship of Jesus in the revivalism of the Presbyterian Charles Grandison Finney, Emerson was scathing. After hearing Finney speak in 1855 he told his wife that that he did not like him any better than he had two decades earlier. "I did not suppose that such a style of preaching still survived. A great parade of logic, to be sure, but all built on a cobweb of church traditions which a child's popgun or a doll's brush would go through." Finney "extolled God's heart at the expense of his head."[37]

All the pushing and shoving among Calvinists and anti-Calvinists to get closest to Jesus made Emerson sick. In the privacy of his journal he uttered words that Tom Paine himself would have thought sacrilegious. "It might become my duty," he raged in 1840, "to spit in the face of Christ as a sacred act of duty to the Soul, an act which that beautiful pilgrim in nature would well enough appreciate." "You name the good Jesus," he complained in 1843, "until I hate the sound of him." In a culture so disarmed and blinded by its personalized Christ, the only way left to convey the actual teaching of Jesus was to do it roundabout, by teaching the cognate ideas of other wise men. "Therefore it is that we fly to the pagans," he wrote in 1838, "& use the name & relations of Socrates, of Confucius, Menu [Manu], Zoroaster; not that these are better or as good as Jesus & Paul (for they have not uttered so deep moralities) but because they are good algebraic terms not liable to confusion of thought like those we habitually use."[38]

Emerson's particular style of devotion to Jesus was now firmly set, and it informed all of his famous essays of the 1840s. His first move had been to de-divinize Jesus, as Jefferson, Franklin, and Paine had done. His second move had been to see him as the wondrously gifted individual who grasped, as Emerson wrote in his journal in 1835, that "God must be sought within, not without." God was within each person not as a fixed moral sense (in Jefferson's conception), and not as a personal spirit (the Methodists' claim), but as the ever-flowing source of one's self-renewal. In his essay "Circles" (1841), Emerson identified the life course with the perpetual creation of wider and wider circles of experience. "The instinct of man presses eagerly onward to the impersonal and illimitable," and carries "the brave text of Paul's" as its guiding principle: "Then shall also the Son be subject unto Him who put all things under him, that God may be all in all" (1 Cor. 15:28). Letting God live in one's self meant increasing one's openness to surprise, novelty, and, paradoxically, self-forgetting. "When these waves of God flow into me," he wrote, he no longer succumbed to the stewing-in-self that especially afflicted writers like him. He stopped fretting about all the squandered days and months when he could have been scribbling more prose. In the "divine moments . . . I no longer reckon lost time." As Jesus taught, you find yourself by losing yourself. Giving yourself over to the impersonal, giving up niggling, calculating self-improvement, did not mean retreating into a contemplative quietism. Emerson tied self-forgetting to the plowing under of atrophied habits and rigid conventions. "The one thing which we seek with insatiable desire," he wrote at the end of "Circles," "is to forget ourselves, to be surprised out of our propriety, to lose our sempiternal memory, and to do something without knowing how or why; in short, to draw a new circle. Nothing great was ever achieved without enthusiasm. The way of life is wonderful: it is by abandonment."[39]

The final step of Emerson's project was to see Jesus as one wise man among others, a sage whose central teachings might be the most sublime of all (as Jefferson had also said), but which could nevertheless be understood by thoughtful people anywhere. Jesus was a contingency of the Middle East and the European West. He was not sovereign; God was. Cultures and languages were historical accidents, not essential carriers of truth. Jesus uttered many truths, "orphic words" such as "God is no respecter of persons," "His kingdom cometh without observation," and "His kingdom is a little child." All of them could be rendered in other languages. Translation worked because the deepest truths were unchanging. Paradoxically, they were immutable only because they required people to change if they were going to live up to them. They were eternal principles because they mandated an open-ended and never-ending striving for virtue as well as knowledge. At the highest level of moral and intellectual attainment—never a final resting place but a platform for further sightings—virtue and knowledge coincided. "The masterpieces of God, the total growths and universal movements of the soul, he hideth; they are incalculable. I can know that truth is divine and helpful; but how it shall help me I can have no guess, for *so to be* is the sole inlet of *so to know*."[40]

Emerson's most famous single term, "self-reliance," comes into much clearer focus when we think about it in relation to his revision of Jesus. As George Kateb has suggested, it is best to pronounce the word *self*-reliance rather than self-*reliance*. The latter suggests independence, even isolation. The former conveys Emerson's essential sense that the goal of the moral life is to protect and develop one's self, allow one's person to grow by embracing the impersonal. Reason and faith, the human and the divine, were ultimately indistinguishable. Pondering "secular personalities" (Socrates, Confucius, Shakespeare, and others) and adopting apparently non-religious stances (praise for the natural world, denunciation of tired religious symbols) could break through the crumbling fortress of historical Christianity and revivify the spirit. But for Emerson there was no virtue in the non-religious as such. There was even a danger that criticizing the church's Jesus too much would promote, as he put it in 1839, the "cold denying irreligious state of mind." Socrates and Confucius were needed because, in what he labeled a "Christized" society, they made Jesus fresh and graspable.[41]

Jesus was the indispensable authority on the impersonal embrace of God. He established, said Emerson, the basic form for all subsequent moral and spiritual aspiration. Jesus resembled a great writer who "established the conventions of composition" that even "the most original" of later authors "feels in every sentence." Self-reliant individuals followed Jesus in looking within, not without, and discovering new and unexplored terrain. They imitated Jesus by refusing to imitate anyone, and finally, ironically, by shutting up about "self-reliance." Words, in the end, were unavailing. One of his greatest verbal flourishes, in his essay "Self-Reliance" (1841), dismisses language about self-reliance in memorable language: "Life only avails, not the having lived. Power ceases in the instant of repose; it resides in the moment of transition from a past to a new state, in the shooting of the gulf, in the darting to an aim. This one fact the world hates, that the soul *becomes;* for that for ever degrades the past, turns all riches to poverty, all reputation to a shame, confounds the saint with the rogue, shoves Jesus and Judas equally aside. Why, then, do we prate of self-reliance? Inasmuch as the soul is present, there will be power not confident but agent."[42]

"Shoving Jesus and Judas equally aside" exhibits Emerson's anti-clerical and anti-iconic-Jesus animus at its most passionate. It is as close as Emerson ever got to publishing the kind of culturally seditious sentiments that dot his journals: spitting on Christ, hating the name of Jesus. Shoving Jesus and Judas equally aside is a double horror in a culture as "Christized" as Emerson's: first pushing Jesus away, then equating Jesus and Judas. Of course Emerson is being ironic. By shoving the socially correct Jesus out of the way he aimed to honor the actual Jesus all the more. To attack Jesus the icon was to defend Jesus the visionary. There is a side of Emerson that imagines a pagan society would do better than a Christianized one at hearing and imitating Jesus. In a pagan society Jesus and his message would stand out in bold relief. In contemporary America, he wrote, confusion was general: unbelievers and believers "often change sides," the former pushing "the cause of Christian love so long as it does not hurt" their "worldly interest," and the latter justifying their dalliances with "the customs of the day" by dressing them up in religious garb.[43]

"Jesus never argued, only affirmed," according to Emerson. Speaking to audiences in the first century, Jesus spoke of himself and his kingdom without being misconstrued as a god. People knew that when he spoke of himself he was conveying his central "discovery": "God must be sought within, not without." In the nineteenth century, people could no longer understand the discovery. When they read his gospel words, they thought he meant that God was in him but not in them. "He said to his age, I," Emerson wrote. "If Jesus came now into the world, he would say, You, You!"[44]

FIVE

THE REAL PRESENCE
OF DISTRESS

I

Picture yourself as an anthropologist from some distant planet setting down in the United States in 1850. It is not long before you notice a great deal of talk about "Jesus"—especially on the one day of
the week when people put down their farm implements and many
of them ride off to church. (Census takers are out and about asking
questions too. They will report that 85 percent of the 23 million
Americans live in rural areas, that 60 percent of the population still
lives in states formed from the original thirteen colonies, and that
only one city—New York—has more than 200,000 people.) Many
people are especially eager to tell you about Jesus when they find
out you are not a Christian. You learn that the words "Jesus" and
"Christ" refer to a historical person at the source of interlocking
traditions, stories, images, and feelings. The already diversified
Protestant Christs of seventeenth- and eighteenth-century America
(formulated in explicit opposition to the Catholic Christ of Europe
and of French and Spanish America) are now commingling with
Roman Catholic and African American Christs. You note that all of
these Christs appear to be socially useful for people attempting to

establish their personal legitimacy. Enslaved or free blacks appear to pray and sing to Jesus for deliverance from oppression as well as from sin. Only a tiny population of Jews, Indians, and freethinkers appear not to subscribe to this cultural program.

While in New York City you visit the magnificent new Astor Library in Manhattan. There you happen upon a book by an earlier visitor to the United States, Alexis de Tocqueville, who toured parts of the country in the early 1830s. You find his two-volume *Democracy in America* riveting, since Tocqueville, like you, was fascinated by popular American ideas and habits. He saw Christianity as the cohesive force in a nation of self-absorbed individuals. Democracy in America after the Revolution had produced a kind of equality that made people pursue their own interests above everything else. Christianity provided a necessary social glue by endorsing individualism while disciplining it—encouraging people to think about others too. Reflecting on Tocqueville gives you a "eureka" moment: familiarity with Jesus facilitates social belonging, but people can use Jesus to extricate themselves from undesired social ties. Jesus is a transferable loyalty: people move around the social arena and take him along. People use him for psychological cushioning when they feel anxious or alone. They offer him as proof of respectability when they need a job, a spouse, or a reputation. And they sometimes take him as a personal moral challenge to give more to others and take less for themselves.

Americans, you learn, revere Jesus as an adult God-man who did miracles, preached wisdom, and sacrificed himself for others, but they also celebrate him as a holy child, especially at the festival of Christmas. He is evidently a symbol of family togetherness, yet he is on occasion a symbol of conscientious rebellion against inherited institutions, including one's family or one's church. A few Christians report to you that they love Jesus even though he does not always make them feel good, useful, or respectable. When he condemns them for their sins of pride, or self-seeking, or sloth, or despair, they suffer from the realization that they are inveterate sinners in spite of all their fine intentions. They say they live in hope of a salvation announced by Jesus. If they receive it, some of them explain, it will be a deliverance that they will have done nothing to deserve.

You are continually struck by the near universality of Christ's appeal. Americans placed high and low in the social order, regardless of their color or place of origin, appear equally likely to invoke the authority of Jesus. Even many of the white Protestant radicals who wish to purify themselves by seceding from the established social order and setting up new, rational communities appeal to Christ's example and wisdom. You soon figure out, however, that intensity of attachment to Jesus varies from person to person. For many people (more often men than women), Jesus is an honorific name they invoke on special occasions, like weddings and funerals. But for many others (more often women than men), he is an intensely sought spiritual "person" whom they try to obey or follow, and with whom some even try to converse. Churchgoing Protestants, you realize, are almost as diverse in their views of Jesus as the non-churchgoing population. Both groups can be plotted at all points along the Jesus-identity spectrum: on the divine side, Son of God, miracle-worker, and healer; on the human side, prophet, philosopher, ethical model, and, increasingly, militant social reformer.

Christ's public role as an advocate of social reform, you learn, is largely a product of the last two decades. Liberal Christians had humanized him before that, putting new emphasis on the earthly life of Jesus so they could elevate the stature of humanity in the overall divine scheme of things. But today they are politicizing this human Jesus in order to promote equality among all men. Slavery now strikes a large and growing percentage of northern Protestants as incompatible with the teachings of Jesus. Catholics and even southerners often agree that slavery is wrong in principle, but they usually disagree with the view that no Christian can tolerate it. Southerners are volubly appealing to the teachings of Jesus too, arguing that he never preached against slavery. Like the northern opponents of slavery, the southern defenders of it are claiming a superior loyalty to Jesus. Each side is giving him a social identity to go with his heavenly identity. He redeems individuals from their sins, but he also eradicates social injustice or bestows social stability.

As you prepare your final report, you think of Tocqueville. His two volumes, published in 1835 and 1840, expressed the fear that American democracy might sacrifice republican virtue to get-ahead individualism. Catholic and Protestant religion might limit the excesses of individualism, but at the cost of spawning a debilitating conformism. Religion might enforce a uniformity of thought compatible with individual economic achievement, but not with individual creative excellence. You shake your head at how quickly times have changed. In 1850 Tocqueville's judgment from the 1830s—that American religion would constitute a unifying force—seems wholly passé. The Methodists and Baptists suffered schisms in 1844 and 1845 over the issue of slavery. The Fugitive Slave Act has just been passed, convincing a broad public of northern Protestants that the defense of freedom and democracy will require not just limiting the expansion of slavery, but eradicating it in the Old South. The name of Jesus may once have been a force for bringing Americans together, but now it magnifies their sectional discord.

II

Using Jesus to further political ends had a long history in America. From the moment of the Europeans' arrival in their New World in the fifteenth and sixteenth centuries, they had invoked him to bless their onslaught against native territories and cultures. Eighteenth-century Christian preachers like John Woolman, Jonathan Edwards, Jr., and Samuel Hopkins had already argued for seeing a contradiction between slaveholding or slavetrading and Christian piety. What was new in the early-nineteenth-century debate over slavery was the politicizing of Jesus within the Protestants' own ranks. For the first time Christ was assuming the mantle of social advocate in addition to that of ethical teacher or holy redeemer. Intriguingly, no one seems to have thought of calling Jesus a "prophet" in the tradition of the Hebrew Scriptures. The continued emphasis on his divinity and his perfectly pure humanity appears to have worked against identifying him explicitly with an earthy, cantankerous Amos or Jeremiah. At the end of the century Social Gospelers such as Walter Rauschenbusch would do just that. Yet with "sin" already commonly seen as a set of discrete actions that a virtuous person could choose to avoid, abolitionists could claim Jesus as an angry judge of any person who sinned by tolerating enslavement. The abolitionists' opponents, whether supporters of slavery or of political compromise between north and south, could take Jesus as a preacher of hierarchical order or social peace.

Northern Methodist Nathan Bangs, editor of his church's official *Christian Advocate*, voiced the majority viewpoint of northerners as well as southerners in 1834 when he chided the abolitionists for misrepresenting the views of Jesus. When the British abolitionist George Thompson came to New York to lecture Americans on the evils of slavery, Bangs instructed him to "imitate the conduct" of Christ by staying out of civil affairs that did not concern him. Jesus had been well aware that "slavery existed all over the Roman empire." It was so pervasive that "about one half of the population of that vast empire," in Bangs's loose estimate, "was in a state of civil bondage." Yet never did Jesus denounce masters for holding slaves, or "tell them that unless they let those oppressed go free, they could not repent and enter into the kingdom of heaven." Jesus cared about the soul, not about society. He kept out of politics.

Bangs was not defending American slavery in principle, just preaching patience while awaiting its eventual dissolution. For the time being, ministers should follow the apostle Paul in teaching "both master and slave how to serve God, and make the best of their present condition, as preparatory to a better state of existence." Bangs's diplomatic middle ground would soon become unpalatable to southern white Methodists as more and more of them joined other southerners in taking slavery as a positive good rather than a tolerable evil. Bangs's views already struck many northern anti-slavery Methodists as a direct attack on the gospel of Christ and on the church's own original Discipline. A group of New Englanders appealed to Bangs to return to one of the founding declarations of 1784, which proclaimed that "slavery is a great evil" and that "no one who enslaves men, women, and children, is truly awakened." There could be no compromise, the writers urged, between "the meek and lowly Jesus" and a system "which defrauds the poor and friendless, destroys feminine modesty, and corrupts all classes of society." In their view Bangs wrongly supposed that Jesus preached love abstractly, without noticing who was oppressing whom. The love of Christ could not be separated from politics because politics had already institutionalized hate.[1]

Abolitionist Angelina Grimké, in her 1836 *Appeal to Christian Women of the South*, pushed these views one step further when she wrote that "the meek, the lowly, and compassionate Savior" could no sooner be imagined "a slaveholder" than "a warrior." The relevant question was not, as Bangs had asked, whether Jesus had ever explicitly condemned slave-ownership, but whether Jesus could plausibly be imagined owning a slave himself. His own human comportment, not his recorded verbal commands, should be the ultimate rule for Christian living. The Word was made flesh in a whole human life, not in a few inspired phrases. For Grimké it was easy to see why Jesus had never denounced slavery. He was a product of his time and place. The servitude he had witnessed in Palestine was wholly unlike the involuntary, hereditary, chattel slavery of modern America, in which, it seemed to her, persons were reduced to things exchangeable in a marketplace. Some ancient Jews had sold themselves into slavery, and some fathers had sold their daughters to prospective husbands. War captives could also be enslaved, and the children born to some slaves could inherit that status (for one generation only). But the Jews considered anyone enslaved through theft—the original condition, Grimké said, of all American slaves—to be illegally held. And all Jewish slaves of whatever type were set free in the year of Jubilee, which arrived at fifty-year intervals.

Grimké conceded that Jesus "did not condemn Jewish servitude." But "this does not prove that he would not have condemned such a monstrous system as that of American slavery." The only way to settle the issue was to judge American slavery by the "golden rule" he had given all Christians "to walk by." "'Whatsoever ye would that men should do to you, do ye even so to them.' Let every slaveholder apply these queries to his own heart. Am I willing to be a slave—Am I willing to see my wife the slave of another—Am I willing to see my mother a slave, or my father, my sister or my brother? If not, then in holding others as slaves, I am doing what I would not wish to be done to me or any relative I have." For Grimké and other anti-slavery advocates, the silence of Jesus on the issue made historical criticism of the Bible essential. They were compelled to define Jesus in his humanness as a first-century Palestinian Jew. That way they could split off his time-bound human consciousness from his time-transcending divinity (or, for those liberals who dropped his divinity, his timeless spirit or teachings). His message was not to be taken literally in all its culturally specific details, but applied anew in each era.[2]

Biblical scholars in New England were simultaneously deciding, thanks to German research, that the human Jesus and the biblical accounts of him were the contingent historical products of first-century Jewish culture. But it was the anti-slavery publicists, not the biblical scholars or the earlier revolutionary rationalists such as Jefferson, who made many American Christians realize that Jesus had been human in the same cultural way they were. He may have been sinless, unlike them—he may even have been divine—but he was culturally as well as biologically human, formed by the outlook of a limited social milieu. Grimké came to her distinction between Christ's human historicity and eternal wisdom not from any study of biblical criticism, but from the needs of her movement.

She scoured Christ's scriptural sayings for proof texts just as American defenders of slavery did. But the proof texts she valued were general injunctions that required new application in each successive culture. Her whole outlook was shaped by the liberal Enlightenment quest for universal human rights, an equality she and a few others wished to extend to both sexes and all races. Such an outlook was progressive by definition: it saw history as the unfolding of liberty. Jesus could be mustered into the progressive march of history, but only by concentrating attention on his overarching principles and his underlying spirit.[3]

Jesus served Angelina Grimké's cause as the preacher and personification of progress. He also stood as a symbolic representative of the anti-slavery movement itself. For Grimké the movement stood in the same relation to the southern slaves as Jesus did to Lazarus. Just as he had uttered "the life-giving command of 'Lazarus, come forth,'" the anti-slavery societies were "taking away the stone from the mouth of the tomb of slavery, where lies the putrid carcass of our brother. . . . They want all men to see how that dead body has been bound, how that face has been wrapped in the napkin of prejudice, and shall they wait beside that grave in vain? Is not Jesus still the resurrection and the life? Did he come to proclaim liberty to the captive, and the opening of prison doors to them that are bound, in vain?"[4]

The "meek and lowly Jesus" and "bleeding humanity" (i.e., that enslaved portion of humanity crucified like Christ) were virtual mottoes of the anti-slavery movement. Frederick Douglass, fearful that his famous *Narrative* of 1845 would be taken as anti-Christian because it disparaged America's "slaveholding religion," added an appendix proclaiming his personal devotion to "the meek and lowly Jesus." His mentor William Lloyd Garrison, Quaker editor of the abolitionist *Liberator*, who attached a preface to the *Narrative*, vouched for Douglass's own "gentleness and meekness." Those Christlike traits did not detract from Douglass's "true manliness of character," said Garrison. He predicted that Douglass would become "increasingly serviceable in the cause of bleeding humanity."

The phrase "meek and lowly" comes from Matthew 11:29: "Take my yoke upon you, and learn of me; for I am meek and lowly in heart: and ye shall find rest unto your souls." Thomas Shepard's congregants spoke often of that verse in their seventeenth-century confessions, but they stressed the offer of rest that Jesus made to "all ye that labour and are heavy laden" (11:28). Jesus offered true rest for the weary because he had subordinated himself to his Father. Douglass passed right by the offer of comfort. He tied Christ's self-description as meek and lowly to his attack on the haughty hypocrites who "bind heavy burdens and grievous to be borne, and lay them on men's shoulders; but they themselves will not move them with one of their fingers" (Matt. 23:4). Where Shepard's faithful saw a promise of spiritual rest for those who abased themselves, Douglass found an injunction to the unrest of militant social action.[5]

William Lloyd Garrison went beyond Grimké or Douglass in the urgency and exuberance of his devotion to Christ. He identified Jesus with the anti-slavery cause, like Grimké, and took the "meek and lowly" position, like Douglass, as a launching pad for prophetic energy rather than gentle forbearance. But he went further by likening his travails as agitator to Christ's own ordeal. At the time his stance struck many Americans north and south as self-righteous at best, sacrilegious at worst. The whole idea of personally "imitating Christ" still connoted irreverent pride in Protestant evangelical circles. Some of Garrison's enemies took pleasure in lampooning his overweening self-dramatization. But from his own standpoint he was honoring Jesus by claiming his mantle and invoking his name. He loved Jesus passionately and fed off the controversies he provoked when he enlisted Jesus in the cause of liberating the slaves. Garrison is well known as the tireless advocate of "immediate emancipation" (by which, in his morally absolutist discourse, he meant unconditional, uncompensated emancipation as well as "freedom now"). But today few people realize that he believed in immediate emancipation from the chains of slavery because of his prior conviction about "immediate emancipation from the chains of Satan." Christ's incarnation was not an announcement of a future world freed from sin, but of a present world freed from sin. True Christians would immediately sever their ties with "slaveholders, warriors, worshippers of mammon, enemies of holiness. . . . The axe must be laid to root of the tree, and total abstinence from sin . . . insisted on as the reasonable duty of every human soul, and as essential to christian character."[6]

In Garrison's view most American churches had made Christianity bland and lifeless by failing to insist on "Christian perfection" as a condition of membership. In 1850 he noted that "a profession of faith in Jesus now costs nothing; for his praises are every where sung and his deeds are every where lauded—by none more loudly than by those who enslave and imbrute their fellowmen." Jesus was so universally "honored and believed on among us," the pacifist Garrison quipped ironically, that he even "occupies the Presidential chair; for President Taylor professes to believe in Jesus, but in a Jesus who enslaves human beings . . . yes, in a Jesus who is for 'giving the Mexicans hell'" (as Taylor was alleged to have said on the battlefield during the Mexican War).[7]

Like Angelina Grimké, Garrison identified Jesus with the anti-slavery movement. But where she saw abolitionists as miracle-workers like Christ, raising a whole people from the tomb of death, Garrison saw abolitionists, like Jesus, as innocent victims of vicious attack. Some would be called "to lay down their lives as martyrs." "What Jesus was to the Jews, unmasking the scribes and Pharisees, rebuking a corrupt church, and [re]proving an oppressive nation, the anti-slavery movement is to the people of the United States." Here Garrison was on the verge of calling Jesus a fiery prophet and defining himself as a prophet for nineteenth-century America. What made him hold back? For one thing, Garrison the pacifist had a hard time appealing to the Hebrew Scriptures, which recorded "exterminating wars . . . expressly commanded by Jehovah." For another, Garrison the Quaker was busy proving that his disparaging of the Protestant churches did not weaken his devotion to the divine Jesus or to the perfectly holy human Jesus. Garrison needed Jesus to be a spotless saint, not a Jewish prophet. And he needed himself to be a respected citizen, not a voice in the wilderness.[8]

Garrison did sometimes refer to the prophets, and to the early Christian martyrs, as precursors to the abolitionists. At a time in America when professing Christianity had become, in his view, "a popular, fashionable, ceremonial act," anyone who truly applied Christ's teaching to the slavery question, north or south, was going to court ostracism, physical violence, or death. When he was accused in 1846 of having made "a special study" of "the science of offense," he compared himself not just to Christ but to "the noble army of martyrs and confessors" in the early church, and to the prophet Isaiah. That "ancient disturber of the peace" had shown, in chapters one and fifty-nine, how to speak to sinners. But Garrison rested his case on his and other abolitionists' likeness to Christ. Jesus might be uniformly "venerated and honored" in 1846, but he and his followers had been castigated as "pestilent and seditious fellows" in their own time. Jesus did not hesitate to respond in kind, calling his detractors "sharply by their proper names": "hypocrites" and "vipers" of "an adulterous and perverse generation." Uncompromising truth-speakers turned the other cheek, but gave verbally as good as they got.[9]

Defenders of American slavery had at least as strong a claim on the support of the biblical Jesus as the anti-slavery forces did. At first they did not appeal to Jesus directly. They just pointed out that the Bible was full of slavery and never condemned it. The Reverend Devereux Jarratt, a slave-owning Virginia Anglican, was attacked by Methodists for holding slaves and engaged his critics in a running debate from the 1780s into the nineteenth century. As he wrote in 1788, the "stations and relations" embodied in the slave system were plainly warranted "under the Gospel, otherwise thirty or

forty verses might as well be blotted out of the New Testament."
Christian practice was unaffected by social arrangements. The love
of God was for everyone, and everyone could know Christ's saving
grace. No doubt slaveholders were sinners, since all human beings
were sinners, but slaveholding was not sinful in itself. It gave rise
to abuses—including the common slave-owner sin of preventing
slaves from hearing the gospel—but so did every other regime of
social relations. If the abuses that occurred under a social system
amounted to grounds for abolishing it, there would be no institutions left at all, north or south.

Jarratt's defense of slavery rested on a rejection of Grimké's
Enlightenment-style progressivism and Garrison's Quaker-style
perfectionism. He dismissed the progressive notion of "different
dispensations," the idea that "what was allowed as consistent with
the dictates of reason and religion" in an earlier period was incon-
sistent with them in a later age. "I never could see the propriety of
such reasoning," he wrote. "The dictates of reason and religion . . .
do not fluctuate." If the gospel itself was satisfied to infuse the hierarchical master-slave, husband-wife, and parent-child relationships
with love (while preserving their reciprocal duties and obligations),
later generations could not appeal to that same gospel for support
in terminating them. The love of Jesus was independent of social
arrangements and unaffected by the passage of time.[10]

In response to the anti-slavery forces' drafting of Jesus, the
southern Christian defenders of slavery appealed directly to his
authority. One of the most articulate was the Reverend James
Thornwell, a Presbyterian from South Carolina. In his 1850 sermon
on "The Rights and Duties of Masters," he responded to the
"golden rule" argument that Grimké had made: you cannot hold a
slave unless you are willing to be one yourself. Thornwell reasoned, on the contrary, that Christ's command "to love our neighbor as ourselves, and to do unto others as we would have them to
do unto us," had nothing to do with a willingness to "turn the tables"
and accept another person's lot as one's own. If that had been

Christ's meaning, then "the rich man could not claim his possessions nor the poor learn patience from their sufferings." Jesus actually commanded "us to do unto others what in their situations, it
would be right and reasonable in us to expect."

Abolitionists were also wrong to assert, Thornwell added, that
southern slavery reduced slaves to the status of "things." On the
contrary, slaveholders considered all human beings, whatever their
status, to be "persons." Everyone had duties and responsibilities
corresponding to their stations in life, and the slaveholders had
God-imposed obligations to care for their slaves. Christians see in a
slave "not a tool, not a chattel, not a brute or thing—but an immortal spirit, assigned to a particular position in this world of wretch-
edness and sin, in which he is required to work out the destiny
which attaches to him, in common with his fellows, as a man." Like
Jarratt, Thornwell conceded that slave-owners did not always live
up to their ideal of reciprocal obligation. But he believed the slave
system was superior to the supposedly "free" contract-labor system of the North since slavery put the Christian ideals of personal
care and responsibility at the heart of its social vision. Jarratt and
Thornwell looked at Jesus and saw a divine man who took for
granted that sin and social status were fixed elements of human
life. Grimké and Garrison looked at Jesus and saw a divine man
who embodied sinless perfection and preached that anyone could
transcend the limits of a prior condition, whether of sin or servitude. Northern abolitionists and southern slaveholders brought all
their profound disagreements about selfhood and society, sin and
progress, to their encounter with Jesus. Each side produced a Christ
it could recognize and revere.[11]

The vast majority of white Americans from the 1830s through
the 1850s were neither slaveholders nor abolitionists. Most northern whites were opposed to slavery, but they were also opposed to
equality for African Americans. Their position was probably close
to that of Nathan Bangs: slavery was wrong in principle, but it was
part of the cultural fabric of the South and should be left there to

collapse eventually of its own weight. One of the most talented exponents of this position was Catharine Beecher, eldest of the many remarkable offspring of the famous, moderately anti-slavery preacher Lyman Beecher. In 1837 she published an *Essay on Slavery and Abolitionism* in response to Angelina Grimké's *Appeal to the Christian Women of the South*. "Christianity is a system of persuasion," Beecher wrote, "tending, by kind and gentle influences, to make men willing to leave off their sins." Unlike the abolitionists, true Christians "imitate the example of the Redeemer of mankind." They employ "gentleness, patience, and pitying love." Beecher conceded Grimké's point that Christians, like Jesus, must sometimes be "reprovers." But finding fault with another person was morally perilous, since it implied the reprover was beyond reproach. Grimké's hero, William Lloyd Garrison, fell short in that respect, Beecher contended, for he lacked the humility and meekness displayed by Jesus.[12]

In her published response to Beecher, Grimké defended Garrison by asserting he was just like the human Jesus in public and private. As public persons Jesus and Garrison naturally delivered "angry passion," for Christianity is "preeminently aggressive." "I came not to send peace, but a sword" (Matt. 10:34) was Christ's own declaration. Beecher wished to remake Christianity into "just such a weak, dependent, puerile creature as thou hast described woman to be. In my opinion, thou hast robbed both the one and the other of all their true dignity and glory." In his private life, said Grimké, Garrison was "a perfect gentleman," not the "coarse, uncouth, and rugged creature" many people assumed him to be on the basis of his public vituperation. Jesus provided the model for Garrison's blend of sweetness and belligerence.[13]

Their tiff over Garrison bespoke a wider disagreement between Beecher and Grimké over how to view the relations between men and women. Here again, as in the slavery debate, Jesus served as supreme symbolic arbiter. Grimké was right that for Beecher Jesus was the figure who modeled perfect womanhood, while for Grimké herself he modeled perfectly androgynous aggression in the public sphere and perfectly androgynous gentility in the private domain. "I know nothing of men's rights and women's rights," wrote Grimké, "for in Christ Jesus there is neither male nor female." Nor did she know anything of divergent male and female experiences or sensibilities. There was a single standard for human beings: moral purity. Human actions were moral when obedient to principle. Calculations of consequences were irrelevant. "Duty is ours," said Grimké, "and events are God's." Ethics transcended prudential calculation. Suffering awaited those who obeyed Christ's golden rule and refused to sanction injustice. Martyrdom would greet a few women and a few men, as it had since the beginning of the Christian era. American women had to stop presuming that they were too weak to withstand the rigors of persecution.[14]

Beecher, meanwhile, assumed a bridgeless gap between men and women, just as many defenders of slavery took for granted an elemental breach between the sensibilities of masters and slaves. In matters of salvation, argued Beecher, there was neither Greek nor Jew, bond nor free, male nor female, but in this world of sin vast differences separated social groups. Beecher's Jesus was a mirror held up to women, revealing to them who they were at their best. "It was woman's place," wrote Beecher, "to win every thing by peace and love; by making herself so much respected, esteemed and loved, that to yield to her opinions and to gratify her wishes, will be the free-will offering of the heart." Women had a special power for public good because they could spark men to rise above the pursuit of self-interest. "All the generous promptings of chivalry, all the poetry of romantic gallantry, depend upon woman's retaining her place as dependent and defenceless, and making no claims." Men could locate Christlike meekness at second remove, in and through their veneration of women. Social order in America depended on women's capacity to rein in the passions of men by seducing them into Christian submission. At a time of social "emergency," when "rancor rules the public sphere," it was especially crucial for "every female instantly to relinquish the attitude of a partisan, in every matter of clashing interest, and to assume the office of a mediator." Jesus modeled the woman's vocation: always "an advocate of peace" whenever he "encountered the weakness, the rashness, the selfishness, the worldliness of men."[15]

The momentous inspiration of Catharine Beecher's younger sister Harriet Beecher Stowe led her to combine Catharine's view that women enshrined Christ's spirit with her own sense that African Americans embodied it too. *Uncle Tom's Cabin: or, Life Among the Lowly* broke like revelation over America (and England) in 1852, because it connected the republican political quest for freedom from oppression to the evangelical religious quest for freedom from sin. The meek and lowly slave Tom was a Protestant saint in the purity of his devotion to Scripture and to Jesus. Even though God "lets us be 'bused and knocked around" by whites, he told a fellow slave, that did not mean "the Lord took sides against us." Mistreatment was no cause for loss of faith in him, since Jesus had been treated far worse. "Have we, any on us, yet come so low as he come? The Lord han't forgot us,—I'm sartin' o' that ar'. If we suffer with him, we shall also reign." Stowe gave many readers a new birth of commitment to Christ. Tom surpassed his station as slave. In the saintly perfection of his character and the brutal horror of his death, he was Christ himself reborn as an outcast American (see fig. 28).

Stowe gave her white characters and readers pious black Christians to be imitated spiritually and rescued bodily. John Bird, her fictional midwestern state senator, thought he would never disobey a law until runaway slave Eliza Harris, fresh from her intrepid crossing of the icy Ohio, landed on his back doorstep. Under the determined moral tutelage of his wife, Mary, he was transformed by what Stowe termed "the magic of the real presence of distress." Eliza was a sacrament for the self-righteous. Her physical endangerment, like Tom's spiritual self-denial, was an occasion for white conversion to Christ's path. Of course Stowe was making evangelicalism serve the anti-slavery cause, but she was also making the horrors of slavery serve the evangelical cause. She was preaching a more intense experience of Christ, just as her illustrious precursors Shepard and Edwards had done. She inflected that experience with a new Romanticism as well as a new politics. For her the love of Jesus resembled the pulsating intimacy between mother and child. When Eliza and her little Harry were in desperate flight, her "maternal love" was "wrought into a paroxysm of frenzy." As the sleeping Harry clung to her chest, "the touch of those warm arms, the gentle breathings that came in her neck, seemed to add fire and spirit to her movements! It seemed to her as if strength poured into her in electric streams."[16]

Stowe shared with most whites, north and south, the belief that African Americans as a people were essentially different from whites because of their African roots. The "negro race" ("race" in her usage included as much of what we would call "culture" as it did "biology") was disposed to embrace Christianity. "In their gentleness, their lowly docility of heart, their aptitude to repose on a superior mind and rest on a higher power, their childlike simplicity of affection, and facility of forgiveness," they displayed "the highest form of the peculiarly Christian life." Stowe elevated African Americans' distinctive traits and historic plight into a special chosenness. "As God chasteneth whom he loveth, he hath chosen poor Africa in the furnace of affliction, to make her the highest and noblest in that kingdom which he will set up, when every other kingdom has been tried, and failed; for the first shall be last, and the last first."

In her *Key to "Uncle Tom's Cabin"* (1853) she noted that God had favored the "cool, logical, and practical" Anglo-Saxon race with a "dominant position in the earth," but he had not favored them with "the doctrine of toleration for the peculiarities of other races." Whites still had to learn that black Christians' religious exercises—full of "outward expressions, violent gesticulations, and agitating movements of the body"—produced conversions as "genuine" as any others. African Americans were like ancient Jews and nineteenth-century Near Easterners in "giving vent to their emotions with the utmost vivacity of expression." Fortunately for the tepid Anglo-Saxons, God had seen to it that the Bible itself would be written in "the fervent language" and "glowing imagery" of the "passionate Oriental races."[17]

Brutalized black slaves and Africans generally were analogous to Christ, Stowe urged, and so were self-denying females like the tubercular Little Eva. Indeed, what helped give Uncle Tom the power to keep resisting slavery *spiritually*—the most potent resistance of all, in his and Stowe's view—was his encounter with the waif-like child whose purity of heart matched his own. An inspired imitator of Christ, Eva took on iconic status for Tom. Tom "loved her as something frail and earthly, yet almost worshipped her as something heavenly and divine. He gazed on her as the Italian sailor gazes on his image of the child Jesus—with a mixture of reverence and tenderness." Stowe gave Tom and Eva an evangelically Romantic moment of spiritual ardor when she seated the two soul-mates in an arbor beside Lake Pontchartrain and let them play at discerning in the clouds the "great gates of pearl" of the "new Jerusalem."[18]

Little Evangeline—like many dying children in whom nineteenth-century parents beheld spiritual greatness—was a little evangelist who wished her death, like Christ's, to lead others to the love of God. She also wished her death to help end slavery. By offering up Little Eva and Uncle Tom as sacrificial lambs, Stowe took a northern Christian audience to a single fever pitch of anti-slavery conviction and evangelical zeal. In a sense she made the American Jesus as feminine and as black as he had always been male and white. She did not literally comment on his skin color, but she did explicitly stress the femaleness of his human personality. As she put it after the Civil War, his human nature exhibited "more of the pure feminine element than . . . any other man" because "he had no mortal father." His humanity "was the union of the Divine nature with the nature of a pure woman."[19]

Yet dwelling on his femaleness established the overall androgyny of Christ the savior. Stowe used women the way she used

African Americans, to renew the experience of Christ's "real presence." And she used Christ to deepen awareness of what she took to be the special gifts of women and blacks. She took the Pauline phrase dear to Angelina Grimké—in Christ there is neither Greek nor Jew, bond nor free, male nor female—and combined it with her sister Catharine's view that men and women, or blacks and whites, diverged culturally while converging spiritually. Their religious practices differed, but their religious experiences did not. Everyone had a heart, and everyone could welcome Jesus into it. In *Uncle Tom's Cabin* Stowe gave moderately anti-slavery American Protestants the mythic story that helped many of them see their divine savior for the first time as a proponent of social justice and political transformation.

III

In a political sense Stowe's Uncle Tom was a majestic gift to enslaved African Americans. His Christlike self-sacrifice unleashed a torrent of anti-slavery sentiment in the North and helped ensure that the war for "Union" begun in 1861 would develop into a war for emancipation. But in a cultural sense Uncle Tom was at best a mixed blessing for African Americans. Stowe could not help implying that blacks were to be valued by whites for their divine chosenness and spiritual perfection, for their capacity to be *better* than whites morally and religiously. African Americans could not demonstrate their moral competence by struggling to succeed, like other human beings. Their moral standing depended on cross-bearing. Stowe saw correctly that black Christianity was different from white Christianity, and that African Americans had been asked to suffer more than most other Americans. But she made the African American difference palatable to white Americans by sanctifying it, in effect constraining blacks to labor religiously for the salvation of whites in place of laboring materially for their former slaveholders.

African American writer and organizer Martin Delany was ex-
aggerating when he remarked to Frederick Douglass in 1853 that
Mrs. Stowe "knows nothing about us." But he was on the right
track, because Uncle Tom was a pure projection of her and her sister Catharine's image of Christ rather than a depiction of an actual
black-slave Christian. He was all "pitying love" and no anger or
bitterness. As historian Donald Mathews has written, the lived experience of Jesus among actual black slaves drew as much on the
Book of Revelation as it did on the Sermon on the Mount. Christ
was the avenging Lord of the final days as well as the forgiving redeemer. And slaves did not experience Jesus in isolation from
Moses, Daniel, and Joshua. Just as Catholics surrounded Jesus with
Mary, Joseph, and the saints, slave Christians beheld a whole
gallery of holy men and spirits. Whatever most slaves may have
thought about Nat Turner's decision to play the part of an avenging angel himself, they certainly grasped that the Lord himself was
as likely to spill the blood of his enemies as he was to die on a cross.
And just as for Catholics there was no sharp boundary between
Jesus and Mary, for slaves the sacrificial lamb could blend effort-
lessly with Moses, who led his people out of captivity.[20]

Harriet Beecher Stowe rightly noted that African American religious practice was different, but neither she nor anyone else in the
1850s was in a position to grasp precisely what was different about
it. She was impressed by "the violent gesticulations," "the vivacity
of expression," and the "lowly docility of heart." She went to great
pains in The Key to "Uncle Tom's Cabin" to prove that, contrary to the
view of abolitionist skeptics in the North, individual slaves as piously submissive as Tom actually existed. (Southern critics of the
novel were glad to concede that slavery had produced saints like
him.) But resting her argument on individual cases showed she had
little awareness of the broad forces shaping slave consciousness.

The actual slaves' experience of Jesus diverged from that of
whites not because it was more emotional and not because they had
a special proclivity for gentle surrender, but because their entire cul-

tural placement and preparation were so different. As Donald Mathews points out, African Americans became interested in Christian preaching only when, in the late eighteenth century, it became evangelical (and emotional) under the aegis of the Methodists, the Baptists, and certain inspired Presbyterians such as Samuel Davies. They had evinced little interest in the dryly propositional catechizing of the Anglicans (who were in any case lackadaisical about missionizing until threatened by evangelical inroads). But the total context of the African American appropriation of emotional Christianity was entirely different from that of their white neighbors, despite the fact that they often prayed, sang, and worshiped together. Blacks and whites decided to be born-again Christians partly in response to the evident spiritual energy of the other group. Blacks were impressed with the anti-slavery convictions as well as the possession-like gesturing of many late-eighteenth- and early-nineteenth-century white evangelicals. Whites took mesmerizing black preaching and singing as evidence of God's unusual wonder-working. These were two peoples in constant religious interchange. They created dissimilar but overlapping sacred practices and divergent yet connected Christs.

Redemption in African-American slave religion joined the Christian yearning for individual salvation to the Jewish dream of collective deliverance from oppression. Old and New Testaments truly formed one Scripture, as the Jewish flight from Egypt intertwined with the approaching New Jerusalem. Where an abolitionist such as Garrison was forced to accentuate the split between Hebrew and Christian Bibles—in order to reconcile a divine judgment upon slavery with Christ's doctrine of nonresistance—the African-American apocalyptic leader Nat Turner beheld a throbbing cosmic web of texts and omens. He did not need slavery defenders such as Devereux Jarratt to tell him that God's Word animated a single holy dispensation. And he did not require abolitionist tracts to instruct him that God would strike down the unrighteous.

While white Christians were harping on Christ's sacrifice as a means of wiping out sin (the Baptists emphasizing his atonement for the colossal original sin of Adam and Eve, and the Methodists his willingness to take believers beyond sinning altogether), slave Christians were feeling Christ's presence as an eruption of the sacred in their midst. Here they drew on and developed a folklore of visions, dreams, and possession-states with African roots as well as premodern-European resemblances. This traditional outlook posited a lively exchange between visible and invisible worlds, between the living and the dead. It envisioned a stark split between good and evil but not between sacred and secular. The idea of a Christ who had died, risen, would come again, and could even now stream into people's hearts posed no conceptual challenge at all to African Americans long accustomed to the notion of migrating spirits taking on mortal form. Nor did the paradox that under his reign the last would be first and the first would be last. The whole people was bound for the promised land, and so were those individuals who avoided sin.

Naturally this summary of antebellum African American Christianity gives too much fixity to a living and evolving faith. It underestimates the crossover between black and white evangelicals, including the inevitable pressure on black Christians in a dominantly white world to learn to speak like whites about sin and salvation. A case in point is the well-known *Narrative* of Sojourner Truth, a northerner who was emancipated from slavery in New York in the 1820s. The theme of learning to speak of Christ as whites did is built right into this text, since it is an "as-told-to" production: the illiterate "Isabella," who took the name Sojourner Truth when she set out on an itinerant preaching mission in 1843, created the *Narrative* in conversation with Olive Gilbert, a white neighbor in Northampton, Massachusetts. The *Narrative* is an account of Truth's gradual emancipation from legal and psychological slavery and her attainment of a mature individual consciousness—the precondition for true freedom in liberal New England. Along the way she tells the story of how she discovered Jesus as the liberator of her soul from sin and dejection. The *Narra-*

tive is a significant document of the American encounter with Jesus because it shows how wrong it is to assume that illiterate or uneducated Christians do not *think* as well as *feel* their faith. Truth's faith, like Benjamin Abbott's, deepened as she increased in her knowledge of Jesus, not just in her closeness to him.

The child Isabella learned of God from her slave mother, and imagined him as "a great man" in the sky who "noted down all her actions in a great book," just as her Dutch master "kept a record of whatever he wished not to forget." She also learned from her mother to ask God for relief from all her cares. Such petitioning had to be done out loud, and Isabella reasoned that the louder she spoke, the more readily God would hear. She arranged a prayer site for herself in the woods on a little island in the middle of a brook. There she recited the Lord's Prayer in the Low Dutch her mother had taught her, and shouted "all her troubles and sufferings" without fear of being heard by anyone but God. The problem with this juvenile scheme, as Olive Gilbert summed up Truth's mature thinking, was that Isabella "felt as if God was under obligation to her, much more than she was to him. He seemed to her benighted vision in some manner bound to do her bidding."[21]

The *Narrative* relates how Truth emancipated herself from the slave condition—in her case both a legal status and a downward spiral of self-disparagement following cycles of abuse and affection from her master. Deliverance from slavery was accompanied by development in her view of God. She had one spiritual insight after another. First came the realization that God was like a person in being aware, but was unlike a person in being "all over." He "pervaded the universe. . . . [T]here was no place where God was not." This thought did not, initially, reassure her. She felt she had been an idolater in all the years spent petitioning him "as if he had been a being like herself." As she fretted over her sinful disregard for God's greatness, she became mired in dark feelings of inadequacy. The cloud lifted when she realized that "if someone, who was worthy in the sight of heaven, would but plead for her in their own name, and not let God know it came from her, who was so unworthy, God might grant it." This desired friend appeared to her in a vision, "beaming with the beauty of holiness, and radiant with love." This "heavenly personage" seemed utterly familiar to her, yet "it moved restlessly about, like agitated waters." She didn't know its name. Finally she heard a voice "saying distinctly, 'It is Jesus.' 'Yes,' she responded, 'it is Jesus.'"[22]

Until that moment she had thought of Jesus as no more than "an eminent man, like a Washington or a Lafayette." But after her vision of him she still did not picture him as a divinity. He was "transcendently lovely," and stood between God and her, loving her so much that God was no longer "a terror and a dread." She imagined she would see him soon in bodily form. She would recognize him instantly and "go and dwell with him, as with a dear friend." Bathed in his love, she grew jealous when she heard others speak of Christ's love for them. She feared that "she would be thrust aside and forgotten, being herself but a poor ignorant slave, with little to recommend her to his notice." One of her acquaintances tried to make her see that Jesus was "God" as well as her friend. Truth was relieved to discover that "the Christian world was much divided on the subject of Christ's nature—some believing him to be coequal with the Father—to be God in and of himself, 'very God, of very God';—some, that he is the 'well-beloved,' 'only begotten Son of God';—and others, that he is, or was, rather, but a mere man." Gilbert quoted Truth's own words in conclusion: "Of that I only know as I saw. I did not see him to be God; else, how could he stand between me and God? I saw him as a friend, standing between me and God, through whom, love flowed as from a fountain."[23]

The cacophony of American theological opinions gave Sojourner Truth the freedom to choose and eventually publicize the Jesus she had met in her own experience—an invisible spirit of love who reconciled her to God and who might any day choose to take her physically by the hand. He was personal like God, but tangibly closer to her than her heavenly master was. He permitted her to let

God be wholly other without having to give up her experience of an immediate heavenly presence. Being in love with Jesus gave her the strength to take to the highways in 1843 speaking of God. Religious assemblies were popping up all over the east in that year of Adventist expectation. William Miller had predicted the end of the world in 1843, and when the appointed day came and went with no cataclysm, he recomputed the day of doom first to the spring of 1844 (wrong again) and then to October 22 or 23, 1844. As the end approached, his followers either gathered in urban chapels or formed rural encampments where (joined by some nonbelievers wisely hedging their bets) they could escape the devastation liable to befall the towns and cities. Truth attended their meetings and debated their doctrines with them. She judged them harshly for failing to "watch and pray" in patient composure. They thought the Lord would take them away "to some parlor away up somewhere" while he reduced the wicked to ashes. As for her, she said, "If the Lord comes and burns—as you say he will—I am not going away; I am going to stay here and stand the fire, like Shadrach, Meshach, and Abednego! And Jesus will walk with me through the fire, and keep me from harm." The Millerites had gone over the edge, she thought, but otherwise she was undogmatic when it came to Jesus. She found "many true friends of Jesus, . . . having no preference for one sect more than another, but being well satisfied with all who gave her evidence of having known or loved the Savior."[24]

IV

Isaac Hecker, a Protestant convert to Catholicism in 1844 (and founder of the Paulist Order of priests in 1858), could have been referring to African Americans when he said of Catholics that "it is the sense of the nearness of the spiritual world, . . . pervading as it does the public worship, the private devotions, and the general tone" of their lives, that made them distinctive. For many black

Americans Jesus was one character in a holy entourage of Old and New Testament figures, all of whom intermingled with an array of other invisible spirits, including the ancestors of the living. For American Catholics, whose numbers had skyrocketed as a result of the Irish famine of the 1840s, Jesus was embedded in his Holy Family and surrounded by the saints. They too occupied an invisible world full of good and evil spirits, along with the souls of the dead. Catholicism was a "communion of saints" like Protestantism, but where evangelical Protestants meant all of "the elect" when they said "saints," Catholics meant the canonized holy men and women empowered to intercede with Christ. Catholics loved mediators, and like African American Protestants took for granted a fluid intermingling among the living and the dead.[25]

White American Protestants since the seventeenth century had proven the purity of their faith by scorning the "superstitious" piety of Catholics and the alleged imperial intentions of the pope. In the 1840s many Protestants rekindled that tradition by rising up to save their pure Protestant Jesus from contamination by the Catholic one. They pushed to keep the King James Bible (abhorred by Catholics) in the public school curriculum, and to allow public school children to sing hymns Protestants considered American, not sectarian. Protestants thought they were defying the Catholic tendency to turn Jesus into an icon, and in the strictly *visual* sense they were right. They managed to restrict the visualization of Christ in their own ranks until the arrival of film at the end of the century. Meanwhile they turned Jesus into a verbal icon of their own resistance to Catholicism. They made him a symbol of their American quest to beat back the religiously primitive and socially reactionary popish forces. By the 1850s the mostly Protestant anti-slavery advocates had another reason to disparage Catholics, and vice versa. Catholics, in the Protestant view, did not understand freedom or democracy, and hence could not be depended upon to defend liberal republican American institutions against attack by slaveholders.

At the time of the Revolution there were about fifty thousand Catholics and about fifty Catholic churches in the American colonies, almost all of them in Pennsylvania and Maryland. One in a hundred Americans was a Catholic, not counting any of the thousands of Spanish, French, and Indian Catholics residing on American land that would become part of the United States in the nineteenth or twentieth centuries. At the end of the nineteenth century one in five American citizens was a Catholic. In 1790 only sixty thousand of the four million Americans were from Ireland, and the vast majority of those were Protestants from Ulster. In 1850, thanks to the potato famine, there were a million Irish in the United States, out of a population of twenty-three million.[26]

A good indication of the contempt with which mid-nineteenth-century Protestants held Irish Catholics in particular is the fact that even the most liberal of them, such as famous Unitarian preacher Theodore Parker, branded the Irish as lazy, filthy, and credulous. He thought the United States had "made a great mistake in attracting them here, and allowing them to vote under less than twenty-one years of quarantine. Certainly it would take all that time to clean a Paddy—on the *outside* I mean: to clean him inwardly would be like picking up all the sands of Sahara. There would be nothing left when the sands were gone." The Irish wallowed collectively in a morass of "bad habits, bad religion, and worst of all, a bad nature." In the 1850s, when he emerged as a leading militant abolitionist, Parker said publicly and repeatedly that the Irish suffered from an absence of Anglo-Saxon blood as much as they did from a presence of Romish superstitions. Protestant Americans, thanks to their "Teutonic veins," had "the strongest ethnological instinct for personal freedom." The Irish, lacking a principle of "individual liberty" in their "ethnological" character or their religion, could be counted upon to lend their support to southern slavery.[27]

In their pitiable languor the Irish could stand, for Parker and many other Protestants, as a symbol of torpid Catholic piety. Protestants had always sneered at Catholic ceremonialism, and

Parker took his turn chastising the Catholic Church for putting pompous display ahead of heartfelt emotion. In Rome on Ash Wednesday, 1844, he witnessed the pope celebrating High Mass in the Sistine Chapel in the presence of cardinals and other officials. A picture of Jesus was hanging above the altar. "I remembered what he said of the temple, of the chief priests, etc. The whole filled me with compassion, and drew tears from my eyes. Is it always to be so, and in Christian Rome, by the head of the Church? The ceremony of kissing the pope's hand or foot, the kneeling before him, and burning incense, and all in the name of the *carpenter's son* at Nazareth,—it is quite too bad." Parker confessed he had "always liked" Catholic "music, architecture, paintings, statues." But the way Catholics used those material aids undermined "conscience," "reason," and "practical good sense."[28]

Most American Protestants were less bothered by the damage Catholics did to "reason" than by Catholic inattention to the new birth announced in John's Gospel. To them the Catholic Jesus looked like a quiescent, seated, mystical Lord, not a bristling, mobile, provocative agent of heart renewal. Catholics lacked urgency about sin or salvation. As Unitarian founding saint William Ellery Channing had put it in the 1820s, Catholic-style complacency resulted inevitably from all Trinitarian faith. Dividing "one Infinite Person" into "three objects in the mind" necessarily "weaken[ed] the energy of religious sentiment." Presented with three alternatives, believers did not know whom to worship. They overcame their confusion the way "the rudest pagans" would, by imagining against all logic that their "Infinite Deity" had put on a body and died on the cross. At that point there was nothing left for them to do but bow down and adore their incarnated God "for his wounds and tears, his agony, and blood, and sweat."

By giving God flesh and then idolizing him, according to Channing, Catholics reversed the "progress" religion had made in "refining" the conception of God. The Jews had taken the first good step in banning "bodily images of God." The early Christians took the next good step by discarding the "grosser modes of describing God," such as imagining him to be a bloodthirsty warrior. Unitarianism completed the march by taking God "under no bodily form" but as "a purely spiritual essence." For Channing the idea of the new birth carried the same weight that it did for any evangelical Calvinist or Methodist. He simply put more emphasis than they did on the growth of mind that went along with the transformed heart. The essence of the faith for him too was the spark of grace crossing the abyss from God to sinner and reigniting the soul. In fact the Unitarians thought they were purifying and intensifying the new birth experience. They claimed to be concentrating the feeling of love and directing it, laser-like, at a single divine target—the Father.[29]

Listening to nineteenth-century northern Protestants bemoan the Roman Catholic presence in America, one realizes how truly affronted they were. Catholic-style piety had been what the Puritans came to America to escape, and it was now oozing up out of the cities of America. Catholics represented a reversion to "grosser modes of describing God": the mystical focus on the "real presence" of Jesus in the Eucharist, the visual iconography of his physical, wounded flesh, and the reliance on nonbiblical prayers in personal and public devotions. Protestants were shocked at Catholics' casual intermixing of "faith" and "works," and their apparent preference for church traditions over the Bible. While Protestants were memorizing sacred Bible verses, they saw immigrant Catholics endlessly repeating Our Fathers, Hail Marys, and Hail, Holy Queens. "Saying the Rosary" included 150 Hail Marys, 15 Our Fathers, and 15 meditations on the life and passion of Jesus. Special devotions to the Blessed Sacrament and the Sacred Heart of Jesus, along with various rites involving Mary, the saints, and souls in purgatory, created a dense set of lived connections between the temporal and spiritual worlds. Catholics appeared to be repopulating the atmosphere with mediating spirits of the sort the Puritans had been trying to stamp out for two centuries. Catholics, for their part, did not think praying to Mary or the saints meant disregard-ing Jesus. They knew that Jesus was greater than the others. They just took for granted that he was enveloped with them in multilat-eral bonds of love. Pious affection directed at one holy person glo-rified them all. Just as Mary said, in Luke's "Magnificat," that her soul magnified the Lord, Catholics thought they magnified the Lord in praising and petitioning her and the saints.[30]

Catholic churches were artifactual and architectural insignias of Christ's, Mary's, and the saints' pervasive presence in believers' lives. A church such as Holy Family in Chicago, founded by Jesuits in 1857, was more majestic than most once its stone Gothic struc-ture was completed in 1860. But it was the model for many other edifices in the Midwest. It contained three altars, the central one de-voted to the Blessed Sacrament and Christ's Passion, and the two on each side given over to Mary and Joseph. Each altar was be-decked with paintings and statues, and the main altar housed sa-cred relics, including the bones of martyrs. An immense Gothic tabernacle lit by candles contained the consecrated eucharistic bread, reminding the faithful that Jesus was mystically present in their midst. This riot of holy objects was designed to prompt heightened affection for Christ and a state of openness to various miraculous healings and methodical deliverances (such as the spe-cial prayers that reduced the sentences of souls confined in purga-tory). It was also a way for the mostly Irish immigrant congregation to preserve a psychic and spiritual tie to the heavily Romanized Catholicism of their ancestral homeland—not to mention making a supportive cultural haven out of their alienation from the Protes-tant Americans who reviled them.[31]

Protestants did not take the Catholic influx lying down. In the most extreme cases actual rioting broke out, as in the Kensington section of Philadelphia in 1844. After Irish youths broke up a meet-ing of the anti-immigrant Native American Party, Protestants set fire to St. Michael's and St. Augustine's Catholic Churches. Deep-seated religious, ethnic, and political animosities all intersected to inflame passions, but the public displays of each side's rituals or beliefs were the flashpoints of discord. Both groups accused the other of imposing their religion on neutral public space. Catholics chafed at the public school requirement that all students recite from the King James Bible and sing Protestant hymns. Protestants complained about Catholics flaunting the cross in public. "The Roman Catholics," editorialized the *Presbyterian,* a weekly Philadelphia newspaper, "have erected political poles surmounted by a cross! This is one evidence of the difficulty with which a Roman Catholic can think of politics except as favouring the advancement of his own peculiar views of religion."[32]

Ironically, the *Presbyterian*'s alarm over the public display of the cross by Catholics was tied to its shock that many Protestant churches were starting to make religious use of it themselves. Lutherans and Moravians had always used crosses, and even crucifixes, but their numbers were too small to bother the *Presbyterian*. The problem was that the Episcopalians were beginning to put crosses atop their churches, and to use the cross in private prayer. Catholics had long before "divested religion of all its spiritualities" by confusing "true religion with merely outward emblems." Now the Episcopal Church was "manifesting symptoms of the same degeneracy. Its veneration for the wooden cross is the first step to a substitution of the emblem for the doctrine of Christ crucified. The Roman Catholic adores the wood which has been made to assume this form; the Episcopalian only venerates it. Veneration, however, is closely allied to worship."

The *Presbyterian* noted a disconcerting report in a recent Episcopal publication. "Written by a young and afflicted maiden," it included the lines "The Cross, sweet emblem of my faith! I bend to thee the adoring knee!" For the *Presbyterian* this was "rank idolatry. . . . Protestantism is certainly in danger if our youth are to be encouraged in bending the adoring knee to a bit of wood." In fact, the Episcopal trend was the first wave of a much wider shift in the biggest Protestant denominations north and south. By mid-century

Episcopalian, Congregational, Methodist, and even Presbyterian churches were adding crosses to the tops of their cylindrical spires. By the end of the century even Baptists were putting crosses on many of their churches. Marking churches with the Latin cross (defined by its shorter horizontal line, as against the equilateral Greek cross) was not a sign that Protestants were moving closer to Catholics in either piety or theology. The Latin cross had simply evolved into a symbol that did not automatically connote Roman Catholicism. In fact Protestants were turning to the unadorned cross as a way of demarcating themselves from the proliferating Catholics, whose ever-offensive crucifix displayed the dying Jesus. Far from being a sign of ecumenical togetherness, the Latin cross was adopted by Protestants only when they were sure it would not be taken as Catholic.[33]

V

The arrival in Theodore Parker's Boston of tens of thousands of (what appeared to him) socially and theologically primitive Catholics starting in the early 1840s coincided with the start of his public campaign to eradicate slavery and modernize religion. Freedom had to be defended in theology as in politics. He gave his first anti-slavery sermon on January 31, 1841, and preached his classic sermon on "The Transient and the Permanent in Christianity" on May 19. In that pivotal work Parker extended Channing's cause of purifying Christianity to its furthest point by applying it to the Word of Jesus. For the "Arian" Channing, the divine Word was still a discrete being, just not a being equal to God. Where Channing had purified God by elevating him above any corporeal "body," Parker, a devotee of Emerson, purified the Word by detaching it from any personal "being" at all, human or divine. The Word could be permanent only when it soared free of any particular historical embodiments, mental or physical. Intellectual constructions like the

feeble-minded idea of the Trinity came and went just as human beings did. Their passing did not matter because "the Christianity
holy men feel in the heart—the Christ that is born within us, is always the same thing to each soul that feels it." Parker did not shy
away from the logical conclusion: he detached the new birth from
the name of Jesus altogether. "If it could be proved," he wrote,
"that the gospels were the fabrication of designing and artful men,
that Jesus of Nazareth had never lived, still Christianity would
stand firm, and fear no evil. None of the doctrines of that religion
would fall to the ground; for if true, they stand by themselves . . .
like the axioms of geometry." In his Christmas sermon in 1844 he
called Jesus "the greatest fact in the whole history of man," since
"he taught the absolute religion, love to God and man." But "that
God has yet greater men in store I doubt not; to say this is not to
detract from the majestic character of Christ, but to affirm the om-
nipotence of God. When they come, the old contest will be renewed, the living prophet stoned, the dead one worshipped."[34]

Parker revealed himself in "The Transient and the Permanent"
to be even more radical than the notorious German biblical scholar
David Friedrich Strauss, whose *Das Leben Jesu* (1835) had raised
eyebrows and anguished souls on both sides of the Atlantic.
Strauss emphasized, on the basis of new German research into the
multiple origins of the gospel texts, the mythic elements of the
Jesus story. Jesus was a historical person, but the gospel character
of Christ and the accounts of his miracles and teaching were creations of the early church. Parker pointed out in his review of *Leben
Jesus* that Strauss had needlessly turned to the idea of myth-making
when there was a simpler explanation that could account for all of
Strauss's data. Jesus of Nazareth could be seen as a real teacher
whose followers tried to do justice to his memory. Inevitably they
amplified his accomplishments and told tales that diverged from
one another in some particulars. The history of culture was made
up not of conspiratorial inventions but of natural magnifications.
Strauss's rationalist campaign to discredit the miracles was beside

the point. Jesus lived at a time when people saw miracles every-where, and Jesus was only one of many miracle-workers. The gospels reported that even his all-too-human disciples "raised the dead" and "healed the sick." First-century Christians naturally told one another miracle stories to express the monumental truth of their encounter with Jesus. Nineteenth-century Christians had other ways of conveying the awesome power of his love.[35]

Parker had arrived, as had Emerson and Thoreau, at an almost completely historical view of culture, rejecting supernaturalism but stopping short of the thoroughgoing naturalism and historicism that would appear in their full-blown modern form only at the end of the century in the imported writings of Nietzsche. Nietzsche gave up the notion of unchanging truth. Parker did not. He could permit historical *culture* to be transitory because he was sure that virtue was safely grounded upon the trans-historical, permanent truths expressed by Jesus. (Emerson tethered virtue to unchanging truths that transcended any one wise man or cultural tradition.) The unchanging creed of Christianity, as Parker wrote in "The Tran-sient and the Permanent," was "the great truth which springs up spontaneous in the holy heart—there is a God. Its watchword is, be perfect as your father in heaven. . . . Its sanction is the voice of God in your heart; the perpetual presence of Him, who made us and the stars over our head; Christ and the Father abiding within us. All this is very simple; a little child can understand it."[36]

Parker the renegade Unitarian, like Garrison the renegade Quaker, was berated by most Christian believers in his own day. Like Garrison, he found strength in Christ's own feelings of be-trayal and abandonment by his disciples and countrymen. Parker in particular was a model for late-nineteenth-century reformers who saw Jesus as a much-needed ally in progressive politics even when they were ready to give him up as their savior. In the breadth of his reform interests and his awareness of labor and urban prob-lems, Parker should even be called a "Social Gospeler," a label historians commonly bestow only upon late-nineteenth-century

Christian activists. They often make the mistake of seeing ante-bellum reformers as "individualists," while postbellum reformers were supposedly "socially" minded. In fact both groups were "individualists," even if early-nineteenth-century rhetoric was understandably awash in talk of "freedom" and late-nineteenth-century rhetoric tilted toward "social control" as a means of restoring order to the capitalist marketplace. Both groups were individualists because they framed personal and public virtue as the spread of love across all human relationships, private and public. In the general durability and persuasiveness of this evangelical motif—the transformed heart as the key to social justice and personal peace—Jesus could rule outside the churches too. Late-nineteenth- and even early-twentieth-century reformers, secular as well as religious, kept appealing to his authority and imitating his example.[37]

In the wake of his 1841 "Transient and Permanent" sermon Parker was thought far too radical even by his Unitarian peers. "I know not," wrote William Furness, a Philadelphia Unitarian pastor who would publish *A History of Jesus* in 1850, "where his eyes are that they are blind to the divine stamp of truth impressed so deeply" on the gospels. "Mr. Parker looks upon all the particular circumstances related of Christ, as mere fables fabricated by one or another and designed to glorify Jesus. If this be so, how is it that mere fictions should harmonize so thoroughly, so profoundly with each other, and with the reality? The consistency and naturalness of the character of Christ, how perfectly are they preserved throughout!" In Furness's estimation, the perfect character of Christ could not be detached from the miracles. It was only through miracles like the raising of Lazarus that the character of Christ was made clear in the first place. "Not the extraordinary physical power which he exerted on that occasion is the wonder, but the wonder is the sublime self-possession, the absence of all vain-glory, all parade, all self-reference." The Lazarus story could not possibly be a fabrication. If it were, "it would belittle him, whereas in fact it gives us a new idea of moral greatness."[38]

The logical circularity in Furness's defense of the supernatural events of the Bible—Lazarus was really raised from the dead because Christ's "physical power" to do it derived from the sublime moral power revealed in stories like the raising of Lazarus—would scarcely have troubled most American Protestants, for whom the Bible could be taken more or less literally. But in the eyes of many orthodox Christians, the special pleading of a miracle-defender such as Furness was no improvement on Parker's naturalism: neither man had anything more than his own opinions to go by. This perception led a few pre–Civil War Protestants to the belief that Protestantism was inherently deficient. They thought the only protection for biblical faith amidst the ravages of sectarian opinion-mongering was an institution established by God to offer authoritative readings of the Bible. Joseph Smith took this realization all the way to the experience of his new revelation from the Angel Moroni. The far more common path out of Protestantism, especially for highly educated Protestants, was conversion to Catholicism.[39]

The prolific writer Orestes Brownson, who joined the church in 1844 along with his friend and protégé Isaac Hecker, was the most articulate of all the Catholic converts. Brownson's lifelong writings on Jesus alone, from his sermon on the new birth when he was a twenty-four-year-old Universalist preacher in 1828 to his *Catholic World* essay on "Nature and Grace" forty years later, would fill several volumes. Brownson came out of the same hardscrabble Vermont background that produced Joseph Smith (two years younger than Brownson). Unlike Smith he was drawn to the popular rationalism of the Universalists, who combined lingering Enlightenment ideals with devotion to Christ. For young men such as Smith and Brownson (both of whom followed the migratory trail into economically and religiously volatile upstate New York), all the disputes among Presbyterians, Methodists, and Baptists about the true meaning of the new birth were baffling and discouraging. Brownson found temporary refuge in the Universalists' appeal to natural reason and ethical striving. Evangelicals failed to agree about the new birth, he told his Ithaca congregation in 1828, because they all made it an "unintelligible" mystery. Christ's own conversation with Nicodemus showed that the new birth was not "a radical change from nature to grace," but the substitution of a new belief for an old one. Jesus was simply telling Nicodemus to give up his Judaism and be baptized ("born of water") so he could "share the blessings of the gospel" (be "born of spirit"). The new birth was a perfectly normal process of "conversion or change of faith," not the cataclysmic emotional deliverance that evangelicals made it out to be. "The design of Christianity is to make us better . . . not in a supernatural, but a natural way."[40]

Brownson went through two more ideological permutations—freethinker, then Unitarian labor radical (a period when he made friends among the Transcendentalists)—before embracing the Catholic Church. All the tempestuous shifting of position made many of his peers doubt his stability as a person and his worth as a thinker—he was "a verbal index of Christianity," Parker said dismissively in 1845. But it was his unwavering commitment to the ever-flexible Jesus that helped make all the switching possible. His Jesus was successively the plain-spoken preacher of love and enemy of theological hocus-pocus, the acerbic critic of capitalist exploitation, and finally the miracle-working healer and redemptive Son of God. His Universalist praise of Jesus as a teacher of moral perfection continued undiminished during his brief period as a freethinking skeptic around 1830. In the early 1830s the Unitarian Brownson and his Jesus became social and political reformers. "Jesus came to introduce a new order of things, to change, to perfect, man's moral and social institutions," he wrote in 1834. Christ gave him the prophetic vantage point from which to assail "a people who worship Mammon." "Going along through the streets of Boston the other day" (he wrote in 1843), he noticed it was now "the fashion to convert the basement floors of our churches into retail shops of various kinds of merchandise. . . . The church is made to rest on TRADE; Christ on Mammon." The "industrial arrangements" of "this huge republic"—"the relations of master-workers and workers, of capital and labor"—were "essentially vicious." They were based on "its forgetfulness of man's brotherhood to man, its morality of Let us alone, Save who can, and the devil take the hindmost; workers no longer finding work to do; master-workers counting their obligations to their workmen discharged in full when the stipulated wages are paid." In 1840 Brownson said he was no less opposed to slavery than any abolitionist, but "as to actual freedom," the slave has "just about as much" as "the free laborer at wages."[41]

By 1844 Brownson was ready for his final move to Catholicism. Only the Catholic Church, he thought, could provide the theological and intellectual foundation for a free republican society. It alone joined an appreciation for the natural capacities of humanity with both a realistic assessment of endemic human failings and a hope of spiritual deliverance from them. Protestant evangelicalism combined with liberal capitalism would destroy the social basis for democracy by rewarding rampant individualism. In one sense Brownson's move from liberal Christianity to Catholicism was not a large one. His enemy remained constant: the mainstream evangelical Protestants who set "grace" against "nature" and in so doing subverted the whole idea of a civic society capable of stable growth toward democratic freedoms. Catholics were supernaturalists too, but their supernatural realm coexisted amicably with the natural human arena.

"The Catholic regards the two orders as mutually corresponding," he wrote in 1856, "and adapted in advance one to the other. The Evangelical regards them as having no relation to one another but that of mutual repugnance." Protestants went through unnecessary hoops trying to figure out how Christ's revelation could come to a sinner who lacked the natural capacity to receive it. "If you condemn natural reason, you might as well talk of making a revelation of the Christian mysteries to an ox or a horse, to a stock or a stone, as to a man. Grace is an aid, an assistance. . . . But if you condemn nature as totally depraved, you leave grace nothing to aid, help, or assist. Indeed, the Evangelical, did he but know it, virtually denies grace, and all works of grace in or by us. He never brings grace and nature together, or permits man by the aid of grace to cooperate with grace. Nature and grace stand always one over against the other, each crying out to the other, 'Die thou, or I must.'"[42]

The Catholic Jesus—divine redeemer and incarnate, sacrificial lamb, whose revealed truths were kept safe by the teaching office of an apostolic church—was perfectly suited to a man like Brownson. He still, as always, put his faith in natural reason, but now his reason led him to embrace a supernatural revelation without which he and the rest of humanity were doomed. There *had* to be a Christ, a divine redeemer who ultimately elevated faithful human beings above sin. "Christ, the literal person we call Christ, is Christianity," he wrote in a famous essay addressed in 1842 to his Unitarian mentor Channing. "All begins and ends with him. To reject him historically is to reject Christianity. . . . It will hardly do to stop with Jesus as an eminent teacher and true model man. . . . As a model man, he serves us very little purpose, because we see him in but a very few of the relations of life, and because his perfections are above, altogether above the reach of us human beings."

Jesus the teacher, reformer, and exemplar did not suffice for Brownson; only Jesus the divine-human mediator would do. Christ "saves the world by communicating to it his life, not as a life for them to look at, to contemplate as an example, and seek to copy, to imitate, but for them literally to live, to be *their* life." First he became "the objective portion" of his disciples' lives, then of every subsequent generation of Christians, since "one generation overlaps another, and thus becomes its objective life." The essence of the Catholic faith was to take Christ as a fixed, supernatural bridge to the natural. His mystical permanence freed the believer from the evangelical Protestant's obsession with achieving an emotional experience of Jesus or with finding some unchanging spiritual message that transcended all the transitory cultural formulations of the

Word. No wonder Parker called the Catholic Brownson "a powerful advocate of material and spiritual despotism." Brownson relied upon the church to guarantee the truth of Christianity, not upon the Bible or the presence of Jesus in the heart.[43]

In 1844 Brownson knew he was *persona non grata* among his former Universalist, Unitarian, and Transcendentalist acquaintances. He fantasized, as he wrote to Isaac Hecker, his fellow apostate from Protestantism, about making "a penitential journey to Europe, even as far as Rome. To work my passage over the sea and to work, walk and beg whatever distance I may go. A better penance I cannot think of." Brownson told Hecker that he had a particular Transcendentalist in mind as a perfect companion for the trip. "I have my eye on one person who can live on bread and water and sleep upon the earth, who can walk his share; if he should consent to go I might go. It is Henry Thoreau I mean."[44]

VI

None of Brownson's former Transcendentalist friends could have had less interest in the Catholic Church than Thoreau. He had known Brownson, fourteen years his senior, since his undergraduate days at Harvard in the 1830s, and they had spent time studying German together. They never embarked on the European trek, but Brownson was surely right about Thoreau's love of walking and readiness to do without. In less than a year—on July 4, 1845—Thoreau would set up camp at Walden Pond. Brownson was also right about being a good match with Thoreau, despite the latter's lack of interest in Catholicism. Had they made the pilgrimage to Catholic Europe they could have spent their rustic nights under the stars counting the reasons why they both disliked the conventional Jesus of Protestant New England. In the 1840s Thoreau may have been the most radical dissenter on the subject of Jesus in all of America. One or two of his Concord neighbors must have quipped that he came from another planet. Emerson was the most influential dissenter from the Christian culture of pre–Civil War Massachusetts, but he remained influential in part because he continued to care so much about Jesus, and to give him so much weight in his thinking. His Jesus was no longer divine, but he still helped rescue people from sin—the sin of sloth, of trespassing against themselves by settling for old versions of selfhood.

Thoreau broke ranks by taking Jesus in a fully detached, anthropological way, and then by letting everyone know that, all things considered, his own favorite wise man was Buddha, not Christ. His 1844 article on Buddhism in *The Dial*, the Boston Transcendentalist magazine, was one early sign of liberal American interest in non-Christian wisdom literature. "The universal favor with which the New Testament is outwardly received," he wrote in 1849, "and even the bigotry with which it is defended," actually kept American Christians from hearing its message or even bothering to read it in the first place. "Really, there is no infidelity, now-a-days, so great as that which prays, and keeps the Sabbath, and rebuilds the churches." Any self-respecting Christians who actually listened to such commands as "Lay not up for yourselves treasures on earth," or "Go and sell that thou hast, and give to the poor," would abandon their meetinghouses for fear of provoking Christ's scathing judgment on their hypocrisy.[45]

For all its admirable spiritual fire, the message of Christ was too relentlessly moral for Thoreau's taste. It centered too singlemindedly on galvanizing the conscience rather than sharpening the mind or softening the heart. At times Jesus did strike Thoreau as "a sublime actor on the stage of the world," as when he said that "heaven and earth shall pass away, but my words shall not pass away" (the same verse that Parker had chosen as the text for his sermon on "The Transient and the Permanent"). "Yet he taught mankind but imperfectly how to live; his thoughts were all directed toward another world." Christianity "has dreamed a sad dream, and does not yet welcome the morning with joy." Thoreau did not wish to substitute Buddha for Jesus or replace the Bible with the "Bhagvat-Geeta" (which he thought surpassed all holy writings in its "pure intellectuality," as the New Testament did in its "pure morality"). His fondest wish was for a printing of "the collected Scriptures or Sacred Writings of the several nations, the Chinese, the Hindoos, the Persians, the Hebrews, and others, as the Scripture of mankind." In the end there was no need to choose between Buddha or Christ. "I know that some will have hard thoughts of me, when they hear their Christ named beside my Buddha, yet I am sure that I am willing they should love their Christ more than my Buddha, for the love is the main thing, and I like him too."[46]

Thoreau's reflection in 1849 that the dream of Christianity was "a sad dream," one that failed to greet the morning with joy, reappeared in one of his later essays in a startling retelling of a famous New Testament story. Like most American writers, whatever their religious convictions, Thoreau made liberal use of the language of the King James Version of the Bible. One scholar estimates that in his classic *Walden* (1854), Thoreau made several hundred tacit or explicit biblical references, an average of about one per page. Writers in any society use the metaphors and tropes that lie culturally at hand. The best authors are those who make the most arresting or unexpected use of them. In his posthumous essay "Walking" (1862) Thoreau picks up the story of Peter's denying Christ three times before the cock crowed (John 13:38, 18:17–27) and turns it upside down. He begins his revision with a standard Transcendentalist gloss on his friend and mentor Emerson: "Above all, we cannot afford not to live in the present. He is blessed over all mortals who loses no moment of the passing life in remembering the past." Who is thus blessed over all mortals? Not some divine being, not some perfect man, but an animal familiar to every farm—and to every reader of the gospel. "Unless our philosophy hears the cock crow in every barn-yard within our horizon, it is belated. . . . He has not fallen astern; he has got up early, and kept up early, and to be where he is to be in season, in the foremost rank of time."

The last shall be first: the rooster is Thoreau's mock guru, the evangelist of "Nature" who authors "a newer testament—the gospel according to this moment." The lowly rooster is blessed over all mortals because his "strain" is free of "all plaintiveness." He never gives way to "doleful dumps," never stops greeting the new day. He is "an expression of the health and soundness of Nature, a brag for all the world—healthiness as of a spring burst forth, a new fountain of the Muses, to celebrate this last instant of time. Where he lives no fugitive slave laws are passed. Who has not betrayed his master many times since last he heard that note?" Thoreau may well be the first biblical commentator in history to make the rooster the hero of the story of Peter's denial. He revised the story not to make fun of it, but to draw out a neglected strand of its spiritual meaning. Like many other secular American moralists who followed him, he thought and wrote with the language and stories of the New Testament engraved upon his brain.[47]

"Where he lives no fugitive slave laws are passed." Like many New Englanders, Thoreau was incensed at the federal law of 1850 that compelled northerners to help return escaped slaves to their owners. In 1859, when anti-slavery warrior John Brown was sentenced to death for leading a raid on the federal arsenal at Harpers Ferry, Virginia, Thoreau and many other abolitionists quickly invoked the trope of the divinely appointed sacrificial lamb. "Think of him," Thoreau declared in a speech he gave as Brown awaited execution. "A man such as the sun may not rise upon again in this benighted land. To whose making went the costliest material, the finest adamant; sent to be the redeemer of those in captivity. . . . You who pretend to care for Christ crucified, consider what you are about to do to him who offered himself to be the saviour of four millions of men." Thoreau was entranced by Brown's vitality, his "manly directness and force." He presented a welcome alternative to the cowering conformism of the "modern Christian," whose prayers all began with "Now I lay me down to sleep." Brown had lifted himself "out of the trivialness and dust of politics into the region of truth" by valuing "ideal things" over "his bodily life." He alone was truly ready to die, since he alone had really lived. He was already immortal. The rest of his contemporaries might be breathing, but they had already passed away. It was of them that Jesus was speaking when he said, "Let the dead bury their dead."[48]

Thoreau and other abolitionists were opposed to a commuted sentence or a judgment of insanity. They said publicly that Brown's severe sentence was far better than a lenient one since it would spur on the anti-slavery movement. Pushing the Jesus analogy was one way to reconcile northerners to the death sentence. But the linkage to Christ was not simply instrumental. His supporters invoked Jesus because identifying him with Brown gave the condemned man the highest anointing they could bestow. In a speech on "Courage" in Boston, the now venerable Emerson said Brown was "the Saint whose fate yet hangs in suspense, but whose martyrdom, if it shall be perfected, will make the gallows as glorious as the cross." Thoreau went further than the others in supposing that Brown, like Jesus, might have known he needed to die so that others could escape their shackles. "Some eighteen hundred years ago Christ was crucified," he said. "This morning, perchance, Captain Brown was hung. These are the two ends of a chain which is not without its links. He is not Old Brown any longer; he is an Angel of Light. I see now that it was necessary that the bravest and humanest man in all the country should be hung. Perhaps he saw it himself."[49]

John Brown did his part in 1859 to encourage the Jesus comparisons. He had earlier been typecast in the North as a very un-Christlike Old Testament prophet, a rifle-toting man of action who had called down Jehovah's wrath on the enemies of freedom in Kansas. In 1856 he had participated (though he later denied it) in the Pottawatomie massacre of five pro-slavery settlers. At Harpers Ferry three years later his small band of eighteen men, including five African Americans, killed five more people. Ten of Brown's men were killed in turn by the small marine force (led by Robert E. Lee) sent to restore federal control. At his trial Brown claimed he had always sought to free the slaves peacefully. From his jail cell in Charlestown, Virginia, he wrote a series of letters (quickly handed to the press) that depicted him as "a most firm and humble believer" in "the holy religion of Jesus Christ." He referred repeatedly to Christ's "most excruciating death on the cross as a felon," and no doubt drew real strength from feeling that "Jesus of Nazareth was doomed in like manner." Many observers, north and south, noted Brown's likeness to Christ as he awaited his end in complete composure. But Brown used Jesus far more inventively when he reinterpreted his own history of public actions, violent and nonviolent, from Kansas to Virginia, as willed by Jesus. "You know that Christ once armed Peter," he told a friend. "So also in my case, I think he put a sword into my hand, and there continued it, so long as he saw best, and then kindly took it from me. . . . I wish you could know with what cheerfulness I am now wielding the 'Sword of the Spirit' on the right hand and on the left. I bless God that it proves 'mighty to the pulling down of strongholds.'"[50]

Brown played shrewdly on the New Testament's own open-endedness, if not confusion, regarding Christ's attitude toward nonviolence. Jesus taught nonresistance in the Sermon on the Mount. But he also said he had come to bring not peace but the sword, as Angelina Grimké had reminded Catharine Beecher. That ambiguity allowed Brown to take up either position at will and believe he had been continuously loyal to Christ. His announced passage from violence to nonviolence actually modeled the path forward for many abolitionists, who simply reversed the direction of Brown's shift. While he was in prison declaring his turn toward the Prince of Peace, they were hailing his earlier readiness to go down shooting. Even William Lloyd Garrison, most famous of the nonresisters, lent guarded support to the Brown arms wagon. Speaking in Boston on the evening of Brown's execution, he reaffirmed his personal aversion to violence but gave his benediction to "all slave insurrections" once "commenced." "Rather than see men wearing their chains in a cowardly and service spirit, I would, as an advocate of peace, much rather see them breaking the head of the tyrant with their chains." Writing on the first anniversary of Brown's "martyrdom," he put Brown alongside George Washington and Nat Turner as freedom fighters. Anyone who praised the patriots' rebellion in 1776 was logically compelled, said Garrison, to laud Turner's revolt in 1831 and Brown's in 1859.[51]

The cultural resonance of the crucifixion story in mid-nineteenth-century America was magnified by the assassination of the president in 1865. Even if Lincoln had not been shot on Good Friday, the very day of Christ's crucifixion, northerners would have rushed to the Jesus story to express the gravity of the moment and the sanctity of their latest and, apart from Christ, greatest sacrificial victim. Boston preacher Warren Cudworth noted in his Easter sermon that the whole preceding week had resembled the "Holy or Passion Week" leading up to Calvary. Both weeks began with festive celebrations—Passover in Christ's day and the fall of Richmond in Lincoln's. Both ended with a Sunday rebirth following the Friday disaster. Lincoln was like Jesus in life as well as death: had he been able to speak after being shot, said Cudworth, there was no doubt "he would have forgiven the cowardly perpetrator of this inhuman act." The very quality that some abolitionists faulted him for—his readiness to forgive wrongdoing—revealed his "final and complete imitation of our Lord's example." Naturally some Christians were wary of identifying Lincoln too closely with Jesus. Congressman (and Union General) James A. Garfield, who would in 1881 become the second assassinated president, voiced the danger when he told a mass meeting in New York City that "it may be almost impious to say it, but it does seem that Lincoln's death parallels that of the Son of God." Baptist minister C. B. Crane in Hartford, on the other hand, assured his flock that "it is no blasphemy against the Son of God and the Saviour of men that we declare the fitness of the slaying of the second Father of our Republic on the anniversary of the day on which He was slain. Jesus Christ died for the world, Abraham Lincoln died for his country."[52]

Harriet Beecher Stowe's fictional comparison of Uncle Tom to Christ made perfect sense to most white northerners and southerners in 1852 because they found him so Christlike. Many northerners affirmed John Brown's likeness to Jesus in 1859 because he gave himself up for others and because he claimed a longstanding love of Christ. Lincoln, however, who had spoken frequently of God's Providence, had rarely mentioned Jesus. His one public statement about his religious beliefs, during his successful congressional campaign against evangelical minister Peter Cartwright in 1846, comprised a string of negatives: he had never "denied the truth of the Scriptures," had "never spoken with intentional disrespect of religion," and had given up an earlier infatuation with "the Doctrine of Necessity" (the idea that "the human mind is impelled to action, or held in rest by some power, over which the mind itself has no control"). After his death, a few people claimed they had heard him testify to his love for Christ. Ministers assured their congregations that he had indeed "closed with" Christ. In Boston the Reverend A. L. Stone quoted words the president had allegedly spoken "a few months ago": "Yes, now I can say that I do from my heart love the Lord Jesus Christ." That (apocryphal) profession compensated in Stone's mind for the unsavory venue, a theater, that the president had selected for his recreation on the evening he was shot.[53]

Lincoln's evident relation to Jesus in death—the savior sacrificed for the people—swiftly eclipsed the issue of his personal relation to Jesus in life. Moreover, his expressed belief in the active Providence of God amounted to an indirect imitation of Christ's own submission to his Father. Yet the ultimate effect of Lincoln's own elevation to quasi-sacred status in the northern pantheon after 1865 was surely to promote a broad, nondenominational view of God's superintendence. Lincoln's God was an umbrella divinity under whose beneficent guidance Catholics and Jews were as welcome as Protestants. This God offered a strategic middle ground between the founders' God of "nature" and the evangelicals' God of the Bible. "He" could truly unify Americans by attracting the loyalty of rationalists and religionists, immigrants and the native-born. Lincoln's Second Inaugural Address in 1865 described him as a personal God who watched over the nation but who refused to give any religious or regional group his exclusive blessing. This judgmental yet forgiving deity would do the bidding of no party, not even the North in its battle with the South. He kept his purposes to himself. Meanwhile, he empowered human beings to pursue the "new birth" of which Lincoln had spoken at Gettysburg in 1863. This new birth was for all citizens of the republic, not just for Christians. In the first birth the nation had been conceived by the holy spirit of liberty and delivered by the fathers in 1776. In the second birth, four score and seven years later, the nation was reborn in freedom "under God."[54]

One might guess that southerners had a harder time praising the Providence of God in 1865 than northerners did. In fact southerners had good reason to insist upon his continuing superintendence. The freed slaves, despite the many uncertainties of their situation, were exuberant, for the Lord (and Mr. Lincoln) had delivered them from bondage. The renowned Brooklyn preacher Henry Ward Beecher, younger brother of Catharine and Harriet, supplied the pulpit of Zion Church in Charleston, South Carolina, on April 16, 1865. An estimated four thousand African Americans attended the service. "When the preacher rose to his climax," a journalist wrote, "and smiting on his breast, said, 'Now you can say, every one of you, "I have a freeman's heart to give to Christ,"' the scene was one chaos of tears and clamorous joy." White southerners, meanwhile, had been devastated by the collapse of the Confederacy and by their calamitous human losses. "The young men of South Carolina were annihilated," the governor told Beecher. "In many places in South Carolina, there was [now] not a young man between the ages of twenty and fifty." Many southern whites turned to their trust in God's Providence as a way of comprehending the disaster. Their suffering, they supposed, fit somehow into God's inscrutable plan. The Lord chastises those whom he loves. Others appealed to the image of Christ scourged and crucified. In 1866 Stephen Elliott, the Episcopal bishop of Georgia, instructed his clergy to remind their "suffering and depressed" flocks that "the Cross" was the "emblem of humiliation and suffering." The idea that the South as a region had been crucified by a materially superior but spiritually degenerate North became one platform of the white myth of the Lost Cause. Southern loyalists repeated it into the twentieth century. For example, the fictional clergyman in the Reverend Henry Wharton's novel *White Blood* (1906) compared the defeated South to "the blessed Saviour who passed from gloomy Gethsemane to the judgment hall, through the fearful ordeal of being forsaken by His friends, and then on to the bloody Cross."[55]

The cross as a postwar instrument of intimidation by the Ku Klux Klan has been engraved in American memory by D. W. Griffith's film *The Birth of a Nation* (1915). He took the idea that southern whites burned crosses right after the war from Thomas Dixon's novel *The Clansman* (1905), on which his film was based. But the Klan may not have thought of burning crosses until after the film appeared. The first documented anti-black cross-burning, according to one researcher, occurred in late 1915. The post–Civil War Klan had other means at its disposal, including the most gruesome and terrifying of all: lynching. Lynching had a long history inside and outside the South, and many victims were white, but it became a major means of racial control in the post–Civil War South. Unlike the later cross-burnings, it did not involve overt Christian imagery. But African Americans did not need to be told that its summary injustice and brutality mirrored the crucifixion (see fig. 33). By the last years of the nineteenth century roughly one hundred African American men were being lynched annually in the South. If white southerners after the war turned to Jesus to cope with their personal and political devastation, black southerners turned to him for sustenance as their new freedom assumed the form of a new oppression.[56]

SIX

HE TELLS ME
I AM HIS OWN

I

The end of the southern whites' War Between the States produced a suffering Jesus who stood for the sacrificial valor of a regional culture. Southerners could construe defeat on the battlefield of war as victory on the battlefield of spirit. Blood sacrifice brought purification, drawing the entire southern people in their devastation closer to Christ their savior. The North had mounted a mighty juggernaut, said southern Christians, but the northern soul belonged to Satan— the same judgment voiced by many southerners from the eighteenth century to the present day. Meanwhile, the end of the northerners' Civil War, and of the anti-slavery movement, released a broader liberalization of Christ than the one already sparked by the abolitionists. They had made him an advocate of equality and distinguished his historical consciousness as a Palestinian Jew from the unchanging truth of his basic principles. Some former abolitionists continued the egalitarian campaign during Radical Reconstruction— keeping Jesus alive as the sword-wielding judge of John Brown's Kansas dreams—but by the mid-1870s their militancy was spent. Liberal Protestants returned to the tranquil mission inaugurated by early-nineteenth-century Unitarians and stalled by the anti-slavery crusade. Jesus modeled and enacted the rule of love in society. Love ruled across the board in all human relations, public as well as private. Love transformed souls and institutions alike. Liberal Christians no longer debated whether Christ had brought peace or the sword. They returned to the effusive, progressive idealism represented by the saintly William Ellery Channing: Jesus was the Prince of Peace and the Apostle of Love.[1]

Like Emerson (and unlike Jefferson), mid-nineteenth-century Protestant liberals wished to break down the barrier between the natural and the supernatural—not to naturalize the divine (the mistake they thought Theodore Parker had made), but to reveal the sacred already instilled by God in the world. Spiritual reality came in a single form—the divine spirit—and ordinary human life pulsed with it. Likewise Christ possessed one seamless "nature"—the spirit of love—not the two ("true God and true man") posited by traditional theology. The liberals presented Jesus as proof that natural and supernatural spheres flowed together. They were not proposing that all reality was spiritual—the formulation chosen by Mary Baker Eddy and her Christian Scientists in the 1870s—but that God had already seeded the very real material world of sin with his spirit. Christ was the living symbol and embodiment of selfless love in a society given over to greed and self-aggrandizement.[2]

The liberals' blissful theorizing about the natural and the supernatural, and about the luminous Jesus who reconciled all good things to himself, comprised one central pillar of a much broader nineteenth-century liberal faith in reason, science, and morality as the motors of American progress. Most liberal Protestants gladly embraced scientific knowledge, including the scholarship of post–Civil War biblical criticism. Nearly all Americans, for that matter, reveled in what they called "science." They rejected only a skeptical science that declared outright war on religion or religious belief—and that kind of anti-clerical science was rare in mid-nineteenth-century America. Most liberal Christians went far beyond preaching harmony between religion and science. Religion actually benefited from the scientific spirit, and vice versa. Dispassionate investigation of religion purified it of irrational contaminants, while faith-informed science celebrated the handiwork of the Creator even as it probed the intricacies of his creation. In particular, religion had nothing to fear from scientific study of the historical identity of Jesus of Nazareth. As a divine-human person, Christ could never be damaged by honest inquiry. His transcendent and immanent "personality" could easily withstand all rational scrutiny.[3]

The mid-nineteenth-century liberal Protestant upswing did meet some resistance. Die-hard traditionalists such as Presbyterian Charles Hodge of Princeton Seminary dug in their heels. Non-Calvinists ranging from working-class Irish Catholics to black and white Methodist farmers saw every reason to keep the supernatural order of grace and redemption distinct from the natural order of suffering and death. People on the social margins were less apt than modernizing middle-class individualists to celebrate signs of the sacred in the secular. They wanted Jesus to deliver them from what Catholics called "this valley of tears," or what Methodists considered Satan's sanctuary. In their eyes liberal Protestants were far too complacent about the opportunities for virtue and fulfillment in the everyday world.

Protestant millennialists also helped keep older sensibilities alive. The Seventh-day Adventists of Ellen White (an outgrowth of William Miller's movement of the 1840s) and Charles Taze Russell's Watchtower Society (later to become the Jehovah's Witnesses) appealed to the many traditionalists for whom the imminence of the end-times ruled out any compromise with the "world." Their New Testament text of choice was the fiery Book of Revelation, especially the twentieth and twenty-first chapters. The "blessed and holy" would be resurrected to reign with Christ for a thousand years prior to the founding of a "New Jerusalem" where "there will be no more death, neither sorrow, nor crying, neither shall there be any more pain: for the former things are passed away" (Rev. 20:6; 21:2, 4). The details of Christ's return, and of who would qualify to reign with him forever, varied from one prognosticator to another. But believers had plenty of incentive to separate themselves from the world, whether or not they were destined for the highest grade of immortality with Christ. For "whosoever was not found written in the book of life was cast into the lake of fire" (Rev. 20:15).

In their fashion the Adventists of White and Russell were as anti-Calvinist as the liberals: they were Arminian in preaching free access to the path of salvation, and Arian in their aversion to the Trinity. Jesus certainly possessed divine powers, and God had created him from the beginning of time, but Christ could not be placed on a par with God. Like the liberals, they found the intricacies of the Calvinists' "new birth" beside the point. Jesus was available to everyone as a healer and savior, and those with the rectitude to withstand bodily and cultural temptation would greet him with relief at the final cataclysm. To the Adventists the cosmic drama of the "new heaven and new earth" promised in the Book of Revelation (21:1) took the place of the Calvinists' inner struggle with unworthiness. The Adventists projected the battle of virtue and vice onto the entire firmament, while many ex-Calvinist liberals remained locked in the individualist psychic terrain of the Calvinists.

The Adventists also diverged from the liberals in their animus against the secular world, their focus on prophetic and healing gifts, and their whole attitude toward time. Their faith exuded an apocalyptic sense of urgency, tempered only by their periodic penchant for making exact calculations of when in the future everything was going to happen. Every time their predictions were proven wrong, some of them rediscovered the deeper faith expressed in the Parable of the Ten Virgins: there is no telling when the bridegroom will arrive, but he is liable to appear when you least expect it. When they managed to tolerate that tension—knowing the end was near, but not knowing how near—they came a lot closer to the sensibility of the earliest Christians than the liberals ever could. Liberals could not hear the state of emergency announced in Christ's final words in the Book of Revelation: "And behold, I come quickly; and my reward is with me, to give every man according as his work shall be. I am Alpha and Omega, the beginning and the end, the first and the last. I Jesus have sent mine angel to testify unto you these things in the churches. I am the root and the offspring of David, and the bright and morning star. Surely I come quickly" (Rev. 22:12–13, 16, 20).[4]

The theological separatism of the Adventists was mirrored by their determined departure from the social mainstream, a withdrawal apparent in the Saturday Sabbath of the Seventh-day Adventists. But their flouting of cultural and religious convention, and of the liberal Protestant Jesus, was far surpassed by the Mormons. Still a tiny group in their postwar isolation beside the Great Salt Lake, they drew the scorn of virtually all Catholics and Protestants, liberal or traditional. "A monster development," said southern writer George Fitzhugh in 1857, and an especially dangerous one since "Mormonism"—of all the faiths born in "Western New York, that land fertile of Isms"—delivered a persuasive vision of "a safe retreat and refuge from the isolated and inimical relations, the killing competition and exploitation, of free society." Their "sensual moral code," the practice of polygamy, was a disgusting barbarism in Fitzhugh's and everyone else's eyes, and their view of Jesus as one "god" among others struck virtually all Americans as a double infraction: a dishonoring of Jesus and a tribalistic rejection of monotheism. In mid-nineteenth-century America, liberal Protestants could relish the righteous modernity of their love-centered Jesus-worship and shake their heads at all the pathetic anachronisms that surrounded them: the apocalyptic Saturday (i.e., Jewish-style) worship of the Adventists, the polytheistic extravagance of the Mormons, the popish superstitions of the Catholics, and the tired creed-worship and guilt-mongering of the Calvinists.[5]

It is easy to miss the radical import of the nineteenth-century liberal Protestant contention that Jesus was the ultimate embodiment of love. The words "Christ is love" have been intoned ritualistically for so many generations that they can seem empty of all meaning. We have as much trouble grasping what those words meant to northern Protestants 150 years ago as we do registering what "freedom" or "liberty" meant to them. To feel the power of the latter terms we have to imagine ourselves in a culture that had only recently disposed of monarchy, that was still trying to throw off constitutionally tolerated enslavement, and that took release from bondage to sin as the virtuous person's highest aspiration. When Henry Ward Beecher staged slave "auctions" at his Brooklyn Church in the 1850s, his parishioners paid for the privilege of ritually emancipating an actual slave (sitting in meek-and-lowly posture before them)—and vicariously releasing themselves from enslavement to sin.[6]

We face a similar difficulty in fathoming nineteenth-century "love." Liberal Christians heard the First Epistle of John, chapter four, differently than most contemporary believers do. John asserts an identity between "love" and "God": "He that loveth not knoweth not God; for God is love" (v. 8); "God is love; and he that dwelleth in love dwelleth in God, and God in him" (v. 16). Thousands upon thousands of Protestants raised in fear of God's ire latched onto John's words as a life preserver in a storm. But where John's Epistle made clear that Jesus (as orthodox theology was still insisting) had been sent as "the propitiation for our sins" (v. 10), the liberals made him the living spirit of love who rendered most creedal formulations, including the substitutionary atonement, poetically serviceable at best and at worst an outright obstacle to faith. David Swing, minister of Chicago's Fourth Presbyterian Church, saw the history of Protestantism as the gradual shedding and simplifying of creeds. Propositional theology of the sort embodied in the Westminster Confession was dry, dead, and diversionary. Arguing over election, immersion, or the Trinity missed the point of being a Christian. "The gate which Christ opened to love we [the misguided historic church] open only to doctrine. Whereas Christ said 'Lovest thou me?,' we say 'Acceptest thou all these things?'"

Swing's heresy trial in 1874 (he withdrew from the presbytery before the synod's guilty verdict came down) was regarded at the time as a pivotal moment in American cultural development. As in the Scopes trial a half-century later, the guilty verdict made conservatives look silly in the eyes of the ever-more-culturally-dominant liberals.[7]

For liberals, taking Jesus as the living spirit of love was a life-altering breakthrough. He promised personal deliverance from accumulated guilt and recurrent panic. As a child, Henry Ward Beecher (the northern liberal preacher of choice after the war) recalled in 1873, "I was always plunged into the depth of despair about my sins." A visiting minister once told him "stories about the Devil and hell until I had got into that state that I now wonder I did not go into convulsions. It was hideous. If he had put me on a hot gridiron and left me there ten minutes, I could have got over that, but this soul-broiling, this torturing a little child's sensitive nature in that way, without presenting any thought of mercy or love or goodness or Christ Jesus—why! The man was a heathen, only he had a Christian coat on him!" In 1872 Beecher still quaked at the thought of Jonathan Edwards's sermon "Sinners in the Hands of an Angry God." "Inventing new horrors for hell," picturing "the Divine Heart as so in love with justice that it rejoices in the merited sufferings of the wicked, was a sad perversion of the functions of imagination. . . . The doom of wickedness is dreadful enough, without the hideous materialism and the horrible buffoonery of justice which prevailed in a former day." But Beecher, like Swing, objected to more than the scare tactics employed by malefactors of orthodoxy. He despised all doctrinal hairsplitting. He went out of his way in 1874 to publicly mock his father Lyman Beecher's late-night debates "in our Litchfield parlor" with his friend Nathaniel Taylor (himself the primary theological defender-adapter of Calvinism in early-nineteenth-century America) over "whether God *could* have had a government in which there should or should not have been sin, and whether or not men could have been free agents."[8]

Horace Bushnell, minister of Hartford's Congregationalist North Church and the most intellectually gifted exponent of the liberal religion of love in nineteenth-century America, put an intriguing twist on the depreciation of creeds. The best way to fight propositional faith was ironically not to condemn creeds but to say "the more, the merrier." Creeds were "so elastic, and run so freely into each other," he wrote, "that one seldom need have any difficulty in accepting as many as are offered him." All language about spiritual matters was approximate anyway. Since no linguistic formulations could ever escape ambiguity about the divine or about the human quest for the divine, it was best to celebrate rather than denigrate the earnest aspiration and aesthetic beauty of all such historic efforts. Even when understood as a cultural-historical product rather than a trans-historical act of divine speech, religious language could still play a role in sparking true piety. Creeds were no different from the Bible itself: the revelation contained in biblical stories or codified in creeds was truly operative in a person's faith only when it touched off an actual experience of divine love. Biblical truth was absolute and unchanging in Bushnell's eyes, but its truth could not be contained in or even communicated through linguistic forms. It could be genuinely known and transmitted only in acts or states of love. "Love," by bridging the transcendent and immanent, the eternal and experiential, allowed liberal Protestants to champion cultural-historical development while affirming the permanence and stability of truth.[9]

A Jesus reconfigured as the symbol and carrier of love permitted northerners long disciplined by the strict moral diet of Calvinist religion and even anti-slavery politics to fully endorse, at long last, some of the everyday joys of secular life and some of the features of the Romantic worldview. Selves could grow by experiencing pleasure as well as discipline. Historians have routinely emphasized in recent years that love in nineteenth-century America was a feminized domestic virtue designed to counteract the brutal selfishness of the male marketplace (see fig. 14). This formulation is true as far as it goes. But it drastically contracts the scope of love as nineteenth-century northern Protestants felt and imagined it. It even distorts the gendered terms of nineteenth-century love.

In liberal Protestant eyes love was much more than a sentimental cushion for capitalism, a Romantic escape from tedium, or a compensatory site of aspiration for women barred from equal opportunities in work. The love made possible by Jesus could lift a man or a woman right out of social conventions, whether based in the family or in the marketplace. In Beecher's preaching men were invited to appropriate the superior care-giving capacities of women and women were invited to take on the superior world-mastering powers of men. Love was androgynous, since in Christ there was neither male nor female. But love was also differentiated by sex, since culture and biology had split men and women apart. The religious goal of meeting Jesus in love was identical for both sexes. Men (like Beecher himself) might find special sustenance in meditating on the lives of piously gifted women (like his friend Elizabeth Tilton or his mother, Roxana). Women were liable to grow spiritually from their encounters with preachers who knew how to put Jesus fully on display in their own personalities. "The truth must exist in him [the preacher] as a living experience, a glowing enthusiasm, an intense reality," Beecher said in 1872. The preacher's goal was "to take the great truths of the Lord Jesus Christ's teachings, and the love of God to the human race, and make them a part of his own personal experience, so that when he speaks to men it shall not be he alone that speaks, but God in him." The "test of pastoral orthodoxy," he added in 1874, should be the preacher's ability to bring souls "into personal love-relationship to the Lord Jesus Christ."[10]

Beecher invoked Jesus even in support of his campaign to loosen up the hard-working urban middle class of Brooklyn by getting them to enjoy time off in nature or society. He spent ten pages of his *Life of Jesus, the Christ* (1871) informing Protestant teetotalers that Jesus probably spent a week at the wedding in Cana, enjoying

festivities that "would seem to our colder manners almost like dissipation." There was no reason to assume that Jesus looked on the
happy proceedings disapprovingly, or even "held himself aloof, . . .
wrapped in his own meditations." Beecher conceded to the temper-
ance establishment of his day (which proposed that the "wine" at
Cana was actually grape juice) that it was impossible to imagine
Jesus "breaking into effulgent gaiety." But surely "he looked upon
the happiness around him with smiles." Unlike "many of the reigning moral philosophers, who despised pleasure, Christ sought it as
a thing essentially good."[11]

II

Horace Bushnell had been preaching a balanced regime of work
and play since the 1840s, and his pivotal book *Christian Nurture*
(1861), the foundational statement of romanticized evangelicalism,
made spiritual growth inseparable from a person's whole development as a natural being. Conversion was no longer to be seen as a
painful confrontation with one's worthlessness (in either the lifelong campaign of a Shepard or an Edwards, or the once-and-for-all
emotional crisis of a Whitefield or a Finney). Coming into proper
relation to Christ was a long-term maturation begun in earliest
childhood. Indeed, the very earliest childhood (in Bushnell's savvy
adumbration of Freud) was most important of all. That is when a
person's basic spiritual tone and attitude were set. Infant baptism
was an indispensable sacrament because it formalized the urgent
responsibility of parents and community to mold the child's soul.
Bushnell saw the communal nurturing of the young Christian as an
organic alternative to the mechanical individualism of the secular
American environment. Widely condemned by his orthodox foes as
a "liberal" and a "rationalist" in theology, Bushnell claimed to be an
enemy of the "liberal" individualism and rationalism that he associated with "naturalists" such as Theodore Parker.[12]

Once evangelical Protestants like Bushnell had come to see infants as emerging Christians, they could finally embrace the age-old Catholic and Anglican representation of the infant Jesus as God. The baby Jesus evoked a worshipful response because his infancy made him fully human—incarnate across the whole temporal spectrum of human life—and because it tied him organically to his family and community. Christmas, long resisted by Puritans and their descendants as a pagan festival, could finally bridge the Catholic-Protestant chasm and become the premier American Christian holiday—though Easter retained its unique aura. A rash of new Christmas carols became Protestant fixtures. "For Christ is born of Mary," wrote the eminent Episcopal rector (of Boston's Trinity Church) Phillips Brooks in his 1868 "O Little Town of Bethlehem." Salvation was from the child Christ: "O Holy Child of Bethlehem / Descend to us, we pray / Cast out our sin, and enter in / Be born in us today." John Hopkins's 1857 carol "We Three Kings of Orient Are," written to accompany a New York Episcopal seminary Christmas pageant, pictured Christian piety as "bearing gifts" to an infant already reigning as king. Even Unitarian Julia Ward Howe's wartime "Battle Hymn of the Republic" (1862) joined the martial vigor of Christ's stomping on the serpent to the Romantic image of "the beauty of the lilies" in which "Christ was born across the sea."[13]

Bushnell's *Nature and the Supernatural* (1858) included a chapter on Christ that was soon published separately as *The Character of Jesus* (and republished several times until World War I). Any reader of the four gospels, said Bushnell, could see that the real miracle lay not in any of the wondrous acts Christ had performed, but in his character. His childhood amounted to "a kind of celestial flower," with "a fragrance wafted on us from other worlds." Of all the biographies ever written, only the gospels began their subject's life story with "a spotless childhood." Normal human growth required a tempering and refining of early wayward impulses. Christ's character, untainted at the start, remained unblemished as he matured.

All of his behavior revealed a holy "innocence" that made the image of the lamb uniquely applicable to him. He was "a perfectly harmless being," yet he displayed no "weakness." Even his apparently violent words and actions—his denunciation of the Pharisees ("Hypocrites! Brood of Vipers!"), and his chasing of the money-changers from the temple—displayed nothing but "the indignant flush of innocence." Everything about him throughout his life bespoke "the natural unfolding of a divine innocence." Jesus lived out a balanced, harmonious, yet uncompromising selfhood.[14]

Christ was natural and supernatural: not two natures in one person, but one undivided person manifesting God in a manner utterly impossible to human beings. Bushnell can sound a great deal like Theodore Parker in his appreciation for the historical vagaries of language and his impatience with any notion of divinity that pulled Jesus out of his fully human life. But the apparent resemblance to Parker was no resemblance at all in Bushnell's view. Where Parker made Jesus a one-time-only human being of unmatched spiritual capacities, Bushnell proclaimed him eternal God-man. Beecher, Bushnell, and Swing all thought they were protecting the divinity of Christ more effectively than the orthodox were able to do with their frozen verbal formulas. "Christ was very God," as Beecher put it, but "when clothed with a human body, and made subject through that body to physical laws, he was then a man, . . . only without the weakness of sin." Not only Jesus, but all human beings shared the same substance with God. "A human soul is not something other and different from the Divine soul. It is as like it as the son is like his father." People could know this empirically through their experiences of love. Love was always the same, whether it was in them or in God. "Man's nature and God's nature do not differ in kind, but in degree of the same attributes. Love in God is love in man." When Jesus displayed "the gentleness, the compassion, the patience, the loving habit, the truth and equity" of his human life, he was actually disclosing the nature of the "Divine Spirit." All that he was on earth "we shall find him to be in heaven, only in a profusion and amplitude of disclosure far beyond the earthly hints and glimpses."[15]

For an unreconstructed Calvinist such as Princeton Seminary's Charles Hodge, the most dangerous enemy was not a Beecher or a Swing, who preached love as a transformative power for individuals. Bushnell was the greater threat because his anti-creedalism rested upon an organic vision critical of liberal individualism. Hodge grasped that Bushnell was attacking Theodore Parker's legacy as much as he was Calvinism. He was proposing a third path, declaring a pox on the language games of Unitarians and Trinitarians alike. He was doing it all in the name of a new conservatism, a new social and psychological stability. He was pushing no radical social transformation of the sort Parker had espoused before the Civil War. And Bushnell rejected revivalist enthusiasm as firmly as he did Parker's Unitarianism. In his eyes they were simply two competing forms of individualist excess. For Bushnell, Calvinism could no longer mount any effective resistance to American individualism run amok. Hodge knew he would have to assault Bushnell's organicism head on if he was to salvage any shred of the Calvinist heritage. Like the Catholic convert Orestes Brownson tilting with Parker before the Civil War, or the orthodox Presbyterian J. Gresham Machen battling liberal Baptist Harry Emerson Fosdick after World War I, Hodge set off to shield the Christian tradition from the acids of modern skepticism.

His effort fell on virtually deaf ears in his own day and ever since, but his intellectual rigor and forceful prose make him an essential source for anyone trying to understand Bushnell and the other liberal Protestants who dominated the northern theological landscape for a solid century after the Civil War. Hodge came as close as anyone in the nineteenth century to asserting (as H. Richard Niebuhr and others did explicitly in the mid-twentieth century) that liberal Protestants, who regarded themselves as champions of the universality and timelessness of Christ, were in fact chaining Christ to the time-bound cultural forms of liberalism.

The best way to protect Jesus against cultural imprisonment in any era, said Hodge, was to pass along the historic doctrines the church had long since reached regarding Christ's identity. They were true not because they were unambiguous (Bushnell was right that language always carried ambiguity), but because they respected the central biblical mysteries about Jesus.

In his review of Bushnell's *God in Christ* in 1849, Hodge noted that the dogmas of the Trinity, the incarnation, and the atonement wisely refrained from trying to *explain* those mysteries. They simply stated them in carefully chosen language that honored all of the relevant biblical statements. The point of doctrine was not to make revelation reasonable, but to use reason to encompass the complexity of the biblical account, to rule out one-sided understandings of revelation. Dogmas were buffers against the common human practice (and sin) of making Christ the servant of culture, turning him into a socially useful badge or psychologically therapeutic tool. The role of the church was to carry forward the doctrines of three persons in one God, of two natures in one Christ, and of Christ's obedient sacrifice and propitiation *because* they surpassed human understanding. Human beings could then be kept aware of exactly who was sovereign and who was subordinate. They should be worshiping God, not praising themselves, Pharisee-like, under the guise of offering their unctuous prayers and breast-beatings to the Lord.[16]

Bushnell, like Beecher, Swing, and many others, was using Jesus to solve an intellectual as well as religious crisis. The classic verbal expressions of theology struck them all as smug. They no longer delivered meaning, much less power. Rather than follow Emerson and Parker in seeing the enlightened human mind and the sympathetic human heart as sources of meaning and power, the liberal Protestants of the mid-century drafted Jesus into their religious and intellectual service, much as the anti-slavery advocates had put him on their moral and political banners. Charles Hodge did more than anyone to clarify exactly what they were doing.

Bushnell, he said, was a mystic and, for all his Romanticism, a rationalist. He was a rationalist because he had no understanding of, or tolerance for, mystery. If a doctrine was mysterious, Bushnell was as quick as any nonbeliever to consign it to the dustbin.

Bushnell was a mystic, said Hodge, because he set the Bible aside and put his faith in "an immediate, continued, supernatural, divine operation on the soul, effecting a real union with God." Biblical Christianity rejected such mysticism. "The Scriptures do indeed teach that, in the moment of regeneration, the Spirit of God acts directly on the soul, but they do not inculcate any such continued direct operation as mysticism supposes." Just as in the life of the church revelation had ceased in the apostolic age, so in the life of the Christian direct divine action stopped at the moment of regeneration. From that point forward, obedience to Scripture took over. True, the Scriptures spoke of the "inspiration" that accompanied such obedience, but inspiration was "an influence on the reason, revealing truth or guiding the intellectual operations of the mind." After regeneration, "all the operations of the Spirit are in connexion with the word; and the effects of his influence are always rational—i.e., they involve an intellectual apprehension of the truth revealed in the Scriptures." Bushnell's path would lead to a "vague ecstasy of feeling, or spiritual inebriation, in which all vision is lost" and in which "the church is nothing"—except a morale-building institution in which preachers try to pump up psychic satisfaction. Hodge was repeating the very points that Shepard in the seventeenth century and Edwards in the eighteenth century had stressed: the Bible as interpreted by a learned ministry was the armor protecting Jesus from assault by self-satisfied sinners.[17]

Naturally Bushnell's cohort of liberals believed their efforts were protecting the spirit of Christ from the dead cultural forms of orthodoxy. Just as Hodge came very close to saying that the church's role was to resist the *cultural* incarnation of Christ by holding to the orthodox *theological* view of his incarnation, so Bushnell came very close to saying that Christ is always incarnated in culture as well as in the person of Jesus. Bushnell understood that cultures evolve and that Christians have no choice but to place their beliefs about Jesus in the shifting linguistic forms available to them. None of those forms was adequate to the task of expressing the reality of Jesus. Nevertheless, as he wrote in *God in Christ*, "we shall delight in truth" as "a concrete, vital nature, incarnated in all fact and symbol round us—a vast, mysterious, incomprehensible power, which best we know, when most we love." The Christian should not bemoan Christ's inevitable adaptation to culture, but rejoice at the glimmerings of him that shine out of every loving human creation or encounter.[18]

Bushnell could have answered Hodge's charge that the liberal religion of love was "a vague ecstasy of feeling" by sending him a copy of a letter he wrote to a worried correspondent in 1860. The troubled individual was stricken with guilt because loving God felt so good. It seemed selfish to derive so much pleasure from it. Bushnell unpacked the writer's moral quandary in a reflection derived from Jonathan Edwards. It *does* feel good to love God, Bushnell wrote, as long as you love him for "his excellence and beauty" rather than for "the state into which he would bring you." Good actions feel good because of the element of "liberty" in them. Liberty of action always contains "the spontaneity of play," a "following after the good for its own sake." Fret not: you are "supposed to please yourself in doing good."

But if Christians can stop worrying about love's being selfish, Bushnell added, they have to beware of loving "only artistically." True, artistic or aesthetic love—as in admiring a landscape or fawning over a beautiful child—*is* an essential part of Christian love. But Christian love always goes further. It "is being joined to Christ so as to be in self-sacrifice with him. . . . It begins in the loss of all things, in the taking up of Christ's cross with him." Plain aesthetic love "rises out of the heart, when it is full and ready." It "requires contemplation only." Christian love, by contrast, "breaks into the heart, when it is emptied and broken." It "requires faith, and is a fire of

God's own kindling in the heart of faith, an inspired or divinely in-
breathed love." The goal of Christian love is to take "deep hold
enough" of a life "to change and work it into the semblance of
Christ's."[19]

Bushnell's two-sided message to his conscience-stricken correspondent is a microcosmic statement of the double task that his cohort of liberal ministers took up in the mid-nineteenth century. On
the one hand, they tried to bury Calvinism, and to help anyone still
overwrought about worldly temptation to taste the beauty of life
and the joy of loving Christ. On the other hand, they tried to prevent their celebration of natural pleasures and pursuits from turning into a denial of the supernatural. They were not "naturalists"
who doubted Christ's miracles or the autonomous power of God's
grace. Beecher's *Life of Jesus, the Christ* insisted on God's continued
capacity to "produce events by the direct force of his will without
the ordinary instruments of nature." The gospels "should be taken
or rejected unmutilated," wrote Beecher. "Sceptical believers" were
attempting to "take from the New Testament its supernatural element." But miracles were "the very spirit of the whole Bible." The
skeptics were welcome to leave the church if they wished, but they
were not welcome to call themselves Christians and gut the Scriptures of the sacred. Charles Hodge could not have agreed more
with that general sentiment. But by the 1860s neither liberal nor orthodox Christians trusted the other party to protect "the very spirit
of the whole Bible."[20]

III

The "real end" of the preacher, Beecher said in 1872, was "soul-
building." It was fine to broach "social questions" in the pulpit, he
conceded, and in some cases (as in the anti-slavery agitation) it was
"a duty." But it was a mistake to put social issues at the heart of
one's message. In that instance one's ministry "will be secular, and

will become secularized." Bushnell's, Beecher's, and Swing's cohort of liberals resisted the "secular" label as much as the "naturalist" one, realizing that traditionalists were eager to use both of those epithets to discredit all world-endorsing or psyche-bolstering moves.[21]

With a century of hindsight we can see that liberal Protestant soul-building formed but one part of a much larger secular soul-reform movement—"secular" in the sense that it went beyond the established churches. Moreover, in the wake of the economic depression of the mid-1870s, liberal Protestants also gravitated toward a secular *social*-reform movement that overlapped with secular *soul* reform. The paradox is that scientific and religious language, motifs, and commitments mixed together in soul-reform and social-reform circles whether based inside or outside the churches. Protestant mindsets persisted even when religious faith was lost, and faith was often not so much lost as transferred to, or revived by, secular purpose. "Jesus" was such a capacious umbrella, and such a useful cultural currency for anyone seeking an audience, that he remained basic to both soul reform and social reform—whether they were religious, secular, or (as was often the case in the United States) a blending of the two.

Soul reformers issued "mind-cure" or "New Thought" books in profusion in the 1860s. Some volumes tendered practical advice, others sought philosophical stature, but all of them merged science with faith. Many harked back to Phineas Parkhurst Quimby, the charismatic mid-century "mesmerist" (hypnotist) who evolved into a spiritual healer relying on talk-therapy rather than mechanical manipulation. Quimby was self-taught, and considered book-knowledge a diversion from experiential learning. Having gotten over his own kidney ailment by believing "that I had no such disease, and that my troubles were of my own make," he began to teach others "to manufacture health" with the techniques of what he already sometimes called "Christian Science." One of his early patients and apprentices was Mary Baker Patterson, later Eddy, founder of the Church of Christ (Scientist).[22]

Jesus, for Quimby, was the first man to grasp that the divine healing power—"the Christ," Quimby called it—resided in every person. New Thought writers such as Warren Felt Evans (another early patient of Quimby, and the author of *The Mental Cure*, 1869, *Mental Medicine*, 1872, *Soul and Body*, 1875, and *The Divine Law of Cure*, 1881) took Quimby's ideas in a "secular" direction, while Christian Science made them "religious" (Eddy's *Science and Health* appeared in 1875, and she revised it seven times, the last in 1907). But both secularists and religionists stood by Jesus. The aim of "the Great Physician," according to Evans, was "to cure the body through the restored soul. . . . We are saved by faith, soul and body." Jesus always tied sick or blind people's cures to their inmost state of belief. "We find no cures were ever wrought by him except through the faith of the patient, or of some one else." His "therapeutical system," summed up in his common healing phrase "Be it unto thee according to thy faith," expressed "a general law of the relation of the body to the sovereign mind."[23]

In *Science and Health* ("with Key to the Scriptures" was added to the title in 1883) Mary Baker Eddy pressed the idea of sovereign mind to its logical limit by denying the reality of matter and body altogether. She called Jesus of Nazareth the first and most perfect practitioner of Christian Science healing, and saw herself as the first to identify and articulate the principles of his practice. Jesus was not God, but since he was conceived by the Holy Spirit (making him, so to speak, half material and half immaterial), he had privileged access to the truth that God was pure mind. Human beings, made in God's image, were in their essence pure mind too. Healing occurred when people woke up to the spiritual character of their true identity. Sin, evil, and death were unreal, though people's misguided belief in those "mortal errors" gave those notions a certain social existence and even power. Jesus was not the only "Christ," or "divine manifestation of God," but he was "the highest corporeal concept of the divine idea." His atonement was neither a propitiation delivering some segment of humanity from the legacy of

Adam's sin nor a moral lesson provoking people to repentance for their own sins. Atonement was simply the scientific demonstration by Jesus of the truth that "the law of divine Love . . . redeems man from the law of matter, sin, and death."[24]

To many liberal as well as orthodox Christians, Eddy's faith was an abomination of the same magnitude as Mormonism, even if her heresy was more recognizably Christian. At the heart of her piety was the liberal Protestant commitment to soul-building: free the higher spiritual faculties from the tyranny of the lower animal passions, and free Christ from his historical incarnation in Jewish culture. Let him flourish as the free-floating human exemplar of the new birth of personality. Eddy followed both Jefferson and Emerson in lifting Jesus out of his historical context. His personal history—life, death, and resurrection—had no redemptive worth in its own right. His contribution was impersonal: he conveyed knowledge of universal truths about spirit. Like the liberal Protestants, Eddy gave no loyalty to the historic creeds of the Christian churches. Like Emerson, however, she faulted the liberals for worshiping the living person of Jesus. Putting him on a pedestal as the *only* "Christ" detracted from the limitless spiritual potential of everyone else.

Of course Eddy went far beyond Emerson by creating both a new church and a new holy writ for that church. Protestants and Catholics alike were aghast at her arrogance in doing again in the 1870s what Joseph Smith had done in the 1820s: treating her own words as incontrovertible truths, putting herself (in effect if not in expressed intention) on the same prophetic pedestal as Jesus himself. In Eddy's eyes *Science and Health* was not quite a latter-day revelation of the divinely chiseled Mormon sort. The text of her book was eminently revisable. The words were not holy; the divine truths the words tried to express were holy. Yet she was the only person empowered to revise that text. From an orthodox or liberal standpoint, she compounded her error on revelation (seeing it as continuous, rather than limited to the apostolic era) by reviving the Gnostic heresy. Matter was evil, and the Creation—which orthodox

Christians thought was followed by the fall of Adam and Eve—already constituted a fall from pure spirit.[25]

Protestants expressed an additional complaint. Eddy had erected an institution that reminded them of the Catholic and Mormon churches: authoritarian and secretive, ill suited to (and hence implicitly corrosive of) what Protestants considered their free, open, and democratic culture. A Presbyterian critic lambasted Eddy for taking the Catholics' veneration of Mary and doing them one better: giving herself "divine attributes." Her opponents could point to evidence such as Eddy's 1893 poem "Christ and Christmas." An illustration published alongside showed a woman labeled "Christian Science" holding Christ's hand. Her head and Christ's were topped with identical halos. Eddy claimed in her defense that the image referred "not to my personality," but to "the womanhood, as well as the manhood of God."[26]

In the 1820s Joseph Smith had believed that a new church with teachings guaranteed by a new prophet could overcome denominational disarray. In the 1870s Eddy believed that a new church with teachings guaranteed by a new healer could overcome therapeutic disarray. America after the Civil War displayed a chaotic religious and secular landscape of practitioners and mediums who claimed special access to divine spirit. Churches, Smith and Eddy understood, were institutions for fighting heresy. One of the heretics, from Eddy's standpoint, must have been Adventist Ellen White, an inspired prophet in her own right. White's Seventh-day Adventists showed as much zeal for a healing ministry as the Christian Scientists, but they took exactly the opposite tack from Eddy on the subject of the body: it was so real that strict dietary rules (no meat, no tobacco, no alcohol) promoted individual health and religious discipline alike. The body was so real that after the final battle with Satan resurrected saints would be with Jesus in the flesh. Where orthodox and liberal Christianity tried to balance the spiritual and the material in their view of Jesus and of human nature, Adventists pressed the material side and Christian Scientists pressed the spiritualist side. Eddy must have taken White's dietary rules and cosmic speculations, not to mention her many trance-visions of Jesus, as pious claptrap interfering with Christ's approach to mental healing. Religion lost its purity as a healing science when it gave so much importance to dream-states (Eddy had insights, not visions), to managing the material world, or to predicting material outcomes for cosmic battles between good and evil. It also lost touch with Jesus himself, who gave no significance to the realm of matter. "Jesus was the most scientific man that ever trod the globe," Eddy wrote. "He plunged beneath the material surface of things, and found the spiritual cause."[27]

While Eddy was busy developing and disciplining the religious side of mind-cure, a strong secular current—indebted explicitly to Emerson—flourished too. Even Eddy made a pilgrimage to Concord in 1882 in apparent search of Emerson's blessing, but he was too decrepit, a few months before his death, to utter more than a few disconnected sentences. Ralph Waldo Trine was the most successful of the string of secular pundits who took Jesus as the master healer and Emerson as his greatest disciple. Trine's parents had named him Ralph Waldo at his birth in 1866 out of veneration for the Sage of Concord. By the time he published the runaway bestseller *In Tune with the Infinite* in 1897, his mass audience had been well prepared for his upbeat message of "Peace, Power, and Plenty." The book performed the inspired feat of fusing Quimby's and Evans's practical Jesus—the layer-on of hands and the speaker of healing words—with a simplified but still recognizable Emersonian Jesus. Trine's Jesus was the philosopher of self-reliance as well as the teacher and practitioner of mind-cure. All human beings needed the lesson of Jesus, whatever their religion or their state of health, because everyone was tempted to stick with the familiar, to rest on the cushion of the past, to make Jesus himself a frozen icon of divinity. Yet "he did nothing for the purpose of proving his solitary divinity. . . . Don't mistake his mere person for his life and his teachings, an error that has been made in connection with most all great teachers by their disciples over and over again." The point of being a Christian was "to live in harmony with the same laws Jesus lived in harmony with: in brief, *to live his life*." The goal was to "study the prophets less and be in the way of becoming a prophet yourself."[28]

For Trine Emerson was "the inspired one, the seer," and much of Trine's text was a direct paraphrase of Emerson's writings. But in the end *In Tune with the Infinite* departed from Emerson and adumbrated the twentieth-century "positive thinking" that often did without Jesus altogether. Trine was preoccupied with manipulating and harnessing the body. Since body responded directly to mind, the path to "the complete realization of this oneness with the Father" was quicker and smoother than Emerson could have imagined. For Emerson the body was a permanent drag on the soul. Human beings were split at the core. Suffering was endemic, as he said in his early "Christ Crucified" sermon. Jesus modeled a path through that suffering but did not promise the elimination of it. The "animal" in human beings struggled against their "thought." In his essay "Fate" (1860), Emerson quoted Jesus saying, "When he looketh on her, he hath committed adultery." "But," observed Emerson, "he is an adulterer before he has yet looked on the woman, by the superfluity of animal, and the defect of thought, in his constitution. Who meets him, or who meets her, in the street, sees that they are ripe to be each other's victim."[29]

Emerson's proposed pursuit of virtue meant not overcoming the split between body and soul, but striving to keep them in balance. Jesus was sublime because he kept his eye fixed on the soul's business, what he called his "Father's business." Human beings should aim for the same goal, knowing they would always come up short. Mind-cure writers such as Trine took Emerson's belief that access to divinity was unrestricted and converted it into the very different idea that the achievement of tranquility was unimpeded. Trine's positive thinking, and Mary Baker Eddy's "science," reveal how much of the Calvinist sensibility Emerson, like Benjamin

Franklin and Abraham Lincoln, preserved. Emerson's Jesus was like us in his full humanity, but unlike us in his pure sublimity. Human beings were stuck in very real bodies, only intermittently capable, as Emerson said dolefully in "Experience" (1844), of transcending the imposed trajectories of "temperament." "I knew a witty physician who found theology in the biliary duct, and used to affirm that if there was disease in the liver, the man became a Calvinist, and if that organ was sound, he became a Unitarian." Body was real, both physically and as metaphor for the Calvinists' deadly sins of sloth and despair. No amount of willpower, or denying the reality of body, could ward off intermittent ebbs in spiritual vigor.[30]

IV

In 1872 Henry Ward Beecher cautioned young preachers against letting "social" concerns impede the slow, delicate soul development of their congregations. The new birth, as he said in his sermon on the topic in 1871, did not come as a "flash of lightning." Like his fellow Romantic Victorians Bushnell and Swing, Beecher saw it as "yielding one's allegiance to God," followed by "a gradual progression from a lower to a higher state." When Jesus said in John, chapter three, that only born-again believers could enter the kingdom of God, he meant that "a man, in his animal being, or in his lower, passional nature, never will come into the experience which belongs to the purity of . . . higher feelings."[31]

Yet for many of Beecher's liberal disciples, the economic depression of the mid-1870s forced the kind of social turn that chattel slavery had provoked a generation earlier. In cities across the North, urban workers commonly faced 25 percent unemployment rates. The Tompkins Square Riot in 1874 pitted thousands of New York City protesters calling for a living wage against an army of baton-wielding police. These events brought many Christians to a new birth of social conscience and a new social definition of the kingdom of God. Lyman Abbott, who replaced Beecher as pastor of Plymouth Church in 1887, recalled later that labor-capital conflict in the 1870s led him to renounce *laissez-faire* economic ideas. Beecher, by contrast, remained "an individualist of the old school," "averse to any increase in the powers of government." For Abbott the Christian's responsibility and the state's responsibility converged. Both were called to active mediation between the warring parties of business and workers. Jesus had always been depicted as the bridge between God and human beings. It was an easy adjustment to see him as the symbolic mediator among social antagonists.[32]

Washington Gladden, who emerged in the 1880s as the leading Social Gospeler, grew up in an anti-slavery Congregational church. To judge from his later recollections, the social focus of his faith simply shifted from slavery before the Civil War to industrial issues after the war. The individual soul-struggles of the "new birth" had never made sense to him in the first place. Though steeped in the Bible—his family had read it aloud in its entirety four or five times during his childhood—he had never had a religious "experience." "It was not an individual pietism that appealed to me; it was a religion that laid hold upon life with both hands, and proposed, first and foremost, to realize the Kingdom of God in this world." He was introduced to labor-capital conflict in North Adams, Massachusetts, in the 1860s, when Chinese strikebreakers were brought in during a lockout at a shoe factory. During the depression of the 1870s he took on the role of mediator in Springfield, where he was a Congregational minister. "The Christian law covers every relation of life," he told the workers and their employers. There was no law of supply and demand operating independently from the law of love. He told the workers to accept lower wages and instructed well-heeled employers to create jobs for the unemployed. His fellow ministers, he said, were obliged to study social questions as well as the Bible; they had "no right to be incompetent" in economic matters. "The church is in the world to save the world."[33]

Out of self-interest alone, in Gladden's view, the church should act to bridge the abyss between labor and capital. If "industrial society plunges into chaos," the church will "go to ruin" with it. If a shell of the church survived, it would bear little resemblance to the Christian church conceived as the moral and religious center for the whole community. But much more than self-interest was at stake. Christians had sworn allegiance to Christ's command "Thou shalt love thy neighbor as yourself." In Gladden's interpretation, the golden rule was the doctrinal basis for social progress as well as individual purity. Christ's teaching staked out the middle ground between self-renunciation and self-concern. The golden rule was not "a maxim of sheer altruism." Christian love "gives ample room for . . . legitimate self-assertion," as it does "for that self-denial which restrains the excesses of self-love." Jesus instructed us to love others the same way we love ourselves. "I ought to have some sense of the value and sacredness of my neighbor's personality." But "I am not to degrade or destroy myself in ministering to him. . . . The gains of cooperation must not be purchased at the cost of the integrity of the individual." Socialism made the mistake, Gladden observed, of excluding "the self-regarding motives." A Christian approach to the industrial problem reconciled self-assertion with "motives of good will" just as it reconciled capital and labor. "I am to identify [my neighbor's] interest with mine, and we are to share together the good which the divine bounty distributes to us all."[34]

The recollections of Lyman Abbott, Washington Gladden, and other late-nineteenth-century Social Gospelers make clear how deep an impact nineteenth-century biblical criticism had on the rise of the Social Gospel. Historical study of the biblical text produced the same effect on their generation of reformers that historical study of the life of Jesus had produced on the anti-slavery cohort: it made them seek out the text-transcending, time-transcending principles of Christ's teaching and living. By the 1870s scholars had access to original manuscripts that forced changes in the King James Version of the Bible. A committee of English and American scholars met in Westminster Abbey to create a revised Bible, and as they worked they delivered some alarming news to believers on both sides of the Atlantic: certain prized passages of the New Testament had to go. The First Epistle of John 5:7, for example, was an interpolation: "For there are three that bear record in heaven, the Father, the Word, and the Holy Ghost: and these three are one." Gladden remembered sitting around a table in Springfield in 1875 with twenty other Congregational ministers and being the only one who thought they should all inform their congregations of what they now knew to be true. Gladden told his flock about 1 John 5:7 and added the bad news about Acts 8:37 for good measure: the faithful eunuch's proclamation to Philip that "Jesus Christ is the Son of God" was not to be found in the earliest manuscripts.

On May 20, 1881, the Revised New Testament was published in the United States. In four days the *Chicago Tribune* sold one hundred thousand copies of a sixteen-page supplement containing the entire text. The Revised Old Testament followed in 1885. The outcome of all the publicity was a crisis of faith for some Christians, along with widespread nostalgia for the beloved language of the King James Version. The loss of the doxology at the end of the Lord's Prayer ("For thine is the kingdom, and the power, and the glory," a late addition to Matthew 6:13) hit believers very hard. "Let us say the Lord's Prayer as we are used to say it," complained a *Washington Post* editorial. Yet most Protestant editors supported the new translation out of explicit devotion to Jesus. The *Evangelical Messenger* applauded the dropping of the doxology, for example, "because the Lord never spoke it." Traditionalists, Catholic as well as Protestant, reassured lay people, as the Presbyterian General Assembly put it in 1893, that the Bible was "the very Word of God and consequently without error." A few conservatives went further, challenging the "lower" textual criticism of the Bible (i.e., correcting the biblical text in accordance with the earliest manuscripts) on the grounds that it led inexorably to a "higher" criticism suspicious or dismissive of the supernatural origins of the Bible. Their efforts laid the groundwork for the reactionary, ahistorical doctrine of "inerrancy" that emerged among fundamentalists in the early twentieth century.[35]

For his part, Washington Gladden encouraged his flock to face the fact that a "fixed and stable foundation" for belief was both impossible and unnecessary. "Some things need no foundations," he said. "Sacred truth needs no such supports. . . . The ground of our faith is not the church nor the bible, but the living God, who as Inspirer and Leader of men is as near to us as He has ever been to the men of any generation, and who, if we will trust Him, will enable us to draw from the messages of the past the truth that we need for the life of today." Gladden eagerly supported the Revised Bible because it respected the textual record and because it brought with it a "considerable relaxation of the rigidity of theological dogmatism, and opened the way for the examination of many traditional beliefs." The truths previously cemented in the unchanging text of the Bible were now to be sought in shifting needs of "the life of today." The Social Gospel did not stem from biblical criticism alone, but it was certainly spurred forward by growing skepticism about finding the "living God" in the exact phrasings of the Good Book. Looking for Jesus in the world rather than seeking him only in the Bible produced a momentous effect: it made many liberal Protestants just as devoted to the imitation of Christ as Catholics had always been.[36]

No author did more to propagate the view that Jesus was to be met in the byways of the real social world than the Reverend Charles M. Sheldon of Topeka, Kansas, whose novel *In His Steps* (1896) may have been the most widely circulated book published in late-nineteenth-century America. Originally released serially in a Chicago church magazine, it was unprotected by copyright and soon appeared under countless imprints at home and abroad. Sheldon said in 1935 that the book had outsold every other book but the Bible itself. But there was no way to tell how many copies had been printed, or even how many publishers had issued it (a five-cent pamphlet edition was released in 1900). Its phenomenal reach can be measured by the commercial production in 1900 of a lantern-slide "picture play" designed for church use. The manufacturer recommended a three-night performance featuring fifty slides on each successive evening. Another sign of the novel's influence is the now virtually universal recognition of its signature phrase, "What would Jesus do?" (see fig. 13).[37]

In His Steps is such a rudimentary literary effort that it is easy to miss its homiletic and even theological contribution. Its unique use of Jesus gets overlooked when the book is set into the stream of late-nineteenth-century novelistic treatments, from General Lew Wallace's hugely popular *Ben-Hur: A Tale of the Christ* (1880) to Archibald McCowan's *Christ, the Socialist* (1894), William T. Stead's *If Christ Came to Chicago* (1894), and Edward Everett Hale's *If Jesus Came to Boston* (1895). *In His Steps,* like the last three books, was an urgent response to economic depression and class conflict, including the Haymarket Massacre (1886) and the Homestead and Pullman Strikes (1892 and 1894). Middle-class northern Protestants and their ministers were overwhelmed by the sufferings of the unemployed and by the specter of revolutionary violence. Some were edging toward "socialism" as a solution, but most, like Sheldon, still followed Washington Gladden in preaching Christlike mediation, and Christ's golden rule, as the practical and peaceable middle ground between self-aggrandizement and utopian self-denial.

In His Steps begins as the fictional Reverend Henry Maxwell, a Congregational minister in the railroad city of Raymond (somewhere in the northern Protestant heartland), is writing a routine sermon on the atonement. His doorbell rings. It is a destitute (and it turns out, dying) tramp in search of work. The shabbily clad young man next appears at the back of the church during the Sunday service. He delivers an impromptu sermon of his own that respectfully calls on the congregation to examine what it means to follow Jesus when there are more than five hundred men in town who cannot find jobs. Before he can finish, he collapses at the communion rail.

Nursed by the Maxwells in the parsonage, he dies three days later. (We suspect that his dying on "the third day," when Christ rose, is not accidental.) The death prompts the minister to challenge his flock: for an entire year they will not take any action in their daily lives without first pondering what Jesus would do in their place. Among the one hundred members of the congregation who take the pledge are a newspaper editor, a railroad shop superintendent, a merchant, a college president, and two young women, one an aspiring singer and the other a wealthy heiress. As the text points out, their oath is slightly different from that of the actual Christian Endeavor Society, a national organization of young Christians founded in Maine in 1881 by the Reverend Francis E. Clark. Christian Endeavor members promised in general to "strive to do whatever He would have me do." The Raymond Congregationalists committed themselves to a more detailed and demanding promise. Every single action they took would be subjected to "a literal testing of their Christian discipleship."[38]

Sheldon's formulation was an ingenious move in light of the recently publicized challenges to the text of the Bible. At the very moment when everyday Bible readers were forced to wonder how literally they could take the words of Scripture, the Reverend Maxwell told the Raymond faithful they could literally follow in Christ's steps. But how could literalism be transferred from text to life? The church members soon realized that no two people were likely to agree on what Jesus would do in any situation. Individuals would have to decide for themselves after praying for guidance from the Holy Spirit. There were no guarantees, Maxwell acknowledged, but whatever action one chose had to be carried out "regardless of the results." Doing the Christlike thing might be inconvenient, painful, or risky to one's peace of mind or personal relationships. Regardless of cost, no prudential compromises were permitted.

Much of In His Steps is a paean to the moral consensus of northern Protestant evangelical culture. One character after another imitates "Christ" by imitating reigning Protestant norms. They have no doubt what his position would be on a whole string of political and cultural issues. The newspaper editor, for example, knows that Jesus, in his place, would refuse to publish whiskey and tobacco advertisements, prize-fight coverage, or a Sunday paper. At a deeper level of Protestant consensus, one character after another imitates Christ by seeking out intense and tearful experiences of "suffering." They immerse themselves in "the real world of the people"—the "diseased and sinful humanity" who frequent the city's saloons and are unacquainted with (yet always moved by) Protestant hymns. The central characters are all conveniently well-to-do and can afford to give up some of their ease in exchange for the good feelings they derive from suffering as Jesus did. None of them is threatened by unemployment, only by making less money than they are used to.[39]

But the novel's apparent complacency in making Christ an honorary middle-American Protestant is challenged again and again by its own author. When an unemployed worker asks the Reverend Maxwell what Jesus would do if he were unemployed, the minister draws a blank. He knows neither what Jesus would do if he were out of work nor what Jesus would say if he were a minister confronted with the question. Other characters decide that the most reliable sign of a decision's being Christlike is that it fills one with foreboding. College President Donald Marsh realizes that he will suffer immense psychic pain when he leaves his scholarly haven to combat "rum and corruption." Granted, he is quickly rewarded with public acclaim, yet it was the feeling of personal discomfort that convinced him he knew what Jesus would do. Several characters also find out that imitating Jesus leads to family disarray. The heiress has "a new birth" following her decision to rehabilitate a drunken woman by bringing her home, but it comes at the cost of losing her grandmother's love. The railroad superintendent alienates his wife and daughter when he takes a stand against illegal rebates that costs him his high-paying job.[40]

Sheldon is relentless in repeating Christ's harsh words on the subject of family: "If any man cometh unto me and hateth not his own father and mother and wife and children and brethren and sisters, yea, and his own life also, he cannot be my disciple." He concludes with his usual preachy didacticism that "obedience to their pledge had produced in the heart of families separation of sympathy and even the introduction of enmity and hatred. Truly, a man's foes are they of his own household when the rule of Jesus is obeyed by some and disobeyed by others. Jesus is a great divider of life. One must walk parallel with Him or directly across His way." If *In His Steps* often glibly equated "Christian" virtue with Protestant-American custom, its stringent adherence to Christ's words about family set it at odds with dominant social norms. Sheldon's Jesus was a culture-buster as well as a culture-booster.

In His Steps manages to combine the individual soul-building of liberal Protestant evangelicalism with the moderate Gladden-style Social Gospel. Individual stewardship was the key to social harmony. The well-to-do had to realize that Christian love infused economic relationships and personal relationships alike. Indeed, economic relationships should be turned *into* personal relationships. The merchant of *In His Steps* becomes a zealous backer of "cooperation" and profit-sharing, gets to know all his clerks, and shares prolonged soulful moments with them. The novel beautifully depicts the tense evangelical oscillation between comfort and unsettledness. The singing of hymns is essential to this endless dynamic. Seven hymns to Jesus are sung in the novel. On the one hand, the moment of song is a moment of melting and restoration. It allows people to come together emotionally and share the burdens of their draining soul-struggles. On the other hand, the hymns prompt reflection even as they permit repose. "Jesus, I my cross have taken / All to leave and follow thee," is the first hymn in the book. "Hark the voice of Jesus calling / Follow me, follow me" is the last. Hymn-singing in the novel offers a much-needed respite, but it announces the first step of another weary pilgrimage.[41]

V

Many secular American writers between the Civil War and World War I were as effusive in their praise of Jesus as the preachers and churchgoers were. After Octavius Brooks Frothingham resigned his Unitarian ministry in 1867 to preach "free religion," Jesus remained his guiding light. There was nothing unusual about that: thousands of former church members clutched Jesus for support as they underwent a wrenching personal crisis. A soft, human Jesus was a cushion for many falling-away Christians. Some said it was Jesus himself—the original rebel against tired rules and rites—whose counsel of perfection ("Be ye perfect, as your Father in heaven is perfect," Matt. 5:48) had made them forsake a very imperfect church. The unusual thing about Frothingham is the originality of his thinking about how Jesus fit into a new American era in which, for many former "theists," "all life becomes worshipful, all service is divine, the distinction between sacred and secular is abolished, all days are holy days, and all work is holy work." One might guess that Jesus would be superfluous in such a seamlessly sanctified and secularized world. Frothingham thought the reverse was true. "Jesus is newly born," he wrote in 1867. "The religion of Christ passes away; the religion of Jesus enters on its career. Christendom declines; Jesusdom awakes."[42]

Orthodoxy was dead on both sides of the Atlantic, Frothingham believed, yet America's shift in faith was distinctive. The particularities of the American anti-slavery movement, and the subsequent "rushing of the mighty wind of moral reform into the hot vacuum of the South," had helped discredit "stationary and stubborn establishments" across the board—intellectually as much as institutionally. Yet in America all of the manic unsettling did not turn people away from the pursuit of spiritual experience. "The people are not unreligious; on the contrary, they are 'very religious'; but they are always desiring 'some new thing.' The word 'progress' is always on their lips. . . . Americans are driven by the Spirit, and go whither they know not. . . . They drift in masses, the sport, apparently, of the winds which blow where they list." Americans were so adrift that many were moving toward "Spiritualism," the fanciful spirit-rappings and séances of the mediums. But even many seekers who remained skeptical of methodically communicating with the dead embraced a generally spiritualist preference for boundlessness rather than fixity. A spiritualist outlook dispensed with a Jesus who mediated between divine and human worlds. There was one world only, already infused with the divine. There was no reason to engage any longer in Horace Bushnell's contradictory special pleading, in which humanity was already bathed in the supernatural but Jesus was somehow still more divine than everyone else. It was more than sufficient to retain Jesus as a peerless model of earnest striving for kindness, tenderness, simplicity, justice, and personal independence. Just as there was no need to make Jesus more than a man, there was no need to tether his humanity to his actual life as a first-century Palestinian Jew. Modern biblical scholarship had shown that task to be impossible—the gospels were not life stories of Jesus, but liturgical and theological documents of the early Christian church. In any case, the quest for a life story of Jesus was beside the point. "The historical Christ is not the real Christ," Frothingham wrote in 1862, echoing Theodore Parker (whose biography Frothingham would publish in 1874). "The real Christ is the spiritual, or the Spirit. Without the Spirit, the historical Christ is naught. Without the historical Christ, the Spirit is himself."[43]

Spiritualism was sweeping the American field because it "encourages the vague, vast longing and aspiration of our time. It does not confine like Theism, nor chill like Atheism." The mass of Americans felt "eternal Arms around them, and the breath of all-pervading Spirit in their very souls." The stringent purity of "theism"—rational, creedal, and doctrinal even if also emotional and heartfelt—was in precipitous decline, but that did not mean Americans were turning to "atheism." Atheism was old hat. It had thrived momentarily during the late-eighteenth-century Enlightenment, when "reason" meant overturning "the idols that men worshipped." Now even scientists were spiritualists. "The number of people who believe in no controlling will or law or intelligence or force, in no personal or impersonal Cause, . . . is diminishing steadily and rapidly." The masses of Americans were making sure that their spiritualism was *not* dry and impersonal. They seeded it with "sign and miracle and angel-forms; skies full of guardian spirits; helpers, inspirers, comforters in the air. . . . Spiritualism has revived under more modern shape the demonology and angelology of the Roman Church; it has set up the Jacob's Ladder again, which Rationalism had pulled down, and has re-established communication with beings in another sphere. For this the millions love it, and cling to it, and give up their old religion for it. Faith in the supernatural has changed its base, but it has not lost its charm."[44]

Jesus fit perfectly into a post-theistic and non-atheistic culture in which "spirit" carried Americans beyond such inconvenient obstacles as their own material bodies or their own stifling traditions. There was not even any need to jettison such now-formulaic doctrines as the "Fall, redemption, incarnation, sacrifice, faith, atonement, endless bliss, and perdition." These ancient ideas had lost their clout as revealed truths, but they could now be spiritualized themselves, made poetically true, venerated in "the popular theology under the form of symbolism." That path had been effectively modeled since the early nineteenth century by the Tübingen school of F. C. Baur and even by the much maligned F. D. Strauss. Spiritualizing the historic doctrines of Christianity did not mean consigning them to worldly irrelevance. On the contrary, they had already undergone a new birth akin to that of Jesus. Already the advocates of "Liberty, Equality, Brotherhood, and Progress" in Europe and America were speaking "the same vocabulary that he [Jesus] used." In particular, "the intelligent and energetic working classes" had joined forces with "a host of reformers" and "the great Masters in social science" to give new meanings to old truths. Together they were "taking to heart the cry of Jesus, "The Kingdom of Heaven is at hand." These modern disciples of Jesus were giving new sense to Scripture as well as doctrine. For example, they reworked Christ's comment to Judas—"The poor ye have always with you"—to make it accord with the overall spirit of Jesus and the pressing needs of the day. It became "The poor ye need not have with you longer than you want them."[45]

Frothingham announced a broad secular progressivism infused with the spirit of Jesus. Every pressing social issue could be connected to Christ. Take the subordination of women. Jesus had explicitly recognized "the sanctity of woman," wrote Frothingham. Hence the "religion of humanity" must press "efforts at improving her personal, social, and legal position, which will not be abated, and will not stop till she has all that belongs to her, does all that may be in her power, and throws her full influence into the mass of opinion of her time." Elizabeth Cady Stanton, America's greatest mid-nineteenth-century feminist thinker, had been making precisely that case since 1848. A vociferous anti-clerical polemicist, she nevertheless found Jesus useful and inspirational. Testifying to the U.S. House Judiciary Committee in 1892 in support of woman suffrage, she delivered an existential meditation on the ultimate isolation of every human being. Since each individual was ultimately alone in the world, women could not rely on men for protection or sustenance. "Self-dependence" was necessary for the fullest growth of human personality, but it was required even for plain survival. Jesus, said Stanton, had been forced to learn this truth the hard way. He had told his disciples, "Bear ye one another's burdens," but they abandoned him again and again. He "felt the awful solitude of self. . . . And so it ever must be in the conflicting scenes of life . . . in the tragedies and triumphs of human experience each mortal stands alone."[46]

In her *Woman's Bible* (1895, 1898), Stanton repeated her conviction that "he is deserving of our love and reverence" because he "was born, lived and died as do other men. . . . By showing us the possibilities of human nature he is a constant inspiration, our hope and salvation." She viewed his evident respect for women as a model for men's behavior and as an indictment of the Bible's general mistreatment of the female sex. Hebrew and Christian Scriptures were an almost unbroken litany of anti-woman propaganda, Stanton thought, but Jesus bucked the tide. Women, like men, were drawn to him by his charismatic speech, "his sympathy with the poor and needy," "his indifference to worldly aggrandizement," and even his "great physical beauty" (she did not explain how she knew what he looked like). Given the cultural conventions of his day, his kind attention to women was a miracle in its own right.

"His patience with women," Stanton wrote, "was a sore trial to the disciples," who tried to whisk him away whenever women accosted or entreated him. But "the woman of Canaan" would not be deterred. She waved the disciples aside and talked back to Jesus, a resilience that he rewarded by healing her daughter (Matt. 15:22–28). Remarkably, the vehemently rationalist Stanton did not "doubt the truth" of such miracles. Like many devotees of reason in the nineteenth century, she merged science and faith with an ease that strikes twentieth-first-century rationalists as credulous if not deluded. Jesus performed the healings attributed to him, she believed, but he could not know, given the cultural development of his age, that these were natural, not supernatural, miracles. "The fact of human power developing in so many remarkable ways proves that Jesus's gift of performing miracles is attainable by those who, like him, live pure lives, and whose blood flows in the higher arches of the brain. If one man, at any period of the world's history, performed miracles, others equally gifted may do the same."[47]

Another Jesus-inspired secular reformer founded Chicago's Hull House settlement in 1889. Jane Addams left the church for a secular vocation explicitly patterned after Christ's example. She regarded the settlement movement as the infusion of the gospel into "the social organism itself." Like Frothingham, she refused any distinction between "religion" and the rest of life. "Jesus had no set of truths labeled Religious," she told a gathering of the Ethical

Culture Societies in 1892. His message did not "belong to the religious consciousness, whatever that may be." To him it was simply "a revelation—a life." Her faith was not doctrinal, she said, but "a bent to express in social service and in terms of action the spirit of Christ." Yet what appeared to her as non-doctrinal, as the simple embrace of "Paul's formula of seeking for the Christ which lieth in each man," did amount to a one-sided interpretation of Jesus. It was the Jesus of Jefferson, not Emerson, the Jesus who had a plan for social order, not the Jesus who preached perpetual self-reformation. Stanton, born nearly half a century before Addams, still saw Jesus as both soul reformer and social reformer. She hailed Jesus as healer and exponent of female equality. Addams looked to him as a model activist for the era of labor-capital conflict. She attended the Oberammergau Passion Play in Germany in 1900, and found the experience entrancing because (in her socially focused vision) it depicted "the Radical who dared to touch vested interests," who was put to death by "the money power which induced one of the Agitator's closest friends to betray him."[48]

For Addams the idea of self-discovery smacked of passive navel-gazing, and worse still, it suggested the passivity imposed with special severity upon modern educated women. They had been raised to care about injustice in the world but then barred, as adults, from taking full responsibility for it. "From babyhood," she wrote, "the altruistic tendencies of . . . daughters are persistently cultivated. They are taught to be self-forgetting and self-sacrificing, to consider the good of the whole before the good of the ego. But . . . when the daughter comes back from college and begins to recognize her social claim to the 'submerged tenth,' and to evince a disposition to fulfill it, the family claim is strenuously reasserted." Christ, for Addams as for Stanton, had a message for these women in particular: take the self-realization that was held up to you in school as a universal promise for all human beings, and make it real in the realm of social action. Men such as Emerson, whose family life had provided material and emotional support for a worldly career, did not need the arena of social action as a proving ground for autonomous selfhood. He could apprehend a self-creation that lay prior to social action, although he knew it would demand social action from time to time. His first responsibility was to protect individuality from the conformism that bedeviled radical movements for change just as surely as it did the rest of society. His Jesus was the master of self-reliance who had no sympathy for the demands of any society, progressive or reactionary. Addams's Jesus was the exemplar of social, transformative action.[49]

Addams and Emerson share more ground than their divergent uses of Jesus suggest. His self-reliance did not imply social isolation, but only individual self-creation within freely chosen social networks. Addams's social action did not imply indifference to the cultivation of the self, but only an equal concern for the self-development of the socially excluded. Neither she nor Stanton had experienced Emerson's privilege: the luxury of staying home in a well-stocked study and preaching freedom from convention, or heralding self-renewal through self-forgetting. To them self-forgetting was a formula devised to keep women on task as Christlike suffering servants within their families. Subordination, not conformity, was the primary problem facing women. An individual could be free only when all other individuals were free, when everyone was granted equal access to socially responsible decision-making. Social justice was a prerequisite for anyone's self-creation. Addams would save Christianity by "socializing" it, redeeming it from its status as "religion" and extending its sway to "life" itself. Inversely, she would improve the world by Christianizing it, seeding it with settlements in which real fellowship could crop up among people of starkly divergent backgrounds. Self-realization would start with social action and culminate when each individual could see, as Jesus did, the beauty of a social whole made luminous by the individually unique beings who composed it.

This intertwining of individual growth and social fellowship also informed the thinking of Eugene Debs, leader of the American

Railway Union in the 1890s and head of the American Socialist Party in the 1900s. He regarded Jesus as "the supreme leader," and constantly invoked his name. "Can anyone doubt," he wrote during a 1902 strike in Terre Haute, "where the living Jesus would stand . . . were he in Terre Haute today? . . . The revolutionary Savior always and everywhere stood with and for the poor." Writing in 1912 in praise of Episcopal priest Bouck White's *The Call of the Carpenter*, a depiction of Jesus as prototypical man of the masses, Debs contended that "Jesus Christ belongs to the working class. I have always felt that he was my friend and comrade." White had asked some laborers what they thought of "the Workingman of Nazareth" and without fail they praised Jesus and scolded the churches. "I don't hold with church-going people at all," one man told him, "but I will say this: I believe Jesus Christ was a downright good fellow." "We used to think that Christ was a fiction of the priests," said another worker. "But now we find that he was a man after all like us—a poor workingman who has a heart for the poor. And now that we understand this, we say, He is the man for us."[50]

Hailing Jesus as friend, comrade, and leader helped White's workingmen sustain awareness of themselves as a working class, not just individual wage-earners. They felt Christ loved them with an intimacy reserved for those persecuted as he was. They identified with him because he identified with them. "The cross that topped Calvary's hill," wrote White, "and the Workingman there put lingeringly to death, typed the lot that has been meted out to the wage class through the long historic story. . . . As the death of the Carpenter gathered up and dramatized the crucifixion of the toiling masses, so his triumph over that death is a forecast of democracy's deathless future. . . . [T]hat Workingman of Galilee has apotheosized the labor movement and has made it earth's holiest holy."[51]

White certainly exaggerated Christ's sway over the American working class. There was a good deal of "freethinking" secularism in labor circles before the Civil War, and so much anti-clericalism after the war that Jesus was sometimes disparaged along with the churches. For example, in 1893 William Stead, the English writer whose *If Christ Came to Chicago* would appear the following year, spoke to the city's Trade and Labor Assembly. Before he mounted the platform he was warned that "not five percent of these men ever go to a place of worship. If you say anything about God or Christ or the churches, you will be hissed off the platform." Yet much nineteenth-century evidence supports White's view that working people venerated Jesus. If nothing else, praising Jesus the carpenter allowed workers to get in a dig at the posh Protestant churches. A report in the *Iron Molders' Journal* in 1896 claimed that New York workers attending a clergyman's speech hissed every time he uttered the word "church" and cheered whenever he said "Jesus." A Baptist minister in Chicago who wondered in 1899 "why so many intelligent workingmen are non-churchgoers" attested to their interest in Christ, complaining only that "the Jesus who is applauded by the average workingman is a minimized Jesus Christ, a fictitious person, not the Christ of the gospels." A piece in *Knights of Labor* in 1886 asserted that "Christ must have been a true Knight of Labor, being a carpenter's son; He was a master of His Father's trade. And this proves all Knights of Labor should be Christ-like."[52]

Many secular working people obviously felt much affection for Jesus because he had been made, and remade, in their image. Drawings and paintings of Jesus as a laborer or radical organizer proliferated. The frontispiece of Bouck White's *Call of the Carpenter* was a painting by Balfour Ker (see fig. 15). It depicted a muscle-bound Christ in his carpenter's workshop. His job was unfinished, but he paused to lift his eyes heavenward. Large pieces of timber loomed ominously behind him, announcing a future rendezvous with the cross. The cover of a 1913 issue of the Socialist magazine *The Coming Nation* (published in the Socialist stronghold of Girard, Kansas) featured a Malcolm Fraser painting of another well-built, proletarian-hero Jesus. This "Carpenter of Nazareth" labored on a mountainside, ax in hand, procuring his own work materials. The same issue launched a ten-part series of articles by Bouck White

touting Jesus as a class-conscious revolutionary. The fourth install-
ment, for instance, was entitled "Why Did Jesus Commend Confiscation?"[53]

A robust working-class tradition of composing songs in verse—
and singing them to hymn melodies as well as secular tunes—further cemented the identification of many laborers with Jesus. Asked
to account for his absence from church, "Brother Jones" replied in
"The Church and the Workingman" (1894):

> And the reason I've quit is this:
> The church has lost its way;
> She follows not the path of old;
> And the cross has lost its sway.
> They follow not the laws of Christ,
> That lowly Nazarene;
> The Bible on the shelf is laid;
> And gold is king supreme.
> You've got a church without a Christ,
> Like a ship without a tiller;
> And wreck you will upon the shores of sin,
> With your load of gold and silver.

In 1890 another resourceful writer found a way to get the usually nonviolent Christ to retaliate against "the heartless spoilers /
Who have not a thought sublime / Or a Christian fellow feeling /
For their neighbor's wants and woes / Who put on their stock-
religion / With their Sunday-meeting clothes." If Jesus had commanded a herd of devil-possessed swine to drown themselves
(Matt. 8:32), why not extend the story to all swine, human as well
as animal?

> What are Christ's apostles doing
> To cast out this devil, GREED
> That's today his hands imbruing

In the poor's life-blood; that feed
On the hearts of widows, orphans,
That have struggled to be free?
Oh for some good Christ to drown them
With the swine beneath the sea.[54]

There is a distinctly modern and cosmopolitan aspect to the common nineteenth- and early-twentieth-century identification of the working class with Jesus. Whereas the early Puritan settlers tended to identify themselves with the ancient Jews, a people chosen by God for special responsibility, and African Americans often joined a Hebrew-Scriptural sense of peoplehood to a deep kinship with the suffering Lord, White and Debs stressed the direct analogy between the workers' situation and that of the human Jesus. They were not a "people" like the Jews, Puritans, or slaves, but a culturally diverse "class" of individuals crucified *en masse* by the malefactors of great wealth. The prophets of the Hebrew Scriptures, tireless advocates of social justice, were certainly crucial to Debs and the labor and Socialist movements. But Jesus the teacher could stand for the prophetic tradition even as Jesus the crucified carpenter exposed the egregious injustice of the modern industrial order. His inconvenient counsel of nonresistance to evil could be overshadowed by his love of the poor and his rage over commerce and money-changing in the temple. As a social symbol the crucifixion appealed to Catholic and Protestant laborers alike. Had Debs's Socialists cared to organize African American workers too, the crucifixion could have been easily applied to the calamity of racial lynching— as African American writer W. E. B. Du Bois and many other black Americans in fact applied it.[55]

Debs went beyond identifying the workers' lot with that of Christ's fate on Calvary. Like John Brown before him and Martin Luther King, Jr., after him, he came to see the narrative of Christ's life as the central story of his own. He too had offered himself up for the liberation of his followers. Like Jesus, John Brown, Elijah

Lovejoy (an abolitionist martyr of the 1830s), and Albert Parsons (an anarchist hung after the Haymarket bombing in 1886), Debs preached the gospel of justice and willingly faced death. In his 1902 article "How I Became a Socialist," he depicts himself as an agitator on a lonely pilgrimage of persuasion. Kicked off a train one day by a conductor, he lands ignominiously in a snowbank. Climbing to the top of it, he runs into a policeman "who heard my story and on the spot became my friend." But successfully converting the Pharisee-lawman came at the price of much suffering. Contemplating Jesus helped give him strength to continue. When he was imprisoned in 1894 for his role in the Pullman Strike, and again when he was incarcerated in 1919 for his opposition to American participation in World War I, he tacked a single image to the wall of his cell: a small black-and-white reproduction of Heinrich Hofmann's painting "The Christ," a favorite of many American Protestants in the late nineteenth century. It shows the sorrowful face of a bearded Jesus, topped by the crown of thorns. His shoulder-length hair is parted in the middle, and a halo hovers behind his head. Jesus is wearing a smock, and additional folds of cloth are draped over his right shoulder. He is looking straight at the viewer.[56]

VI

Debs's self-image as a suffering servant of the people reinforced his alienation from the Protestant churches—in his and many workers' eyes the pusillanimous lackeys of the capitalist class. But his attachment to the Hofmann "Christ" reproduction marks him as typical of his Protestant American contemporaries. By the end of the nineteenth century the Protestant majority had abandoned the old Calvinist strictures on visual representations of Christ. Some Protestants, including Lutherans, Episcopalians, and Adventists, had always leaned to the Catholic side on the propriety of images of Jesus. The shift in the nineteenth century took place in the mainstream denominations: the historically Calvinist Congregationalists, Presbyterians, and Baptists, and the historically anti-Calvinist (but still evangelical) Methodists. As with their adoption of the cross in the pre–Civil War period, these Protestants could endorse portraits of Jesus only when they no longer connoted "Catholic." Like the earlier church crosses, Christ images were still barred from the worship space. Evangelical Protestants kept up their vigilance against adoring them as icons. The antebellum crosses had been put on exterior spires. Postbellum depictions of Jesus were printed on lesson cards in Sunday School rooms and placed on the walls of church offices and domestic parlors.[57]

Woodcuts of Christ and other biblical figures were already widely available in printed books (and as separate reproductions) before the Civil War, but Protestants appear to have made broad use of them only after 1860. The quality of low-cost engravings (and then halftones) improved dramatically, and printers could rely on a massively growing Catholic immigrant market while Protestants hemmed and hawed about whether to buy images. Famous Protestant preachers and writers (such as Henry Ward Beecher and his sister Harriet Beecher Stowe) traveled to Europe and wrote about their love for the masterpieces of Christian art. Having images of Christ in one's family Bible or framed on one's parlor wall gradually became a sign of cultivated character, not of Catholic leanings. Beecher's *Life of Jesus, the Christ* (1872) was just one of many illustrated biographies published in the late nineteenth century. The images contributed to the book's basic goal: to overturn "the skeptical school of [biblical] criticism." That school's detached analysis might "lead scholars from doubt to certainty," but it led "plain people from certainty into doubt." Beecher aimed "to produce conviction" by painting a living portrait of Christ's personality. To aid in that effort he used five wood engravings of classic European heads of Christ along with a gorgeous steel-engraved frontispiece copied from his favorite Jesus image: Rembrandt's "Last Supper" (see figs. 29–30).[58]

As Beecher's chosen portraits indicate, Protestants typically restricted their Christ imagery to the Lord's head. That way they
could distinguish themselves from Catholics, who liked to depict
the pulsating, blood-red "sacred heart." The Protestant impulse
was to seek out Christ's full personality in the soft, sorrowful look
of his eyes or the tender tilt of his head. But even after mobilizing
artistic support in his own book, Beecher expressed ambivalence
about visual representations of Jesus. Those who knew Christ by
faith could never be satisfied with a mere human likeness. There
was no way to return in imagination to Jerusalem and see Jesus the
way people had seen him then, as a fellow human being. Even if
the gospel writers *had* described his appearance, the resulting images of him would still divert people from the real Christ. For "it is
not the Jesus who suffered in Palestine that we behold, but the
Christ that has since filled the world with his name.... His very
name is a love-name, and kindles in tender and grateful natures a
kind of poetry of feeling.... We cannot change at will our yearning
and affection for Christ, so as not to see him in the light of our own
hearts." Too much interest in the physical look of Christ's historical
person blocked the actual experience of his eternal personality. "It
is impossible," Beecher wrote, "for art to combine majesty and
meekness, suffering and joy, indignation and love, sternness and
tenderness, grief and triumph, in the same face at one time."
Christ's uniqueness, as Jonathan Edwards had noted, lay in his reconciling of contradictory character traits. Any single visual image
was bound to get him wrong.[59]

If the most worldly of post–Civil War Protestants, Henry Ward
Beecher, was still of two minds about images of Jesus, it comes as
no surprise that most Protestants were dead set against representing him on the stage. Ever since the Puritans, members of Calvinist
churches had found the mere idea of *anyone* acting in the theater
suspect at best, diabolical at worst. Slipping identities on and off as
"roles" suggested frivolous disrespect for the soul, God's seed in
the self. The identity-slippage built into acting was exacerbated by

the unsavory behavior that theaters invariably spawned in the audience as well as the neighborhood. Putting Jesus himself in the floodlights was beyond most evangelical Christians' power to contemplate. Give physical form to the unchanging Word of God? Place that physical form in a theatrical hall? The obscenity of it was dizzying. And a moral cataclysm awaited any actor with the hubris to take on the identity of the savior. Evangelical America had always walked a fine edge: pushing the freedom of individuals to meet Jesus in their individual hearts, then asserting clerical control over the meaning and validity of the meeting. Campaigning against allowing Jesus on the stage was a last-ditch effort to keep control of the Christ image—and of people's encounters with Jesus—inside the churches.

A theatrical producer named Salmi Morse found out how Protestants felt when he tried to mount a reverential Passion Play in San Francisco in 1879 and in New York in 1880. A Jewish convert to Christianity (born Solomon Moses in Germany in 1826), he had studied the Passion Play genre in Jerusalem and Oberammergau, Germany, to be sure his production would follow traditional models. In San Francisco the Catholics were supportive but the Protestants were not. "For one dollar per head," wrote one minister, Morse "would trample under foot the blood of the crucified, and present to the prurient gaze of an unhallowed throng the strange, deep, holy mysteries of our religion." Multiple worries collided in that statement. Selling tickets to a Jesus performance was literally sacrilegious: it exposed sacred things to secular, uninstructed view. It took the holy out of sacred space and abandoned it to the mockeries of the crowd. It put a price on the supposed sight of Christ. For all his purported reverence, Morse was undermining authoritative control of the name of Christ. All admiring speech about Jesus was not equal. To put Christ in the theater was to declare him free of biblical protection. It was to make him incarnate in secular culture and to lose sight of his mysterious transcendence of all culture. In response to Protestant pressure, the Board of Supervisors enacted

a law barring "any play or performance or representation displaying or intended to display, the life of Jesus Christ" from any
"theater, or other place where money is charged for admission."
Morse managed to put on a few performances—minus the crucifixion scene, to placate opponents—before the city ordinance took effect.[60]

In New York Morse's plan to produce the play met even more
opposition, since Catholics and Jews—apparently concerned about
the possible magnitude of the Protestant uproar—were cool on the
idea themselves. The Catholic Church made no official comment,
despite the pleas of the press. Rabbi Gottheil of Temple Emmanuel
said the play was "calculated to stir up the embers of religious hate,
which we have tried for so long to cover up. . . . It will offend the
Jews, and do the Christians no good." The *New York Times* added a
chauvinist tone to the chorus of opposition. It was one thing to attend a Passion Play performed by "ignorant German peasants" at
Oberammergau, where the ritual could be regarded with "sympathetic curiosity." But involving "professional theatrical people" in a
New York City performance "we should resent as an insult to the
common sense of decency." After lengthy legal wrangling, Morse
finally put on a free performance of the play in 1883 in a hall he had
had certified as his "private" residence. But Protestant opposition
succeeded in blocking public performances for many years to
come. After Morse's death, the Irish actor playing Jesus (James
O'Neill, father of Eugene O'Neill) tried unsuccessfully to get permission to produce the play in Omaha (1889) and Waterbury, Connecticut (1891). The only nineteenth-century American commercial
productions of a Passion Play were far off the beaten track of publicity. In Athens, Georgia, for example, an African American company performed it for a black audience in 1888.[61]

For Protestants the late-nineteenth-century stage may have
been the paramount representational threat to Christ's sovereignty,
but the practice of photography also proved worrisome. The most
highly publicized case concerned an elite Anglo American Bosto-

nian named Fred Holland Day. Day was a fine-arts photographer and publisher well known for his association with Oscar Wilde, Aubrey Beardsley, and other British "decadents." In July 1898 he dressed himself up as Jesus, mounted a cross he had erected on a Norwood, Massachusetts, hillside, and (thanks to a concealed cable) shot images from every angle of a tired, thin, but otherwise unblemished Christ. This Jesus was obviously victimized and forsaken, but he was not sweating or bleeding. His crown of thorns had done no more damage to his skull than a Greek wreath. No lance had pierced his side. Day emphasized the sinuous beauty of the torso and the composed tapering of the legs. A loincloth hid the belt that secured his buttocks to the vertical post of the cross. Large nails were positioned to suggest pierced appendages, but the feet rested upon a large wedge of wood and the fingers were still mobile, expressing longing as much as pain. This Christ was strangely comfortable as he waited disconsolately for the end. In some of the images the camera angle accentuated the New England countryside—trees, shrubs, and fields. This dying savior was not a nameless actor calling to mind Jesus in Old Jerusalem. It was F. Holland Day in Norwood asserting some undisclosed connection to Jesus as inherited image or living reality. At the very least it was Day in Norwood pointing out that Christ had come to America culturally and spiritually even if he had come personally and physically only to first-century Palestine (see fig. 32).

Another series of seven images showed Day's head in close-up, topped by the wreath-like crown of thorns, acting out "The Seven Last Words" of Christ (see fig. 31). These photos were displayed in a single rectangular mount, each of the seven frames set off from the others by a classical column. To a twenty-first-century eye they suggest a succession of film frames. Above the pictures each of the seven last words was written out in capital letters, starting with "Father, forgive them, they know not what they do" and ending with "It is finished." In the fall and winter of 1898–1899, Day put "The Seven Last Words" and several crucifixion images on view in

Boston and Philadelphia, and over the following two years displayed them in New York, London, and Paris. Opinions were divided and opinions were strident. Day polled over two hundred
guests he had invited to a private Boston showing. He reported
that two-thirds of them had come "to see the pictures with a very
strong prejudice against them," but that only "one single individual left the exhibition with those same prejudices." Published reviews and comments were all over the spectrum, from disgusted
condemnation to avid support.[62]

These photographs of "Jesus" were not the first to be exhibited.
Several American images of Christ had been produced at least as
early as 1850, when Gabriel Harrison shot a boy (of about ten or
twelve) with a cross resting on his shoulder and called the photo
"The Infant Savior Bearing the Cross." Salmi Morse photographed
his lead actor, James O'Neill, made up as Jesus in 1880, causing a
stir in San Francisco and New York. But Day was the first respected
American art photographer to follow the example of Italian,
French, and Belgian colleagues in trying to treat Jesus as the Renaissance painters had done. Day professed no conventional religious faith, but like many English literary figures going back to
John Keats (whom Day venerated), he saw the artist's sensibility—
and the artist's social isolation—as akin to Christ's. Taking photos
of a sacred subject could promote photography as an art, rather than
the merely "realistic" and technical instrument most people still
took it to be. Sacred photography also let him mark his affection for
his two fellow Keats-lovers and Christ-admirers: Wilde, whom Day
published in America, and the recently deceased Beardsley. Wilde,
Beardsley, and Day all thought Christ modeled suffering as a way
of life that attained beauty and passion despite dislocation and
alienation. The body itself—even the suffering body—deserved
adoration. Unlike Nietzsche, who sensed that the ideal of suffering
had reduced Christianity to a slave religion, Day and his fellow aes-
thetes joined the suffering-servant persona to the celebration of
physical-spiritual beauty. Products of an already heavily secular

formation, they saw no reason to choose between Greek love (eros) and Christian love (agape). Like his early hero Emerson, Nietzsche felt his Christian cultural heritage as stifling—as an obstacle to heroic striving—and did everything in his unprecedented rhetorical power to give it an indecent burial. He shared an ironic accord with Washington Gladden and the entire Calvinist tradition on the incompatibility of the aesthetic life and the Christian life. The Christian's "master passion" was "the love of righteousness," said Gladden in 1884, not "the love of beauty."[63]

Critics at the time were split on the propriety of photographing "Christ" on the cross in the first place. Some objected to all representations of Jesus in photographic form. Painting and sculpture could capture "Divine Inspiration" in a face of Christ, said the editor of *Photogram,* but delivering that kind of "living Jesus" seemed "beyond the power of the camera." Sacred painting and sculpture relied upon the artist's internal inspiration: a vision of Christ took possession of the artist's soul and was transferred to canvas or marble. That representation, already a mere approximation of the original soulful encounter, pointed beyond itself to the real Jesus, who could not be represented. Photography seemed to these critics incapable of pointing beyond itself; it necessarily reduced the invisible to the visible and the ideal to the real. Other negative commentators did not mind photographic images of Christ, any more than putting him on the stage at Oberammergau (Day himself had been there to see the pageant in 1890). But they thought a bohemian such as Day acting the part of Jesus—whatever his intentions—necessarily mocked the sacred.[64]

Even most of those who applauded Day's overture in photographing sacred subjects, and in putting himself in front of the lens, judged the outdoor shots artistic failures. Those photos seemed too barren and cold, as well as poorly shot. They were as unheroic, critics thought, as Thomas Eakins's spent and drooping Christ in his 1882 painting "Crucifixion." Day's outdoor images lacked the tonal and compositional vitality of "The Seven Last

Words." But these pro-Day, anti-Norwood-crucifixion reviewers missed the point that this secular aesthete had made a resolutely orthodox theological claim, however unintentionally. The "Jesus" crucified on a Massachusetts hillside may not have been bleeding from his wounds—the photographer wanted to accentuate the beauty of his body—but he was still defeated and resigned. He was about to give up the ghost. It was a barren and cold moment, undeserving of the vibrant tones that softened the beatific, contorted, ecstatic row of Christ heads uttering the seven last words.[65]

The critics also missed the theological and cultural importance of Day's showing Jesus crucified upon an obviously American landscape. Day rooted the story of Christ's suffering for humankind in American soil. The Norwood photographs insist on locality: Jesus is incarnated culturally, not just biologically, wherever and whenever he is believed in, not only in America but anywhere in the world. All of the cultural incarnations of Christ throughout history are a sign of the power of the Christ story and of the missionaries and armies and governments who have implanted him in human societies. One implication of the Day photos (whether Day intended this message or not) is that cultural incarnation always poses a threat to the integrity of the Christ story. People may prefer to dress Jesus up as a cultural totem rather than embrace a suffering like his. F. Holland Day realized that photography was essentially no different than painting or sculpture. It was an art capable of expressing the photographer's vision of sacred things as well as secular things. Day helped establish photography as an art by showing it was equipped to probe the weightiest of paradoxes: that the sacred was embodied in, yet circumscribed by, culture.

Day's "Jesus" images mark a pivotal moment in the history of photography and the history of artists as a social group, but they also illuminate the cultural history of Christ in America. At the moment when his photos were displayed, American Protestants were fretting about whether, in the words of the Reverend Frank Samuel Child, they had let Jesus become too "weak," too "effeminate," too "etherealized into a beautiful abstraction which has no flesh and blood reality." A wave of Protestant books and sermons faulted the churches for purveying a namby-pamby Christ, a misrepresentation they blamed for the paltry participation of men in religious services and organizations. The church writing of the time appeals for religious "muscularity" as the alternative to stasis or decay (thus seconding the general call for martial vigor that swept through American culture in the 1890s). "The Master was himself thoroughly a man," the Reverend Child kept repeating in his 1894 book. "Jesus is the highest type of manliness . . . , a thoroughly manly man." R. Warren Conant, author of the 1904 volume *The Manly Christ* (reissued in 1915 as *The Virility of Christ*), added that "ancient miracles do not interest the modern man, but he would be interested in a manly Christ who fought his way up and through just as he himself has to do. . . . The men of a strenuous age demand a strenuous Christ."[66]

The theological implication of Day's 1898 photos was that the strenuosity vs. effeminacy tug-of-war, however relevant to the churches' problem of attracting male adherents, was irrelevant to an understanding of Christ. Whether Jesus of Nazareth was muscular or not prior to encountering Pilate (and the gospel writers were notably uninterested in any aspect of Christ's physical frame or appearance), he had been physically vanquished upon the cross. He saved humanity by being overpowered. There was human beauty to be celebrated even in his crucified frame, but the beauty in it had nothing to do with muscularity. It concerned flesh composed, the body in spiritual equipoise. From an orthodox Christian standpoint Day's crucifixion photos erred in making Christ's crucified body smoothly marbled, but they properly conveyed the stark desolation of the Good Friday scene. The crucifixion was a moment of defeat and hopelessness. The disciples scattered in disarray. Resurrection was three days away.

VII

The flurry of enthusiasm for masculinizing images of Jesus flowed from genuine and repeatedly expressed clerical fears that the Protestant churches were themselves losing strength. It is unclear whether the huffing and puffing did much to change either Christian practice or the gender breakdown of the faithful. Some small but culturally revealing shifts certainly occurred. For example, the YMCA refurbished its hymnbook in 1907. Old favorites from the 1867 version, such as "Sweet Hour of Prayer" (1845) and "He Leadeth Me! O Blessed Thought" (1862), were judged too sentimental. They were dropped to make way for "Social Gospel" songs "in which the emphasis is put upon the heroic, active masculine qualities rather than upon the passive virtues and states of mind and feeling." The purest example of such a song may have been "Men Are Wanted," published in the 1910 collection *Manly Songs for Christian Men*.

> *The days are evil and forces mighty*
> *Against the Christ now stand array'd*
> *And He is calling for manly workers,*
> *The strong of heart and unafraid.*
> *Ye men of purpose, arise and serve Him,*
> *The manly man of Galilee,*
> *That you may hasten the day of promise,*
> *The golden day that is to be.*
> *The noise of battle, the clash of armies,*
> *The din of strife, will not be long;*
> *For men are waking to high endeavor*
> *And soon shall swell the victor's song.*
> *Then let our banner, the cross of Jesus,*
> *Be lifted high till all shall see*
> *And hail as Saviour and King all-glorious*
> *The blessed Christ of Galilee.*[67]

But for every "Men Are Wanted" penned to seduce men into the pews, many more new hymns of the old variety were also written, embodying what the YMCA and many Americans, female and male, now considered merely "passive virtues." The old-style hymns were written because many other Americans still believed that the gospels and church tradition rightly emphasized submission to God, a posture that was self-denying but active, not passive. These traditionalists kept alive the eighteenth-century evangelical insistence on meeting Jesus in what the YMCA now deprecated as mere "states of mind and feeling." One of the most popular of the new-yet-old creations was "In the Garden," composed by Charles Austin Miles in 1913. It tells the story of a submissive yet hardly passive disciple of Jesus who happened to be female: Mary Magdalene. It was her faith, not her sex, that mattered. Like many Protestants historically barred from making visual representations of Jesus, Miles compensated by creating a verbal-aural representation whose narrative detail allowed singers and listeners to imagine visual scenarios on their own.

Early on the first day of the week after the crucifixion, according to John's Gospel, Mary went to the sepulcher seeking Christ's body. She saw a man, and "supposing him to be the gardener, saith unto him, Sir, if thou have borne Him hence, tell me where thou hast laid Him, and I will take him away" (20:15). In a single intimate word—"Mary"—Jesus let her know that it was he. Taking Magdalene's reported experience at the tomb, Miles could restate in story form the evangelical longing for an intense encounter with Christ—a meeting so intense as to be wholly unique in every instance. The venerable Puritan and Catholic tradition of seeing oneself (whether one is male or female) as a bride of Christ is transposed in Miles's story into a passionate and secret garden meeting in which "He tells me I am his own." The Puritans' knowledge that Christ will keep his distance even from his intimate beloved is captured in the final verse. You enter the garden alone, and for all the ecstasy of the meeting, you depart alone. You do not get to "have" your lover. You are left with your yearning, a voice in your ear and a melody in your heart.

> *I come to the garden alone*
> *While the dew is still on the roses*
> *And the voice I hear falling on my ear*
> *The Son of God discloses.*
> *Refrain: And He walks with me, and He talks with me,*
> *And He tells me I am His own;*
> *And the joy we share as we tarry there,*
> *None other has ever known.*
> *He speaks, and the sound of His voice,*
> *Is so sweet the birds hush their singing,*
> *And the melody that He gave to me*
> *Within my heart is ringing.*
> *Refrain: And He walks . . .*
> *I'd stay in the garden with Him*
> *Though the night around me be falling,*
> *But He bids me go; through the voice of woe*
> *His voice to me is calling.*[68]

SEVEN

JESUS WAS CERTAINLY NOT A CHRISTIAN

I

The invention of moving pictures in the 1890s had a dramatic effect on the cultural incarnation of Jesus in America. Remarkably, the concerted Protestant effort to keep him off the stage did not turn into a campaign to bar him from the screen. Protestants were not even neutral on the question: they joined Catholics in welcoming Christ to cinema. Jesus films were good evangelizing tools, especially among urban immigrants with limited English-language skills. And Jesus films gave upright Protestants a chance to enjoy movies, otherwise off-limits for the pure and respectable. Picture houses raised the moral hackles of even the most liberal ministers. Baptist preacher Harry Emerson Fosdick, a modernist who welcomed all Christians to his communion table in Montclair, New Jersey, resisted even the creation of a movie theater in 1911. He changed his mind only when he realized that Montclair youths were going elsewhere for their viewing pleasure. Much as he disapproved of "the photo-play invasion," he concluded that "properly regulated exhibitions . . . would obviate the necessity of young people going to Newark, where temptation assails them."[1]

Film historian Charles Musser has shown that early Jesus movies—including a film version of Salmi Morse's Passion Play shot on a New York City rooftop in 1898—struck Christians across the Catholic-Protestant spectrum as both respectable and compellingly spiritual. The movies seemed respectable because the way had been prepared by high-brow lecture-slide shows presenting photographic images of the Oberammergau Passion Plays of 1880 and 1890. (The Bavarian players performed it at ten-year intervals.) When the Morse film was shown, its separate reels—hard to watch for more than a few minutes at a time because of the jumpy projection—were intermixed with familiar music, slides, and commentary. The very same middle-class Protestants who turned up their noses at working-class nickelodeons around the turn of the century streamed into auditoriums featuring certifiably moral fare such as the film of Morse's Passion. Thirty thousand people saw it during its twice-a-day, three-month run at Manhattan's Eden Musee in 1898. The show would have gone on longer had the battleship *Maine* not blown up in Cuba. Films of the Spanish-American War soon swept other shows off the screen. The Musee still put on periodic performances of the filmed Passion Play, and two touring companies took the spectacle to the provinces.[2]

The first experience of seeing a person moving across a screen seemed miraculous to many viewers. Imagine the spiritual sensation for believing Christians when that person happened to be Jesus. Audiences were awed as Christ came startlingly to life in a darkened room on a two-dimensional surface. Spiritualist mediums had produced "spirit photographs" that enjoyed a faddish currency in the mid-nineteenth century, but film made the spiritual visible without apparent trickery. When a Bohemian Passion Play film was shown in Boston in 1898, accompanied by a fastidious lecture and choral music, the *Boston Herald* reported a transfixed clientele. It was composed of "not only regular theatergoers, but a considerable contingent of people who are much oftener to be found at church than attending a play." The "cinematographic

Fig. 27— **Fourteen Stations of the Cross**, James S. Baillie Company, 1845

CHAPTER XXXVIII.

THE VICTORY.

"Thanks be unto God, who giveth us the victory."

AVE not many of us, in the weary way of life, felt, in some hours, how far easier it were to die than to live?

The martyr, when faced even by a death of bodily anguish and horror, finds in the very terror of his doom a strong stimulant and tonic. There is a vivid excitement, a thrill and fervor, which may carry through any crisis of suffering that is the birth hour of eternal glory and rest.

But to live, — to wear on, day after day, of mean, bitter, low, harassing servitude, every nerve dampened and depressed, every power of feeling gradually smothered, — this long and wasting heart martyrdom, this slow, daily bleeding away of

Fig. 28—**Jesus and Uncle Tom**, *Uncle Tom's Cabin*, John P. Jewett, 1853

And as they were eating. Jesus took bread and
blessed it, and brake it, and gave it
to the disciples. *Matt. XXVI. 26.*

Restored. Painted. & Engraved. after. Leonardo da Vinci's Milan Fresco.
"THE LAST SUPPER."
BY W.E. MARSHALL.
EXPRESSLY FOR H.W.BEECHER'S. LIFE OF JESUS THE CHRIST.

Fig. 29—Head of Christ Modeled on Leonardo Da Vinci's "Last Supper,"
frontispiece to Henry Ward Beecher, *The Life of Jesus, the Christ* (1871)

1. EARLIEST KNOWN, FROM CATACOMBS OF ST. CALIXTUS

2. FROM EMERALD INTAGLIO OF EMPEROR TIBERIUS

3. AFTER FRANCISCO DI FRANCIA

4. AFTER ALBRECHT DÜRER

5. AFTER PAUL DE LA ROCHE

HEADS OF CHRIST

Fig. 30—**Assorted Heads of Christ,**
Henry Ward Beecher, *The Life of Jesus, the Christ* (1871)

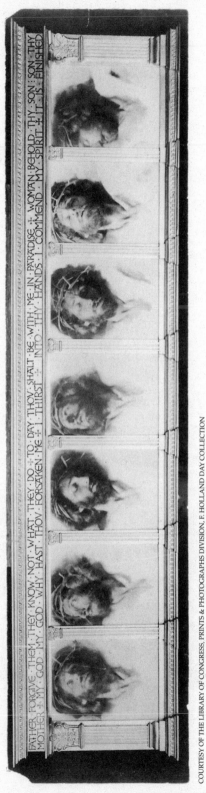

Fig. 31—**Seven Last Words**, F. Holland Day

Fig. 32—**Crucifixion,** F. Holland Day

Fig. 33—**Drawing** by Charles Cullen,
frontispiece to Countee Cullen, *The Black Christ and Other Poems*,
copyright 1929 by Harper & Brothers, renewed 1957 by Ida M. Cullen.

What Would Jesus Drive?

To some, the question might seem amusing. But we take it seriously. As our Savior and Lord Jesus Christ teaches us, "Love your neighbor as yourself." *(Mk 12:30-31)*

Of all the choices we make as consumers, the cars we drive have the single biggest impact on all of God's creation.

Car pollution causes illness and death, and most afflicts the elderly, poor, sick and young. It also contributes to global warming, putting millions at risk from drought, flood, hunger and homelessness.

Transportation is now a moral choice and an issue for Christian reflection. It's about more than engineering—it's about ethics. About obedience. About loving our neighbor.

So what *would* Jesus drive?

We call upon America's automobile industry to manufacture more fuel-efficient vehicles. And we call upon Christians to drive them.

Because it's about more than vehicles— it's about values.

Rev. Clive Calver, Ph.D.
President, World Relief

Rev. Richard Cizik
Vice President for Governmental Affairs, National Association of Evangelicals

Loren Cunningham
Founder, Youth with a Mission
President, University of the Nations

Rev. David H. Englehard, Ph.D.
General Secretary, Christian Reformed Church in North America

Millard Fuller
Founder & President, Habitat for Humanity International

Rev. Vernon Grounds, Ph.D.
Chancellor, Denver Seminary

Rev. Steve Hayner, Ph.D.
Past President, InterVarsity Christian Fellowship

Rev. Roberta Hestenes, Ph.D.
International Minister, World Vision

Rev. Richard Mouw, Ph.D.
President, Fuller Theological Seminary

Rev. Ron Sider, Ph.D.
President, Evangelicals for Social Action

Sponsored By THE EVANGELICAL ENVIRONMENTAL NETWORK
10 East Lancaster Ave., Wynnewood, PA 19096   www.WhatWouldJesusDrive.org
Partial list of signatories. Affiliations listed for identification only.

Fig. 34—**A 2002 updating of the 1896 novel** *In His Steps*

Fig. 35—**A 1998 addition to "The Apple Celebrity Collection"**

method," wrote the *Herald*, "showed its advantage for a sacred play over both living figures and mere pictures in panorama." For film "disposes forever of the objection of irreverence."

At first the moving images struck the Boston viewers as nothing but "a representation of a representation," pictures of Bohemian peasants acting out the Passion. The audience braced itself for the usual sacrilege of an actor "suggesting in flesh and blood what Christ might have looked like when he was on earth." But, said the *Herald*, they soon realized that moving images extracted "the flesh and blood" from the representation without imposing the "dead calm" of a still photo. Film made the body of Christ spiritual, took out "the personal element" while adding "an element of mystery." "So absorbing become the pictures that the onlooker, from merely regarding the figures as the real, live people who acted the play in Bohemia, begins to forget all about what was done in Bohemia and henceforth is lost in the thought that the faces and forms before him are the real people who lived in Palestine 2000 years ago, and with their own eyes witnessed the crucifixion of Christ." From the *Herald*'s description of Christ's spiritualized body, this filmed image actually sounds much more like a rendering of the resurrected Jesus than of the crucified Jesus. As in F. Holland Day's photos, the crucified body is aesthetically purified rather than waled and punctured.[3]

The first feature-length life of Jesus on American screens, *From the Manger to the Cross* (1912), took the opposite tack, depicting the Passion in disturbingly graphic detail. The scourging of Jesus is so violent and prolonged that the Roman soldier whipping Christ's back has to quit from exhaustion. Jesus is severely bloodied and bowed before he gets to Calvary. Yet he still has enough energy to squirm in pain and fright when his feet and hands are nailed to the cross. Once he is on the cross the camera lingers on his physical and mental suffering, and the last image in the film is of Jesus expiring. (The Eden Musee production, and French Passion films shown in America before 1912, all included the resurrection.) The crucifixion sequence was "almost too ghastly in its strict realism" for one industry reviewer, but another said that all of the film's seventy-five scenes, including the suffering and death, were marked by "chaste decorum." The many clergymen who attended an invitation-only premiere in the auditorium at Wanamaker's Department Store in Manhattan were apparently pleased with the film, though some feared it would be distributed to common-garden "picture houses." Those venues featured contaminating vaudeville acts along with projected images. As one of the reviewers put it, "it would be both bad taste and artistically ineffective to sandwich [*From the Manger to the Cross*] between a juggler's act and a Broadway song and dance, just as it would be absurdly out of place to read Milton's poems in the subway."[4]

There is no telling whether these viewers in 1912 were still awed by the magic of film itself, or whether the believing Christians in the audience felt that a Jesus on film was truer, more spiritual, than a Jesus on the stage or in a still photo. We can guess from the contemporary reviews that most Protestant onlookers were by this time as comfortable as the Catholics with moving images of Jesus. By 1912 the view that visual representation of the sacred was necessarily irreverent seems to have dissipated. Those who still had doubts about putting Jesus on the screen may have been mollified by two prominent features of *From the Manger to the Cross*. First, it was filmed entirely on location in Palestine—for Protestants as for Jews an emotionally gripping spiritual homeland. (Catholics loved the Holy Land too, but their attachment to Rome made them much less passionate than Protestants or Jews about biblical sacred places.) Second, the visual images in the film were interspersed with the written Word. Long quotations from the King James Version introduced each scene. In a sense the film took its cue from the massive illuminated Bibles that piled up in affluent Protestant parlors in the late nineteenth century. The images illustrated the text. The movie opened with a detailed map of Palestine, followed by the words of Luke 1:26–27 introducing Mary and Joseph. The final shot, after Christ's chin had dropped to his chest, offered the culturally holy benediction of John 3:16: "For God so loved the world, that he gave his only begotten Son, that whosoever believeth in him should not perish, but have everlasting life." Far from simply replacing words with images, *From the Manger to the Cross* systematically interlaced them.[5]

The film must have displeased Christian critics of "the pictures of Christ which traditional art has furnished us—a feminine face, hair parted in the middle, long flowing locks, all gentleness, tenderness, femininity," as Lyman Abbott complained in 1893. Jesus movies in the silent era were positively retrograde from the standpoint of muscularity. Filmmakers may have been so intent on justifying visual representations of Christ, and on using Christ to help clean up the image of the movie industry, that they gave viewers only the most saintly and ethereal depictions of him. Even D. W. Griffith's masterpiece of filmmaking (and heinous celebration of white supremacy), the Civil War and Reconstruction saga *The Birth of a Nation* (1915), got into the act. Griffith capped off his rousing finale—"The Parade of the Clansmen," set to the tune of "Dixie"—with an appearance by a thoroughly feminized, resurrected Christ. This giant-sized but "gentle Prince in the Hall of Brotherly Love in the City of Peace" was superimposed by double exposure over an idyllic vision of an all-white gathering. The jubilant, energetic crowd stood for Griffith's hope of reconciliation between white peoples north and south, and Jesus blessed them with an approvingly raised hand. This hope of tranquil white rebuilding was shared by Baptist preacher-turned-lecturer Thomas Dixon, Jr., author of the book *The Clansman* (1905), from which *The Birth of a Nation* was adapted. Before writing the novel he had himself traveled around the northeast presenting "The Story of Jesus," a lecture accompanied by music and illustrated with slides of a European Passion Play.[6]

Griffith's films remind us that anti-progressives can trot Jesus out as a social advocate just as easily as progressives can. Christ was not the sole property of liberal reformers in the early twentieth century any more than he was of abolitionists before the Civil War. In *The Birth of a Nation* Griffith shrewdly used a feminized Christ's pacifism as a weapon against northern agitators, armies, or carpet-baggers who preferred conflict to accommodation. The anti-reform "Nazarene" in Griffith's innovative film *Intolerance* (1916)—a dazzling, unheard-of interweaving of four independent narratives, one of them the Passion story—was also tailored to vilify the morally strident interventions of northern do-gooders. This dainty-looking Christ was set off against the stony, hypocritical Pharisees (one of them played by Erich von Stroheim, later a famous actor and director), who vaunted their own piety and faulted everyone else. It was brilliant interpretive legerdemain to take the nonresisting Jesus and make him, instead, nonjudgmental. His unmuscular bearing corresponded to his morally *laissez-faire*, anti-reformist bent—a perfect double inversion of the northern Social Gospel's he-man Christ as symbol of ardent social interventionism.

The Jesus of *Intolerance* threw down a judgment on the modern Pharisees whose separate story opened the film. These tight-lipped "ladies banded together for the 'uplift' of humanity" were devious plotters, just like the holier-than-thou abolitionists whom Griffith placed at the start of *The Birth of a Nation*. Both groups turned against Jesus, in Griffith's rendition, by provoking violence. His sanctimonious abolitionists in *Birth of a Nation* brought about the Civil War. His even more cartoon-like early-twentieth-century female reformers caused industrial violence: their campaign against working-class drinking, prostitution, and crime siphoned off so much money in donations from hard-pressed industrial magnates that they had to cut workers' wages. The result was strikes and pitched battles in the streets. Let Jesus be a lesson, said a Griffith caption, to those unsexed women who "turn to reform as a second choice . . . when they cease to attract men." Far from passing judgment upon the habits of others, Jesus defended even "the woman taken in adultery." And he gladly turned the water into wine at the marriage in Cana. Griffith had no qualms about drafting Christ into political service against the Prohibitionists and other redeemers of working-class culture. But he was very careful to keep Jesus personally dry. His Christ hovers beatifically on a stairway while the marriage guests imbibe his miraculous wine. When one of his disciples later offers him a goblet, he waves it off. He does not object to drinking—he just has better things to do, such as pondering his fate. Charles Sheldon's parishioners in *In His Steps* asked, "What would Jesus do" about saloons? They replied without a moment's hesitation that he would shut them down. D. W. Griffith gave the opposite answer in *Intolerance:* Christ would let the substantially Catholic working class enjoy its beer and whiskey.[7]

The blockbuster Jesus film of the silent era was Cecil B. DeMille's *The King of Kings* (1927). Like Fred Niblo's equally fabulous *Ben-Hur* (1925), it played in high-fare commercial theaters rather than picture houses, reducing its reach but protecting its purity. At first glance H. B. Warner's Jesus looked like one more feminized Christ, composed, serene, languid. But reviewers at the time had trouble deciding what to make of the tall, stately, and facially chiseled Warner, who was fifty years old when the movie was shot. (Jesus was only about thirty-three at the time of the crucifixion.) *Variety*'s reviewer thought that "Mr. Warner is the accepted likeness of Christ," but his *New York Times* counterpart felt that "Mr. Warner's countenance is not the general conception of that of Jesus." DeMille said in his memoirs thirty years later that Warner's Christ countered all "the effeminate, sanctimonious, machine-made Christs of second-rate so-called art. . . . This Man of Nazareth was a man, with a body hard enough to stand 40 days of fasting and long journeys on foot and nights of sleepless prayer." But he shot Warner in soft focus and kept a spotlight on the top of his head, as if he were transfigured all the time, not just during the Transfiguration on the mountain (described in the synoptic gospels—e.g., Matthew 17:1–8—but not shown in the film). This ploy to make him look both divine and human succeeded only in making him look odd, disembodied, and detached from his surroundings. No wonder the

critics could not decide if this was a credible Christ. He was stat-
uesque rather than intimate. His generally cool mien, combined
with the facial sags of a fifty-year-old (his gaunt lines only partially
obscured by the makeup and soft focus), made him look much
more like the usual image of God the Father than God the Son.[8]

DeMille thought he was masculinizing Jesus, but the character he actually masculinized was the young, virile, and handsome
Judas. This actor looked like a member of *Stover at Yale*'s football
eleven rather than Christ's evangelical twelve. (After the Last Supper he morphed into a tousle-haired madman, writhing in guilt
for having sold Jesus out.) DeMille gave unusual plot prominence
to this athletic, affluent Judas and to a Mary Magdalene who at the
start of the film is wealthy, frivolous, and barely clothed. DeMille
ingeniously began the story not with the usual Nativity sequence—Mary and Joseph in search of a room for the night, the
wise men seeking their star—but with a wholly nonbiblical fantasy about this classic "fallen woman." The fleshy and exuberant
Mary Magdalene lounges in her ornate palace stroking her pet
tiger and taking bets from her male admirers: Will she succeed in
winning back her lover Judas from his recent infatuation with a
healer-carpenter from Nazareth? She sets off in her zebra-driven
chariot to deprogram Judas, only to fall under Christ's spell herself. Of course Jesus deprograms *her*, exorcising the Seven Deadly
Sins that hold her in their collective grip. Each of the sins is depicted as a writhing female ghost struggling to stick with Mary.
Finally vanquished by Christ's power, they let go. Suddenly shamed,
Mary covers her exposed flesh. Christ has cleaned her up, and by
extension has helped clean up the film industry. DeMille, meanwhile, got to have the cake of high-mindedness while eating it too.
The bawdy opening created the same aura of titillation he had
generated with sexual innuendo in his earlier lavish spectacle *The
Ten Commandments* (1923).

Like *From the Manger to the Cross*, *King of Kings* used captions
from the King James Version of the New Testament. But DeMille

freely adapted his captions and used them out of their original contexts. *King of Kings* is not an illuminated Bible on the order of *From the Manger to the Cross*. His scenes are not visualizations of New Testament passages. Many of his captions quote the gospel, but many others express DeMille's opinions. The script is especially single-minded about making villains out of Caiaphas, the Jewish high priest, and his entourage. The script played to standard anti-Semitic stereotypes by instructing viewers that "Caiaphas cared more for revenue than religion." The anti-Semitism gets worse, if that is possible. In an invented conversation with Judas, Caiaphas threatens to kill all of the disciples. And one of his lieutenants accosts a small boy whose broken leg Jesus has healed. This stock villain is about to strike the boy with a cane when Peter overpowers him. At the end Caiaphas's temple goons bribe the Jewish populace to get them to demand the execution of Jesus. B'nai B'rith told its members to boycott the film because it treated the Jewish authorities of Christ's time "with hatred and contempt."[9]

In his 1959 memoir DeMille voiced shock that anyone, especially Jews, should have faulted his movie. After all, his film had featured "the greatest Jew who ever lived." He claimed to have gone to "great lengths to show that the Jewish people of Jesus' time followed and heard Him gladly, that His death came at the hands of a few unrepresentative, corrupt religious leaders and the cowardly and callous Roman government." But DeMille entirely missed the point of the criticisms a string of writers had made of *King of Kings*, of earlier Jesus films, and of the Passion Plays at least since 1901, when Philadelphia Rabbi Joseph Krauskopf published his book *A Rabbi's Impressions of the Oberammergau Passion Play* (which went through at least eight printings). Anti-Semitism was structured into the genre even when vicious ethnic stereotypes or global indictments of the entire Jewish people were avoided or downplayed. To depict Pilate as "cowardly" was already to arbitrarily accept the Gospel of John (which says Pilate was "afraid" [19:8]) over the other gospels, which never assert or imply that he was cowardly. To make Pilate a coward bossed around by Caiaphas was to make an unjustified choice, even if a conventional one.

The anti-Semitism of *King of Kings* lies in the obvious exaggerations and inventions regarding Caiaphas and his thugs, but it resides even more in DeMille's unquestioning embrace of traditional characterizations. Readily available scholarship, such as Jewish scholar Joseph Klausner's *Jesus of Nazareth* (1925), made it plain that the gospels quite likely exaggerated the Jewish responsibility for the crucifixion—and minimized Pilate's role—in order to placate the Roman authorities of their own time. At the very least there was ample reason in the 1920s to make Pilate co-responsible for the execution of Jesus, rather than putting all the blame on a venal Caiaphas and his malicious cronies. *King of Kings* embraced the long Passion Play tradition of blaming the Jews and did so in utter assurance of its own innocence.[10]

DeMille's abundant captioning from the King James Bible might lead one to suspect that *King of Kings* is a merging of the biblical Word with visual imagery. But the film set a new precedent that later Jesus films would follow: much more weight is assigned to Christ's miracles than to his teachings. The miracles are far more impressive on film, whether silent or sound, than the often elliptical sayings are. Even the pithy Sermon on the Mount is a dramatic bore. *The King of Kings* does not show it, and many later Jesus films follow suit. DeMille's script offers a caption at one point that implies we are going to see some "preaching," but what we get is Jesus gathering the little children around him, the raising of Lazarus, and the cleansing of the temple. DeMille, master of crowd scenes, never supplies a crowd listening to Jesus speak and never has Christ utter a parable. Twentieth-century visual culture does not eliminate the written word, any more than the pre-modern spread of literacy eliminated oral performance. But visual culture does influence which written words get retained and repeated, just as literacy reshaped the formation and reception of the spoken word.[11]

In *King of Kings* the public words that survive are the terse phrases that accompany visually exciting healing miracles. "Be thou clean," Jesus tells Mary Magdalene as the Seven Deadly Sins struggle for her soul. "Lazarus, come forth," he says to the entombed, bandaged man. In both cases the assembled onlookers then watch the miracles unfold in silence. By contrast, Christ's post-resurrection appearances are wordy and look completely unmiraculous. Jesus shows himself to the tight circle of Mary Magdalene and the disciples in order to praise those who believe in him *without* having seen him (unlike the spiritually challenged Thomas, who doubts what he cannot see with his own eyes). And he gives the disciples their marching orders for the evangelization of the world. He looks no different resurrected than when he was alive, since DeMille made his mortal body glow too. In a wonderfully oxymoronic phrase, the *Variety* reviewer praised *King of Kings* for being so "realistically supernatural." DeMille evidently made the supernatural seem real for some viewers. The question remained whether the mechanical reproduction of images of the supernatural would ultimately seem so "real" as to be boring, just as onscreen preaching already was. Vital preaching may require a live interaction between orator and audience. The mystery of the supernatural may require the real presence of invisibility.[12]

Of course Christ the teacher had taken a backseat to Christ the person in some brands of American Protestantism long before the arrival of film. DeMille supported that trend by putting substantial emphasis on Christ's looks. The Jesus of *From the Manger to the Cross* had been hailed for being impersonal, hence universal. By contrast, H. B. Warner's Jesus in *King of Kings,* while glowingly supernatural, was fully individualized. His image came close to being a stationary, Catholic-style icon. Our first sight of him—in an inspired use by DeMille of visual language to develop plot and disclose character—is through the eyes of a faithful young girl whom Jesus is curing of blindness. We watch with her as she first makes out a ray of light. Cut to a caption with Jesus saying, "I come a light into the world, that whosoever believeth in me shall not abide in darkness" (John 12:46). Then we squint out with her as she gradually picks up his face. First it is a vague halo, then the head and shoulders of a beaming, bearded Christ. The scene calls to mind those stupefied movie viewers at the Eden Musee in 1898 for whom Jesus came into focus on film for the first time.

II

Two of DeMille's advisers on *King of Kings* were the father-son team of the Reverend William E. Barton, a Congregational minister, and Bruce Barton, a magazine writer and advertising man. Barton the elder was the well-known author of *Jesus of Nazareth: His Life and the Scenes of His Ministry* (1903), and of a popular biography of Lincoln. Barton the younger, author of *A Young Man's Jesus* (1914) during the prewar masculinity craze, was riding high in 1927. His best-selling book *The Man Nobody Knows: A Discovery of the Real Jesus* (1925) had become a topic of general cultural debate, and his follow-up work on the Bible, *The Book Nobody Knows* (1926), was selling briskly. *The Man Nobody Knows* asked, What would Jesus do if he were trying to spread the Word in 1920s America? "He would be a national advertiser today, I am sure," Barton wrote, "as he was the great advertiser of his own day." Barton—cofounder of the ad firm Batten, Barton, Durstine, and Osborne in 1919—was plainly Christ's equal at creating buzz: "The parable of the Good Samaritan," his book asserted, "is the greatest advertisement of all time." *The Man Nobody Knows* became a best-seller because catchy provocations like that made it a *cause célèbre* for two large groups: Christians of all stripes who thought Jesus was endangered in modern America, and secular critics who thought modern America was endangered by the Christians' Jesus.[13]

His kowtowing to "business" made Barton the writer many politically liberal Christians loved to hate in the late 1920s, but his theological liberalism made him the one they hated to admit they loved. The *Christian Century* derided his indifference to the Social Gospel but said that *The Man Nobody Knows* "in many respects is really an admirable piece of work." The book was so profoundly emblematic of liberal Protestantism that they could not help but like it. For all his laughable sales pitches about Jesus as a businessman, Barton also presented Christ as a modern, cosmopolitan cultural hero. What made the Jesus saga the "finest, most exalted success story," in Barton's words, was Christ's skill at meeting the problem faced by "so many small town boys." Jesus "was not at all sure where he was going when he laid down his tools and turned his back on the carpenter shop." But like "each of us [who] has to venture on Life as on to an uncharted sea," he overcame his doubts about himself and forged a firm adult identity. Barton's Jesus migrated from country to city, left localism and parochialism behind. Christ was admittedly a first-century Palestinian Jew, but he transcended his upbringing by attaining critical self-consciousness and discovering a trans-historical, universal truth: the good life was the life committed to "ideals."[14]

That formulation was a near-perfect encapsulation of much early-twentieth-century liberal Protestantism. For liberal Christians Barton's book seized the ground of modernity abandoned by evangelical Protestantism (in the person of William Jennings Bryan) at the Scopes Trial in 1925. Jesus was not an apocalyptic prophet, not a charismatic healer, not a dazzling miracle-worker, not a submissive Son obeying a sovereign Father, but a peace-loving exponent of rational and humanitarian ideals. The ideal that Jesus cherished above all others, said Barton, was "service." And the ultimate test of his commitment to that ideal came when "the people" (John 6:15) prepared to "come and take him by force, to make him a king." At that tense moment Christ faced a decision confronted by very few small-town boys. "Why not be their king?" Barton has him ask himself. He could become another Solomon or David. But accepting the call to be king would compel him to rule rather than humbly serve. So Jesus reconciled himself to dying. That was the only alternative to self-contradiction. He did not want to die. Barton was sure of that because the old image of Christ as "weak and unhappy and glad to die" had been so thoroughly buried by the muscularity campaign. His Jesus manfully accepted death as the lesser of two evils. He died not out of loyalty to his Father, not to redeem the world from sin, but out of uncompromising devotion to his chosen ideal of service.[15]

Traditionalist Christians often liked the book for its no-nonsense endorsement of business, and all of them savored its old-fashioned individualism and avoidance of the liberals' Social Gospel. But they were still put off by its theological liberalism. Before the book was published William Jennings Bryan himself complained to Barton's publisher about the short shrift it gave to the supernatural character of Christ. Other conservatives agreed that Barton was a "modernist of the rank type," as one Arno Gottschall expressed it in a self-published attack on the book. Modernists such as Barton, in Gottschall's view, attacked the gospel by denying its historicity and its miracles. But Barton was so blasé about the miracles that he did not bother even to deny them. Take them or leave them, he said. Just be sure that if you take them, you do not arbitrarily exclude the wine miracle at Cana because of your niggling aversion to alcohol. A handful of conservatives did decry Barton's claim that Jesus "thought of his life as *business*." "Can the conception of Christ as a business man . . . bring us nigh unto God?" asked Arno Gaebelein, editor of *Our Hope* and author of *The Christ We Know* (1927). "No! Nothing but the blood of Jesus." Jesus, said Gottschall, "did not leave Heaven and come to earth in order to teach men the tricks of trade, or how to promote commercial enterprises." Here conservative dismay overlapped with liberal outrage at Barton's inducting Jesus into the Chamber of Commerce. "Under Mr. Barton's hand," editorialized the *Christian Century*, Jesus "is in fact reduced to moral proportions which make him a kind of sublimated Babbitt . . . the typical Rotarian go-getter who knows how to work and how to make other people work for him."[16]

But liberal critics, thanks to the priority they assigned to biblical scholarship, had a more devastating criticism to make. It was bad enough that Barton had made Jesus pro-business. Still worse was his portrayal of Christ as an advocate of worldly success in the first place. As the *Christian Century* put it, "the gospel of Jesus is not a gospel of obvious success, but of ultimate success through obvious failure." Barton asserted that Jesus "picked up twelve men from the bottom ranks of business and forged them into an organization that conquered the world." But "the real Jesus" whom Barton claimed to have discovered built no such organization. That achievement was the work of Paul, Peter, James, and the local leaders, male and female, who created an organized Jesus movement of Jews and Gentiles after the resurrection. Barton's most outrageous move, from a Christian standpoint, was to commandeer one of Christ's favorite paradoxes—"He that findeth his life shall lose it; and he that loseth his life for my sake shall find it" (Matt. 10:39)—and use it as the key to self-advancement. Barton construed selflessness as the way to get ahead. "Whoever will find himself at the top must be willing to lose himself at the bottom." Forgetting about one's salary, privileges, or prestige was a winning strategy. Judas, the disciple who "looked out for Number One," lost everything. Barton gathered testimony from Charles Evans Hughes, Henry Ford, and other great men of accomplishment to prove that Christ's plan worked. If a man "gives his whole self" to being productive, Ford told him, "the money will roll in so fast that it will bury him if he doesn't look out."[17]

Perhaps the most astute Christian critic of *The Man Nobody Knows* was Reinhold Niebuhr, a rising-star liberal preacher from Detroit. His biting assessment, entitled "Jesus as Efficiency Expert," showed how cultural groups—in this case, businessmen—exploited Jesus under the guise of praising him. "Through Mr. Barton the business world looks upon Jesus and makes a frantic effort to preserve its moral self-respect in investing his life with the 'success' ideals which it so passionately cherishes." Barton was doing for business in general, and the advertising profession in particular, what DeMille was doing for the motion-picture industry with *The Ten Commandments* and then *The King of Kings:* using Jesus to upgrade its image. But Niebuhr's critique cut much deeper. The danger posed by Barton went beyond his manipulation of Jesus in the service of a narrow interest group. The real problem lay in his complacency about the ideal of "service." Ideals were always at risk of degenerating into smokescreens concealing "the most predatory practices of industrial and commercial life."[18]

When he wrote this response to *The Man Nobody Knows* in 1925, Niebuhr had many reasons to be insistent about the moral threat posed by hypocritical idealism. He knew from firsthand observation that Barton's hero Henry Ford, a self-proclaimed Christian idealist, was speeding up his assembly line and laying off workers, all the while hailing the generosity of his five-dollar-a-day wage. Niebuhr had been to Germany in 1923 and 1924 and found Christian pacifist ideals hard to reconcile with the suffering and dislocation of the German people. How self-serving, he thought, for American Protestants to congratulate themselves for renouncing violence when they were the prime beneficiaries of a structurally unjust global status quo. Domestic and international affairs were both pushing Niebuhr toward a break with the main body of liberal Protestants, and with their idealistic Jesus. Barton's book was one more pebble on the balance scale, tipping Niebuhr and many other liberals toward radicalism. The fissure between him and his liberal friends deepened after 1927, and finally exploded when Niebuhr published *Moral Man and Immoral Society* in 1932. He took a sizable cohort of Protestant radicals with him when he declared that pursuing Christ's ideals of love and justice might well mean setting aside Christ's objections to violence. Niebuhr's rejection of pacifism and turn to socialism helped effect a major realignment in American Christian attitudes toward religion and politics. The place of Jesus in American culture would never be quite the same.[19]

The ground for Niebuhr's shift from "idealism" to "realism" had been prepared by the great Social Gospeler Walter Rauschenbusch a decade before World War I. Rauschenbusch had reached the brink of embracing socialism in his *Christianity and the Social Crisis* (1907). The experience of watching New York City workers go broke during the depression of the 1890s taught him that the industrial system was "underpaying, exhausting, and maiming the people." Where Washington Gladden had preached social peace through aggressive mediation between labor and capital (and Charles Sheldon had stuck with heroic acts of self-abasement on the part of the rich), Rauschenbusch did not believe the capitalist class would ever voluntarily relinquish its stranglehold over the nation's wealth. Yet he was still confused about how to proceed. He was convinced on the one hand that social justice required the church to support labor in its standoff with capital, yet sure on the other hand that Jesus barred Christians from approving such coercive measures as strikes and boycotts. Meanwhile, it was inconceivable to Rauschenbusch, a devoted evangelical as well as a committed social reformer, that Jesus did not point the way forward.

His analysis of the parable of the Good Samaritan revealed how close he had come to asserting that Christ's teaching was irrelevant to the solution of modern social problems. The humanitarian universalism of this parable (Luke 10:25–37) had made it one of the liberal Christians' favorites since the mid-eighteenth century, when John Woolman invoked it in his anti-slavery writing. American Christians in earlier centuries, and traditionalists in the modern era, gave much more prominence to such parables as the Ten Virgins (Matt. 25:1–13), which taught the faithful to be ready for the sudden appearance of the savior. Modern liberals liked the Good Samaritan story because it featured the sudden appearance of an opportunity to do good. Rauschenbusch naturally cited it to solicit liberal support for his ever-more-radical position. But he managed only to expose the parable's shortcomings for such a purpose. "The good Samaritan did not go after the robbers with a shot-gun," Rauschenbusch wrote, "but looked after the wounded and helpless man by the wayside. But if hundreds of good Samaritans traveling the same road should find thousands of bruised men groaning to them, they would not be such very good Samaritans if they did not organize a vigilance committee to stop the manufacturing of wounded men. If they did not, presumably the asses who had to lug the wounded to the tavern would have the wisdom to inquire into the causes of their extra work." The "if they did not" was the giveaway: there was no reason to think that first-century Good Samaritans, or first-century prophets such as Jesus, could have imagined a "committee" to "stop" injustice or brutality. If anything, the gospel suggested that Jesus would react to thousands of bruised men the same way he reacted to a single one: bind as many wounds, find as many beds, as you can.[20]

The First World War interrupted the socialist advance among Protestant liberals. They turned to debating whether Christ's doctrine of nonresistance ruled out all wars or only wars of aggression. Catholics and conservative Protestants had no doubt that some wars were "just." Of course many Irish American Catholics objected to the war not because of anything Jesus said, but because they could not imagine fighting side-by-side with the British. On the whole, liberal Protestants came to the same conclusion that conservatives did. Christ's pacifism was not absolute. He preached nonresistance to evil when the only sufferer was oneself. But he demonstrated a willingness to use force in the temple. Nations were positively obligated to defend their citizens against aggression. Washington Gladden, Lyman Abbott, and other Social Gospel stalwarts took their virile Jesus straight from the campaign for justice at home to the battle for democracy abroad. The Book of Revelation, Abbott pointed out, portrayed Christ "as a conqueror on horseback in righteousness to make war." Jesus "taught not that it is wrong to use force in resisting evil, but that love, not selfishness, should resist evil. . . . It is sometimes Christian to fight; it is sometimes unchristian not to do so. . . . We do not hate the German militarists; we do not want to wreak vengeance on them; we do not even want to hurt them. But we want to compel them to stop killing women and children." Ex–Republican President and recent Progressive Party candidate Theodore Roosevelt concurred. He spoke for all Christian interventionists when he asked how Jesus had expelled the money-changers from the Temple. He went for a weapon. "The Saviour armed himself with a scourge of cords" and "drove" them out.[21]

Young Reinhold Niebuhr, in 1917 a twenty-five-year-old pastor in a heavily German American denomination, took a leading role in justifying the American war effort (and in "Americanizing" his German Evangelical Synod of North America). Rauschenbusch, despite "being a hater of war," as he put it shortly before his death in 1918, thought "a victory for the Central Powers" (Germany and its allies) would be "a terrible calamity." He privately expressed grudging support for the American cause—grudging because he was not "as sure as others that a victory of the Allies would of itself free the world from imperialism." The Versailles settlement, widely regarded by liberal idealists as a vindictive repudiation of their hopes for democratic progress, gave renewed life to pacifist idealism in the early twenties. A large group of liberals, secular as well as religious, committed themselves to "the outlawry of war." Some, such as Unitarian John Haynes Holmes of New York's Community Church, joined the historic peace churches, the Quakers and Mennonites, in claiming Jesus as an absolute nonresister. Even Harry Emerson Fosdick, a vociferous war supporter who refused to mount the pacifist bandwagon after the war, agreed that Jesus had left no doubt about his own position: "When a man takes Jesus in earnest," Fosdick wrote in 1923, "he must see that war is the most colossal social sin against him of which the world is guilty, that it is absolutely, irrevocably unchristian, that it means everything that Jesus does not mean and means nothing that Jesus does mean."[22]

The stage was set for some liberal idealists, once they felt compelled to take sides in the intractable "warfare" of the industrial arena, to return to Rauschenbusch's position of 1907 and take the final step: cross over the line to socialism and embrace the cause of labor in its class struggle with capital. In the late 1920s and early 1930s they did so in substantial numbers, taking either of two courses. The smaller of the two groups, led by Harry F. Ward, a Methodist professor of ethics at Union Theological Seminary in Manhattan, proclaimed that Christ was a revolutionary and that imitating him in the modern world meant countenancing violence in the social struggle. The second and much larger group, led by Reinhold Niebuhr (also a professor at Union as of 1928), agreed with the first that Christian responsibility entailed a willingness to use force, coercion, and perhaps violence in certain emergencies. But Niebuhr's cohort did not try to bring Christ with them. They conceded to the radical pacifists that Jesus was an absolutist in his ban on violence. Jesus was simply no longer relevant in some political or social situations. This group's position had momentous consequences for American politics and culture since it meant that many socially alert Christians would no longer be asking "What would Jesus do?" about public questions. The realists' romance with socialism did not survive the mid-1930s, but their view of Jesus as politically unhelpful—even dangerous—persisted as they marched into the New Deal fold.

As early as 1923 Niebuhr began breaking the spell of postwar liberal pacifism. Christ's principle of nonresistance might be "too ideal for a sinful human world," he wrote. "It might fail if it were tried." That seed of doubt about imitating Christ grew in Niebuhr's thinking as the 1920s progressed. By 1928 he was contending that while Jesus was not a "revolutionist"—he would have refused "to participate in a revolt against the oppression of the Romans"—he was a "radical" who knew that "the good life could not be achieved within the limits of conventional society." Christ's perfectionism, Niebuhr said in 1932, supplied "an absolute standard by which to judge both personal and social righteousness." But one could not "draw from the teachings of Jesus any warrant for the social policies" needed to establish a "modicum of justice." The idea of a

"Christian social order" was oxymoronic. Christ's "law of love," he wrote in 1935, made social sense only as an "impossible possibility." In a typically Niebuhrian paradox, Jesus remained relevant because he offered a prophetic indictment of the human sinfulness that would inevitably make his law of love irrelevant in certain situations.[23]

The Niebuhrian realists removed Jesus from the scene of daily decision-making about politics and society, but not from their hearts. Many remained just as attached to a "personal" Jesus as the revolutionary Methodist Harry Ward or the liberal pacifist John Haynes Holmes. The realists wished policy decisions to be secularized, reached by the same pragmatic problem-solving methods employed by secular liberals. Decisions about the use of force, whether violent or nonviolent, would depend on prudential assessments, not a reading of the Sermon on the Mount. The Niebuhrians' elevation of Jesus to the role of transcendent prophetic judge was designed to protect society from his ethical absolutism. But it was also intended to protect Christ from the machinations of Jesus boosters such as Bruce Barton. Putting some distance between Christ and everyday human affairs did not indicate secularization, in the Niebuhrians' eyes, but a strategy of faithfulness in the orthodox tradition of Shepard and Edwards. Relocating Jesus to the transcendent realm freed social policy-making from pacifist literalism while helping to free Jesus from cultural exploitation by any individual or group.[24]

The decision by the mostly northern and midwestern Niebuhrian liberals to limit the social application of Christ's love doctrine magnified the force of a second shift in the cultural incarnation of Jesus. As a publicly proclaimed cultural hero, "Jesus" was taking on an ever more southern and western resonance. This trend had begun long before, at least as early as the late nineteenth century, when a defeated South praised the crucified Lord as a regional symbol of hope and perseverance. (Southern blacks had made Jesus a symbol of their hope for survival and deliverance long before the

Civil War.) After the Scopes Trial, when Clarence Darrow made William Jennings Bryan look ridiculous (at least in the eyes of most northerners), southern and western conservative evangelicals embraced Jesus all the more firmly as their cause and inspiration.

Northern liberals liked to think that at the Scopes Trial the fundamentalists, while technically victorious (the Tennessee teacher John Scopes had been judged guilty of teaching evolution), had actually lost the larger battle. Evangelical Christianity had been shown up as primitive, laughably out of touch with modern scientific rationality. But as Garry Wills has noted, the real loser at the Dayton courthouse was not conservative evangelicalism but the *liberal* evangelicalism that for a century had been mobilizing Jesus on behalf of social justice. Bryan's career had been spent fighting for equality with Jesus at his side. The Scopes Trial made people forget that Bryan had been a liberal in his prime, not a conservative. The public humiliation he suffered at the hands of Darrow and H. L. Mencken cemented the linkage between secularism and liberalism, on the one hand, and evangelicalism and conservatism on the other. Meanwhile, the conservative evangelicals, far from accepting the place northerners assigned them—extinction—went about raising money and radio antennae. They built regional networks around Bible schools and summer institutes, and prepared for the national resurgence that would come with Billy Graham at mid-century. They gladly hailed the name of Jesus, causing liberal realists—already reticent for political reasons about proclaiming Christ in public—to speak of him less and less frequently. As a result of their silence, "Jesus" uttered in public came more and more to connote anti-modernist convictions.[25]

Of course the secularization of northern liberalism, assisted by many liberal Protestants and given a major boost by the Scopes Trial, stemmed from many other sources too, including the discoveries of modern science, the rise of the research university, and the emergence of professional communities of authoritative opinion in many fields of knowledge (including critical biblical scholarship).

But one additional change had direct bearing on the cultural place-ment of Jesus in America: the gradual admission of Jews into main-stream northern cultural life. The arrival of distinguished Jewish scholar-refugees from Nazi Europe in the 1930s only heightened a trend that had begun long before. The demographic facts were irre-sistible. In 1850 there had been only fifty thousand Jewish Ameri-cans. By 1880, thanks largely to emigration from Germany, there were 250 thousand. By the mid-1920s, when Congress restricted immigration, there were four million American Jews. Over three million Russian and Eastern European Jews had emigrated to the United States since 1881, when the Russian pogroms had begun.[26]

On the issue of assimilating Jews into American intellectual and professional elites, a wide range of liberal Protestants in the 1920s proffered voluble support. Such committed adversaries as Reinhold Niebuhr and Unitarian John Haynes Holmes, at war over the place of pacifism (and therefore of Jesus-the-nonresister) in so-cial ethics, saw eye to eye on welcoming Jews into the American mainstream. Along with liberal Rabbi Stephen Wise and many oth-ers, they campaigned for a ban on Christian efforts to convert the Jews. The idea of a "Judeo-Christian" tradition began to take off, vying for supremacy with the common nineteenth-century notion of the United States as a "Christian nation." Jesus would henceforth share his spot as American sacred hero with Moses. (African Amer-ican Christians had put them both in the same elevated pantheon since the early nineteenth century.) The publication in 1955 of Will Herberg's *Protestant-Catholic-Jew* capped the liberal Christian and Jewish project of pluralizing the symbolic sacred core of America. Catholics and Jews could join the mainstream: they just had to demonstrate to the satisfaction of Protestants that their primary loyalties were not to Rome or Israel but to "American freedom." Of course the northern liberal rejection of the "Christian nation" con-cept only made it more appealing to many conservative evangeli-cals and even to some conservative Catholics.[27]

III

Events in the second quarter of the twentieth century produced a more secular and pluralistic northern Protestantism. Liberal Christians continued to extol the authority and grace of Christ—the realists noting especially his searing judgment on human pride and pretentiousness, the idealists dwelling on his rejection of the world's violent methods and unprincipled compromises. But liberals of both types eagerly pursued other sources of earthly wisdom. Marx, Gandhi, Freud, and the neo-Freudian psychologists were special favorites, while Buddhist and Hindu sages—always of interest to a small group of liberals since the early nineteenth century—drew major interest after mid-century. The liberal Christians' intellectual eclecticism encouraged non-Christian Americans to nod in agreement at the perennial value of Jesus as philosopher. Liberal Jews such as Stephen Wise joined the chorus, calling on all Americans, Christians as well as non-Christians, to take Christ's tenets more seriously.

In his talk on "Jesus, the Jew" at Carnegie Hall on the Sunday before Christmas 1925, Wise hailed Christ as a great Jewish prophet and universal teacher whose wisdom everyone, Christian and non-Christian, should revere. Wise was shocked when he read in the *New York World* that he had urged Jews to convert to Christianity. "I never said such a thing at all," he wrote to a friend. The Union of Orthodox Rabbis was disturbed enough to ask him to resign as chair of the United Palestine Appeal. He sent in his resignation letter, but the Appeal's Board of Directors refused to accept it. The important revelation of the flap was that the liberals' Jesus was passing into modern "Judeo-Christian" civilization as one significant symbol of an open-ended, pluralistic modernity. As Rabbi Krauskopf had written in 1901, there was no reason that "those who have been separated" by "Jesus, the Christ" could not be "reunited" by "Jesus, the man." Thomas Jefferson would have been pleased.[28]

Meanwhile, the liberal gesture of inclusiveness—Jesus as one wise man among many, even if *primus inter pares*—spurred conservative Protestants to reaffirm his exclusive, sovereign, supernatural power. Evangelical zeal for "the name of Jesus" had never let up since the eighteenth-century revivals, but praising Jesus nevertheless evolved as a cultural activity. After the Scopes debacle, amplifying Christ's name became a shorthand way to signal one's righteous disenchantment with northern scientific modernism. Among anti-modernists "Jesus" figured as a religious proclamation and a cultural password. For some it verged on becoming a talisman, possessing magical properties for warding off humanistic secularism. Uttering the name of Jesus carried such power because behind the name stood a real Son of God who could vanquish a resourceful enemy. Conservatives knew that secularism (loving the world and its pleasures too much) and modernism (either historical analysis of the Bible or, worse, the ideas of Darwin and Nietzsche, well-publicized demons at the Scopes Trial) were liable to infiltrate their own ranks. Christ's divine help was essential because human beings were weak, unable on their own to resist a downward spiral of cynical, self-regarding temptation. Many liberals supposed that self-mastery was straightforward, built up by rational acts of mind and caring acts of heart, but many conservatives sensed that the struggle against the devil could easily be lost—if indeed it had not already been lost. The most apocalyptic of the conservatives awaited Christ's immediate Second Coming: the world already belonged to the devil. God had promised the ultimate victory, but Armageddon came first. Across the conservative Christian spectrum battles of eternal significance were being fought against a real anti-Christ. The Jesus preached by the more apocalyptic conservatives ruled as an avenging warrior.[29]

Even among the non-apocalyptic traditionalists there were major variations of doctrine and sensibility. Fundamentalists, themselves split over whether to convert the whole nation or withdraw into sectarian purity, often differed from Pentecostals. The fundamentalists

took a more doctrinal approach to the faith and stuck to the old orthodox view that miracles happened in Christ's time but not in ours.
Yet with respect to Jesus, what the fundamentalists and Pentecostals
shared far outweighed their differences of style or belief. They all
saw liberal modernist Christianity as a sellout of Christ. They were
aghast that liberals seriously debated whether Jesus truly said what
the Bible said he said. They were shocked that liberals seriously wondered to what degree Jesus was relevant to thinking about everyday
life. *Everything* depended on him, from eternal salvation to getting
along with one's spouse. A few conservatives, such as Carl F. H.
Henry at Fuller Seminary in Pasadena, California, thought that when
enough individuals chose Jesus as their personal savior real social reform could occur. But most conservatives were wary of social-justice
appeals, partly because so many liberals who preached them were
silent about seeking Christ as their personal savior. The Reinhold
Niebuhr of 1927 typified the gathering liberal legion for whom talk
of "giving one's heart to Jesus" connoted blindness to social responsibility. Liberals detached themselves more and more completely
from evangelical piety. The modernist liberals (whether realists or
idealists) and the anti-modernist conservatives (Pentecostals, Adventists, or fundamentalists) were settling into a state of mutual distaste
if not enmity. That standoff has come to be one major fault line—if
not the major fault line—of modern American culture.[30]

Pentecostals (and Adventists, including the "Jehovah's Witnesses," the name as of 1931 for the post–Civil War Watchtower Society of Charles Taze Russell) were premillennialists. So were the
"dispensationalists" among the fundamentalists. For the premillennialists, the prospective return of Jesus rendered gradualist social
reforms beside the point. The "dispensationalists" divided salvation history into a sequence of distinct eras. In their view each of
the five completed phases had come to a smashing conclusion with
a disastrous event (the Fall, the Flood, the Tower of Babel, the
Egyptian captivity, the crucifixion). The present sixth phase would
culminate in a great tribulation, a seven-year eruption of calamities.

Some dispensationalists thought the tribulation would include a rapture, in which those chosen by God would disappear suddenly—instantaneously—and be elevated to God's domain. These "rapture" believers, like the apocalyptic Adventists, were the purest anti-moderns of all, since they disputed the bedrock liberal assumption—shared by many conservatives too—that fundamental social changes always occurred gradually, even glacially. Despite their differences, Christian conservatives shared a divine, miracle-working Jesus revealed in an inspired Bible, sending his spirit into the believer's heart, and promising eternal salvation to his chosen ones. What made many fundamentalists and Pentecostals distinctively *modern* traditionalists was their self-consciousness about dissenting from modern liberal religion.

J. Gresham Machen, Princeton Seminary professor and champion of Presbyterian orthodoxy, typified this self-conscious antiliberalism. His influential book *Christianity and Liberalism* (1923) presented a masterful polemic against the modernism of such liberals as Harry Emerson Fosdick. As early as 1916 Machen had assailed Fosdick's "pitiful" and "undogmatic" preaching. Fosdick, then a surging presence among liberal Baptists, had followed in the Henry Ward Beecher and David Swing tradition of taking Jesus as the embodiment and exemplar of love, tolerance, and personal growth toward selflessness. By 1923 Fosdick was the preaching pastor at Manhattan's First Presbyterian Church and a national leader of liberal modernist Protestantism. When the *New York Times* wanted a liberal response to William Jennings Bryan's 1922 article on "God and Evolution," the paper picked Fosdick, who repudiated Bryan's "medievalism." He promised a protracted battle to defend "scientific freedom of investigation" in the name of "religion" and "God."[31]

In Machen's eyes liberal modernists overlooked the disabling weight of human sin and exaggerated the power of human reason. In *Christianity and Liberalism* he delivered a stinging rebuke to their positive thinking while exempting the positive thinking of popular evangelism. The liberals were eating away at the essence of Christianity, he thought, while popular fundamentalists such as William Jennings Bryan were merely diluting the gospel in their zeal to Christianize the nation. Machen himself had no interest in converting the nation, defending Prohibition, banning evolution, or depreciating careful biblical scholarship. In the tradition of his Princeton predecessor Charles Hodge, Machen aimed to shore up belief in the supernatural essentials of Christianity: the virgin birth of Christ, his nature miracles and healing miracles, his physical resurrection, his substitutionary atonement, and the inspiration of Holy Scripture.[32]

Christianity and Liberalism tacitly conceded the mounting cultural power of religious liberalism by calling on all supernaturalists, whatever their differences, to arrange their wagons in a single circle. Catholics and Protestants, Calvinists and Arminians, post- and premillennialists—anyone who believed in Christ as "the object of faith," not just as "example for faith," was welcome to join the alliance. Machen gave them all an incisive, if oversimplified, picture of their liberal enemy. Liberals loved Jesus, said Machen, because he was "the fairest flower of humanity," the "mild-mannered exponent of an indiscriminating love." For them he was "the first Christian," the original practitioner of self-sacrifice in the service of ideals. But Jesus "was certainly not a Christian," Machen announced. "Christians" were all sinners for whom Christ was crucified. Jesus never sinned; he practiced a religion of "untroubled sonship." It was all right to take Christ as "the supreme example for men" as long as imitating him meant living always, as Jesus did, in "the conscious presence of God." The "monstrous perversion" of liberalism was to reduce the imitation of Christ to "a life of humanitarian service outwardly like the ministry of Jesus." Liberals committed the corrosive error of assuming that "nearness" to Christ entailed "likeness" to him. They brought him down to the familiar level of "Brother" when in fact, as presented in Paul's epistles, he remained as distinct from and superior to his worshipers as a human father does to his son. Above all else, liberalism lost sight of sin. Christianity rose or fell on its doctrine of sin. Human beings were either inveterate sinners in need of redemption, or they were good-natured strivers in need of education. Divine revelation of supernatural grace made no sense to those who had not "faced the problem of evil in their own lives." For liberals, a "sage of Nazareth" sufficed. True Christians would hold out for a Son of God who took away the sins of the world.[33]

Machen's ideal-type "liberalism" minimized sin and rejected the supernatural. Actual liberal Protestantism since the nineteenth century had claimed to revitalize the supernatural by joining it to the natural and deepening awareness of sin by uncovering its social roots. Machen wholly missed the depth of liberal Christians' attachment to Jesus. They believed Christ had called them to witness the supernatural in the natural and to perceive sin in human institutions as well as hearts. If many liberals harped on the humanity of Jesus, it was because his full humanity had been so thoroughly neglected in the Calvinist churches in which so many of them had been raised. Fosdick was typical of many modernist Christians who praised a tender, loving Jesus for rescuing them from the guilt-inducing Christ of childhood. "What present-day critics of liberalism often fail to see," he wrote in his 1956 autobiography, "is its absolute necessity to multitudes of us who would not have been Christians at all unless we could thus have escaped the bondage of the then reigning [turn-of-the-century] orthodoxy." As a child he had been "morbidly conscientious, . . . weeping at night for fear of going to hell. . . . In those early days the iron entered my soul and the scene was set for rebellion against the puerility and debasement of a legalistic and terrifying religion." Like the young Henry Ward Beecher three-quarters of a century earlier, Fosdick was saved from self-loathing by a brotherly, companionate Christ.[34]

Machen derided liberal humanism as "paganism," the "view of life which finds the highest goal of human existence in the healthy and harmonious and joyous development of existing human faculties." But to liberals the open-ended cultivation of one's natural talents formed part of God's own plan for human redemption—not a substitute for divine grace but one manifestation of divine graciousness. They considered the cherishing of human reason fully compatible with the recognition of human sinfulness. Liberalism adapted itself to new conditions much more successfully than Machen could understand. In the wake of *Christianity and Liberalism* Reinhold Niebuhr and other liberal realists took a page from Machen himself and spoke passionately about the deep roots of sin in all human endeavor, social and individual. The realists made Machen's sin-consciousness palatable to modernists by stressing the interpenetration of social and individual sin. That perspective permitted religious liberals to enter the Depression decade of the 1930s as advocates of social justice but opponents of the idealism associated with either John Haynes Holmes's pacifism or Harry Emerson Fosdick's "personal" religion. H. Richard Niebuhr, Reinhold's younger brother and a professor of ethics at Yale Divinity School, summed up the liberal realists' position on Jesus when he wrote in 1934 that "the characteristic deed of Jesus was not enacted in the temple but on Golgotha." Christ may have swept the money-changers out of the temple, but that action was a minor note in his overall preaching of submission to the Father. Jesus "did not say: Love your enemy in order that you may convert him to your point of view," but "Love your enemies in order that ye may be sons of your Father in heaven who maketh his sun to shine on the evil and the good." Liberals had wrongly turned Christ into an aggressive fighter for humanistic ideals. It was high time to sweep this idealist Jesus out of the American political arena.[35]

IV

The most vibrant force within Machen's imagined supernaturalist coalition of the 1920s may have been the Pentecostal churches, then commencing their rapid twentieth-century growth. The Pentecostal movement derived from the Methodist "holiness" preaching of such nineteenth-century evangelists as Phoebe Palmer, who gained a following because the Spirit so evidently informed her speech. Her holiness teaching focused on the sanctification that could take a believer beyond the reach of sin. The early-twentieth-century Pentecostals extended holiness practices by taking literally the second chapter of the Book of Acts, where "Luke" (the same author who put together the final arrangement of the Gospel of Luke) described the original Pentecost. The Holy Ghost enabled 120 Galilean disciples of Jesus assembled in Jerusalem after the resurrection to speak suddenly in the native languages of "the multitude" of foreigners who had come to town from "every nation under heaven." Modern Pentecostals combined the second chapter of Acts with the words attributed to Jesus in Mark 16:17–18 (though their authenticity had been challenged by scholarly authorities): "And these signs shall follow them that believe: In my name shall they cast out devils; they shall speak with new tongues; they shall take up serpents; and if they drink any deadly thing, it shall not hurt them; they shall lay hands on the sick, and they shall recover." In effect Pentecostals responded to liberal biblical critics—who seemed eager to take some of Christ's most cherished words *out* of the Bible—by taking his purported utterances even more literally than they had been taken before.[36]

Liberal Social Gospeler Walter Rauschenbusch assured his fellow modernists in 1897 that the phenomenon of "speaking in tongues" was of no more than historical interest. "This is not a live question," he announced. "In an age of red-hot questions this one is refreshingly cool and dead." Yet around 1901 a Methodist healer in Topeka, Charles Parham, began preaching an "Apostolic Faith" in which speaking in tongues was proposed as part of a "Holy Ghost Baptism." This third stage of Christian faith came after justification and sanctification. African American preacher William Seymour learned the Apostolic Faith from Parham and took it to Los Angeles, where he launched a revival in a converted barn on Azusa

Street in April 1906. The newsletter Seymour began publishing in September 1906 included testimonies and reports about how the Holy Spirit had been going about his work on Azusa Street since the previous spring. The Spirit was performing miracle after miracle, and doing it far into the night. Seymour quipped that the Spirit had led him to choose a decrepit barn in a nonresidential part of town because holy hollering would respect no curfew.[37]

The most noteworthy of the Spirit's miracles may have been to make the most socially disadvantaged of Americans miracle-workers in their own right. "The work began among the colored people," the first newsletter explained. "God baptized several sanctified wash women with the Holy Ghost, who have been much used of Him." Then a white woman also received "the Pentecost and gift of tongues." It was soon evident that "God makes no difference in nationality, Ethiopians, Chinese, Indians, Mexicans, and other nationalities worship together." The gift of tongues was plainly a way for the Holy Spirit to get a socially and linguistically varied gathering of souls to understand one another and to experience a unifying spiritual force. Instant translation took place. First the living Christ, the source of grace, passed the baton of spiritual power to the Holy Spirit, who proceeded to fill the faithful with languages they had never studied. This new power of speech took over people's emotions as well as their tongues. One person taken over by the Spirit could heal another person's physical ills:

> On August 11, a man from the central part of Mexico, an Indian, was present in the meeting and heard a German sister speaking in his tongue which the Lord had given her. He understood, and through the message that God gave him through her, he was most happily converted so that he could hardly contain his joy. All the English he knew was Jesus Christ and Hallelujah. He testified in his native language, which was interpreted by a man who had been among that tribe of Indians. This rough Indian, under the

power of the Spirit was led to go and lay his hands on a woman in the congregation who was suffering from consumption, and she was instantly healed and arose and testified.

In most Protestant churches, liberal or conservative, the Spirit moved from minister to congregation as the Word was preached. In Azusa the Spirit surged from person to person via speech and touch. The preacher might set off the chain reaction, but he scarcely controlled it. The Spirit blew where it listed. It was the well-advertised power of speech and touch to transform bodies that brought this assembly together in the first place. Some people in this crowd knew that Jesus could heal them, body and soul, and they taught that belief to others—along with the proper ritual signs for identifying and conveying the belief. Of course many of the sick and dispossessed of all evangelized nations have found hope in stories of Christ's healings ever since Jesus himself performed them. American Protestantism has been so word-centered that it was easy for American evangelicals to forget that the original Jesus cured as well as preached. The Pentecostals revived an ancient hope.[38]

They did so in a fully Protestant fashion: the spoken word healed as surely as touch. The Pentecostals did not have the Catholic option of taking Christ's flesh by mouth into their bodies. So they took in his words as if they were physical. Seymour's newsletter made a point of identifying "Theosophy, Christian Science, Magnetic Healing, Spiritualism, and Hypnotism" as "works of the devil." From the Pentecostal point of view they were either too mechanical (magnetic healing) or they detached the Spirit from the tangible, earthly body and its needs. But the newsletter was no more enchanted by Catholicism or the general run of Protestant churches. "A young man who a year ago was in the chain gang, is now baptized with the Holy Ghost and preaching everywhere," the paper recounted. "He was a Catholic but God took all the Romanism out of him. He is telling the Catholics to get their own Bibles and the Protestants to get to God and not lean on preachers." This reformed Catholic—who must have learned in his Catholic years that Jesus was strong in spirit even when weak in body—could also have told the YMCA to stop fretting about Christ's muscle tone. The young man was "powerfully built," but "God has so taken the fight out of him that when he was struck and spit upon in the face, he went home and was so blest that he prayed all night and said he loved the people who persecuted him more than if they had asked him to pray for them." From the standpoint of the Azusa revival, Protestant ministers were no different than Catholic priests: they were all obstructing people's access to Jesus and to the holy work they could do for each other.[39]

Among the languages spontaneously spoken at Azusa were all the living and dead European languages. The newsletter exudes a tone of pride that Greek, Latin, French, and German, normally a sign of elite education, were freely accessible to some participants. So were Chinese and Tibetan. A group of Russians broke down in tears when they heard their native tongue perfectly pronounced by a non-Russian who had had no training in the language. In addition, said the newsletter, "there are a good many Spanish speaking people in Los Angeles." God "has been giving the language, and now a Spanish preacher, who, with his wife, are preaching the Gospel in open air meetings on the Plaza, have received their Pentecost." The couple's "testimony" was printed in Spanish in the newsletter, followed by the English version. The experience of immediate verbal translation displayed at Azusa directly influenced how the newsletter responded to modern biblical scholarship. One article said that the final verses of Mark's Gospel (16:15–20), suspected of being spurious because they were missing from an ancient manuscript, were verifiably "the words of Jesus." For at Azusa the verses had been spoken "again and again by the Spirit in unknown tongues," then translated into English by assorted interpreters in everyone's hearing. The Spirit was not simply giving the gifts of healing and speaking. The Spirit was certifying the inerrancy of the scriptural passages that announced those gifts in the first place.[40]

The words spoken in the revival seemed like meaningless syllables to members of the press. The *Los Angeles Daily Times* reporter wrote that during the "pandemonium" of "prayer and testimony" he heard one "old colored 'mammy'" say "you-oo-po goo-ioo-ioo come under the boo-oo-oo-boo-ido" while "swinging her arms wildly about." To judge from the newsletter, the faithful spoke actual words that were regularly repeated. "Jesus is coming" was a particular favorite. The Spirit harped on the central messages of the Pentecostal faith. Like Thomas Shepard's congregants almost three centuries earlier, these faithful followers of Jesus entered their meetings knowing what sorts of public testimony—Christ sayings and sayings about Christ—they were going to hear. The spontaneity resided not in the content of the message—well-rehearsed at previous meetings—but in who would speak, which language would be spoken, and how much fire would inform the delivery.

One day young Sister Keyes got up to speak and sing in tongues, and then Sister Mead—for twenty years an African missionary—rose to say that Keyes had spoken in the very African dialect Mead had mastered. It was "a beautiful language, but one that is very difficult for English-speaking people to acquire, but the Holy Ghost, through the young lady, had given the perfect accent." With those few words Sister Mead had already—before giving the translation—conveyed the essential news: the Spirit had spoken miraculously. She then added the expected content of the message: what Keyes had said was "Jesus is coming again, coming again soon, and we shall meet him then . . . ye know not the hour. If you are not prepared, you will not go with Jesus. . . . The love of God is so great. He says, 'Come unto me; come unto me, and I will give you rest. . . . O, Jesus is such a wonderful Savior." Christ's gospel promise of rest for the weary had been the favorite phrase of Shepard's flock in their seventeenth-century testimonies. One reason Jesus is so deeply grounded in American soil is that verses such as Matthew 11:28 have been read, spoken, and sung so often by so many Americans for nearly four centuries. Protestants like to think it is only Catholics who pray repetitively—"Hail Mary, full of grace, the Lord is with thee; blessed is the fruit of thy womb, Jesus"—but Protestants filled the American atmosphere to overflowing with their favorite biblical phrases long before the radio waves became charged with them in the 1920s.[41]

There were major differences, naturally, between Thomas Shepard's seventeenth-century testimonies and those of the Pentecostals. The most basic was that Shepard's testifiers said that self-doubt and self-abasement formed a part of their Christ-elevating faith. The Pentecostals at Azusa thought that faith banished doubt. "If God for Christ's sake has forgiven you your sins," said the newsletter, "you know it. And if you do not know it better than you know anything in this world, you are still in your sins." And if "He has given you a clean heart and sanctified your soul, you know it. And if you do not know it, the work is not done." The Holy Ghost baptism—speaking in tongues—was surefire proof that God had transformed the self. No one could doubt the magnitude and finality of "know-so salvation." The delivered soul knew it had changed and so did everyone watching the speaking and healing. "When He comes and covers you over and around and about, people know it." Pentecostalism was a high-wire act as a religious practice: some of those who could not manage to speak in tongues or to be healed would blame themselves for inadequate faith. But those who did receive special gifts could exult in the feeling of salvation. The Catholic Mass has the congregation say to Christ, just before ingesting his body and blood, "Speak but the word, and my soul shall be healed." The genius of Azusa Pentecostalism was to have the Spirit pass through worshipers' bodies while they did the speaking and healing themselves.[42]

V

Revivals are by definition temporary. Worshipers cannot sustain the fire forever. Radical Christian communities either disband or metamorphose into established institutions with set routines. In the case of Azusa, bickering among Parham, Seymour, and other local leaders discouraged the Spirit. Or perhaps it was the dwindling spiritual fire that caused the feuding. By 1923, when the itinerant Pentecostal preacher Aimee Semple McPherson decided to settle down in Los Angeles—her newly built Angelus Temple in sedate Echo Park seated 5,300 people—radical Pentecostalism was just a memory in the city. It soon became just a memory in McPherson's own ministry. She had tempered her pious practices even before putting down roots in California. Her Foursquare Gospel preserved three potentially unruly Pentecostal elements—Jesus the healer, Jesus the Coming King, and Jesus the Spirit-baptizer—but subordinated them in practice to the mainstream evangelical staple of Jesus the personal savior. Her controversial ministry offers a case study of how Jesus was reborn and newly institutionalized as a mass savior-hero in twentieth-century America.

After 1923 the Canadian-born McPherson, already a nationally known revivalist, emerged as a major religious force in an explosively growing and very religious Los Angeles. The city's population had risen from 760,000 to 900,000 in the single year preceding the Temple's opening. Sixty new churches were built in 1924 to accommodate all the new arrivals, mainly midwestern Protestants but also many Catholics from the U.S. and Europe. When Reinhold Niebuhr passed through town in the summer of 1925 to address the Pacific Palisades Chautauqua, he noticed only that southern California had surrendered to a "paganism of pleasure." Californians "vegetate on these pleasant shores" in a "state of complete relaxation." McPherson's success at Angelus Temple confirmed Niebuhr's observation but also belied it. California Protestants were in a state of spiritual hunger and even agitation, not relaxation. Yet the

gospel McPherson preached was designed to go down easy. She es-
chewed the fire-and-brimstone that Billy Sunday had thrown down
in his urban revivals of the 1910s. Castigation of sinners gave way to
upbeat reassurance. McPherson's maternal succor, joyous singing,
and playful antics drew a devoted clientele that knew what to expect but was surprised every time. The audience watched their "Sister" perform. The surprise now lay not in who would speak in
which language with how much fire, but what kind of costume or
skit Sister would come up with next. One Sunday she dressed up as
a traffic cop and preached beside a police motorcycle on the topic
"Stop! You're Under Arrest!" Recorded sirens accompanied her
message that the unfaithful were speeding down life's highway in
the wrong direction. Another Sunday she had the assembly sing
new verses to the tune of "It's a Long Way to Tipperary":

> It's a grand thing to be a Christian,
> It's the best thing I know;
> It's a grand thing to be a Christian
> Wherever I may go.
> Goodbye, sin and sadness,
> Farewell all that's bad.
> It's a grand thing to be a Christian
> For it makes my heart glad.[43]

Sister still preached about healing and speaking in tongues, but
she exiled these practices from the regular meetings. "Tarrying"
(waiting expectantly for the gift of tongues) took place in evening
sessions, and healing occurred at special times set aside for that
purpose. Sunday services culminated in a ritual of audience participation: the old evangelical "altar call" in which sinners came forward to accept "salvation." Here McPherson was placing herself in
the long American Protestant revivalist tradition going back to
George Whitefield in the eighteenth century, Charles Grandison
Finney before the Civil War, and Dwight Moody after the war. The

two essential features of that tradition remained constant, whether the preacher stressed hellfire or love, and whether the proceedings were sedate or raucous. First, the communal context exercised a subtle coercion on the individual's decision for Christ. From the beginning, orthodox clerics complained about the durability of conversions that owed so much to the compulsions of the immediate setting. In 1835 the Reverend Albert Dod of Princeton Seminary complained about Finney's revivals because they virtually compelled audience members to go to "the anxious seat." People stopped dwelling on the gospel when they started worrying about "who else will go? What will they say of me?" They could not help assuming that "to go to the anxious seat is 'to do something for Christ' and that it is impossible for him who refuses to go to be a Christian."

Second, the revival emerged for many evangelical Protestants as the event where Jesus was felt to be most fully present, and the revivalists tended to become the most favored instruments of Christ's spirit. Revivalism flowed out of the evangelical quest to magnify the *feeling* of being wedded to Christ. Revivalists exuded intensity of feeling in order to stimulate and convert their audiences. They had no choice but to measure their success by the number of spectators who got up and joined the march to the altar or the anxious bench. They had no choice but to become celebrities of the spirit. Sister Aimee institutionalized revivalist methods at Angelus Temple and brought Hollywood-style performance into the celebrity revivalist's repertoire.[44]

McPherson was often attacked by secular and religious critics (liberals and conservatives alike, including other Pentecostals) for turning the Foursquare Church into a cult of her own personality. Los Angeles fundamentalist Bob Shuler (as "Fighting Bob," he was a local celebrity himself) alleged in 1924 that "whatever her lips may say, the fact remains that thousands of people sit in Angelus Temple and worship Aimee McPherson, even as we are supposed to worship Jesus Christ." Thousands more, he might have added,

worshiped her on the radio. She began broadcasting her church services in 1924, adding markedly to her local celebrity. There is no
doubt that she loved performing, and she took every chance to
speak about her own life experiences. Some suspected that she
staged her own disappearance in 1926—she claimed to have been
kidnapped—as a publicity stunt. But for all her gleeful and compulsive self-promotion, she also inveighed against anyone mistak-
ing her authority for God's. She and everyone else knew she had a
rare gift of persuasion and reassurance, but she took pains to dissociate that gift from any virtue residing in her. Meanwhile, she saw
no reason not to use the culture-wide hunger for new celebrities to
call attention to Christ's gospel. Evangelical Protestantism had always depended upon regular infusions of spiritual enthusiasm to
prove that it was not reverting to Catholic-style sloth. McPherson's
special talent lay in using her life experience as an instance of pious
vitality. She made a version of the imitation of Christ available to
ordinary twentieth-century Americans who swayed to her anthem:

> We're a happy lot of people, yes we are!
> We're a happy lot of people, yes we are!
> For our sins are all forgiven,
> And we're on our way to heaven;
> We're a happy lot of people, yes we are!

It is easy to mock the Angelus Temple hoopla (including the
massive sets rolled onto the stage for McPherson's dramas and op-
eras) and easy to fault her for giving people a comfort they craved.
Her preaching avoided hell and issued a gentle invitation to a recently migratory Protestant audience to remember their roots in
Jesus. She could make herself and others weep to the words "Give
me that old-time religion." Her preaching was as apolitical as Bruce
Barton's writing. The difference between her and Barton was that
she explicitly banned politics from Angelus Temple while he appeared oblivious to the subject. When she preached on the Good

Samaritan parable she stripped it of social content. She saw it as a tale about a "backslider" who "went down" from the spiritual heights of Jerusalem to the moral cesspool of Jericho. Jesus, the Good Samaritan, rescued the sinner from "the devil and his imps" who had left him half dead by the side of the road. McPherson's preaching, like William Seymour's, featured deliverance from suffering as well as sin. His meetings gave people relief from their physical suffering, while McPherson centered her campaign on spiritual anxieties. Like Barton, she preached a Jesus who wished Americans to feel better about themselves. The imitation of Christ did not entail imitating his suffering. Her audience, like Seymour's, had had enough of suffering; they wanted some power and glory for a change. And her audience, like Barton's, had had enough of a weak and resigned Jesus.[45]

Yet when one has added up all the ways in which McPherson risked trivializing the gospel, one has still not accounted for her success. It is not plausible to dismiss her thousands of followers as simple-minded buffoons, unable to distinguish spiritual pap from true Christianity. It is not enough to note that many admirers were seduced by her self-presentation as a starlet. Even one visiting Protestant pastor critical of her ministry could not help himself. "Let no man venture to deny," he wrote in 1928, that "she is a beautiful woman . . . with the soft spotlight shining upon her. . . . The writer has seen screen beauties in his day, and confesses to [having felt] a slight clutch of the heart as he watched her superb entrance." But the starlet also knew something about preaching. She gave a new look to revivalist celebrity. In addition to the traditional altar calls and untraditional theatricality, she created a public persona who seemed especially close to Christ. As always, evangelical Protestant audiences wanted to sit at the feet of preachers who depicted an intense engagement with Jesus. McPherson let everyone know that she knew Christ intimately because she had suffered (among other painful reverses, she had lost her first husband to malaria in Hong Kong) and because Jesus had come to her and delivered her from that suffering. Her life story served as her perennial sermon text. Her message gripped audiences not because her life was special, but because it was ordinary. She offered a personal account but the upshot was impersonal: Jesus saves anyone who comes to him. Salvation was available for the taking, as long as one avoided conscious sin.[46]

At the heart of McPherson's sermonic message was her special vulnerability as a woman. She was not angry about that vulnerability or troubled by discrimination against women. On the contrary, she always subscribed to the doctrine of "where there's a will . . . ," as she titled one chapter of her 1951 autobiography. But she communicated a fragility that was gendered female. Her constant references to it may help explain her preaching success at a cultural moment when male preachers were outdoing one another in professions of toughness. Her particular vulnerability was that of a woman victimized by love. McPherson was married three times, widowed once and divorced twice, and her last two misadventures in love were duly savored in the press. By her own account she could not stop falling in love—"My poor lonely heart again throbbed," she wrote of her third relationship—but this love was doomed like the others. Jesus, of course, offered male companionship to be counted on. She depicted her relation to Jesus as that of a woman to a man who protected and loved her. She made her celebrity human and accessible by dramatizing the power of her explicitly female feeling for Jesus in relation to the futility of her human loves. She gave new life to the old Puritan and Catholic notion of the spousal relation to Christ by recasting it as a sentimental tale of true, if wholly spiritual, romance.[47]

Her sermon "They Have Taken Away My Lord" illustrates her talent at bringing Jesus home as faithful lover. McPherson built on the foundation of Charles Austin Miles's 1913 hymn "In the Garden." The hymn's own sentimentality was perfectly mirrored in McPherson's earnest, melodramatic style, full of prolonged vowels and lilting intonations. "The day had not yet begun to dawn," she began calmly, "and the Sacred City was wrapped in slumber. The frightened guards had taken their departure, and there was silence in the Garden." Then her voice tightened. "Silence did I say? But no—what is that sound? 'Tis more than the whispering of the olive trees. . . . 'Tis a sound that strikes a chill through the heart of the listener—the sound of a woman weeping—heartbrokenly, inconsolably, and repeating over and over again in hopeless tones: 'They have taken away my Lord, and I know not where they have laid him!'"

One wonders if any male preacher had ever pictured Mary Magdalene quite the way McPherson did: "There is a lump in our throat and a catch in our heart as we gaze upon that poor little disconsolate figure clad with the garments of grief, rocking herself to and fro." Had any other preacher even brought to consciousness the image of Mary rocking to and fro as she wept? "Poor Mary!" McPherson went on. "Dear Mary, forgiven much, loving much, her heart was well nigh broken as she sat weeping at the empty tomb." McPherson continued milking the scene for pathos. "Oh I want Him!" she has Mary cry. "I want to hear His voice! I want to feel the touch of His hand on mine! I want to feel the warmth of His fires burning on the altars of the church!" Had any other preacher in the history of American Protestantism ever given such explicit voice to the desire as well as the dejection of Mary Magdalene?

When Jesus first approaches Mary, in McPherson's rendition, she looks at him but cannot see him because "her eyes are too blurred with tears, her ears too dull from the agony of her aching heart." Then McPherson gives the resurrected Jesus some passionate feelings too. After he says, "Woman, why weepest thou? Whom seekest thou?" he is moved by her pain. "How the heart of that Man must have throbbed as the strangled, little choking voice of Mary made answer: 'Sir, if thou hast borne Him hence tell me where thou hast laid Him, and I will take Him away.'" Mary is determined to take the body away even though she fears she is too weak physically to manage the task. Had any other preacher ever let Mary mull over how she would gather the physical strength to carry him off? "I can't—I can't go on without him! I must find him! And, though I'm only a woman, my love shall make me strong and in these two arms of mine I shall take Him away." In a deft homiletic stroke McPherson then got in a dig at liberal, modernist Bible scholars. "Higher criticism" had "taken away the Lord," saying "that You have changed, Jesus dear, that You are far away beyond that dome of blue; that You are no longer the miracle-working healing Christ of the Bible." In place of "the old-time glory of a Christ who lives and moves in the midst of His people" the modern church had substituted "moving pictures in the parish-house, chicken suppers, festivities, preaching of psychology, community uplift and social reform."[48]

McPherson ended her autobiography, published seven years after her death in 1944, with a reflection about her being a woman overcoming weakness. Trying to explain the success of her ministry, she contended that "the secret of power lies, not in oneself or one's surroundings, but in the message which is borne; not in personality, but in the Christ which shines above the personality." Jesus was responsible for "the power of the message, even when spoken by the lips of a woman." At a time when male preachers, liberal and conservative, discountenanced any appearance of weakness, for fear of seeming effeminate, McPherson could embrace female submission rhetorically and use it contrastively to emphasize the power of Christ.[49]

EIGHT

FOR ALL YOU CARE, THIS WINE COULD BE MY BLOOD

I

I spent the spring of 1965 in Washington, D.C., working as a student intern at the U.S. Senate. Every day I rode the underground tram linking the Senate office building to the Capitol. One morning in April, as the tram approached the Capitol stop, I noticed a crowd surrounding someone in the waiting area. I wondered who could have set so many tourists atwitter at such an early hour. It could not be the usual senator or congressman. Maybe it was LBJ, or Robert McNamara. Before the tram came to a stop I could see, at the center of the circle, a tall, tanned, smiling, smartly dressed Billy Graham, then in his late forties. People pressed up to him to get a touch or a handshake and to hear his voice. In an instant I understood one reason why he had developed such a phenomenal international following. He was magnetically attractive, a charismatic presence even before he opened his mouth. Then he opened his mouth. His lilting North Carolina accent disclosed just a hint of "South." Northerners like me could sense him as intriguingly "other," yet reassuringly cosmopolitan.

Graham had burst onto the national stage with an unexpect-
edly rousing revival in Los Angeles in 1949. Organizers had
planned a three-week event, but Southern Californians were still
squeezing into the circus-style tent at the downtown corner of
Washington and Hill five weeks after the anticipated closing date.
"Christ in This Crisis," Graham titled the crusade. The *Los Angeles
Daily News* identified the crisis in question: "the worldwide crisis of
fear, of atomic warfare, . . . of moral degeneration in this country."
Graham made the crisis personal: "The only time a man can decide
for Christ," he told the six thousand listeners, "is when the Holy
Spirit of God has brought conviction to his heart. If God is bringing
conviction to your heart you dare not say 'no.' This is your moment
of decision." Nine thousand people crowded into the reconfigured
"canvas cathedral" for the final session. *Time* and *Newsweek* announced the arrival of "the new evangelist." Graham was launched.
His rise in the 1950s was mirrored, and immeasurably intensified,
by the rise of television. "I feel so undeserving of all the Spirit has
done," he said after Los Angeles. "I want no credit or glory. I want
the Lord Jesus to have it all."[1]

Graham, raised a Presbyterian but a Southern Baptist in adulthood, preached an immediately accessible Christ who promised a
place in heaven to everyone who chose to believe in him. "Salvation is yours for the taking," he told a New York City audience in
1957, "only you must reach out and take it." At the end of each
night's meeting he would address the crowd (attendance at Madison Square Garden averaged seventeen thousand for the six weeks)
with some version of his signature appeal, accompanied by a large
volunteer choir softly singing "Just As I Am." He spoke with gentle
insistence, like a kindly, concerned father instructing his children:

I am going to ask you to come. Up there—down here—I
want you to come. You come—right now—quickly. I am
going to ask you to get up out of your seats from all over
the place—quietly and reverently—and come and stand

here for a moment. Say, "Tonight I receive Christ. I give my life to Christ. I will serve and follow Him from this moment on." If you are with friends or relatives, they will wait for you. . . . It's a long way, but Christ went all the way to the Cross because He loved you. Certainly you can come these few steps and give your life to Him. It's an act of your will. You come right now! . . . You can make a decision tonight that will change your life. You can be born again and you'll never be the same.

During the six-week revival some fifty-six thousand people came forward and signed "decision cards" expressing their acceptance of Christ's offer.[2]

On one evening of the New York crusade, Graham gave an extended sermon on "the new birth." He sampled the many biblical references to sinfulness and regeneration, including Hebrew scriptural verses such as Jeremiah 17:9 ("The heart is deceitful above all things and desperately wicked") and Ezekiel 36:26 ("A new heart also will I give you and a new spirit will I put within you"). He staked out the interdenominational ground: "Every denomination, every catechism, teaches something about the matter of the new birth. Different terminology may be used, but the facts are always there. We that have been born the first time into the physical world can be born the second time, we can be changed, translated into the Kingdom of God." He made clear that being born again was not a kind of self-help. "It must come from above, from God." The only love people could attain without divine help was a love of self. "After the new birth, you will love with all your heart, soul, and mind your neighbor as yourself. The new birth is a change of direction and change of affection. It's a union of the soul with Christ. Christ comes to you through the Holy Spirit and you become a partaker of God's life." Graham stressed that accepting Christ as your personal savior "doesn't remove your problems. Your problems may be even greater after you come to Christ, but you will have a capacity and power to face them. You have a new life, you have God's life."[3]

Graham was aware of the danger that he was finessing difficult theological issues and resorting to hortatory solutions for intractable problems. He kept repeating the words "Ye must be born again" as if clarity would spring from reiteration alone. In his diary during the crusade he confessed he found it "difficult to understand the difference between the sovereign, irresistible Grace of God and man's free will. It seems to me both are involved." He would "preach directly to their wills" while nevertheless being "certain that I am preaching to people whom God has chosen." Still, he found it hard "to put in chronological order just which comes first, repentance, faith, or regeneration. It's like saying: which comes first, the chicken or the egg? They all seem to be happening simultaneously." In the "new birth" sermon, he settled on a logical but decidedly "will"-centered resolution of the dilemma. He did tell the audience that "the whole operation of the new birth is done by the Holy Spirit," and that the wind of Spirit "bloweth where it listeth," without regard for "our wishes." But then Graham equated the Holy Spirit's action with a person's conscious repentance and conscious choice of Christ over Satan. You knew the Holy Spirit had entered your heart once you overcame your sinful resistance and stood up for Jesus. The Presbyterian-turned-Baptist Graham had taken a Methodist turn, as any popular American revivalist had to do. Salvation had to be within the reach of all individuals who set their minds and hearts on being with Jesus.[4]

Graham did all he could to ensure that his listeners' lives would be disrupted if they turned their backs on Christ. In the early 1960s he told his biographer that "I have a responsibility . . . to give people the opportunity to decide 'Yes' or 'No,' and when a man deliberately faces Christ and turns Him down, he can never be the same again." Graham strove to plant seeds of psychic turmoil in those who said no to Jesus. "People say, 'Those who leave our meetings and don't make a decision have emotional and psychological reactions.' Of course they do. When you face Jesus Christ and reject Him, you are going to have a disturbance. . . . This is the work of the Holy Spirit. He is a disturber. Christ said, 'I didn't come to bring peace, but a sword.' He said, 'I came to divide families and communities and nations.' His Gospel is divisive." Graham spurned Billy Sunday–style tirades and Aimee Semple McPherson–style special effects. That reticence did not stop him (or his main nineteenth-century model, Dwight Moody) from preaching doom to unrepentant sinners, or from striving to make them feel horrible. The results spoke for themselves. He found that preaching a sermon on the Great Judgment provoked many more decisions for Christ than a sermon on the Prodigal Son, which stressed "the love, mercy, and grace of God." Graham told the crowd that much as he disliked the subject of hell, it was "an act of mercy to warn men when they face anything so terrible."[5]

Graham's popular version of the gospel as sure deliverance from sin and anxiety—including the anxiety intentionally induced by Graham—drew repeated fire from Reinhold Niebuhr. His weekly journal of opinion, *Christianity and Crisis,* called Graham's faith "a compound of pietistic escapism, 'peace of mind,' and American self-righteousness." Niebuhr said privately that Graham was far better than those who backed him, but in print he took him to task for his offer of easy salvation and his minimal attention to social issues. "This new evangelism," Niebuhr noted in *Life* magazine, "promises a new life, not through painful religious experience but merely by signing a decision card." In the *Christian Century* Niebuhr wrote that while "the great [Charles Grandison] Finney" made the abolition of slavery "central to the religious experience of repentance and conversion," Graham, though publicly opposed to racial discrimination, failed to incorporate racial justice directly into his evangelical appeal. He did not understand that "the soul, confronted with the judgment and forgiveness of Christ, should regard racial prejudice as an element in the 'life of sin' from which the conversion experience redeems." Graham's personal "sense of justice" was "well developed," but he was programmed by the well-grooved practices of revivalism to oversimplify and individualize moral issues "for the sake of inducing an emotional crisis."[6]

Niebuhr identified two additional deficiencies in Graham's mass evangelism. First, it threatened to undo the liberal realists' quarter-century campaign to get Jesus and his pacifism out of social policy-making. "Graham honestly believes," wrote Niebuhr, "that conversion to Christianity will solve the problem of the hydrogen bomb because really redeemed men will not throw the bomb." Graham had succumbed to "perfectionist solutions for the problems of an atomic age," solutions similar in the end to those offered by pacifists ever since World War I. He was oblivious to "the serious perplexities of guilt and responsibility, and of guilt associated with responsibility, which Christians must face." Second, by promoting Jesus as the solution to social as well as personal challenges, Graham and other mass evangelists were in effect excluding Jews and other non-Christians from the civic battle for justice. Paradoxically, said Niebuhr, the deepest loyalty to Jesus in the social realm—i.e., actually bringing social justice about—meant not making too sharp a distinction between the "saved" and the "unsaved." The Reformation's insistence on the persistent sinfulness of the "saved" offered a better foundation for social ethics than Graham's "perfectionist" linkage of individual conversion and social virtue. The United States had never been a "Christian nation." Christians should concentrate on "the precariousness of the virtues of the redeemed" and build bridges to Jews and "decent secularists" with whom struggles for justice must always be fought.[7]

The recent revelation that Billy Graham, during a private 1972 meeting with President Nixon, uttered a series of vehement anti-Semitic remarks lends graphic support to Niebuhr's contention that only a Reformation-based faith can account for the temptations to which "even the most devoted Christians" are liable to succumb. But the continuous fire he directed at Graham in the late 1950s prevented Niebuhr from identifying what Graham achieved at his best. Nor did Niebuhr's friend and colleague Henry Van Dusen, who defended Graham in 1956 against Niebuhr's strictures, get to the bottom of Graham's accomplishment. Van Dusen thought Graham admirable because he delivered "the pure milk of the gospel in more readily digestible form" than Niebuhr did. Van Dusen noted that he himself would never have come within the reach of Niebuhr's "sophisticated interpretation of the gospel" had he not "been first touched" by the simple pieties of an "earlier Billy," revivalist Billy Sunday. But Graham was no more offering pure milk than Niebuhr was. His gospel preaching took a particular slant on the gospel, just as Niebuhr's did. Graham's special gift—communicating reassurance tinged with admonishment—roused millions of ordinary Protestant Christians to the conviction that a supernatural Christ really did care for them personally and really would forgive their sins. No doubt Graham even sparked a few of his listeners to lives of sacrificial service, even if most heard only the offer of relief from anxiety or a free pass to heaven. At its best Graham's message contained a measure of challenge along with the free-flowing comfort. "Jesus could have healed the man with the withered arm by saying, 'Be healed,'" Graham told the New York throng. Instead, "Jesus said to him, 'stretch it forth.' The man looked at Jesus and, upon the authority of the word of God, he stretched it forth. And he was healed! I'm asking you to stretch your life forth and commit it to Christ. Surrender your life to Him to serve and to follow Him. Let Him wash your sins away and make you a new creation."[8]

II

One evening session of Billy Graham's New York crusade opened with a prayer by a twenty-eight-year-old African American preacher from Montgomery, Alabama. Martin Luther King, Jr., had been much in the news as the Montgomery Bus Boycott unfolded over the previous year. In 1957 he was already dining with heads of state, but no one could yet foresee that as the leader of a major social and political movement, King would bring Jesus back into liberal public discourse. King put a stop to the liberal realist program of banishing Jesus from politics so as to protect politics from pacifism. Perhaps only a southern African American religious leader, supported by a cross-racial and cross-denominational coalition, could have managed to resurrect the ethical idealism of Jesus as a major social force. In respectable northern culture, the publicly uttered name of Jesus had come to connote either a dangerously utopian pacifism or a primitively provincial anti-modernism. For over two decades liberal Protestants of Reinhold Niebuhr's stripe had conceded the public name of Jesus to a handful of northern Quakers and Mennonites and a mass of southern and western evangelicals. King retrieved Christ as the standard-bearer for a new democratic movement bridging South and North.

It comes as no surprise that a black political leader would express earnest devotion and indebtedness to Jesus. King stood in a long line of Jesus-heralding African American leaders, secular as well as religious. With the exception of Elijah Muhammad of the Nation of Islam, subsequent Black Muslim spokesmen, and the black-power activists of the 1960s, every major African American leader in the nineteenth and twentieth centuries appealed to Jesus for leverage against injustice or deliverance from oppression. It could scarcely have been otherwise given the deep penetration of Christ into black American consciousness since the early nineteenth century. No one could emerge as a credible leader among African Americans without displaying extensive knowledge of if not commitment to Jesus. Elijah Muhammad relied on the Bible too. Even if he had been educated in the Koran himself, he would have been forced to use the Bible to make contact with his faithful, virtually all of whom had been raised Christian. Secular leaders without obvious Christian credentials—Frederick Douglass, Booker T. Washington, W. E. B. Du Bois, and Marcus Garvey, for example—

strove all the harder to demonstrate familiarity with Jesus. Douglass added an appendix to his published *Narrative* to make clear that his denunciation of the southern slaveholders' religion did not imply "infidelity"—the early-nineteenth-century term for religious unbelief. Attachment to Jesus allowed Douglass to liberate himself from the folk beliefs and licentious practices that enchained his fellow slaves. The moral discipline and wisdom of Christianity could reverse the dissipation and ignorance imposed on the slave quarters by professedly Christian slave-owners. Jesus delivered slaves from cultural as well as legal and political servitude.[9]

Booker T. Washington of the Tuskegee Institute modified Douglass's position by seeing southern black devotion to Jesus after the Civil War as a primitive folk belief in its own right, and an obstacle to practical community development. "The Negro has been satisfied with 'Jesus,'" he said in 1888, "and the white man has gotten all the cotton." Yet Washington came back around to a version of Douglass's position by using Christian religion as an instrument of modernization. In an address to a national gathering of Unitarians in 1894, he described southern black culture as so steeped in emotionally charged religious feelings that African Americans took one of their favorite song lines literally: "You may have all de world, but give me Jesus." They actually "like to live in the next world" right now, talking incessantly about "heavenly mansions," "golden slippers," and "milk and honey." Since hopes for the future were already so present and so tangible, reformers could appropriate them as tools for change. The material longings voiced in the old Christian framework could be put to new purposes. "We teach that the way to have the most of Jesus, and to have him in a substantial way, is to mix in some land, cotton and corn and a good bank account; and we find, by actual experience, that the man who has Jesus in this way has a religion that you can count on seven days in the week."[10]

W. E. B. Du Bois, the greatest African American intellectual of the twentieth century and a founder of the NAACP, gave up belief in Jesus as a young adult, but that personal shift only made him more intrigued by the staying power of Christ in black American consciousness. His classic *Souls of Black Folk* (1903) is a passionate meditation on the constitutive power of Christianity in African American experience—it preceded even the family, he argued— and on the historic role of spirituals in lending comfort and hope to a people victimized beyond normal powers of endurance. "The Negro church made the Negro race in America," he wrote in 1916. Like his sometime-nemesis Booker T. Washington, with whom he disagreed politically, the secular Du Bois employed Jesus as a bridge to white as well as African American Christians. Unlike Washington, he invoked Jesus to condemn the American national failure to protect its citizens' basic rights. He often made the point generally and hopefully, as in his Christmas message in 1910. "This is the month of the Christ Child. This is the month when there was reborn in men the ideal of doing to their neighbors that which they would wish done to themselves. It was a divine idea—a veritable Son of God. . . . God grant that on some Christmas day our nation and all others will plant themselves on this one platform: equal justice and equal opportunity for all races." And he made the point specifically and irately, as in his 1913 vision of Jesus coming to America: "Jesus Christ was a laborer and black men are laborers; He was poor and we are poor; He was despised of his fellow men and we are despised; He was persecuted and crucified and we are mobbed and lynched. If Jesus Christ came to America he would associate with Negroes and Italians and working people; He would eat and pray with them, and He would seldom see the interior of the Cathedral of St. John the Divine."[11]

Jamaican immigrant Marcus Garvey, the intellectually eclectic head of the Universal Negro Improvement Association in the 1920s, could not abide Du Bois's interracial approach to justice. Jesus provided the proof of its inadequacy. "The salvation of this race cannot come through the admixture of black and white people working toward that end, because the mass of white people everywhere are the same today as they were when Jesus visited this world; and Jesus tried to bring humanity together but failed. . . . If Jesus Christ failed, I do not see how Du Bois can do it." Garvey disputed Du Bois's view of how to build a movement, but he saw eye to eye with him about the relevance of Jesus to the black American experience of victimization. "Our Blessed Redeemer," he wrote in his Christmas message in 1921, was killed by the same sort of "wild and wicked men" who "seek the lives of Negroes today, and burn and lynch and kill them" (see fig. 33).[12]

Garvey knew how to build a following. Martin Luther King later called him "the first man of color in the history of the United States to lead and develop a mass movement," the first "to give millions of Negroes a sense of dignity and destiny and make the Negro feel he was somebody." Garvey drew thousands of African Americans to a vision of trans-Atlantic racial pride and unity. And he achieved that remarkable result in part by appealing to Jesus as a symbol of a racial unity that specifically involved color while also transcending it. It was evident, said Garvey, that Jesus was not white. White people had devised that idea, just as they had colored the devil black. Not being white, however, did not make Jesus a black man. "Jesus Christ was not white, black, or yellow. . . . The line from which He came had connection with every race existing, hence Jesus Christ is the embodiment of all humanity." Indeed, God could not have given the Son any one color, since God, being a spirit, "has no color." Garvey preferred to visualize Jesus as a blend of hues ("colored"). But he added that if whites continued to present Christ as white, he would restore some balance by shading him black. Since "in America the man who has any colored blood in his veins is regarded as a Negro," he noted in 1927, it would be especially (and ironically) appropriate for Americans to depict him as a Negro. In fact, of course, Jesus was just plain "colored . . . as much a Mongolian, a Caucasian as he was African. The idea of Christ being a black man is simply being enunciated in keeping with the idea of white men making Him white. . . . Christ came to save all mankind. He, therefore, took in everything that was human, from white to black—and everything in between."[13]

Like Garvey, Martin Luther King placed his social and political activities on a theological foundation. Like Du Bois, King envisioned an interracial movement for justice. Unlike any of his predecessors, he rode his charisma, courage, intellect, and political talent to an unprecedented position of national leadership as a moral and religious interpreter of "the American dream." He had an uncanny sense of how Jesus could and could not serve that cause. Like Washington Gladden and Walter Rauschenbusch between the 1880s and 1910s, he brought the militant idealism of Jesus to bear on the social struggle. But he went beyond them in explicitly rejecting the idea of the United States as an actual or potential Christian nation. In his single most important oration, the "I Have a Dream" speech on the centenary of Lincoln's Emancipation Proclamation, he said nothing about Christ. Instead he quoted the Declaration of Independence (as Lincoln had done at Gettysburg) and cited two Hebrew prophets, Amos ("We will not be satisfied until justice rolls down like waters and righteousness like a mighty stream," 5:24) and Isaiah ("Every valley shall be exalted, and every hill and mountain shall be made low; the rough places will be made plain, and the crooked places will be made straight; and the glory of the Lord shall be revealed, and all flesh shall see it together," 40:4–5). The last phrase from Isaiah was the key theme of the speech: all Americans shall see the glory of equality together. His individual dream, he said, was "deeply rooted in the American dream." That dream concerned "all God's children, black men and white men, Jews and Gentiles." America was Judeo-Christian, King thought, not Christian. The God of the Hebrew Scriptures would supply the strength to move mountains of prejudice and exclusion.[14]

Yet Jesus permeated King's self-understanding, just as he did African American identity. King's brother, father, grandfather, and great-grandfather were all preachers. He could hardly help seeing his life and America's future in relation to Jesus. He performed the virtual miracle in mid-twentieth-century America of mobilizing a new imitation of Christ for the purpose of civil freedom for all. He worked out the theological dimension of that imitation as a student at Crozer Seminary and as a young preacher in Montgomery. As a twenty-one-year-old at Crozer he freed himself from the constraints of Reinhold Niebuhr's anti-pacifism while retaining Niebuhr's sense of "the reality of sin on every level of man's existence." He realized that Niebuhr's longstanding repudiation of "the false optimism" of liberal Protestantism had been so overpoweringly effective that most young theological students held all social idealism in suspicion. Studying Gandhi gave King a transformative insight: nonviolent social action could be both realistic and idealistic. Nonviolent resistance to evil could combine worldly political tactics with a spiritual discipline based on Christ's love-commandment. King thought Niebuhr was right to reject Christ's doctrine of complete nonresistance to evil. Gandhi showed how to reconceive Christ's "turning the other cheek" so that it became a vehicle of justice as well as love. Everything hinged on Gandhi's conviction that "it is better to be the recipient of violence than the inflictor of it, since the latter only multiplies the existence of violence and bitterness in the universe, while the former may develop a sense of shame in the opponent, and thereby bring about a transformation and change of heart."[15]

For a time, according to King, his insight remained strictly intellectual. He had no idea he would soon be applying it to an actual social struggle. The Montgomery Bus Boycott of 1956 changed all that. It refined his understanding of Christ's love-commandment while confirming his commitment to nonviolent social action. The 1957 sermon he preached on "Loving Your Enemies" shows how his viewpoint had developed. He argued that Jesus, often dismissed as "an impractical idealist," was in fact "the practical realist." King identified several stages on the difficult path to achieving love of enemy. First came analyzing yourself to uncover any aspect of your own behavior that might have contributed to another person's or group's hatred of you. Next came an effort to detect possible elements of good in the enemy. For "within the best of us, there is some evil, and within the worst of us, there is some good." The goal is to perceive "God's image" in the other person, "no matter what he does." The goal is achieved when you realize that you do not wish "to defeat your enemy," but only "to defeat the system" in which your enemy "happen[s] to be caught up." The love that Jesus preached—"agape" in Greek—asked nothing from another person, unlike "eros" (romantic love) or "philia" (friendship). The love of enemies was "agape": "You love men not because they are likable, but because God loves them. You look at every man, and you love him because you know God loves him. And he might be the worst person you've ever seen." Jesus never said you had to like your enemy personally. You only had to love him impersonally.[16]

The intensity and intricacy of King's experience of Jesus came into sharp and final focus the night before his death, when he delivered his "I've Been to the Mountaintop" address to the striking Memphis sanitation workers. Toward the end of the speech he retold the parable of the Good Samaritan as a nondenominational call for all Americans to stop what they were doing and fight for justice. The priest and Levite worried about what would happen to them if they stopped to help their fellow Jew wounded by the side of the road. The non-Jew Samaritan put ethnic division aside and bound the injured man's wounds. King the preacher announced the moral upshot: imitate the Samaritan by doing the right thing, not the safe thing.

Then King entered the parable personally. It became a summary of his own life as spiritual leader and prospective victim. He recalled renting a car and driving with his wife down the road from Jerusalem to Jericho. "It's a winding, meandering road . . . conducive to ambushing." He had journeyed on such a road in the past: in 1958 a "demented woman" had stabbed him in the chest with an eight-inch letter-opener as he sat in a Harlem bookstore signing copies of his *Stride Toward Freedom: The Montgomery Story*.

He came within a sneeze or a cough of dying, the doctors told him. "If I had sneezed," King declared to the Memphis audience, "I wouldn't have been around" for the sit-ins in 1960, for the freedom rides in 1961, for Albany, Georgia, in 1962, for Birmingham and "I Have a Dream" in 1963, for Selma in 1965, or for Memphis in 1968. The very morning of his speech, he reported, his plane from Atlanta had been delayed for a bomb search. Whether he lived or died now mattered little. God's will be done. The road to Jericho beckoned, and King was traveling it as Good Samaritan (he had stopped in Memphis to help the sanitation workers) and as innocent voyager about to be set upon by thieves.

In Christian sermons going back to the early church, Jesus too was described as both Jew by the side of the road (the sacrificial victim) and compassionate Samaritan (the savior). King drew on that long tradition, and on secular American predecessors such as Eugene Debs, in voicing his readiness to give himself up for his people. In the Memphis oration King taught his fellow citizens how best to worship Jesus in a religiously plural nation: you display your intimacy with him, but you never suggest he loves you more than he loves everyone else. You show in your tone as much as your words that being intimate with him has prepared you for suffering as well as joy. Being intimate with him has opened you up to the wisdom of Christ's own tradition, the Jewish tradition. King makes that point emphatically at the end of the speech by likening his role to that of Moses: "I just want to do God's will. And He's allowed me to go up to the mountain. And I've looked over and I've seen the Promised Land. I may not get there with you. But I want you to know tonight that we, as a people, will get to the Promised Land."[17]

III

Martin Luther King was shot and killed the following day, Thursday, April 4, 1968. Catholic writer Dorothy Day, founder of the

Catholic Worker movement in the 1930s, remarked at the spiritual discipline with which he had approached his martyrdom. "He knew he would be killed for the faith that was in him. . . . [He] died daily, as St. Paul said." How appropriate, she observed, that the following day was Good Friday, "when Jesus Christ, true God and true man, shed His blood." For the Catholic Dorothy Day, King belonged to the company of the saints. "The courage with which he expected his own martyrdom," she wrote in 1978, two years before her own death, placed him alongside such early martyrs as St. Polycarp, St. Ignatius of Antioch, St. Perpetua, and St. Blandina. She was fascinated by the "joy and patience" with which martyrs met their fates. At the end, they "did not seem to suffer." She took the sacrificed Martin Luther King, along with the others, as an actual revelation of the living Christ. Saints imitated Christ, but more important they manifested him. "When the martyr suffers and dies," she wrote, quoting Father Louis Bouyer's *Liturgical Piety*, "it is so truly Christ Who suffers and dies, that the suffering is transcended, and the risen Christ is revealed in the martyr's very death." Dorothy Day's response to the death of King exhibits a mystical strain of Catholic thinking and feeling about Jesus that can be traced back to Sister Marie de St. Joseph in seventeenth-century Quebec and beyond. Orestes Brownson converted to Catholicism in 1844 because the church offered intellectual certainty and an unchanging supernatural Christ. Dorothy Day converted to Catholicism in 1927 for much the same reason Elizabeth Seton did in 1805: because the church offered a living Christ who died daily and invited her to a strenuous life of "holy obedience." Their faith took a mystical and ethical turn, while Brownson's moved in a logical and philosophical direction. His faith stood as a bulwark against secularism and naturalism, while theirs sanctified the secular and the natural. Yet all three of them demonstrated how a Catholic Jesus, in his impersonal supernatural glory and his intimately personal physicality, offered many nineteenth- and twentieth-century American Protestants an alternative path to God.[18]

As a young woman Day had gravitated to Greenwich Village, worked for the radical magazine *The Masses,* and experienced the "desires for freedom and for pleasure" that marked a unique generation of cultural and political revolutionaries. She felt tugged by her "own gropings for the love of others," but she sensed something missing in the freedom preached by John Reed, Max Eastman, and Emma Goldman. She was "revolted" by the "promiscuity" she associated with the "free lover" Goldman (though the anarchist Goldman explicitly rejected promiscuity and said "free love" simply meant getting the state out of the love-regulating business). But Day's deeper complaint concerned too much self, not too much sex, and on that score she indicted herself as much as the others. She dove into doing "works of mercy" for the down-and-out and wanted "to go on picket lines, to go to jail." But she was afflicted by "how much ambition and how much self-seeking there was in all this." She groped for a love that permitted self-surrender, the kind of losing oneself, according to Jesus, that permitted finding oneself. But she never imagined how immense the physical and spiritual force of love could be until her daughter, Tamar, was born. Her breathtaking state of union with this helpless little being made her forget her preoccupation with freedom. Now she wanted to adore rather than seek. She entered the Catholic Church because "I had reached the point where I wanted to obey. . . . I was tired of following the devices and desires of my own heart, . . . which always seemed to lead me astray."[19]

The Catholic mystical tradition gave Day the framework she needed for her half-century of service to the poor. The people she served were revelations of God just as the saints were, holy creations made in his image. Day liked to recount "the vision of Saint Elizabeth of Hungary, who put the leper in her bed and later, going to tend him, saw no longer the leper's stricken face, but the face of Christ." Day had no visions herself. There were no halos around the heads of the poor she met, "at least none that human eyes can see." Since she thought the homeless urban poor were especially despised in America, she saw them as the special recipients of and exhibits of Christ's love. In her view, Jesus of Nazareth expressed his radicalism in his general call for justice and in his personal association with the despised—the poor, the Samaritans, the prostitutes, the tax collectors. Like Martin Luther King seeking God's image in the enemy, Day went out of her way to counsel love for the tax collectors with whom she and the Catholic Worker movement tangled. After one meeting with the IRS, Day wrote that "our struggle is with principalities and powers. . . . As peacemakers we must have love and respect for each individual we come in contact with."[20]

When she started the Catholic Worker movement during the depression of the 1930s, she thought of it as a beacon of justice, a means of "building up a new social order" through journalism, discussion, and action. But "God . . . made it a place for the poor." Catholic Worker Houses of Hospitality provided food and clothing to anyone, no questions asked and no reformation required. Critics suggested that this charity was "contributing to laziness," or that the recipients of free clothes were exchanging them for alcohol or drugs. Day responded that "the reason for our existence is to praise God, to love Him and serve Him, and we can do this only by loving our brothers." Once a well-to-do woman came by the Catholic Worker house in Manhattan to donate a diamond ring to the cause. Rather than sell it for much-needed money, Day bestowed it on a solitary old woman. A staff member complained that the money could have paid the woman's rent for a year. "Do you suppose," answered Day, "that God created diamonds only for the rich?" The woman could herself decide whether to sell it or enjoy seeing it sparkle on her finger. Sometimes Day took a hard line with the poor, but only when they threatened the order of the house. One day she evicted a slovenly and obstreperous woman, but before doing so she took the woman in her arms, kissed her, and told her she loved her—loved the person she really was underneath, the one temporarily hidden by the disturbing behavior. Participating in the mystical body of Christ, for Day, meant partaking of his body in the sacrament and touching his body in those of the poor.[21]

Dorothy Day's life with the poor in New York resembles that of Jane Addams at Hull House a half-century earlier. Both women were inspired by Jesus, and both were reborn as adult women when they created novel communities of service. But the Catholic Day and the liberal Protestant Addams diverged dramatically in their assumptions about culture and politics. Hull House's service to the poor formed part of a campaign for cultural education of both the poor and her own middle-class residents. Addams wished ultimately for a democratic society providing equal access to the means of self-development and equal appreciation for everyone else's way of life. Fellowship in a democratic society meant that everyone would grow in cultured conversation, discussing the arts, history, literature, and science as well as debating the public good in politics. Service for Addams did not entail "reforming" the poor any more than it did for Day, but Addams always tied it to individual and communal transformation. This endeavor amounted to a secularizing of the old Calvinist urge to heighten everyone's heart-experience of God. It also restated the old republican ideal of citizen equality and the old Enlightenment hope that everyone could grow in grounded knowledge of the world. Jesus functioned for Addams as a model of sacrificial service and as a theorist who erased any firm line between sacred and secular. He roamed the entire world, seeking disciples in every realm of experience. The virtue he taught was not "religious" but "social."

Day's conception of the good life differed considerably from Addams's. She shared Addams's commitment to pacifism and social justice, and put as much energy into political action as Addams did. But Day's politics protested against the brutalities of power; it did not mobilize people for wider participation in an ongoing cultural conversation. Education as such did not figure as a significant goal for Day. She sought sanctity. The Catholic Church drew her in the 1920s because it gathered the uneducated masses, not the

highly schooled elites. Unlike Addams, Day had inherited no culture she wished to pass on to the poor. On the contrary, she
yearned for their imagined simplicity and even poverty—not abject
poverty, but a poverty of spirit in which "things" were not one's
prime possessions. For Addams the passionate life combined learning with service, while for Day it followed service to the point of
self-surrender—the point where the old meaning of "passion," the
suffering of a martyr, was reborn. Day pictured Jesus as both a social radical and a mystical Christ, but his radicalism witnessed to
truth and justice rather than trying to build a new society. Indeed,
Day's spirituality and social action were both driven by the desire
to apprehend Christ beyond culture altogether, by apprehending
herself and her contemporaries *sub specie aeternitatis,* in their eternal
aspect as sons and daughters of God. The power of her witness lay
in her insight that one could undertake sacred work in the everyday alleyways of the world. Living in voluntary poverty in Manhattan presented the same opportunity for holiness as withdrawal
to the desert or the convent.[22]

Much of the Catholic radicalism of the 1960s (unlike the liberation theology of the 1970s) shared Dorothy Day's enthusiasm
for witnessing over educating for a new society. Father Daniel
Berrigan, who with his brother Philip (also a priest) and seven
other protesters applied homemade napalm to the draft-board
records of several hundred Catonsville, Maryland, men in 1968,
spoke with unusual clarity about the radicalism of witness. A few
weeks after the Catonsville incident, Daniel Berrigan came to say
Mass at Dorothy Day's new Catholic Worker house in New York.
Afterward someone asked him why he believed burning draft
records would be effective. He replied, in a journalist's summary of
his words, that "of course it had not been a useful act, a political
act. . . . How useful were the acts of the martyrs? How many martyrs ever had programs for reforming society? Since politics
weren't working anyway, one had to find an act beyond politics: a
religious act, a liturgical act, an act of witness." The model was

"Christ over-throwing the tables of the moneychangers. There were times in history when men had to destroy false idols to jolt people into justice. . . . If only a small number of men could offer this kind of witness, it would purify the world." Berrigan felt empowered to resist civil laws because that resistance concerned only his citizenship, not his "membership in Christ's body." He did not place himself above *all* law. He felt answerable only to the same judge Jesus answered to. "I will welcome the judgment of my fellow Christians," he wrote in 1970, "on my life, my sins, my lovelessness, my intemperate speech, my lassitude and fear. . . . The true God judges you and me and our works." Where Martin Luther King approved of choosing God's law over civil law only when a lawbreaker accepted the civil penalty—thus, in King's view, reaffirming the overall integrity of the civil legal system—Berrigan erected a wall of separation between civil action and holy witness.[23]

Naturally many twentieth-century American Catholic writers, thinkers, and educators followed Jane Addams rather than Day or Berrigan in working for a unified democratic-ethical citizenship rather than resisting the status quo through radical witness. Two of the most influential Catholic thinkers of the twentieth century were the priests John A. Ryan and John Courtney Murray. Both devoted their careers to reconciling Catholic tradition with American democracy. But what has united virtually all Catholics, conservative, liberal, or radical, and distinguishes them from many Protestants, evangelical and non-evangelical, is their deep-seated sense that Christ is a living presence continuously in their midst. Despite the rise of a "charismatic" movement among American Catholics in the late twentieth century, Catholics are much less likely than Protestants to crave a rebirth of spirit. Jesus was never absent, so why would he need to transform a person's heart? Catholics are also much less likely to probe the gospel accounts for compelling evidence that what they recount about Jesus is factually "true." Many Catholics look on in detachment if not amusement as evangelical Christians proclaim the unerring truth of biblical passages, and as liberal

Protestants in the "Jesus Seminar" (joined by an occasional liberal Catholic such as John Dominic Crossan) respond by weighing the evidence that Jesus actually said or did the specific things the gospels claim he said or did. All this intense Protestant dissecting of the biblical text is beside the point for most Catholics, who believe that the church was empowered by Jesus to promulgate his ever-living truth. Catholics shake their heads at the anti-intellectualism or hyper-textualism to which many Protestants are forced by their skepticism about the church as the body of Christ persisting in the world. Without a church that reinterprets the Bible as time passes, Protestants are led (or so it seems to many Catholics) to worship the Bible more consistently than they worship the living Christ.

The Catholic standpoint is well expressed by theologian David Tracy in his pivotal book *The Analogical Imagination* (1981), one of the most widely hailed works of American Catholic theology in the late twentieth century. "Our primary understanding of the Christ event," Tracy writes, "is fundamentally a present experience—a realized experience of recognition of that event's disclosure of God." That experience is "mediated to us, directly or indirectly, through the . . . whole church as the living tradition re-presenting that Christ event" in "word and sacrament." Individuals meet Christ directly in their experiences of faith, just as Protestants do, but the "tradition" embodied in the church "challenges every individual response with its centuries-long memory and its fundamental fidelity to the authoritative apostolic witnesses to the event itself." The church's memory includes all the "saints and witnesses to that event, the reformers, mystics, theologians, activists, prophets, sages" as well as "the outcasts in every period whose memory, often effaced, cannot be forgotten." In the wake of the reforms of the Second Vatican Council in the 1960s, Catholic theology and much Catholic practice stress more clearly than ever the centrality of Jesus among all those saints and wise men and women. All of them "come to us now in the light of the church's primary apostolic memory of this one person, Jesus of Nazareth."[24]

Since Vatican II American Catholics are in some ways closer to Protestants than they used to be. Jesus gets more exclusive attention as the center of the faith, and he is worshiped in English rather than Latin (apart from the Latin traditionalists, such as actor Mel Gibson, who have mounted resistance to what they consider the Vatican's Babel-of-tongues pluralism). Mary and the saints are downplayed in church theology and in church interior decorating: thousands of statues of the Virgin, St. Anthony, St. Christopher, and others disappeared from Catholic churches after the 1960s. Mary continues to flourish in many Latinos' piety, especially among Chicanos for whom the Virgin of Guadalupe is a national as well as religious symbol. But if a Protestant-style concentration on Jesus is now more explicit in Catholic thought and practice, most Catholics of all ethnic groups and all political persuasions still feel Christ in a markedly different way than most Protestants do. He is the suffering Lord on the cross, the living presence of the divine, and the mystical Body of the whole church. For most American Catholics he is still surrounded by his saints and his Holy Family, as he was in the seventeenth century (see figs. 1–3). His exact historical identity in the first century, his precise spoken words, his comings and goings into and out of human hearts are all less important than his continuous physical gift of himself in the eucharistic ritual administered by his one holy and apostolic church.[25]

IV

One might suspect that the development of mass popular culture in America in the twentieth century would have homogenized conceptions of Jesus, breaking down sharp distinctions between Protestant and Catholic experiences of him. Certainly the rise of film loosened if it did not eliminate the evangelical objection to making images of Jesus. Evangelical Protestants still strenuously avoid the use of visual images in collective worship. But in their private devotions many Protestants have incorporated representations of Christ, greatly reducing the distance between their worship of Jesus and that of their Catholic neighbors. Art historian David Morgan contends that American Protestants from Calvinist traditions (the Reformed churches, the Presbyterians, and the Baptists, along with the Congregationalists now subsumed into the United Church of Christ) have largely set aside their historical fear that praying in front of an image of Jesus puts his Word at risk. Many now join Episcopalians and Lutherans in taking for granted the spiritual benefits of pictures. By the mid-twentieth century, Morgan suggests, large numbers of Protestants, mainly women, had adopted the Catholic practice of venerating Jesus images. These images had become virtual icons, avenues to the divine if not sacred objects in themselves. Even in the nineteenth century many Protestants had hung images of Christ in their living rooms as signs of their piety and of the sacredness of home. New to the twentieth century, according to Morgan, was the use of the pictures in prayer and meditation.

The picture most favored by Protestants, hands down, is the "Head of Christ" painted by Warner Sallman in 1941 and distributed in millions of copies since then throughout Catholic as well as Protestant America (see fig. 16). Many adults now cherish the picture because they grew up with it and associate it with their families of origin. One of Morgan's five hundred respondents explained that the image still brings "instantaneous peace to my mind" because he had gotten such comfort from it as a child. Peace of mind was equally important to another respondent. "When I'm feeling stressed out, I look on my wall and know I'm not alone. It has a very calming effect on me." But the image, she wrote, "also helps me when I pray. It makes me feel, because I see him, that he is really here with me." Prayer operates here on a typically Protestant track of trying to overcome separation from Jesus. Lacking the sacramental infusion available to Catholics, evangelical Protestants have to meet Jesus in their heads and hearts. On Sundays they can meet Jesus in the Word preached and sung, but during the week many now rely on visual assurance that Jesus is "really here with me." Still, they know the Protestant drill and keep repeating it: "Of course it's true," wrote one respondent, echoing the sentiments of many others, "that we worship the Saviour and not his picture."[26]

Morgan reports that many Protestants continue to be apologetic about their craving for such imagery, sensing the scowl of some long-buried Calvinist ancestor. But they justify their practice in much the same way that Catholics have always defended iconography. Bringing Jesus close through visual imagery is perfectly compatible with the knowledge that he transcends any representation. The interesting irony suggested by Morgan's data is that some Protestants appear to have given Jesus a mediating role akin to the one Catholics have long given to Mary and the saints: petitioning him to intercede with God. There is nothing new for Protestants in seeing Jesus as mediator. For them he is the one legitimate "midman," as Thomas Shepard put it, between themselves and God. But orthodox Protestants have always talked directly to the Father in prayer, just as they have to the Son. Indeed, Shepard was on more intimate daily terms with the Father than he was with Jesus, for all Christ's importance to him as the mediator of God's grace. What may be new in twentieth-century Protestantism is the spread of explicit personal prayer to a visualized mediator who is asked to intervene with the Father. If the experience of one Protestant mother is typical, Protestants are now a good deal more like Catholics than they used to be. When her daughter was seriously ill, Sallman's "Head of Christ" became her "confidant" and "crutch." "I talked, cried, and pleaded with it for strength, not only for my daughter, but for all of us to cope with the pain and agony. . . . Every day I asked God, through the portrait, to keep her with us."[27]

But twentieth-century mass culture, rather than breaking down Catholic-Protestant differences, has simply given Catholics and Protestants a wider variety of representations of Jesus than ever before. They can use those images as occasions for reaffirming, refining, or modifying their beliefs, an open-ended process that accentuates variations among groups as often as it attenuates them. Jesus films continued in the late twentieth century to be the primary arena of culture-wide discussion about images of Jesus. Early Jesus films, like Cecil B. DeMille's *King of Kings* (1927), established the propriety of visualizing Jesus, in part through their explicit piety and in part through their heavy emphasis on the written Word. Naturally a silent film like *King of Kings* relied heavily on verbal text—the captions were essential to the storytelling. The 1961 remake of *King of Kings* by Nicholas Ray still highlighted the Word. In fact it did much more than DeMille's film to present Jesus as a preacher and teacher, featuring an elaborate Sermon on the Mount. But Ray's *King of Kings* was anachronistic in its sanctimonious religiosity. It was still trying to uplift and purify by presenting a perfect holy man, a gesture that succeeded only in divesting him of his humanity. George Stevens's epic box-office failure *The Greatest Story Ever Told* (1965) suffered from the same wooden sanctifying. Max Von Sydow's Jesus was even more spiritless than Jeffrey Hunter's in the second *King of Kings.* Audiences in the 1920s were moved to tears by the holier-than-thou self-distancing of H. B. Warner. Audiences in the 1960s were bored by such one-note beneficence. The only things truly made holy in *The Greatest Story Ever Told* were the gorgeous Technicolor mesas of the American Southwest. Where Ray's *King of Kings* improved most upon DeMille's was in blaming the Romans as much as the Jews for the death of Jesus. If anything, the 1961 version tried too hard to correct DeMille's anti-Semitic characterizations by opening with a scene of Roman soldiers crucifying an entire landscape of Jewish rebels. But the film wisely presented a decisive Pilate and avoided blaming the Jewish crowd for collaborating with or intimidating the high priest Caiaphas.[28]

The long-needed corrective to the on-screen Christs of the 1960s came with the Jesus films of the 1970s and 1980s, most notably *Jesus Christ Superstar* (1973) and *The Last Temptation of Christ* (1988). These

Hollywood productions followed Italian filmmaker Pier Paolo Pasolini's *The Gospel of Saint Matthew* (1964) in offering a Jesus whose humanity was credible to late-twentieth-century audiences (though the American films spurned Pasolini's populist-reformer Jesus). Holy Christs floating piously above their peers had still seemed human in the 1920s—as long as they were physically imposing. By the 1960s, psychological intensity (or, in Pasolini's case, radical politics) had trumped august authority, whether effete or muscular. *Jesus Christ Superstar,* Norman Jewison's film of the Andrew Lloyd Webber and Tim Rice Broadway play of 1971, was especially imaginative in depicting the humanity of Christ in recognizably late-twentieth-century terms. Ted Neeley's Jesus was presented as a celebrity desperately seeking relief from fame.

"Celebrity" had become a widely discussed social phenomenon in twentieth-century America, and Jesus was inevitably invoked to help illuminate it. The humanity of Jesus has evolved over the centuries in response to social developments of that sort. People in Christianized societies naturally grasp emergent social and cultural phenomena—the anti-slavery movement, the labor movement—in relation to him. The process works in two ways at once. People utter the name of Jesus as a means of lending authority to their views. Some individuals then realize that the new realities demand a new view of Jesus, or a return to an old one that has been forgotten. They use newly prominent social issues to reconfigure his identity and to restore his authority. The first explicit use of the modern celebrity concept with respect to Jesus may have been Beatle John Lennon's 1966 remark that the Beatles were "more popular than Jesus." His comment certainly first brought the idea of Jesus as a celebrity to wide public attention. Conservative Christians took Lennon's quip as an attack upon their faith. Even much of the mainstream press was shocked, along with being entertained. Commentators were unable to decide which was worse, illiberal Christians burning Beatle records or a megalomaniac Lennon putting Jesus and celebrities like himself on the same scale.

Lennon was made to look as ridiculous as the record-burners. He made an abject public apology at a press conference in Chicago. "I'm not anti-God, anti-Christ, or anti-religion," he said in his meek-and-lowly response to the withering criticism. "I was not saying we are greater or better." But he was saying that attachment to Jesus was like attachment to any cult hero. The applause meter could measure both preferences.[29]

Four years later, the libretto of the rock opera *Jesus Christ Superstar* made the notion of Jesus as celebrity explicit. The Webber/Rice album was an instant and massive hit when Decca released it in the fall of 1970. The Broadway show in 1971 benefited from the general perception that the play concerned a "hippie" Jesus band, and to that extent it reflected the "Jesus people" segment of the counter-culture. In fact, *Godspell*, an off-Broadway production in 1971, came a lot closer than *Superstar* to representing the "Jesus people." *Superstar* neither advocated nor reflected any social movement. It used countercultural trappings, standard Webber melodies, and occasionally inspired Rice lyrics to present a serious Passion Play within a play. The actors arrive on a bus, put on their theater, and then (except for the actor playing Jesus, who is unaccounted for) depart again on the bus. In the last scene a shepherd is seen leading sheep across a hillside, with a cross in the distance. Is that shepherd Jesus, making a post-resurrection appearance? There is no telling.

Ted Neely's Jesus did exude contemporaneity. He was young, and his long hair brushed against his robe. ("One thing I'll say for him," sings Caiaphas in *Superstar*, "Jesus is cool.") But he stood for something deeper in the culture than hipness, and helped expose it to view. Tim Rice's Jesus was above all exhausted and beaten. In part he was beaten by the "system"—the utterly evil Jewish and Roman authorities. Caiaphas considers Jesus a threat to the nation. The high priest believes that the Jesus movement will unleash a Roman attack. Better that one man should die than an entire people. Caiaphas needs Jesus to die for political reasons. But even more important than the system in bringing Jesus to his end was his own fame. It devoured him and made him yearn for his own death. Tim Rice's Caiaphas has a politics, but his Christ has none. Jesus listens to Simon the Zealot's plea that he seek the power and glory of political leadership but rejects it vehemently. In 1971 *Superstar* delivered an indirect but nonetheless stinging judgment on the political sixties: cease and desist; seek your salvation in another world; resign yourself to the fate God has in store for you. Tim Rice's Jesus teaches no doctrine of revolution or reform. He does scarcely any teaching at all: the "end" he preaches is his own end, his own death, not the end of the world or the end of the reign of death. Granted, *Superstar* was a Passion Play, not a full life of Christ. But Rice worked scenes from the healing ministry of Jesus into his story, and he could have included parables or wisdom sayings if he had wished.

Superstar delivered a wrenching depiction of Christ's degeneration as he cultivates and is destroyed by celebrity. Judas, who in Rice's vision becomes the beloved disciple who sees what is happening to Jesus and tries unsuccessfully to stop it, degenerates too. He alone grasps what celebrity is doing to the Jesus movement and its leader. *Superstar* appealed to what everyone already knew about the cost of modern celebrity in the lives of Marilyn Monroe, who died in 1962, and many others. (Elvis Presley, who died in 1977, would join Marilyn in the upper pantheon of celebrity's victims.) In the celebrity-as-victim trope, audiences eat stars alive and then cast them aside. Stars are defined by their suffering. But the pain of Jesus in *Superstar* only superficially resembles the pain of the gospel Jesus. In *Superstar* the suffering of Christ is no more redemptive than that of Judas. Like the suffering of modern celebrities, it is a waste of precious psychic resources. In Tim Rice's remarkable Gethsemane scene, Jesus does come finally to accept whatever God has in store for him, but he has no sense of what good might come of it. It only fills him with terror. "Show me there's a reason for you wanting me to die," he wails to the Father. "You're far too keen on where and how, and not so hot on why."

The power of the celebrity-victim linkage was heightened in *Superstar* when Rice tied it to the gospel story of the Last Supper. The night before his crucifixion, Jesus taught his followers to consume bread and wine in remembrance of him. (In the Catholic rite, worshipers affirm that they are consuming his actual body and blood.) In Rice's reimagining of the gospel account, Jesus says to his disciples, "For all you care, this wine could be my blood, for all you care, this bread could be my body." *Jesus* is not the one claiming it is his body and blood; he accuses *them* of wishing it were his body and blood so they could cannibalize him. The celebrity strikes back and accuses his audience of being all appetite. They, his devoted fans, are as much the cause of his bodily destruction as the Jewish and Roman officials or the Jewish crowd. Rice's Jesus soon snaps out of it and proceeds to the orthodox Christian version of the Supper command: "This is my blood you drink. This is my body you eat. If you would [i.e., would you please] remember me when you eat and drink." But he concludes by tossing out that pious hope: "I must be mad thinking I'll be remembered."

Of course we viewers know he will be remembered. *Superstar* shrewdly combined what everyone knew about modern celebrity with what everyone knew about Jesus. Celebrity means sacrifice and defeat as much as it means fame and success. But celebrity is not always fleeting. At its core, celebrity is not so much transitory as corrosive. Immortality—as Jesus, Marilyn, and (a few years later) Elvis demonstrated—is possible, but its price is unbearable physical and psychic suffering. *Superstar* drew on cultural feelings about celebrity to revivify popular attachment to Jesus. Conversely, the libretto suggested that the Jesus of the gospels had long ago laid out the true trajectory of human celebrity. "Then, I was inspired," Jesus reflects in the Garden of Gethsemane; "now, I'm sad and tired."[30]

Jesus Christ Superstar displayed plenty of divinity. It was simply located in the Father, not in Jesus. With *The Last Temptation of Christ* (1988), based on Greek novelist Nikos Kazantzakis's 1955 work of the same name, Martin Scorsese tried to imbue Jesus with real divinity and full humanity (or at least full blue-eyed, blond-haired humanity). Willem Dafoe's Christ, like Ted Neeley's, is psychically disturbed; unlike Ted Neeley's, he performs miracles. In one scene, which only a pre–Vatican II Catholic like Scorsese could possibly have imagined, Dafoe reaches into his chest and yanks out his blood-red heart for everyone's spiritual edification. Scorsese's Jesus makes straightforward divine claims for himself. "When I say 'I,'" Jesus tells Caiaphas, "I am saying 'God.'" All of his direct assertions and demonstrations of divinity contrast with and compensate for the emphatically tormented psyche of his human self. Ted Neeley's Jesus suffers mentally from the incessant hero-worship of his admirers and disciples. Willem Dafoe's Christ is afflicted by doubts about his worth and about his ability to hold body and soul in balance.

Webber and Rice capitalized on the cultural fascination with celebrity and its discontents—using Jesus to illuminate celebrity and celebrity to reconfigure Jesus—while Scorsese capitalized on misgivings about the stability of modern selfhood. If Jesus was fully human in all things save sin, then he must have been as messed up psychically as the rest of us in the post-Freudian West think we are. As a young man he must have been assailed with sexual urges like everyone else. In itself sexual desire is natural, not sinful, so Jesus would have undergone the usual battle to tame and mold his instincts. As he languished on the cross, he could not help imagining himself in another life. In that alternative life he is married twice, fathers children, and relishes the pleasures of physical, familial love. Jesus realizes that the devil, having earlier tempted him in the desert, has returned to try it again. He wants Jesus to renounce his sacrificial divine calling in favor of physical love and domesticity. In the end Jesus resists the last temptation and embraces his atoning death. As he had earlier told Judas, "I am the sacrifice . . . I have to die on the cross . . . We're bringing God and man together. They'll never be together unless I die."

Many Christians of all denominations—Catholic, Protestant, and Orthodox—were outraged by the film. "7,500 Picket Universal Over Movie About Jesus," announced a *New York Times* article. The crowd outside Universal Studios in Los Angeles chanted J-E-S-U-S and then "assembled under several hundred multicolored helium-filled balloons tied together to form the word 'Jesus' 50 feet above their heads." Two days earlier demonstrators led by the Reverend R. L. Hymers of the Fundamentalist Baptist Tabernacle "formed a tableau outside Universal in which Lew Wasserman, the [Jewish] chairman of M.C.A. [Universal Studios' parent company] was represented as nailing Jesus to a cross." In Chicago, Greek Orthodox Christians in picket lines and ticket lines "traded insults in Greek." Most protesters were upset about Jesus' having a last-minute fantasy life involving married sex and fatherhood. Novelist and sociologist (and Catholic priest) Andrew Greeley took a different tack. There could be nothing wrong with Jesus imagining himself marrying and procreating. The Christian tradition, according to Greeley, grasped bodily urges as wholly natural. They were no more sinful than spiritual urges. Physical or spiritual states were sinful only when they put selfishness ahead of love. *Last Temptation* erred not in letting Jesus dream of an alternative moral life, but in depicting him as bedeviled by psychic doubt. Catholic theologian David Tracy agreed. While he respected Scorsese's "religious seriousness," he found his reduction of the human Jesus to "a troubled Romantic hero" both "unpersuasive" and "unbiblical."[31]

The publicity furor over *The Last Temptation of Christ* conveyed a valuable lesson to future filmmakers such as Mel Gibson, whose *Passion of the Christ* (2004) had already become a *cause célèbre* by mid-2003. In 1988 Universal saw that the pre-release ruckus over Christ's sexuality could be turned to its advantage. A low-budget film destined for art theaters might emerge as a major hit. The film was issued early to benefit from all the press and to prevent Christian opponents from coordinating large-scale picketing on opening day. Universal demonstrated that Jesus the cultural symbol could be effectively mobilized to ensure a profitable reception. Gibson's publicity campaign built upon his own mega-celebrity to focus attention on his film's prospective portrayal of Jewish responsibility for the death of Jesus. The Anti-Defamation League appealed to the Catholic Gibson to heed the lessons of modern scholarship (give the Roman prefect Pontius Pilate at least as much responsibility as you impute to the Jewish high priest Caiaphas) and the injunctions of the Catholic Church (avoid centuries-old stereotypes of Jewish venality or maliciousness). The controversy sparked frenzied national debate about Gibson's impending response, and ensured an immensely lucrative opening. (I treat the film in the new Postscript to this book.)[32]

The Passion of the Christ struck many reviewers as *schlock* art—in aesthetic terms a kitschy and unimaginative work. But it makes equal sense to see the film as *shock* art from the Right. Like F. Holland Day and more recent radical artists, Gibson used Jesus to test the bounds of cultural decorum while trying to represent the sacred. The Brooklyn artist Andres Serrano did the same thing in his 1987 photograph "Piss Christ"—a crucifix obscured by and glowing within an amber-reddish medium. As the title suggests, it turns out to be urine illuminated by red light. The image itself looks positively holy. The title, however, is designed to provoke, and to force a decision on the viewer's part: Do I take urine as an unobjectionable, natural bodily fluid, or do I take it as a culturally inflected symbol of profanity? Do I take the title itself, wholly aside from the image, as obscene speech? Serrano forces observers to answer the question whether what they see with their eyes is overruled by what they are told in writing. He also provokes thought about whether there is any justifiable limit to a community's tolerance for free speech and free art. Along the way he makes viewers realize that Jesus is one of the few remaining cultural symbols that most Americans consider sacred and that almost all Americans would refuse to profane. Of course what is "profane" to one generation is often unobjectionable to the next. Most Americans in the 1950s would have gagged at seeing the American flag emblazoned on articles of clothing, a practice now associated with patriotism. Today, when most people are used to seeing the flag or Jesus Christ on T-shirts (see fig. 20), they nevertheless object strenuously to a photograph such as "Piss Christ" or "Yo Mama's Last Supper," Renée Cox's depiction of a nude female Christ dining with her twelve disciples displayed at the Brooklyn Museum in early 2001. Most Americans probably object with equal vehemence to performances of Terrence McNally's 1998 play *Corpus Christi*, which features a Christlike gay man (Joshua) and his twelve gay followers. *Corpus Christi* tests cultural boundaries via satire as well as sexuality: the Last Supper, for example, is punctuated by a food fight.[33]

V

There is nothing new about Jesus' serving as a charged symbol in American culture wars. The novel departure at the very end of the twentieth century may have been his explicit appearance as a campaign issue in presidential politics. The reemergence of a consciously evangelical Protestant voting bloc, thanks to Jerry Falwell's Moral Majority in the 1970s and Pat Robertson's presidential campaign in 1988, prepared the way for an unexpected invocation of Jesus during the Republican primary season of the year 2000. Six candidates had assembled at the Des Moines Civic Center for a televised debate before the Iowa vote. They tussled genially on abortion, school violence, and ethanol. Then local TV reporter John Bachman livened things up by asking the candidates which "political philosopher or thinker" they "most identif[ied] with." "John Locke," said Steve Forbes. "The founding fathers," said Alan Keyes. "Theodore Roosevelt," said John McCain. "Abraham Lincoln and Ronald Reagan," said Orrin Hatch. Governor George W. Bush of Texas took another tack. "Christ," he answered, "because He changed my heart." Bachman asked Bush to say "more on how he's changed your heart." Bush explained that "when you turn your heart and your life over to Christ, when you accept Christ as a savior, it changes your heart, and changes your life, and that's what happened to me." The upstaged "evangelical" candidate Gary Bauer, speaking last, scrambled to establish that he liked Jesus just as much as Bush did.[34]

Much of the press scoffed at Bush for what seemed an obvious appeal to Iowa's evangelicals, or worse, a stab in the dark by an intellectual lightweight who could think of no real philosopher to name. *Boston Globe* columnist James Carroll called it "a breathtaking display of ignorance" to invoke Christ "in the context of political philosophy." *New York Times* columnist Maureen Dowd saw the crassest politics at work: "W. is checking Jesus' numbers, and Jesus is polling well in Iowa. Christ, the new wedge issue." Both writers missed the larger cultural revelation in Bush's response. Most Americans do not have a favorite philosopher and look skeptically at egghead candidates like 2000 Democratic hopeful Bill Bradley who do (John Dewey is Bradley's favorite). They have a redeemer who lives in their hearts, not in their minds. Bush's answer was certainly politically motivated, but there is no reason to doubt the sincerity of his belief. A majority of Americans would answer the question just as he did, in the same "heart" language. Jesus is their hero, their staff and support, their personal savior, as he has been for most Americans since at least the early nineteenth century. And evangelical born-again rhetoric is if anything more prevalent across the country at the start of the twenty-first century than it was at the start of the nineteenth or twentieth, when highbrow Protestants were better positioned to resist it than they are today. Bush's answer in Des Moines is a sign of the partial return of evangelical language to the respectability it enjoyed in northern Protestant culture before the Scopes Trial and the Niebuhrian liberal realists banished it from the cultural mainstream. Bush got political mileage out of his words because he showed he can speak a pious language of the heart and do so, to all outward appearances, from the heart.[35]

The irony of Bush's answer, and of the critical response it provoked, is that no one seemed to notice that he had an illustrious
predecessor in the "Jesus is my favorite philosopher" camp. Thomas
Jefferson asserted repeatedly that Jesus was the greatest thinker of
all time. Of course Jefferson's devotion to Christ was strictly moral
and intellectual, not religious. Jesus was a sublime teacher, not a divine redeemer. Jefferson abhorred the evangelical movement that
was already beginning to roll up conversions, even among Virginia
planters, before his death in 1826. He saw evangelical Christianity
as a new outbreak of superstition, a sign of Americans turning
away from science and reason. He naturally rejected any explicit
government endorsement of Jesus or faith in Jesus. He certainly
spun in his grave when Governor George W. Bush of Texas officially designated June 10, 2000, as "Jesus Day" in Texas. "People of
all religions recognize Jesus Christ as an example of love, compassion, sacrifice and service," the official statement said. "Jesus Day
challenges people to follow Christ's example by performing good
works in their communities and neighborhoods."

Governor Bush did not think up "Jesus Day." It developed out
of an annual "March for Jesus" that began in Austin, the state capital, in 1991. By 2000 the event had spread to 180 counties. The
governor simply put an official seal of approval on a popular
statewide church and community initiative. The Texas proclamation was carefully phrased to sound secular and inoffensive to
non-Christians. Who could object to "good works" done in Christ's
name? Founders Thomas Jefferson and James Madison would have
loved the communally generated works of mercy, but they would
have cringed at the government endorsement. All official supports
for particular religious beliefs, in their eyes, were dangerous in-
fringements upon the sacred private encounter between God and
believer.[36]

Southern evangelical religion had gone national in the 1950s
with the creation of television and the crossover charisma of Billy
Graham, whose stylish attire, measured cadences, and simple-yet-

challenging message attracted masses of white Protestants, north, west, and south (not to mention the rest of the world). But Graham was diligent about keeping out of politics—apart from his denunciations of Communism, which endeared him equally to Democrats and Republicans. Martin Luther King, by contrast, had brought a hybrid of Social Gospel liberalism and African American religion into national politics in the 1960s. King's approach was evangelical in the sense that he applied the gospel to moral and political issues—justice and equality before the law. But it was not evangelical in Billy Graham's sense of seeking conversions to Christ. King was explicitly pluralistic. Anyone who understood, as he put it in his "Letter from Birmingham Jail" (1963), that "the time is always ripe to do right" was his political ally. King had learned from Reinhold Niebuhr that politics needs religion to keep it pointed toward justice. But he had also learned from Niebuhr that to stay pointed toward justice, politics needs protection against religious sectarianism. Too much dogmatic purity undermines broad-based alliances essential to political or economic equality. From King's and Niebuhr's standpoint, Graham was too aloof from politics, but the later politicking of Falwell and Robertson would probably have struck King and Niebuhr as going too far. Jesus had to be let into politics as a prophet passing judgment on everyone's failure to measure up to his love-commandment, but kept out of politics as a policy-maker or as a judge of *other* people's sinful behavior.[37]

Within the broad evangelical Protestant community, the political route to the kingdom of God is frowned upon by Graham and many others. But a large coalition of fundamentalists, Pentecostals, and other evangelicals has modified Graham's old idea that moral reform will result only from an accumulation of religious conversions. They believe that serious followers of Jesus must struggle politically to enact laws to purify the nation. Abortion and homosexuality continue to be the issues of most heated discussion. Catholic and Protestant conservatives join hands to battle Catholic and Protestant liberals on both questions. Each side must cope with the same problem confronted by pro-slavery and anti-slavery Christians in the nineteenth century: Jesus was silent about abortion and homosexuality just as he was about slavery. Both sides implicitly invoke Charles Sheldon's 1896 test of "What would Jesus do?" Sheldon designed that question for Christians facing problems unknown to first-century Palestinians such as Jesus. There could be no certainty, Sheldon said, about which course Jesus himself would have chosen, but responsible Christians had to make up their minds anyway. "What would Jesus do?" was a reminder that everyone faced unavoidable moral and political choices every day.

The Evangelical Environmental Network made Sheldon's point in 2002 when it took out an advertisement entitled "What Would Jesus Drive?" (see fig. 34). Much of the press guffawed at the ad, assuming its backers really thought the question concerned the historical Jesus of Nazareth, or really thought there was a single legitimate answer. But the text of the ad was pure Sheldon in its openness to different choices about vehicles themselves. What Jesus would do is love his neighbor. The "moral problem" facing Christian consumers of fossil fuels concerns that love-commandment. The global warming aggravated by auto emissions should preoccupy Christians as well as scientists—not because Jesus had an opinion about it himself, but because he was a zealot on the matter of love. Global warming becomes a religious issue because love for the entire creation is now the only way in practice to truly love one's neighbor. The stewardship for the poor that evangelical preacher Charles Sheldon pushed in 1896 is preserved in the Evangelical Environmental Network's campaign since it is the poor (along with the young, the sick, and the aged) who suffer disproportionately from environmental damage.[38]

The "What Would Jesus Drive?" ad shows that not all evangelicals embrace political conservatism. Other evidence supports the same conclusion. *Sojourner* magazine and its editor, James Wallis, kept up a steady call throughout the 1980s and 1990s for economic and racial justice in the name of Jesus. In 2002 Wallis organized a

"Faith-Based Peace Initiative" to try to head off the American invasion of Iraq. And many American evangelicals all over the world,
whatever their politics may be, are imitating Christ by performing
medical and humanitarian relief tasks in the face of grave personal
danger. *New York Times* columnist Nicholas Kristof, a longtime critic
of evangelicalism, announced in 2002, after visiting courageous
evangelical workers in the Philippines, that his attitude had
changed. Evangelicals were living out Christ's injunctions to feed
the hungry and heal the sick, asking nothing in return—not even
conversions, although they obtained some of those. In 2003 he observed the same trend in Africa. "We should all celebrate the big
evangelical push into Africa because . . . it will mean more orphan-
ages, more schools and, above all, more clinics and hospitals." In
the midst of an AIDS epidemic, "those church hospitals are life-
savers." If Kristof is right, more and more young evangelical
missionaries abroad are learning the pluralistic lesson that many
missionaries from the liberal denominations learned in the late
nineteenth century: Christian responsibility begins with meeting
urgent human needs, not changing people's beliefs.[39]

The Reverend T. D. Jakes of the Potter's House church in Dallas
illustrates a related trend in contemporary evangelicalism. Just as
evangelical missionaries are addressing immediate physical crises,
Jakes urges preachers to target their congregation's psychological
and material as well as spiritual needs. *Time* magazine put this formerly Pentecostal African American preacher from West Virginia
on its cover of September 17, 2001, along with the question "Is This
Man the Next Billy Graham?" The answer may well be yes if the
question concerns oratorical prowess. But Jakes takes Graham's
message much further toward psychological therapeutics than
Graham has done. Graham does not dwell upon the power of sin,
but he still mentions sin. Jakes follows the example of liberal
preacher Robert Schuller by avoiding the word altogether. The goal
is empowerment, not repentance. Jakes is following in the path
of Aimee Semple McPherson, cultivating Christian celebrity by

presenting marvelously staged performances of heightened feeling. Like McPherson and Graham, he eschews politics. He will comment on an occasional issue like homosexuality (he is against it), but in the social realm he concentrates on building a massive relief and self-improvement operation in Dallas to go with an important national prison ministry. Jakes also writes best-selling books, produces Grammy-nominated gospel music, fills superdomes with his fans, and has a syndicated television talkshow seen on cable stations around the world.

Anyone who sees T. D. Jakes in person, as I did at a Potter's House Sunday service in April 2001, will be struck by his unique verbal acuity. He is a master orator who uses his whole body to act out his message. Like Martin Luther King, he begins slowly, with a few erudite references to establish his scholarly credentials. Before long he is prowling the stage with startling juxtapositions of Bible texts and everyday experiences. He invokes the story of Ruth to examine the issue of loyalty, asking people to touch each other if they have ever needed help being loyal. The audience (disproportionately female, like all Protestant and Catholic congregations) stirs with approval. "Touch someone and tell them, 'I need help being loyal.'" The audience complies. Then he reverses the thematic flow. "Touch someone if you've ever needed someone to leave you and they just wouldn't go. Touch five people and say, 'I need you to go.'" The audience roars its approval. Jakes plays the congregation like an instrument. "Are you ready to go deeper?" he asks. They cry out in concurrence. He turns the sermon into a disquisition on suffering. "Christians think they've got it made when they get saved," he says. But "their problems have just begun. Save your tears. You're going to need them." The sermon indeed centered on self-help, but the self-help was administered collectively and it was filled with gospel-based wisdom. This empowerment advice passed through a Calvary of suffering and reversal. Jakes dwelt on the drag in our spirits that keeps us from worshiping God solely because he is God, not because of what he can do for us. Jonathan Edwards would have pricked up his ears. Jakes is forthright about dispensing self-help advice and psychotherapy along with insights drawn from the Hebrew Scriptures and the New Testament. His African American congregation, he told an interviewer, cannot afford to get their practical advice or psychotherapy from fee-charging professionals. If he continues to develop biblical themes with the skill and passion he displayed on my visit, he will have created a remarkably potent Christian ministry. Nothing could be more American: coming up with a new way of thinking about and marketing Jesus. Jakes's ministry starts with people's everyday problems, sheds gospel light on them, and mobilizes people to draw on all their powers—including the power of Jesus—to solve them.[40]

At the Potter's House in Dallas, in keeping with Protestant evangelical tradition, no images of Jesus are to be found. Jesus is represented in the Word spoken by T. D. Jakes—a word spoken, in revivalist and Pentecostal fashion, with full participation by his animated physical frame. Jakes reminds us that the most celebrated Protestant evangelical preaching in the twentieth century, from McPherson to Graham to Jakes, combines resourceful communication of the Word with an inspired performance of spirit. Jesus may not be visualized in worship, but the preacher conveys the actual experience of being swept up in the Holy Spirit. Graham does it with regal reserve, Jakes with rapid shifts of tone, flawless pantomime, and uncanny streams of language and song. Contemporary Protestant evangelicals are used to images of Jesus in film, in advertising, and in private prayer, but in worship they differentiate themselves from most Catholics by adhering to the minister's verbalized and performed Word, not the visualized icon. Catholics, like Eastern Orthodox Christians, find visual images indispensable for the life of faith, in and out of church. One does not miss icons when a perspiring T. D. Jakes, resting momentarily on an assistant's shoulder, sings a contemplative rendition of "Will the Circle Be Unbroken?"

Naturally it was a Catholic newspaper that came up with the idea of a millennial art contest called "Jesus 2000." A prize of two

thousand dollars would go to the artist who created the most compelling new visual representation of Christ. "The era of the blond,
blue-eyed Jesus is over," said the *National Catholic Reporter*'s editor,
Michael Farrell. The winner and runner-up, selected by celebrity art
critic Sister Wendy Beckett, demonstrated his point (see figs. 21–22).
"Jesus of the People" fit Marcus Garvey's prescription for blending
the colors of all racial groups. "Yeshua" took a different tack, planting Jesus emphatically in his first-century Jewish cultural context.
The two images express opposing approaches to imagining a
human Jesus for our age, one universalist (make Jesus stand for everybody) and the other localist (make him humanly real via historical authenticity). Both visions aim to make Jesus newly available
for our time, but "Jesus of the People" does so with determined inclusiveness. Artist Janet McKenzie says that "the essence of the
work is simply that Jesus is all of us," and to that end she gave her
figure a prescribed mix of human characteristics. She made him
multicultural and gave him a "feminine aspect" by using a female
model. With his "Yeshua" portrait, by contrast, Peter De Firis embarked upon a visual version of the "quest for the historical Jesus,"
which he has followed since the 1970s. Contemporary scholars
agree that we can know very little in a historically documented
fashion about the life of Christ, but they emphatically concur about
his Jewish identity. De Firis's painting emphasizes that consensus
viewpoint on the historical Jesus. After picking the top winners,
Sister Beckett confessed that "for myself, I have no image. I cannot
even begin to visualize the Jesus in whom and through whom I
live. But the very act of trying to envisage him is deeply fruitful. . . .
Every viewer will understand our Lord more deeply as he or she
. . . responds to what the artists have made visible."[41]

   Sister Beckett's ambivalence about representations of the divine
mirrors that of Henry Ward Beecher in the nineteenth century. In
their view Jesus surpasses all image-making, but representations of
him can still provide an important reminder about the limits of representation. Beecher put five different heads of Christ on a single

page of his *Life of Jesus,* as if to say, "None of these is really him" (see fig. 30). The problem is built into Christianity, a religion in which God briefly took on human form. Christ's humanity makes him seem close by. Believers are tempted to turn their closeness to him into secure possession of him. The historical quest for Jesus the Palestinian preacher and miracle-worker can offer the same kind of reminder that Beecher presented with his five heads of Christ: the actual Jesus confounds all of our efforts to locate him historically. From a Christian standpoint, scientific investigation ends up by supporting faith. It is faith alone that provides assurance about the truth of God's revelation.

In an era of apparent trivialization of the Jesus image, when he turns up on T-shirts and in advertisements, and in the lyrics of hundreds of popular songs, one might conclude that his divinity has been fatally compromised and his humanity woefully abused. But as Emerson understood, Jesus is a renewable cultural figure precisely because Christians can become critically aware that they have neglected or exploited him. The Eastern Orthodox tradition has understood for many centuries that there are two kinds of icons, both of them salutary for the life of the believer. One kind of icon is a representation of Jesus, a saint, or anything else created by God. This positive icon leads believers directly to the mystery of the divine. The other kind of icon is a representation of something insulting, scandalous, disfigured, scatological, or otherwise profane. This negative icon leads believers indirectly to the divine, by reminding them that God is imageless, transcendent, unrepresentable even by ostensibly reverent portrayals.[42]

Some Christian viewers will think Kevin Stacy's 1998 "Think Different" is irreverent, while others will judge it unobjectionable or even pious (see fig. 35). Stacy found an old engraving of Jesus in the Garden of Gethsemane on the Internet. Jesus is kneeling, leaning forward against a small boulder that supports one elbow, looking up into a ray of heavenly light. The fingers of his two hands are loosely interlocked, angling down toward his knees. He is tired, questioning, a bit disconsolate. Christians know that at this moment he is supposed to be whispering a set of words: "Father, if it be possible, let this cup pass from me; nevertheless not as I will, but as thou wilt." But behind his head are the emphatic, printed commercial words "Think Different." Stacy's image was a contribution to the Apple Computer "Celebrity" Web page. But with the Eastern Orthodox conception of icons in mind, it scarcely matters whether one takes the image as holy or profane. Either way, it conveys multiple meanings. Jesus is thinking differently by pursuing his self-sacrifice. Kevin Stacy is thinking differently by reimagining a holy card as a trade card. We viewers are thinking differently if we respond to the picture by rethinking our relation to Jesus iconography.

One day I asked the students in my "Jesus in American History and Culture" class, "What would Emerson do" if he saw Kevin Stacy's Jesus-in-Gethsemane advertisement? A lively discussion ensued. The group came up with two main ideas. First, Emerson would smile at the words "Think different" and then counter with "Think different, but think true." For him neither difference nor passion counted as virtues in themselves. Only truth made them virtuous. Genius was a function of truth, not of inspiration alone. Second, Emerson would have loved the ad so much he would have tacked it to his icebox. It perfectly expresses his view of celebrity philosophers. They were effective spokesmen for their own ideas for a limited period of time, but people started worshiping them instead of appreciating their wisdom. When people had bowed down to him for too many centuries, Jesus became routine, calcified. Then you had to go to Zoroaster or Mencius or Swedenborg to find out what Jesus really meant. Christ had difficulty delivering the new birth under his own name. "Think differently" about me, Jesus is saying, and you can know me again.

VI

Four centuries of Jesus in America: so many Christs, so many cultural incarnations, secular and religious alike. Legions of Americans have embraced the God-man from Galilee as their personal savior and cultural hero. Many Americans have craved his new birth because it spurred them to embark on uncharted futures while maintaining a respectful attachment to tradition. Jesus let them cherish local or ethnic allegiances and at the same time seek a cosmopolitan makeover. Jesus has been just all right with Americans, to paraphrase the Doobie Brothers 1970s hit "Jesus Is Just Alright," because he has tied them to their past and empowered them to leave it behind. The tonal shift in the middle of the song catches the complexity of Americans' attachment to Jesus. The jaunty, compulsive affirmation of the chorus (chanting the name of Jesus to the point of exhaustion) is suddenly interrupted by a pensive gospel-solo interlude. This contemplative ballad-within-the-anthem speaks of Jesus as the friend who takes one's hand and leads one to a far different place—an unspecified realm, except that it lies beyond this present state of disappointment or suffering or routine. Jesus saves because he purifies. He can deliver you back to simple beginnings, and from that place you can depart for a better self or a better world.

For many generations the Protestant American majority has summed up its faith by asking, "What would Jesus do?" No phrase could better exhibit the distinctiveness of the American evangelical conception of Jesus in the nineteenth and twentieth centuries. "What would Jesus do?" puts all the weight on action, not contemplation, intellection, or submission. And it makes Jesus the ultimate authority on ethical action—not the church, not even the Bible (which lost its cachet as a flawless ethical guide when slavery, polygamy, and other Old Testament practices slipped beyond the moral pale of modernity). Now that the historical Jesus is widely understood to have been Jewish, not Christian, he can be situated at the fountainhead of the broad "Judeo-Christian tradition" that many political and cultural conservatives have embraced in place of the now anachronistic "Christian nation" concept. Politically conservative evangelicals can finally ally Moses with Jesus, just as liberal Christians have done since the early twentieth century. In 1995 Roy Moore, then a rural Alabama judge, showed he was a man of contemporary evangelical action when he mounted a plaque of the Ten Commandments—not a cross or an image of Jesus—on his courtroom wall. Eight years later, still a man of action and also the elected chief justice of Alabama, he installed a 5,280-pound granite monument of the Ten Commandments in the lobby of a state government building. After defying a federal court order compelling him to remove it, he was removed from office himself by the unanimous decision of a nine-member Alabama state panel.[43]

Evangelical Protestants like to ask, "What *would* Jesus do?" but many Catholics and non-evangelical Protestants prefer to ask, "What *does* Jesus do?" In their eyes Christ makes his body and his Holy Spirit available to believers in the sacraments, and he models selfless surrender to his Father's will. Since the nineteenth century, Word-centered Protestant evangelicals have focused on Jesus as speaker and doer, not mystical presence or submissive servant. Jonathan Edwards in the eighteenth century had seen Christ in all those aspects, but his layered vision of Jesus as manifesting both the "infinite highness" of God and "lowness and littleness before God" made less and less sense to evangelical Protestant thinkers over the next two centuries.

The prime twentieth-century American evangelical teacher who still celebrated Edwards's dialectical conception of Christ as incomprehensibly grand and humble, high and low, was H. Richard Niebuhr. He was the lesser known of the two Niebuhr brothers who, with Paul Tillich (the eminent German émigré theologian of the 1930s), formed the great American theological triumvirate of the century. Niebuhr found no use for the question,

"What would Jesus do?" but in the wake of the phenomenal Billy Graham revival in New York City in 1957 he did ask, in effect, "What would *God* do" about what Americans had done to Jesus. For decades H. Richard Niebuhr had been composing memorable dismissals of liberal Christianity, putdowns that far surpassed those of J. Gresham Machen in rhetorical firepower. "Liberalism," Niebuhr wrote in his classic book *The Kingdom of God in America* (1937), imagined that "a God without wrath brought men without sin into a kingdom without judgment through the ministrations of a Christ without a cross."[44]

But more significant than Niebuhr's inspired phrasemaking was the depth of his thinking about the fate of Jesus in twentieth-century America. Unlike Machen, he did not let mass evangelists off the hook when he condemned liberal modernizers of the gospel. An Aimee Semple McPherson or a Billy Graham might *say* they subscribed to a supernatural view of Christ, according to Niebuhr, but they could not automatically be taken at their word. Machen was naïve, he thought, to attack liberalism without also taking on the popular revivalists who did as much to undermine a proper respect for the supernatural as the liberals did. Revivalists too were reducing the gospel to a self-help creed, an empowerment doctrine adorned in pious trappings.

Niebuhr used the occasion of the bicentenary of Edwards's death in 1958 (the year after Billy Graham's New York City crusade) to take a swipe at modern American Christianity, liberal or conservative. Modern American Christians usually disliked Edwards, said Niebuhr, and thought they objected to him (as Henry Ward Beecher had in the nineteenth century) because of his supposedly obsessive emphasis on hell and damnation. In fact, said Niebuhr, they were blissfully unaware of their most basic divergence from Edwards. His God was "eternal, immortal, invisible" (adjectives that Niebuhr took from 1 Tim. 1:17). The God of modern Americans "is someone we . . . use for solving our personal problems, for assuring us that we are beloved." This crutch-God was a concoction of Americans' own making. Edwards, by contrast, beheld a God of "holy love" with "the power that can set us free to be free indeed"—free of the bedrock American conviction that "freedom" meant pursuing one's individual self-interest or creating oneself *ex nihilo*. Real freedom, as Edwards taught, *followed* rather than *preceded* the establishment (via Christ's gift of grace) of a right relation to God. Americans mistakenly thought they were free from the start, and in their freedom made the choice to accept God. But that sort of self-interested choosing was a decision to love themselves, not God. Real love of God flowed from acknowledgment of one's dependence on one's Creator and from repentance for believing oneself ever to have been free of God's care and chastisement.

Niebuhr speculated that by 1958 Americans had experienced so much hot and cold war, so much unprecedented horror in the Nazis' Auschwitz and in their own Hiroshima, that they were perhaps more willing than ever before to take the position that "man is as wicked" as Edwards himself believed. The question remained whether the mass religious revival of the 1950s, encompassing Catholics as well as conservative and liberal Protestants, would bring them any closer to knowing that "God is as holy as Edwards knew him to be." Niebuhr concluded in a signature Niebuhr-style jeremiad, arguing that

> a holy God will not suffer his plans for a vast, stupendously intricate, marvelous creation ... to be flouted and destroyed by self-willed and proud little delinquents, aged 60 as often as 16, called nations or civilizations as often as persons. ... [Americans suppose] there is no wrath in heaven directed against us, [and they mistakenly suppose it] because there is no holiness [in us]. ... [S]ince there is no holiness there is no hope for us except the hope that we'll get by a little longer with our compromises and our superior animal cunning. Edwards used to say that the trouble with men was not that they had no ideas of God, but that they

had little ideas of God. We might add that they are ideas about little Gods.[45]

What would God do? asked Niebuhr. He would deliver judgment upon the American delinquents (himself included among the sixty-year-olds) for hypocritically praising Jesus while disregarding his preaching. In *Christ and Culture* (1951) Niebuhr bemoaned the degeneration of Christian faith "into a utilitarian device for the attainment of personal prosperity or public peace" through the creation of "some imagined idol called by his name [who] takes the place of Jesus Christ the Lord." Niebuhr could not stomach the tribalism—Jesus as totem of a self-proclaimed Christian civilization. But for Niebuhr the alternative to cultural tribalism was not a transcendent encounter with Christ that occurred in some pure place beyond culture. "Christ claims no man purely as a natural being, but always as one who has become human in a culture; who is not only in culture, but into whom culture has penetrated. . . . [T]he forms and attitudes of his mind which allow him to make sense out of the objective world have been given him by culture." Even the most radically sectarian Christians, who often imagined themselves separated from the "institutions and expressions" of their society, were forced to "confess Jesus . . . by means of words and ideas derived from culture." They might "speak as though they were separated from the world," but they could not escape the problem faced by Christians in every era: "the necessity of translating into the terms of [their] own culture what was commanded in the terms of another."[46]

The ironic fate of Jesus in America, or in any culture, was to end up being worshiped by many Christians who thought they were solely submitting to his authority when they were actually subjecting him to the authority of their personal obsessions or their culture's norms. Modernist Christians who grasped the historical contingency of human consciousness had a special responsibility: to debunk the posturing of any person or group (including themselves, the modernists) that claimed to occupy a universal, transcultural viewpoint. In Niebuhr's view, knowing Christ by faith conducted believers to a standpoint not of universality, but of privileged suffering and submission—a position from which to honor God's sovereignty by judging themselves harshly before passing judgment on anyone else. Remove the two-by-four from your own eye before worrying about the splinter in your neighbor's.

Modernists were correct to insist on the historicity of Scripture and of all culture: hence they should stop reducing Jesus to a universally applicable wise man or ethical perfectionist. Conservative evangelicals and fundamentalists were correct to note the pervasiveness of sin and the limits constraining human reason: hence they should cease imagining that they could trump culture by returning to the Bible. The Bible could not save people from culture because "many cultures are represented in the Bible. . . . [T]here is no single Biblical language [and] no single Biblical cosmology or psychology. The word of God as it is uttered to men comes in human words; and human words are cultural things, along with the concepts with which they are associated." The biblical Christ mocked the culture-escaping schemes of modernists and fundamentalists alike. Jesus remained the mysterious divine person whose excellences surpassed all logic, all expectation, all human culture. But human beings adored him from their human place, not from the heavens. The God-man they cherished was a being of awesome variety, one who in his unanswerable power condescended to take humanity's weakness on himself. "The supernatural being was a man of flesh and blood; the mystic [was] a teacher of morals; the moral teacher [was] one who cast out demons by the power of God; the incarnate spirit of love [was] a prophet of wrath; the martyr of a good cause [was] the Risen Lord."[47]

One of the important legacies of H. Richard Niebuhr for our day is his reminder that Jesus outdistances all efforts to contain him: think twice, therefore, before you dismiss someone else's view of him. Martin Luther King, Jr., applied that insight in his "Love Your Enemies" sermon. The pursuit of justice, he said, entailed noticing the image of God even in one's social or political opponent. Dismiss the argument, not the person making it. Jane Addams preached a related doctrine at Hull House: self-development could occur only when one saw that the community was composed of multiple excellences stemming from many cultural traditions. Her philosophical hero William James had offered a memorable statement of that position in his 1899 essay "On a Certain Blindness in Human Beings." In this secular version of Christ's beam-in-the-eye injunction, overcoming blindness meant respecting "those whom we see harmlessly interested and happy in their own ways, however unintelligible these may be to us. Hands off: neither the whole of truth, nor the whole of good, is revealed to any single observer, although each observer gains a partial superiority of insight from the peculiar position in which he stands. . . . It is enough to ask of each of us that he should be faithful to his own opportunities and make the most of his own blessings, without presuming to regulate the rest of the vast field."[48]

Niebuhr, King, Addams, James, and others have led me to my own answer to the question, "What would Jesus do?" What would he do if he were a historian looking back at the cultural history of Christ in America? My guess is that he would listen in wonder, joy, confusion, and dismay to all the things Americans have said about him for four hundred years. (If believers are correct about his being God, these are things he had already been hearing for sixteen centuries from his followers, ever since he emerged from the tomb and heard Mary Magdalene crying in anguish for him.) I have tried to listen to many of those American voices in this book, taking William James's warning to heart. We can overcome our blindness about others, past or present, only if we try to see and feel things as they did. We have to pass over, James said, from "hard externality" to a "gleam of insight" into "the vast world of inner life beyond us, so different from that of outer seeming." We will still have enemies on occasion, as Martin Luther King understood. If we are followers of Jesus, we do not have to like them. We just have to love them, and loving them entails listening.[49]

A vast gap separates liberal Christians from traditionalist Christians. (The adjectives are slippery, but they do point to real groups exhibiting real differences.) "Every generation is called to something new," said the Reverend Robert Kinloch Massie in his sermon at St. James Episcopal Church in Cambridge, Massachusetts, on November 2, 2003. "We are self-weaving tapestries, free every day to add new colors to the emerging pattern of our lives." Jesus lends his divine-human support to that liberal program of self-creation. "We are repeatedly being shown," said Massie, adding an organic metaphor to go with his textile analogy, "that at the heart of the universe lies forgiveness and joy, and we are repeatedly offered the chance . . . to struggle out of the dull cocoon that we have spun of our fears into brilliant color and open flight." Many American Christians will gravitate to Massie's Emersonian Christ, the preacher of a metanoia (transformation) that emphasizes open-ended innovation.[50]

Many others will opt for a traditional Jesus who warns against open-ended growth and recommends or commands long-cherished practices and convictions. An anonymous but well-informed advertiser in the *Los Angeles Times* in November 2003 announced "8 Compelling Reasons Why: Christ Is Coming Very Soon! How to Be Prepared for History's Greatest Event." This newspaper preacher used standard end-time signs (from "Israel's rebirth" and "plummeting morality" to "the new world order" and the "increase in both apostasy and faith") as a hook to spark interest in a broadly evangelical message: repentance for sin followed by the subsequent gift (guaranteed to "all who put their trust in Him") of undeserved grace. There is only a little common ground between the viewpoints of Massie and the unnamed apocalyptic evangelical. Both proclaim their allegiance to Jesus. One believes following Jesus involves a state of perpetual, indeterminate growth toward new experiences of love and joy; the other sees Scripture as a source of certainty about a fixed-for-all-time "escape plan" from "the wages of sin." There will be no overcoming this yawning gap: many liberals thrive on uncertainty and revision, while many traditionalists depend on certainty and fixity. Historians can express their awe at the diversity of American faiths that call on the authority of Jesus. Christians, meanwhile, can remind themselves that Jesus said to look for the beam in your own eye and get busy extracting it.[51]

That strenuous project of self-criticism was brought home to me as I finished writing this book while reading another one: the phenomenally popular novel by Dan Brown, *The Da Vinci Code*. As of December 21, 2003, it has ridden at or near the top of the *New York Times* best-seller list for eight months. Its premise that Jesus married Mary Magdalene and became a father—a claim that Nikos Kazantzakis entertained in *The Last Temptation of Christ* only as a fantasy Jesus savored on the cross—prompted ABC to televise a one-hour special investigation. Reporter Elizabeth Vargas inquired into the possible truth of the Jesus–Mary Magdalene connection—along with a number of other theories embraced by Brown, such as the existence of a secret society committed to protecting the Holy Grail, which according to Brown is not a literal chalice but the sacred bodily vessel through which Mary delivered the holy child, Sarah.[52]

Brown's book is a novel, but in interviews he has expressed his personal belief in the historical truth of these theories. He told ABC's Vargas that on the marriage and family of Jesus and Mary Magdalene he had gone in as a "skeptic" and come out a "believer." Rather than dwell on the splinter in Brown's eye—his apparent over-eagerness to adopt some tenuous positions—I want to applaud his book for forcing many readers like me to think further about inherited American—and Western—cultural images of the divine. Why are they so overwhelmingly male? Even the Holy Spirit has been given male characteristics in some Christian iconography (see fig. 3, where the Trinity is depicted as a band of brothers). Why has the figure of Mary Magdalene come down to us as a redeemed prostitute rather than as the apostolic authority that some leading scholars, liberals and evangelicals alike, contend she may have been? What would Jesus say about the elevation of his mother Mary to special prominence in the Christian pantheon while the other Mary, one of his trusted companions and perhaps one of his most respected followers, was consigned to relative insignificance?[53]

Historians intrigued, as I am, by the project of listening to the full range of voices embedded in the historical record confront a major obstacle when they discover that whole classes of people have been excluded from, or underrepresented in, the record. How can historians listen when people are deprived of speech, not to mention authority? They can praise fiction-writers such as Brown for imagining alternative histories, including that of a *sub rosa* secret society devoted to the prospect of female as well as male sacred authority. They can try to find evidence in the historical record of women who did manage to speak and even lead despite the opposition they faced. And they can note that in the history of American and world Christianity many female and male voices have proclaimed that what Jesus would do about Paul's Epistle to the Galatians (3:27–28) is apply it socially as well as spiritually. The new birth in Jesus, according to Paul, creates a new being who has "put on Christ. There is neither Jew nor Greek, there is neither bond nor free, there is neither male nor female: for ye are all one in Christ Jesus." Paul meant that social distinctions are irrelevant when one has put on Christ. For a century and a half, a train of American women and men have contested Paul's position. Social distinctions should not be relevant to the putting on of Christ, they concede, but they become relevant whenever individuals find themselves arbitrarily excluded from giving their own best gifts back to the Lord.

EPILOGUE
JUST TELL THE LOVE OF JESUS

One of the most revered spirituals in the African American Christian tradition is "Balm in Gilead":

> There is a balm in Gilead
> To make the wounded whole;
> There is a balm in Gilead
> To heal the sin sick soul.

> Sometimes I feel discouraged,
> And think my work's in vain,
> But then the Holy Spirit
> Revives my soul again.

> If you can't preach like Peter,
> If you can't pray like Paul,
> Just tell the love of Jesus,
> And say He died for all.

It is tempting to suppose that Christian belief has had such staying power in America because it provides respectable conformity, relief from anxiety, or a promise of eternal happiness. Yet some people find Christianity compelling because it provides an alternative to conformity, or a correction to their complacency. Christianity of Catholic and Protestant varieties, along with Russian and Greek Orthodoxy, the Latter-day Saints, and other smaller groups, is so deeply plowed into American soil that contradictory impulses can easily be accommodated under the Christian rubric. For instance, those who wish to shore up family values can appeal to Christ, while those who challenge family loyalties in the name of individual purity—like some of the characters in Charles Sheldon's "What Would Jesus Do?" novel *In His Steps*—can call on him too.

There is at least one more reason for the lasting power of Christian belief in America: so many Americans have known holy people who loved Christ so fully that they seemed to spend their days, in action as much as in speech, "just telling the love of Jesus." Saintliness is awe-inspiring, and many people gravitate toward the faith of the saint they witness. One may encounter secular saints too. In the 1920s the young preacher Reinhold Niebuhr was overwhelmed by the passion for justice displayed by his Detroit friend Fred Butzel, an unbelieving Jewish lawyer who labored for the poor and disadvantaged. Butzel made Niebuhr wonder if a secular commitment to justice was a purer form of Christ's ethical calling than Christianity could ever muster. Fred Butzel had no thought of what was in it for him, making his self-renunciation complete. Niebuhr knew plenty of Christian saints too. He especially liked to tell the love of Jesus manifested by a "faithful old woman" in his church. She greeted her final years of physical pain with repeated thanksgiving for all the gifts God had bestowed on her. Her unusual love of Christ, Niebuhr said, was surely made possible by Christ's love of her. Niebuhr could preach like Peter and pray like Paul—his spoken prayers at the end of his sermons, like those of Henry Ward Beecher, are works of art. But one of his favorite themes in preaching and prayer was the love of Jesus displayed in the lives of secular and religious saints, Jewish and Christian.

I cannot separate my own affection for Jesus from my affection for certain saints, living and dead, who told me their love of him.

The one who influenced me most was Michael Peterson, not because he was the greatest saint, but because he could not help telling the love of Jesus. With him it was organic, urgent. I knew Michael first-hand for only six months, when I was a sophomore in college and he was a senior. The year was 1963. We were studying at Stanford University's campus in Tours, France. It was a wonderful time to be young American Catholics, like Michael and me, exploring Europe for the first time. The Catholic Church was humming with new ideas and attitudes. France was an American hitchhiker's paradise, even before President Kennedy's assassination made French drivers want to pick up every American student with an outstretched finger (the French did not use thumbs). All over Europe American students spelled out "USA" on their suitcases with reflecting duct tape.

In early November Michael and I went to Rome and got tickets to attend the Wednesday afternoon public audience with Pope Paul VI. Two or three hundred Catholics from all over the world had assembled in a stone-gray, rectangular hall in the Vatican. The atmosphere was somber until a bubbly, multilingual Monsignor strode out of the shadows to liven us up. "How many people came here from the United States?" he asked. Several dozen people clapped (no whooping in those days). "Combien viennent de la France?" brought a smaller round of applause. He asked the question in a good ten languages, to excited if sometimes minimal applause. "Now I invite you to sing the Credo with me to welcome his Holiness," the priest said. Hundreds of voices joined his, proving that Catholics can sing if they are about to meet the pope. "Credo in unum Deum, Patrem omnipotentem, factorem coeli et terrae, visibilium omnium et invisibilium ..." ("I believe in one God, the Father almighty, maker of heaven and earth, and of all things visible and invisible ...")

The singing echoed warmly off the chilly walls. By the time we had gotten to "visibilium omnium et invisibilium" (one of my favorite phrases from childhood: the implausible length of the words, the beauty of their sound, the notion of invisible things!), I was smiling at the magic of so many strangers from so many places knowing the melody and words to the same sonorous chant. When we finished we were all aglow and ready to salute the pope. Four bearers carried him around the room on a portable canopied throne. He passed about ten feet away, and as he waved and half-smiled with a Cheshire cat grin, I snapped his picture. As the blue flashbulb popped and fizzled, I felt very lucky to be a Catholic. The whole experience seemed to me a sign of the love of Christ for humankind. He established his church to make his unifying love continuously available. The Roman Catholic Church brought everyone together, whatever their race, country, or language. The afternoon in the Vatican permitted me to believe that deep down I was just human, not American, French, or Italian. My elation was much more intellectual than Michael's. He loved the singing, and afterward he was shaking from his near encounter with the pope.

We had such a good time in Rome that we planned a Christmas trip to Algeria via Marseille. We hitchhiked across France, and every morning we recited Michael's favorite prayer of St. Francis (in French, at my insistence). The first half of it went "Lord, make me an instrument of your peace; where there is hatred, let me sow love; where there is injury, pardon; where there is doubt, faith; where there is despair, hope; where there is darkness, light; and where there is sadness, joy." On a frigid evening shortly before Christmas, we paid twenty dollars each for overnight passage to Algiers. Our third-class tickets gave us a cot in the ship's hold, where a few water spouts and toilets were shared by thirty or forty male passengers. All of the other passengers were Algerian laborers headed home on vacation from France and Germany.

The gregarious workingmen spoke better French than we did, and we talked far into the night about their families, their work, and the general state of the world after Kennedy. Finally everyone turned in. Naturally a storm came up shortly after we had fallen asleep. The Mediterranean made the ship heave and roll. The Algerian men saw no reason to be silent about their seasickness. I thought I had been deposited in a biblical epic with moaning and weeping and gnashing of teeth. I buried my head as far as I could inside my sleeping bag to escape the stench and the wailing. I lasted only a few minutes in that state of suffocation. I slowly stuck my head out looking for Michael on the cot next to me. It was empty. I thought he must be sick in the lavatory, and went looking for him there. No sign of him. One of the workingmen tapped me on the shoulder and pointed to a corner of the hold. Michael was there tending to a sick passenger. He had been walking back and forth from the water spout to the Algerians' cots giving them sips of water. It did not take long to see the link between our morning prayer of St. Francis and what Michael was telling me silently in the storm about the love of Jesus.

After graduating from Stanford, Michael went off to medical school, and we stayed in touch with occasional letters. I knew that he became a doctor, a psychiatrist, and finally a Catholic priest. I heard from mutual friends in 1981 when he founded the St. Luke Institute, a treatment center in Maryland for priests addicted to alcohol and drugs. I did not hear from anyone in the mid-eighties when he came out as gay. Michael had concealed his homosexuality for fear of undermining the work at St. Luke, but having contracted AIDS, he could hide it no longer. In 1986, when I was teaching at Reed College in Oregon, I got a letter from him telling me his parents had moved to the Oregon coast and he might be passing through Portland sometime. I wrote back saying how glad I would be to see him, and reminding him of our long night on the Mediterranean in 1963. I never heard from him again. He died in 1987. He had written me, it turned out, to say goodbye. At his memorial service in Washington, D.C., bishops, priests, and lay people praised him for his service. Back in Oregon I was remembering his spontaneous charity to the Algerians in the ship. I reread the St. Francis prayer. The last half says, "O Divine Master, grant that I may not so much seek to be consoled as to console; to be understood, as to understand; to be loved, as to love; for it is in giving that we receive, it is in pardoning that we are pardoned, and it is in dying that we are born to eternal life."

In 1993 the entire AIDS quilt—hundreds of colorful panels produced across the country over many years in honor of AIDS victims—was assembled over a huge expanse of the National Mall between the Washington Monument and the Lincoln Memorial. The organizers said this might well be the last time the entire quilt could ever be displayed. It was getting too big for any available urban or suburban space. I had no idea whether anyone had made a quilt panel for Michael, but I looked up his name in the directory. There were two Michael Petersons listed, Michael "L" and Michael "R." The "R" rang a bell, so I checked out that one first. It was his, and I could tell he had designed it himself. It showed a large black cross superimposed on a pale-blue-and-red banner. He had written "Father Michael R. Peterson" across the top of the cross, and hugging the trunk of the cross he had written a passage from St. Augustine. It resembled the St. Francis prayer in its yearning for consolation, but it went beyond St. Francis in speaking of fear. "What I am for you terrifies me—What I am with you consoles me—For you I am a Priest; but with you I am a Christian" (see fig. 25).

Looking at his panel, I found myself wondering what Michael had thought about his physical deterioration. His message on the quilt showed that like Niebuhr's faithful old woman he had kept thanking God for multiple gifts as his body wasted away. I wanted to know if Michael had felt his body's decline as a gift in itself. That was a common sentiment in an earlier Christian culture. Marie de St. Joseph in seventeenth-century Quebec, like the Protestant Abigail Hutchinson in eighteenth-century Massachusetts, had seen her physical decay as a special instance of the love of Jesus. Hutchinson, according to Jonathan Edwards, thought God had chosen her body as a vehicle for telling her community about the love of Jesus. Marie de St. Joseph, according to her Mother Superior Marie de l'Incarnation, felt that Christ was telling *her* of his love. While she was praying in 1646, before getting sick, her soul appeared to her under the form of a charming castle; and at the same time the Bridegroom, the Son of the Almighty, presenting himself at the door, made himself apparent to her spirit. . . . He was so bright and full of glory, and of such ravishing beauty, he held out his arms and threw her such fond glances, that she would have died of joy and love if he had not sustained her. At length, holding her in his arms and taking full possession of her soul, he said to her: "My daughter, take care of the outside of the castle, and I will guard the interior."

She spent two years in a state of recurrent ecstasy. "Her well-beloved instructed her in all the mysteries of his adorable humanity, clothing her with his Spirit and changing her entirely into a new creature. From that time, her heart was no longer her own; and one could not speak of Jesus Christ in her presence without causing her soul to soften and melt with love."

Marie de St. Joseph's new birth was matched by Christ's own:

Our Lord often talked with her, in language heard only by the inner ear. Singing the Credo one day at holy Mass, she lapsed into a state of amorous delight on uttering these words, *Per quem omnia facta sunt* [by whom all things were made], rejoicing in her heart that all things had been made by her Bridegroom. And, when that joy and that delight made her almost swoon away, he said to her: "Yes, my daughter, all things were made by me, but I am recreated in thee." She thought she would expire on hearing these words, which signified nothing less than a holy transformation in him in whom she lived more than in herself.

Of course Marie de St. Joseph soon discovered what her Ursuline training had prepared her for. Christ had told her of his love as "a nutriment and support" for the suffering to come. He announced to her in 1648 "that she would thenceforth live only by faith and crosses." Her last four years brought her spiritual as well as physical suffering. At times she was forced to wonder why Jesus "torments me in an inexplicable manner." She longed to die "in order to enjoy him whom she had seen in such ravishing beauty." In 1652 he gave her that wish.[1]

I like to think that Michael felt some of what Marie de St. Joseph felt. I like to think he knew her story. In the end none of that is important. What matters is that Michael just told me and many others the love of Jesus.

NOTES

INTRODUCTION

1. Robert H. Schuller, "The Hour of Power," June 3, 2001. In his autobiography, *My Journey: From an Iowa Farm to a Cathedral of Dreams* (San Francisco: HarperSanFrancisco, 2001), Schuller notes that Pentecostal televangelist Jimmy Swaggart, critical of Schuller's "nonbiblical" ministry, embarked on a campaign to displace him from the airwaves (p. 418).

2. The church council at Chalcedon came up with a formula—Christ was one "person" with two "natures"—designed to protect his unity as a single person against both the previously condemned Nestorians (who believed he had two separate identities) and the countervailing Monophysites (who believed he had one nature, his divinity having intermingled fully with his humanity). From a cultural standpoint, one suspects that when contemporary Americans say Jesus is both human and divine, most are not interested in propositional precision or even in the question of who Jesus is in himself. If asked, they would probably say they want to protect their *experience* of Jesus as both human and divine. Western intellectual culture shifted so profoundly after the eighteenth century that even many theologians began viewing propositions about the person or nature of Christ as poetically true rather than metaphysically true. An excellent introduction to the various meanings given to such terms as "Messiah," "Son of man," and "Son of God" in early Jewish and Christian usage is E. P. Sanders, *The Historical Figure of Jesus* (1993; New York: Penguin, 1995).

3. Christine Heyrman's marvelous book *Southern Cross: The Beginnings of the Bible Belt* (Chapel Hill: Univ. of North Carolina Press, 1997) discusses the gendered contours of "democracy" in early-nineteenth-century evangelical religion. See especially p. 322, n. 1. She shows how the "popular" style of an explosively expanding Protestant evangelicalism was quite compatible with hierarchical organization and anti-democratic social views on the position of blacks and women. The same points could be made about an explosively expanding Irish American Catholicism beginning after the 1840s. Popular religion was "democratic" but only partially "egalitarian."

4. A perspicacious study of the unique complexities of the Catholic case is John T. McGreevy's *Catholicism and American Freedom: A History* (New York: Norton, 2003). For the nineteenth-century American Jesus, see pp. 28–29.

5. On the Latino Catholic experience of Jesus, a fine place to start is Roberto Goizueta's essay, "The Symbolic World of Mexican-American Religion," in *Horizons of the Sacred: Mexican Traditions in U.S. Catholicism*, ed. Timothy Matovina and Gary Riebe-Estrella (Ithaca: Cornell Univ. Press, 2002), pp. 119–38.

6. A survey in the 1980s showed that 48 percent of African Americans read the Bible at least once a week, compared to 32 percent of all Americans. Given a choice in 2001 between describing themselves as "religious" or only "somewhat religious," 49 percent of non-Hispanic black American adults chose the former, compared to 37 percent of non-Hispanic white Americans, 30 percent of Hispanic Americans, and 28 percent of Asian Americans. George Gallup, Jr., and Jim Castelli, *The People's Religion* (New York: Macmillan, 1989), p. 122; The American Religious Identification Survey (ARIS), City University of New York, 2001 (www.gc.cuny.edu/studies/aris_index.htm). To my mind the most profound treatment of the intersections between African American and white southern experiences of Jesus is still Donald G. Mathews's wonderfully written and conceived *Religion in the Old South* (Chicago: Univ. of Chicago Press, 1977). Contrary to the dominant trend among contemporary historians of American religion, Mathews grasps that conceptions of Christ are integral to people's experiences of Christ. Ideas cannot be sequestered from "practice." Many religious historians, rightly rejecting an exclusive interest in the lofty thoughts of intellectual elites, have gone too far in the other direction. Mathews offers an important corrective by showing how ordinary believers make ideas about Jesus an essential element of their experiences of him. The next step is to insist that the ideas of innovative intellectuals (Jonathan Edwards, Ralph Waldo Emerson, and others) exert tremendous influence—through their own writings and oratory and through their chain-reaction impact on a large cohort of popularizers—on the ideas of many ordinary believers.

7. "Religion and Public Life Survey," Pew Research Center for the People and the Press, July 24, 2003 (www.people-press.org). Gallup and Castelli, *The People's Religion*, p. 64 , reported half of Americans were "born-again" in 1988, while in the mid-1970s "Poll Finds 34% Share 'Born Again' Feeling," *New York Times*, Sept. 26, 1976, p. 32 ("tried to encourage someone"). Polling data on church attendance are probably inflated, because respondents are thinking about how they wish they acted, not only about how they do act. The same may be true about belief in Jesus. People may be thinking about what they sense they are supposed to believe rather than about what they do believe. Even if that is the case, the data are still very revealing about American attitudes about Jesus. A sizable majority of Americans either believe he is divine or think they should believe it. Andrew Greeley, *Religious Change in America* (Cambridge: Harvard Univ. Press, 1989), p. 13, reports that 77 percent of Americans believed in the divinity of Christ in 1952, and a virtually identical 76 percent did in 1983. On a 10-point scale measuring how "important" God was in

the lives of Europeans and Americans, Americans ranked at the top with a figure of 8.2, followed by the Irish (8), the Italians (6.9), the Spanish (6.4), the British and Germans (5.7), and the Swedes (3.9). On a 10-point scale measuring "certainty" about the resurrection of Christ, 65 percent of Americans were dead certain (10), another 11 percent almost certain (8 or 9). Internationally, the only national population rated more "religious" than Americans are the Indians. Kenneth Briggs, "Gallup Poll Finds Evidence of Pervasive Religious Character of U.S., With Only India More Committed," *New York Times,* Sept. 12, 1976, p. 25. Figures on European church attendance are supplied by Sheena Ashford, *What Europe Thinks: A Study of Western European Values* (Brookfield, VT: Dartmouth Publishers, 1992), p. 46. Canadians diverge from their neighbors to the south as much as western Europeans do. Only 30 percent of Canadians say religion is important to them, and only 21 percent claim to go to church or synagogue regularly—figures one-half or lower than U.S. percentages. Clifford Krauss, "In God We Trust . . . Canadians Aren't So Sure," *New York Times,* Mar. 26, 2003, p. 4. In the 2003 "Religion and Public Life Survey," 60 percent of Americans said religion was a "very important" part of their life, and another one-fourth said it was "fairly important."

8. ARIS, City University of New York, 2001; Michael Hout and Claude S. Fisher, "Why More Americans Have No Religious Preference: Politics and Generations," *American Sociological Review* 67 (Apr. 2002): 165–90.

9. ARIS, City University of New York, 2001. On the "new" American religions—Islam, Buddhism, and Hinduism—see Diana L. Eck's important book *A New Religious America: How a "Christian Country" Has Become the World's Most Religiously Diverse Nation* (San Francisco: HarperSanFrancisco, 2001).

10. No doubt verses about Jesus have been added to "Amazing Grace" over the last two centuries. In the seven-stanza early-nineteenth-century version (the seventh stanza was added to Newton's original six stanzas by an unknown author), Jesus is not mentioned. It is available online at www.cyberhymnal.org, where the hymn's universal American reach is affirmed by the printing of Cherokee, Choctaw, Creek, Kiowa, Navajo, and Spanish translations of the lyrics. On the commercialization and mainstreaming of contemporary Christian music, consult Jay R. Howard and John M. Streck, *Apostles of Rock: The Splintered World of Contemporary Christian Music* (Lexington, KY: Univ. Press of Kentucky, 1999), and Neil Strauss, "Christian Bands, Crossing Over," *New York Times,* Jun. 10, 2003, p. E1. Of course contemporary Christian music sells records that protest against secularizing Christ's message. See Jacob's Trouble's song "The Church of Do What You Want To," which laments the churches' choice of doctrinal ambiguity and liturgical entertainment over the Bible, the Savior, and absolute right and wrong. Thanks to Nicholas Lopez for this reference.

11. A good entry point into the vast sociological literature on American Christian social life is James P. Wind and James W. Lewis, *American Congregations,* 2 vols. (Chicago: Univ. of Chicago Press, 1994). English scholar and Anglican churchman N. T. Wright reflects helpfully on American-European differences regarding Jesus in "The Great Debate," *Bible Review,* Aug. 1999, pp. 12, 54.

12. On the complexities of the Mormon understanding of Jesus, whom many contemporary Latter-day Saints view as "literally our elder brother," since all human beings are "begotten and born of heavenly parents" (God being married himself), see the trenchant treatment by Richard N. Ostling and Joan K. Ostling, *Mormon America: The Power and the Promise* (San Francisco: HarperSanFrancisco, 1999), p. 325 and passim. It makes sense that contemporary Americans devoted to the sanctity of the family would turn to the LDS Church—which values Jesus but does not worship him with the same exclusive intensity that marks Catholic and Protestant piety—since Jesus, for all his passionate strictures against divorce, was decidedly of two minds about the family. Some of his sayings suggest that leaving family behind in a life of holy itinerancy was the spiritual path of choice. On the general question of how culture shapes religion I concur with H. Richard Niebuhr, whose books *The Meaning of Revelation* (1941) and *Christ and Culture* (1951) seem to me right on target. Religion is decisively molded by culture, but the power of culture to delimit the range of religious expression and feeling does not reduce religion to a function of culture. I discuss Niebuhr's views in "The Niebuhr Brothers and the Liberal Protestant Heritage," in *Religion and Twentieth-Century American Intellectual Life*, ed. Michael J. Lacey (Cambridge: Cambridge Univ. Press, 1989), pp. 94–115.

13. "The Divinity School Address," in *Ralph Waldo Emerson: Essays and Lectures*, ed. Joel Porte (New York: Library of America, 1983), p. 79; Peter Dickson, "Fame by the Book," *Washington Post Book World*, Sept. 12, 1999, p. 7. Throughout this book I use the King James Version of the Bible, since it is the translation that has had the most significant impact on American culture, secular and religious, to this day. Even the Puritans, we now know, cited the KJV along with the Geneva Bible. A complete history of Jesus in America would have to trace the history of the various translations of the words the gospel writers attributed to him. That history would address at least two collateral histories: the cultural trajectory of "literalism" in general, and the cultural shift in the weight Americans have assigned to Christ's words as such, compared to his deeds and to his physical image. The first of those collateral histories is addressed by Vincent Crapanzano, *Serving the Word: Literalism in America from the Pulpit to the Bench* (New York: New Press, 2000). The second awaits its undaunted chronicler. One of his or her major topics will need to be the simplification of the gospel text in recent editions of the Bible.

14. Joseph Klausner, *Jesus of Nazareth: His Life, Times, and Preaching* (1925; New York: Macmillan, 1927), pp. 373–76. An excellent study of American cosmopolitan patriotism is Jonathan M. Hansen, *The Lost Promise of Patriotism: Debating American Identity, 1890–1920* (Chicago: Univ. of Chicago Press, 2003).

15. See Jay P. Dolan's *Catholic Revivalism: The American Experience, 1830–1900* (Notre Dame: Univ. of Notre Dame Press, 1978) on Catholic efforts to reinvigorate piety. A telling instance of the Catholic tendency to believe that "the real Jesus" is always available, and that efforts to decipher his actual first-century words and deeds (as the "Jesus seminar" of the 1980s attempted to do) are beside the point, is Luke Timothy Johnson's *The Real Jesus: The Misguided*

Quest for the Historical Jesus and the Truth of the Traditional Gospels (San Francisco: HarperSanFrancisco, 1996). To understand Catholics' relation to Jesus in America or anywhere else, it is essential to realize that their "pro-life" instincts are not limited to the abortion issue, but extend to cloning, genetic engineering, environmental damage, and all other basic alterations of the "natural" human order—God's creation. Catholic emphasis on the divine child Jesus and even divine fetus Jesus is part of a broader commitment to him as a fully natural being whose integral humanity is biological as well as historical. Those who believe in him must therefore respect the integrity of all human bodies. "Human rights" include the protection of the human body against any tampering; those who wish to tamper with it have no natural or human right to do so. Conservative Protestants may join conservative Catholics in opposing liberal abortion laws, but they often do so out of a desire to protect the family as a social and religious institution, not out of a "natural law" commitment to preserving the created biological and natural order as ordained by God.

16. *The Journals of Ralph Waldo Emerson,* ed. Ralph H. Orth and Alfred R. Ferguson, vol. 9 (Cambridge: Harvard Univ. Press, 1971), p. 7; *Journals of Ralph Waldo Emerson,* ed. Merton M. Sealts, Jr., vol. 10 (Cambridge: Harvard Univ. Press, 1973), p. 389.

17. "State Fair's Masterpiece in Butter," *Omaha World-Herald* (Iowa ed.), Aug. 14, 1999, p. 1.

18. Consult Frederic Cople Jaher, *A Scapegoat in the New Wilderness: The Origins and Rise of Anti-Semitism in America* (Cambridge: Harvard Univ. Press, 1994), for evidence that nineteenth- and even twentieth-century American anti-Semitism was significantly based on a specifically Christian (i.e., religious) animosity toward the Jews.

CHAPTER ONE

1. This chapter and the next contrast the Catholics of New Spain and New France to the Calvinist Protestants of New England. A comprehensive treatment of early European-Indian contact in North America would obviously need to examine Virginia too, from Thomas Harriot's *Briefe and True Report of the New Found Land of Virginia* (1588) to Pocahontas's trip to England in 1616 and the killing of three hundred English Virginians in 1622, an event that cooled the English on evangelizing the Indians. The Puritans, whose numbers swelled after their arrival in Salem and Boston in 1629–1630, left us a rich body of reflections on the problem of bringing Christ to the Indians (see Chapter Two).

2. Oliver Dunn and James E. Kelley, Jr., eds., *The Diario of Christopher Columbus's First Voyage, 1492–1493* (Norman: Univ. of Oklahoma Press, 1989), p. 19; Joseph Jouvency, "An Account of the Canadian Mission" [1710] in Reuben Gold Thwaites, ed., *The Jesuit Relations and Allied Documents: Travels and Explorations of the Jesuit Missionaries in New France, 1610–1791,* vol. 1 (Cleveland: Burrows Bros., 1896), p. 211. On the cultural intricacies of "possession," Stephen Greenblatt's *Marvelous Possessions: The Wonder of the New World*

(Chicago: Univ. of Chicago Press, 1991) is very suggestive. See, for example, pp. 58–60, 167 (n. 7).

3. Álvar Núñez Cabeza de Vaca, *His Account, His Life, and the Expedition of Pánfilo de Narváez,* ed. Rolena Adorno and Patrick Charles Pautz (1542; Lincoln: Univ. of Nebraska Press, 1999), vol. 1, p. 173; Thwaites, ed., *Jesuit Relations* 38:115, 117, 139; 2:52. When I cite an even-numbered (French language) page of *Jesuit Relations,* it means I have made my own translation; when I cite an odd-numbered page, I have used Thwaites's English translation from a century ago. His translation is sometimes off the mark, as Joseph P. Donnelly, S.J., shows in his *Thwaites' Jesuit Relations: Errata and Addenda* (Chicago: Loyola Univ. Press, 1967).

4. Greenblatt, *Marvelous Possessions,* p. 63.

5. The Europeans often called the Indians "savages," but in the seventeenth century they usually meant by that term "wild" or "uncivilized," not "subhuman." And the wild members of their own societies frequently struck them as less salvageable than the Native Americans. "The savages are brighter ["ont plus d'esprit"] than our ordinary peasants," wrote Father Paul Le Jeune in 1634; Thwaites, ed., *Jesuit Relations* 6:230. James Axtell discusses "savage" and other related terms in "Forked Tongues: Moral Judgments in Indian History," in his *After Columbus: Essays in the Ethnohistory of Colonial North America* (New York: Oxford Univ. Press, 1988), pp. 39ff.

6. Thwaites, ed., *Jesuit Relations,* 35:204.

7. Cabeza de Vaca, *His Account,* 1:153, 177, 195.

8. Cabeza de Vaca, *His Account,* 1:107, 219.

9. Rolena Adorno, "The Negotiation of Fear in Cabeza de Vaca's *Naufragios,*" in *New World Encounters,* ed. Stephen Greenblatt (Berkeley: Univ. of California Press, 1993), gives a cogent analysis of Cabeza de Vaca as shaman. See esp. p. 58.

10. Garcilaso de la Vega, "La Florida," in *The De Soto Chronicles: The Expedition of Hernando De Soto to North America in 1539–1543,* ed. Lawrence A. Clayton et al. (1605; Tuscaloosa: Univ. of Alabama Press, 1993), p. 434.

11. Jacques Cartier, *The Voyages of Jacques Cartier* (Toronto: Univ. of Toronto Press, 1993), pp. 61, 63–64. François-Marc Gagnon, *Jacques Cartier et la découverte du Nouveau Monde* (Quebec City: Musée du Québec, 1984), offers a magnificent interdisciplinary assessment of Cartier's voyages—archaeological, anthropological, material-cultural, artistic, and historical.

12. Cartier, *Voyages,* p. 26.

13. Thwaites, ed., *Jesuit Relations,* 4:35, 37; *Diario of Christopher Columbus's First Voyage,* pp. 157, 219.

14. Thwaites, ed., *Jesuit Relations,* 41:150. In the Catholic ministry "secular" priests are distinguished from "regular" clergy. Franciscans and Jesuits, as members of international orders, are regular clergy; secular priests are appointed by diocesan bishops to serve within that diocese only. David E. Stannard's *American Holocaust: Columbus and the Conquest of the New World* (New York: Oxford Univ. Press, 1992) is an example of legitimate outrage tethered to the view that missionaries (and Christianity) were the wholehearted

handmaidens of genocide. See James Axtell, "Columbian Encounters: 1992–1995," *William and Mary Quarterly* 52 (Oct. 1995): 684.

15. Fray Alonso de Benavides, *A Harvest of Reluctant Souls: The Memorial of Fray Alonso de Benavides, 1630,* ed. Baker H. Morrow (Niwot, CO: Univ. Press of Colorado, 1996), p. 72. David J. Weber, *The Spanish Frontier in North America* (New Haven: Yale Univ. Press, 1992; chap. 4 ("Conquistadores of the Spirit") is a finely balanced overview of the Franciscans' presence in Florida and New Mexico. Like most of the scholarly and popular literature published on the occasion of the sesquicentennial of Columbus's voyage, Weber's book rightly stresses the Europeans' imperial disregard for whatever stood between them and the riches or lands of the New World. But Weber does not let the coercive character of Spanish rule—religious and secular—blot out the concurrent fact that the seventeenth-century Franciscans in New Mexico got their conversions only when the "Indians cooperated," and that the cooperation occurred "only when they believed they had something to gain from the new religion" (p. 115). Those gains, he notes, combined spiritual and material benefits.

16. Bartolomé de las Casas, *In Defense of the Indians* (1552; DeKalb: Northern Illinois Univ. Press, 1974), pp. 178–80. See also Luis N. Rivera, *A Violent Evangelism: The Political and Religious Conquest of the Americas* (Louisville: Westminster/John Knox Press, 1992), and David M. Traboulay, *Columbus and Las Casas: The Conquest and Christianization of America, 1492–1566* (Lanham, MD: Univ. Press of America, 1994).

17. Alonso de Benavides, *A Harvest of Reluctant Souls,* p. 82. J. Manuel Espinosa, in the "historical introduction" to his collection *The Pueblo Indian Revolt of 1696 and the Franciscan Missions in New Mexico: Letters of the Missionaries and Related Documents* (Norman: Univ. of Oklahoma Press, 1988), pp. 19, 33, estimates that there were thirty-five thousand "Christianized Indians" in New Mexico in 1629, and that the number was down to twenty-five thousand in 1680. David Weber gives the figure of thirty-five thousand for the entire New Mexican Pueblo population in the early 1600s, and believes the number was down to about half of that (mainly because of disease) by 1680. "Blood of Martyrs, Blood of Indians: Toward a More Balanced View of Spanish Missions in Seventeenth-Century North America," in *Columbian Consequences,* ed. David Hurst Thomas (Washington, D.C.: Smithsonian Institution Press, 1990), vol. 2, p. 436.

18. Alonso de Benavides, *A Harvest of Reluctant Souls,* pp. 83–84.

19. Alonso de Benavides, *A Harvest of Reluctant Souls,* pp. xix–xx, 30–32; Ramón Gutiérrez, *When Jesus Came, the Corn Mothers Went Away: Marriage, Sexuality, and Power in New Mexico, 1500–1846* (Stanford: Stanford Univ. Press, 1991), pp. 73–74.

20. Alonso de Benavides, *A Harvest of Reluctant Souls,* p. 80; Weber, *The Spanish Frontier in North America,* p. 107. Of course, the European interest in the "fabulous" was not limited to the invisible world of spirits. The Spanish friars would never have gotten to New Mexico if adventurers and government officials had not been seduced by tales of untold riches waiting for them in "the Seven Cities" of "Cibola" in the Zuni country. George P. Hammond, "The

Search for the Fabulous in the Settlement of the Southwest," in David J. Weber, ed., *New Spain's Far Northern Frontier* (Albuquerque: Univ. of New Mexico Press, 1979), p. 21. The impressive work of William A. Christian, Jr., on sixteenth-century Spanish piety suggests that the New Mexico Indians had plenty of support for their magical visions from the secular as well as clerical Spaniards in their midst: *Apparitions in Late Medieval and Renaissance Spain* (Princeton: Princeton Univ. Press, 1981) and *Local Religion in Sixteenth-Century Spain* (Princeton: Princeton Univ. Press, 1981).

21. Alonso de Benavides, *A Harvest of Reluctant Souls*, pp. 64, 68, 72.

22. Louise M. Burkhart, *The Slippery Earth: Nahua-Christian Moral Dialogue in Sixteenth-Century Mexico* (Tucson: Univ. of Arizona Press, 1989), pp. 173–74, 183. See also Susanne Klaus, *Uprooted Christianity: The Preaching of the Christian Doctrine in Mexico Based on Franciscan Sermons in the Sixteenth Century Written in Nahuatl* (Bonn: Sauerwein, 1999).

23. Alonso de Benavides, *A Harvest of Reluctant Souls*, p. 42. Spanish formalism is well described by Stephen Greenblatt in his discussion of Columbus's ritual proclamation claiming possession of New World real estate. Saying the right words was the substance of the transaction, whether of secular ownership or religious assent. *Marvelous Possessions*, p. 59.

24. Gutiérrez, *When Jesus Came*, pp. 86–88, 137. During the Pueblo Revolt twenty-one Franciscans were killed. Gutiérrez calculates that of the roughly one hundred priests who served in the pueblos in the seventeenth century, forty-nine met the martyrdom that Franciscan tradition cherished. It takes nothing away from Gutiérrez's massive intellectual achievement to note that he sometimes subverts the delicate interpretive balance of religious and political meanings that his book, at its best, achieves. In order to underline the Franciscans' or the Spanish officials' destructive impact on Indian culture, he sometimes needlessly doubts the sincerity of their religious professions. Why suggest, for example, that the governor's pious self-flagellation in 1598 may have been a "purely political ploy" (p. 88)? It accords better with Gutiérrez's overall perspective to assert that it was probably *not* a ploy. The brutality of Spanish political power, he notes again and again, is perfectly compatible with genuine religious convictions on all sides. Gutiérrez shows better than anyone else has managed to do that the fateful drama of Christ's introduction into the Indians' Old World and the Europeans' New World includes *both* Christ's cross-cultural religious appeal and the aggressive use of him by Europeans to modify or extirpate Native American cultures.

25. Alonso de Benavides, *A Harvest of Reluctant Souls*, p. 76; Espinosa, ed., *The Pueblo Indian Revolt of 1696*, p. 120. According to Espinosa (p. 27), the conflict between Franciscans and local Spanish government officials from 1610 to 1680 was an "almost endless confrontation." When the Franciscans returned to the Pueblos from their Texas exile in 1694, they found the Indians notably uninterested in sanctifying their sexual unions with the sacrament of marriage (pp. 116–44).

26. Espinosa, ed., *The Pueblo Indian Revolt of 1696*, pp. 122, 124–25, 137.

27. Marc Lescarbot, *The Conversion of the Savages Who Were Baptized in New France During This Year, 1610* (Paris: Jean Millot, 1610), reprinted in Thwaites, ed., *Jesuit Relations*, 1:54, 58–59, 61; Biard in *Jesuit Relations*, 1:162–63. A few English Jesuits preached to the Indians in Maryland between 1634 and 1645, but they did little living among Indians or learning of native languages. In those years there were never more than five Jesuits in Maryland at a time; in Quebec there were never fewer than twenty, along with numerous lay brothers. James Axtell, "White Legend: The Jesuit Missions in Maryland," in *After Columbus*, p. 83.

28. Thwaites, ed., *Jesuit Relations*, 5:168; 7:55, 145, 147, 150.

29. Thwaites, ed., *Jesuit Relations*, 5:159, 161, 224.

30. Thwaites, ed., *Jesuit Relations*, 11:193; 17:124, 126.

31. Thwaites, ed., *Jesuit Relations*, 22:60; 27:189–93, 200.

32. Thwaites, ed., *Jesuit Relations*, 10:168; 6:182, 185.

33. Thwaites, ed., *Jesuit Relations*, 8:161.

34. Thwaites, ed., *Jesuit Relations*, 10:13, 39, 49; 8:134.

35. Thwaites, ed., *Jesuit Relations*, 7:101, 103.

36. Thwaites, ed., *Jesuit Relations*, 8:37, 127–29.

37. Thwaites, ed., *Jesuit Relations*, 8:129, 144–46.

38. Thwaites, ed., *Jesuit Relations*, 10:25–26; 41:148; 11:230, 232. Karen Anderson's *Chain Her By One Foot: The Subjugation of Women in Seventeenth-Century New France* (London: Routledge, 1991) rightly notes that the Jesuits' very male God in Jesus helped extend patriarchal structures already well cemented in Montagnais and Huron cultures. The Jesuits often regarded Indian women as Jezebels who threatened the virtue of Indian men, and failed to realize that the campaign to end polygamy had disastrous material effects on wives let go by Christianized husbands. Anderson might have added that the Jesuits also thought that Indian men threatened the virtue of Indian women, and that the Jesuits' male God in Jesus could unsettle gender relations by giving new spiritual authority to individual women as well as men. Carole Blackburn, in *Harvest of Souls: The Jesuit Missions and Colonialism in North America, 1632–1650* (Montreal: McGill-Queen's Univ. Press, 2000), concurs with Anderson's judgment about the Jesuits' view of women but offers a much more nuanced analysis of gender and power relations between colonizers and colonized. She shrewdly observes that "the expression of dominance in the *Relations* is not necessarily equivalent to dominance in their actual relations with Native people" (p. 12). Her Introduction shows why a "post-colonial" perspective is indispensable to a full understanding of the cultural transfer of a figure such as Jesus. On "cultural transfer" as an alternative to "acculturation" in social theory, see the Introduction to Laurier Turgeon et al., eds., *Cultural Transfer, America and Europe: 500 Years of Interculturation* (Laval: Les Presses de l'Université Laval, 1996), pp. 33–54.

39. Thwaites, ed., *Jesuit Relations*, 8:151, 166–67.

40. Thwaites, ed., *Jesuit Relations*, 11:214–19; 17:63–65.

41. Thwaites, ed., *Jesuit Relations*, 34:29, 31.

42. Thwaites, ed., *Jesuit Relations*, 10:118, 120, 211; 20:70.

43. Thwaites, ed., *Jesuit Relations,* 66:265.
44. Thwaites, ed., *Jesuit Relations,* 3:153; 15:79–81, 95, 97.
45. Thwaites, ed., *Jesuit Relations,* 16:115–17.

CHAPTER TWO

1. John Cotton, *Gods Promise to His Plantation* (London: William Jones, 1630), p. 17; [Thomas Shepard], *The Day-Breaking, if not the Sun-rising of the Gospell with the Indians in New-England* (London: Richard Botes, 1647), p. 15. Thomas Shepard claimed that the Spanish colonization "in the southern parts of this vast continent" had been "laid in the blood of nineteen millions of poor innocent natives (as Acosta the Jesuit, a bird of their own nest, relates the story)": *The Clear Sunshine of the Gospel Breaking Forth Upon the Indians in New England* (1648; Boston: Doctrinal Tract and Book Society, 1853), p. 489.

2. *Winthrop Papers,* vol. 2 (Boston: Massachusetts Historical Society, 1931), p. 126.

3. *The Journal of John Winthrop, 1630–1649,* ed. Richard S. Dunn and Laetitia Yeandle, abridged ed. (Cambridge: Harvard Univ. Press, 1996), p. 93. Richard W. Cogley's excellent *John Eliot's Mission to the Indians before King Philip's War* (Cambridge: Harvard Univ. Press, 1999) shows that the Puritans also went slow on Indian conversions because some ministers, such as Eliot and Roger Williams, were millennialists who believed that until the Jews were gathered in, Gentiles such as the Indians could not be converted.

4. Edmund S. Morgan, *Visible Saints: The History of a Puritan Idea* (1963; Ithaca: Cornell Univ. Press, 1965), is a fine introduction to the Puritan conception of faith. Charles E. Hambrick-Stowe, *The Practice of Piety: Puritan Devotional Disciplines in Seventeenth-Century New England* (Chapel Hill: Univ. of North Carolina Press, 1982), and Charles Lloyd Cohen, *God's Caress: The Psychology of Puritan Religious Experience* (New York: Oxford Univ. Press, 1986), show how the conception was lived out in experience.

5. *Winthrop Papers,* 2:111; Thwaites, ed., *Jesuit Relations,* 17:122; 24:62.

6. Cotton Mather, *Magnalia Christi Americana* (1702), and Mather, *Christianity to the Life* (1702), quoted in Richard F. Lovelace, *The American Pietism of Cotton Mather: Origins of American Evangelicalism* (Grand Rapids: Christian Univ. Press, 1979), pp. 116–17. See pp. 165–66 for a discussion of these texts.

7. [Thomas Weld, Hugh Peter, and Henry Dunster], *New England's First Fruits* (London: Henry Overton, 1643), pp. 6–7.

8. Roger Williams, *A Key into the Language of America* (London: Gregory Dexter, 1643), in *The Complete Writings of Roger Williams,* vol. 1 (New York: Russell and Russell, 1963), pp. 26–27.

9. Henry W. Bowden and James P. Ronda, eds., *John Eliot's Indian Dialogues: A Study in Cultural Interaction* (1671; Westport, CT: Greenwood Press, 1980), p. 66; John Eliot and Thomas Mayhew, Jr., *Tears of Repentance* (London: Peter Cole, 1653), pp. 4, 7; [John Eliot], *A Further Accompt of the Progresse of the Gospel amongst the Indians in New-England* (London: M. Simmons, 1659), p. 9 (for Waban's comment on Jesus healing "both soul and body").

10. Eliot and Mayhew, *Tears of Repentance,* pp. 17–18, 39. Charles L. Cohen, in his "Conversion Among Puritans and Amerindians: A Theological and Cultural Perspective," in Francis J. Bremer, ed., *Puritanism: Transatlantic Perspectives on a Seventeenth-Century Anglo-American Faith* (Boston: Massachusetts Historical Society, 1993), pp. 253–54, gives further examples of Native American interest in Jesus as healer.

11. [Shepard], *The Clear Sunshine,* pp. 459–60.

12. [Shepard], *The Clear Sunshine,* pp. 470–72.

13. [Shepard], *The Clear Sunshine,* pp. 474, 476; Eliot and Mayhew, *Tears of Repentance,* p. 8.

14. [Shepard], *The Clear Sunshine,* pp. 481–82. In New France weeping was common in Indian mourning rituals even if it was not in cases of torture. See *Jesuit Relations,* 40:61. Shepard may have exaggerated the rarity of weeping among Indians in New England, but his (and Eliot's) main point was that Indians had learned under Puritan tutelage to weep over their sins.

15. Bowden and Ronda, eds., *John Eliot's Indian Dialogues,* pp. 88–89; [Shepard], *The Clear Sunshine,* p. 465.

16. James Axtell, "The English Colonial Impact on Indian Culture," in his *The European and the Indian: Essays in the Ethnohistory of Colonial North America* (New York: Oxford Univ. Press, 1981), p. 270, and especially "Some Thoughts on the Ethnohistory of Missions," in *After Columbus,* pp. 48–57.

17. Jacques Mathieu, "French Settlements," in Jacob Ernest Cooke, ed., *Encyclopedia of the North American Colonies,* vol. 1 (New York: Scribner, 1993), p. 136 ("war sticks"); Lescarbot, *The Conversion of the Savages,* in *Jesuit Relations,* 1:79 (Chkoudun).

18. Edward Winslow, ed., *The Glorious Progress of the Gospel amongst the Indians in New England* (London: Edward Winslow, 1649), pp. 12–13; *Of the Conversion of Five Thousand and Nine Hundred East-Indians . . . with a Post-script of the Gospels good successe also amongst the West-Indians in New England* (London: John Hammond, 1650), pp. 20–21; [Shepard], *The Clear Sunshine,* p. 485.

19. On the wonder-lore and its relation to magic, see David D. Hall, "Magic and Witchcraft," in Cooke, ed., *Encyclopedia of the North American Colonies,* vol. 1, pp. 653–64; Hall's innovative study of "lived experience," *Worlds of Wonder, Days of Judgment: Popular Religion in Early New England* (New York: Knopf, 1989); Richard Weisman, *Witchcraft, Magic, and Religion in Seventeenth-Century Massachusetts* (Amherst: Univ. of Massachusetts Press, 1984); and Richard Godbeer, *The Devil's Dominion: Magic and Religion in Early New England* (Cambridge: Cambridge Univ. Press, 1992).

20. Samuel Willard, *The Danger of Taking God's Name in Vain* (Boston, 1691), p. 10, and Increase Mather, *Essay for the Recording of Illustrious Providences* (Boston, 1684), p. 261, both quoted in Godbeer, *The Devil's Dominion,* pp. 40, 61. The toothache cure, as given by Godbeer and presumably Mather, "In Nomine Patris, et Spiritus Sanctis" ("in the name of the Father, and Holy Spirit") actually dropped the Son ("et Filii") from the Catholic sign of the cross.

21. Andrew White quoted in Edwin Scott Gaustad and Philip L. Barlow, *New Historical Atlas of Religion in America* (New York: Oxford Univ. Press, 2001), p. 52.

22. Jacobus Arminius was a Dutch Reformed theologian, and a notorious defector from Calvinism, who died in 1609. The label "Arminian" entered American evangelical Protestant usage as a term of revulsion. Forgotten today, it was a virtual Protestant household term well into the twentieth century. Alien though the term may be, I will employ it throughout the book to designate the anti-Calvinist position of Catholics, Anglicans, Methodists, Unitarians, Universalists, and others, all of whom stressed the freedom of people to choose, and the power of believers to navigate (with God's help), the path of salvation in Christ.

23. Henry Dunster quoted in Philip F. Gura, *A Glimpse of Sion's Glory: Puritan Radicalism in New England, 1620–1660* (Middletown: Wesleyan Univ. Press, 1984), p. 121.

24. Gura, *A Glimpse of Sion's Glory*, p. 125, gives a good discussion of the Baptists' individualist critique of the Puritan "federated covenant."

25. Marmaduke Stephenson quoted in Hugh Barbour and J. William Frost, eds., *The Quakers* (New York: Greenwood Press, 1988), p. 52; William Robinson quoted in Carla Gardina Pestana, "The Quaker Executions as Myth and History," *Journal of American History* 80 (Sept. 1993): 447. Mary Dyer was on the scaffold with Stephenson and Robinson, but was reprieved and banished from Massachusetts. She promptly returned to Boston and was executed in her turn.

26. James Nayler and George Fox quoted in Leo Damrosch, *The Sorrows of the Quaker Jesus: James Nayler and the Puritan Crackdown on the Free Spirit* (Cambridge: Harvard Univ. Press, 1996), p. 94. Damrosch provides an excellent introduction to the Quaker idea of the "Christ Within," pp. 92–97.

27. Perry Miller, *The New England Mind: The Seventeenth-Century* (1939; Boston: Beacon Press, 1961), p. 45. Miller shows how central Christ was to the Puritans' covenant theology on pp. 405ff., and to what Miller calls their "practice of piety" on p. 55.

28. John Cotton quoted in Richard Godbeer, "'Love Raptures': Marital, Romantic, and Erotic Images of Jesus Christ in Puritan New England, 1670–1730," *New England Quarterly* 68 (Sept. 1995): 365, n. 31; Edward Taylor, *Preparatory Meditations* 116 and 80, in *The Poems of Edward Taylor*, ed. Donald E. Stanford (New Haven: Yale Univ. Press, 1960), pp. 295, 230. I am indebted to Godbeer's article for alerting me to the meditations of Taylor on the Song of Songs and the Gospel of John. But I think he exaggerates how "vividly sexual" they are (p. 368) by abstracting from the biblical context and by piling up erotic-sounding phrases from separate poems. It is also worth noting that Taylor's meditations went unpublished in his lifetime, and that he barred his heirs from publishing them. They were first printed in 1937. Thomas Shepard's marriage ceremony is described in Charles E. Hambrick-Stowe, *The Practice of Piety: Puritan Devotional Disciplines in Seventeenth-Century New England* (Chapel Hill: Univ. of North Carolina Press, 1983), pp. 121–22. Hambrick-Stowe's informative introduction to his edited volume *Early New England Meditative Poetry*

(New York: Paulist Press, 1988) ties the Christ imagery of Puritans Edward Taylor and Anne Bradstreet to their Catholic and Protestant predecessors.

29. Edward Taylor, "Meditation on Song of Songs 4:8," in Hambrick-Stowe, ed., *Early New England Meditative Poetry*, pp. 190–91.

30. Thomas Shepard, "The Autobiography," in Michael McGiffert, ed., *God's Plot: Puritan Spirituality in Thomas Shepard's Cambridge*, rev. ed. (Amherst: Univ. of Massachusetts Press, 1994), pp. 48, 74–76.

31. Shepard, "Autobiography," p. 44.

32. Shepard, "The Journal," in McGiffert, ed., *God's Plot*, p. 100.

33. Shepard, "Autobiography," pp. 72–73.

34. Shepard, "Autobiography," pp. 47, 57.

35. Shepard, "Autobiography," p. 75.

36. Shepard, "The Journal," p. 119.

37. Shepard, "Autobiography," p. 70.

38. Shepard, "Autobiography," p. 68.

39. David D. Hall, *The Antinomian Controversy, 1636–1638: A Documentary History*, 2nd ed. (1968; Durham, NC: Duke Univ. Press, 1990), p. 337.

40. Michael P. Winship's *Making Heretics: Militant Protestantism and Free Grace in Massachusetts, 1636–1641* (Princeton: Princeton Univ. Press, 2002) challenges the received wisdom that puts Anne Hutchinson at the center of the Antinomian Controversy. Consult David D. Hall's probing review essay "Orthodoxy and Heterodoxy on Trial," *Harvard Theological Review* 95 (2000): 437–52, which puts Winship's important book in the context of Puritan historiography.

41. Shepard, "Autobiography," p. 68.

42. John Shepard's confession, in McGiffert, ed., *God's Plot*, p. 211.

43. Elizabeth Cutter's confession, in McGiffert, ed., *God's Plot*, p. 196.

44. Mary Sparrowhawk's confession, in McGiffert, ed., *God's Plot*, pp. 171–72.

45. Roger Williams, *George Fox Digg'd out of his Burrowes* (1676), quoted in Glenn W. LaFantasie, ed., *The Correspondence of Roger Williams*, vol. 2 (Hanover: Brown Univ. Press/Univ. Press of New England, 1988), p. 651.

46. Robert Holmes's and Barbara Cutter's confessions, in McGiffert, ed., *God's Plot*, pp. 183–84, 186, 195. Michael Winship notes that Shepard's position on doubt and assurance was common, and perhaps typical, among early-seventeenth-century Puritan ministers in England. *Making Heretics*, p. 18.

CHAPTER THREE

1. Mary Rowlandson, *The Sovereignty and Goodness and God*, ed. Neal Salisbury (1682; Boston: Bedford Books, 1997), pp. 88, 112.

2. The Indian population estimates are discussed by Russell Thornton, "Health, Disease, and Demography," in *A Companion to American Indian History*, ed. Philip J. Deloria and Neal Salisbury (Malden, MA: Blackwell, 2001), p. 69. A superb treatment of Moravian overtures to the Indians is Jane T. Merritt's "Dreaming of the Savior's Blood: Moravians and the Indian Great Awakening in Pennsylvania," *William and Mary Quarterly* 54 (Oct. 1997): 723–46.

3. Vernon Louis Parrington, *Main Currents in American Thought,* vol. 1 (New York: Harcourt, Brace and Co., 1927), p. 165 (Franklin), p. 162 (Edwards).

4. Benjamin Franklin, *Writings* (New York: Library of America, 1987), pp. 1385, 1392–93. Part 2 of the *Autobiography,* which concludes with his list of virtues, was completed in 1784. The best source on the history of Franklin's religious opinions, and the long history of disagreement about them, is Kerry S. Walters, *Benjamin Franklin and His Gods* (Urbana: Univ. of Illinois Press, 1999). See also Alfred Owen Aldridge, *Benjamin Franklin and Nature's God* (Durham, NC: Duke Univ. Press, 1967), and Douglas Anderson, *The Radical Enlightenments of Benjamin Franklin* (Baltimore: Johns Hopkins Univ. Press, 1997), esp. chap. 2. Myra Jehlen offers intriguing ideas about Franklin in relation to Rousseau, Bunyan, and other thinkers in "'Imitate Jesus and Socrates': The Making of a Good American," *South Atlantic Quarterly* 89 (Summer 1990): 501–24.

5. Franklin, *Writings,* p. 1321 (Socrates), p. 1408 (Whitefield); Whitefield to Franklin, Nov. 26, 1740, Aug. 17, 1752, in Leonard W. Labaree, ed., *The Papers of Benjamin Franklin* (New Haven: Yale Univ. Press, 1960), vol. 2, p. 270, vol. 4, p. 343.

6. Franklin, *Writings,* pp. 475–77.

7. Franklin, *Writings,* pp. 638–41. Franklin also toiled at modernizing the Book of Common Prayer, a task of which Jesus, he believed, would have approved, since the latter was on record in favor of "short prayer." Labaree, *Papers of Benjamin Franklin,* 20:346. I comment on the current assumption that irony is inherently cynical or nihilistic, rather than sincere, in my review of Andrew Delbanco's *The Death of Satan: How Americans Have Lost a Sense of Evil* (New York: Farrar, Straus, 1995), "Speak of the Devil: Popular Religion in American Culture," *American Literary History* 9 (Spring 1997): 181–95. Compare Delbanco's chap. 6 ("The Culture of Irony") to Reinhold Niebuhr's treatment of irony in *The Irony of American History* (New York: Scribner, 1952), which I summarize in my *Reinhold Niebuhr: A Biography* (1985; Ithaca: Cornell Univ. Press, 1996), pp. 244–47.

8. Of course the Calvinist Whitefield never meant to say that anyone's salvation was guaranteed. All he said was that no one could be saved without the grace of God made manifest in the New Birth. That double negative amounted to a necessary-but-not-sufficient argument. Being born again in the Spirit provided the only kind of assurance human beings had access to: not a guarantee but a greater probability of salvation. Franklin simplified and distorted Whitefield's position, equating it with a promise of automatic salvation. That made his own secular-religious stance substantially more attractive to a skeptically minded but spiritually curious individual like him.

9. Franklin, *Writings,* pp. 1179–80.

10. Interpretation was essential to a correct reading of the Bible, said Edwards, because the Holy Scriptures were not clear at all points. The Bible was full of metaphors ("similitudes") whose full meaning was hidden. Belief was a double vocation: accepting the truth of a metaphor like "ye are the temple of the Holy Ghost" (1 Cor. 6:19), then using one's reason to make as much

sense of it as one could. Indeed, Scripture had to be filled out by reason if it was to be the revealed Word of God in the first place. The doctrine of the Trinity, in his view, was never "said in Scripture in express words," but it emerged theologically thanks to "safe and certain" deductions of reason. Edwards, "Entry dd" ("similitudes"), "Entry 94" ("express words," "safe and certain"), and "Entry 104" (second Trinity) in Thomas A. Schafer, ed., *The Works of Jonathan Edwards: The "Miscellanies,"* vol. 13 (New Haven: Yale Univ. Press, 1994), pp. 181, 257, 273.

11. "The Surprising Work of God in the Conversion of Many Hundred Souls in Northampton" was the subtitle of Edwards's first report on the Connecticut Valley awakening: *A Faithful Narrative of the Surprising Work of God* (published in London by John Oswald in 1737 and in Boston by Samuel Kneeland the following year). Whitefield gave three other talks to Edwards's congregation during his visit in October 1740, and Edwards later wrote that "the congregation was extraordinarily melted by every sermon; almost the whole assembly being in tears for a great part of sermon time." Edwards to Thomas Prince, Dec. 12, 1743, in C. C. Goen, ed., *The Works of Jonathan Edwards: The Great Awakening,* vol. 4 (New Haven: Yale Univ. Press, 1972), p. 545.

12. Edwards, "A Sermon Preached on the Day of the Funeral of the Rev. Mr. David Brainerd," in Norman Pettit, ed., *The Works of Jonathan Edwards: The Life of David Brainerd,* vol. 7 (New Haven: Yale Univ. Press, 1985), p. 547; "An Appendix," in Pettit, ed., *Life of David Brainerd,* p. 503 ("pleasant warm feeling").

13. Edwards to Lady Mary Pepperrell, Nov. 28, 1751, in George S. Claghorn, ed., *The Works of Jonathan Edwards: Letters and Personal Writings,* vol. 16 (New Haven: Yale Univ. Press, 1998), p. 418; Edwards, "The Sweet Harmony of Christ," in M. X. Lesser, ed., *The Works of Jonathan Edwards: Sermons and Discourses, 1734–1738,* vol. 19 (New Haven: Yale Univ. Press), p. 442.

14. Charles Chauncy, *Seasonable Thoughts on the State of Religion in New England* (1743; Hicksville, NY: Regina Press, 1975), pp. 96, 217.

15. Edwards, "The Sweet Harmony of Christ," p. 447 ("will-worship"); Edwards, "A Divine and Supernatural Light," in Wilson H. Kimnach et al., eds., *The Sermons of Jonathan Edwards: A Reader* (New Haven: Yale Univ. Press, 1999), p. 126. Ann Taves, *Fits, Trances, and Visions: Experiencing Religion and Explaining Experience from Wesley to James* (Princeton: Princeton Univ. Press, 1999) is an especially probing analysis of the debate over "enthusiasm" and "experience" in the eighteenth and nineteenth centuries. Her insightful treatment of Edwards in relation to Chauncy and Wesley (pp. 15–75) needs to be put in the larger context of Edwards's campaign to deepen cultural awareness of human sin and divine sovereignty.

16. Edwards, "Some Thoughts Concerning the Present Revival of Religion in New England (1742)," and "A Faithful Narrative," in Goen, ed., *The Great Awakening,* pp. 312, 158, 200, 204.

17. Edwards, "A Faithful Narrative," pp. 195–96, 198.

18. Edwards, "Some Thoughts Concerning the Present Revival of Religion," pp. 332–35; Edwards, "Christ, the Light of the World," in Wilson H.

Kimnach, ed., *The Works of Jonathan Edwards: Sermons and Discourses, 1720–1723,* vol. 10 (New Haven: Yale Univ. Press, 1992), pp. 542, 540.

19. Edwards, "Some Thoughts Concerning the Present Revival of Religion," pp. 332, 334–35, 341; Sarah Edwards memoir, in *The Works of Jonathan Edwards, with a Memoir by Sereno E. Dwight,* vol. 1 (1834; Edinburgh: Banner of Truth Trust, 1974), pp. lxiii–lxiv. C. C. Goen notes (*The Great Awakening,* p. 341, n. 9) that Edwards was not fair here to Wesley, who should not have been identified with enthusiasm. The Christian perfection that Wesley preached was not an absence of "corruption" or "rottenness." Those terms were part of Edwards's Calvinist scheme, which Wesley not only rejected but, as an Anglican, had never imbibed in the first place. Raised an Anglican, he pictured sin as a willed offense against God and his law. "Holiness" was logically possible since a saintly person could choose not to sin. As an empirical matter, humanity was corrupt because so many people preferred sinning to obeying God's law.

20. Edwards, "Some Thoughts Concerning the Present Revival of Religion," pp. 334–35. In his *Seasonable Thoughts,* pp. 104–05, Charles Chauncy contended that women comprised a majority of those given to "fits and screams." In his mind, that supposed fact showed the illegitimacy of the revivals. If the bodily seizures had been divinely caused, he argued, they would have affected men and women equally. There is much evidence that women outnumbered men in religious practice in colonial America (as elsewhere), but the revivals tended to draw more men than usual into the churches. Whether they expressed themselves physically and vocally as much as women did once they were there is another matter. See Catherine A. Brekus's discussion in *Strangers and Pilgrims: Female Preaching in America, 1740–1845* (New Haven: Yale Univ. Press, 1998), pp. 44ff. Richard D. Shiels documents the overrepresentation of women in New England churches in "The Feminization of American Congregationalism, 1730–1835," *American Quarterly* 33 (Spring 1981): 46–62.

21. Edwards, "The Excellency of Christ," in Kimnach et al., eds., *Sermons of Jonathan Edwards,* pp. 163–64, 166, 181. Edwards explicates "the sense of the heart" in "Entry 782" of Ava Chamberlain, ed., *The Works of Jonathan Edwards: The "Miscellanies,"* vol. 18 (New Haven: Yale Univ. Press, 2000), p. 459. James L. Hoopes does a fine analysis of Entry 782 in "Jonathan Edwards's Religious Psychology," *Journal of American History* 69 (Mar. 1983): 849–65.

22. Edwards's 1739 sermon on Luke 22:44, in *The Works of Jonathan Edwards,* vol. 2 (1834; Edinburgh: Banner of Truth Trust, 1974), pp. 869–70 [the sermon is also published in *The Works of President Edwards,* vol. 10 (1847; New York: Burt Franklin, 1968, pp. 248–80)]; Edwards, "Entry 205," in Schafer, ed., *The "Miscellanies,"* 13:341.

23. Edwards's sermon on Luke 22:44, *Works of Jonathan Edwards* (1834), 2:868.

24. John E. Smith, ed., *The Works of Jonathan Edwards: Religious Affections,* vol. 2 (1746; New Haven: Yale Univ. Press, 1959), pp. 214–15; Thomas Shepard quoted by Edwards, p. 214. On the "image" of Christ, and "seeing" the image, see also Edwards's discussion in "Entry 777" of Chamberlain, ed., *The "Miscellanies,"* 18:429ff.

25. Edwards, "Some Thoughts Concerning the Present Revival of Religion," pp. 353–55.

26. John R. Wilson, ed., *The Works of Jonathan Edwards: A History of the Work of Redemption*, vol. 9 (New Haven: Yale Univ. Press, 1989), pp. 433–34; Edwards, "To the Mohawks at the Treaty, August 16, 1751," in Kimnach et al., eds., *Sermons of Jonathan Edwards*, pp. 107–09.

27. Wilson, ed., *A History of the Work of Redemption*, pp. 406, 431–32. On the intricacies of the original Arian and Socinian positions, consult Jaroslav Pelikan's magisterial *The Christian Tradition: A History of the Development of Doctrine* (Chicago: Univ. of Chicago Press, 1971), vol. 1, pp. 193–200 (Arius), and vol. 4, pp. 322–32 (Socinus).

28. An excellent discussion of the New Divinity in relation to Edwards is found in William Breitenbach, "Unregenerate Doings: Selflessness and Selfishness in New Divinity Theology," *American Quarterly* 34 (Winter 1982): 479–502. Original sin was virtually impossible to defend persuasively by the late eighteenth century, when leading religious as well as secular opinion found "imputed" responsibility nonsensical. How could a modern person still be guilty for something Adam had done? Edwards had countered brilliantly in *Original Sin*. As he put it in his notebook, "It is no more unreasonable that we should be guilty of Adam's first sin, than that we should be guilty of our own that we have been guilty of in times past. For we are not the same we were in times past," despite how much "we please to call ourselves the same. For we are anew created every moment." But that Augustinian view of contingent selfhood, in which people needed God to hold them in existence just as much as they needed Christ to redeem them from sin, was out of tune with the times after Edwards died, and probably during his lifetime too. Edwards, "Entry 18," in Schafer, ed., *The "Miscellanies,"* 13:210. For the latest contributions to the vast literature on Edwards, his successors (the New Divinity theologians), and their successors (the New Haven theology of Nathaniel Taylor and others), consult the richly informative endnotes in Douglas A. Sweeney, *Nathaniel Taylor, New Haven Theology, and the Legacy of Jonathan Edwards* (New York: Oxford Univ. Press, 2003), and the comprehensive *Jonathan Edwards: A Life*, by George M. Marsden (New Haven: Yale Univ. Press, 2003).

29. Of course churchmen throughout Christian history have kept women subordinate, and they have done so in part by preaching a higher soul-equality that conveniently diverted attention from day-by-day inequalities of power and responsibility. But the doctrine of soul-equality cut the other way too, continually prompting some women and men to challenge male domination. The historian's goal must be to do full justice to the complexity of the marital metaphor, rather than reducing it—as scholars in our own day often do—to a mechanism by which gender inequality was reproduced. Catherine Brekus, for example, gives several instances of eighteenth-century men using the bride-bridegroom metaphor to describe their relation to Christ (*Strangers and Pilgrims*, pp. 38–39). She rightly notes (p. 38) that "there was nothing inherently feminine about this marital language," but then unaccountably concludes that

"nevertheless, men who described themselves as brides implicitly subverted their status as men."

30. Stephen J. Stein, *The Shaker Experience in America: A History of the United Society of Believers* (New Haven: Yale Univ. Press, 1992), pp. 16, 36–37.

31. The Methodists' complex relation to the American Revolution is treated in Dee E. Andrews's excellent book *The Methodists and Revolutionary America, 1760–1800: The Shaping of an Evangelical Culture* (Princeton: Princeton Univ. Press, 2000).

32. Donald G. Mathews, *Religion in the Old South* (Chicago: Univ. of Chicago Press, 1977), pp. 19–20, offers an insightful treatment of the relation between individualism and community in Methodist religion.

33. Benjamin Abbott, *Experience and Gospel Labors of the Rev. Benjamin Abbott*, ed. John Ffirth (New York: Mason and Lane, 1836), pp. 35, 93–96.

34. Abbott, *Experience and Gospel Labors*, pp. 6–7, 226.

35. Abbott, *Experience and Gospel Labors*, pp. 13, 25, 38, 53, 112.

36. Abbott, *Experience and Gospel Labors*, pp. 6, 27, 214.

37. Abbott, *Experience and Gospel Labors*, pp. 60, 63.

38. "Memoir of Old Elizabeth, a Coloured Woman," in *Six Women's Slave Narratives* (1863; New York: Oxford Univ. Press, 1988), pp. 6–7, 10, 13. Catherine Brekus notes how commonly in the late eighteenth and nineteenth centuries women preachers expressed doubt about their vocations. Brekus, *Strangers and Pilgrims*, p. 190.

39. "Memoir of Old Elizabeth," pp. 8–9.

40. "Memoir of Old Elizabeth," p. 18; John Woolman, "Some Considerations on the Keeping of Negroes" (1754), in *The Journal and Major Essays of John Woolman*, ed. Phillips P. Moulton (1971; Richmond, IN: Friends United Press, 1989), p. 208.

41. [Benjamin Rush], "An Address to the Inhabitants of the British Settlements, on the Slavery of the Negroes in America," 2nd ed., 1773, and "A Vindication of the Address," 1773, both reprinted in Rush, *An Address on the Slavery of the Negroes in America* (New York: Arno Press, 1969), pp. 12–13 ("Address") and p. 9 ("Vindication"). On Rush's anti-slavery statements (or any other aspect of religion in relation to anti-slavery), see the indispensable book by David Brion Davis, *The Problem of Slavery in the Age of Revolution, 1770–1823* (Ithaca: Cornell Univ. Press, 1975), pp. 533–37 and passim.

42. Jon Butler, *Awash in a Sea of Faith: Christianizing the American People* (Cambridge: Harvard Univ. Press, 1990), is excellent on Philadelphia (pp. 118–28) and on the concrete connections between revolution and religion (pp. 194–224). On Richard Allen and the African American population of the city, consult Gary B. Nash, *Forging Freedom: The Formation of Philadelphia's Black Community, 1720–1840* (Cambridge: Harvard Univ. Press, 1988). Gordon S. Wood offers a comprehensive review of the religion-as-cause-of-the-Revolution question in "Religion and the American Revolution," in Harry S. Stout and D. G. Hart, eds., *New Directions in American Religious History* (New York: Oxford Univ. Press, 1997), pp. 173–205. For examples of revolutionary sermons drawing analogies to the Old Testament, see Conrad Cherry, ed., *God's New Israel:*

Religious Interpretations of American Destiny, rev. ed. (Chapel Hill, Univ. of North Carolina Press, 1998), pp. 67–109. Tom Paine's revolutionary pamphlet *Common Sense* (1776) concludes with an extended attack on those Quakers who thought "the light of Christ Jesus" left political questions to be resolved by the appropriate authorities, in this case the king. But many other Quakers, while remaining pacifists, strongly supported independence. On millennial appeals to Jesus after the war, see Ruth H. Bloch, *Visionary Republic: Millennial Themes in American Thought, 1756–1800* (New York: Cambridge Univ. Press, 1985), pt. 3.

43. *The Autobiography of Benjamin Rush,* ed. George W. Corner (Princeton: Princeton Univ. Press, 1948), pp. 164–65, 224, 339–40.

44. "The Journal of John Woolman," in *Journal and Major Essays of John Woolman,* ed. Moulton, p. 31.

45. Timothy Dwight, *Travels in New-England and New-York,* vol. 4 (New Haven: Timothy Dwight, 1822), pp. 207–08.

CHAPTER FOUR

1. An earlier version of parts of the Jefferson and Emerson sections of this chapter appeared in *Raritan* 22:2 (Fall 2002). My thanks to *Raritan* editor Jackson Lears for his searching comments, which have improved my discussion immensely. In *The Lustre of Our Country: The American Experience of Religious Freedom* (Berkeley: Univ. of California Press, 1998), John T. Noonan, Jr., offers a fine discussion of Jefferson's and Madison's opposition to state supports for religion.

2. Alexis de Tocqueville, *Democracy in America,* vol. 1 (1835; New York: Vintage Classics, 1990), pp. 308, 314; vol. 2 (1840), p. 6; William Adam, "The Moral Character of Christ," *Christian Examiner* 39 (Sept. 1845): 263.

3. Clement C. Moore quoted in Eugene R. Sheridan, "Introduction" to Dickinson W. Adams, ed., *Jefferson's Extracts from the Gospels* (Princeton: Princeton Univ. Press, 1983), p. 12. Jefferson expressed his notorious claim about blacks in *Notes on the State of Virginia* (1782) in these words: "I advance it therefore as a suspicion only, that the blacks, whether originally a distinct race, or made distinct by time and circumstances, are inferior to the whites in the endowments both of body and mind." Jefferson, *Writings* (New York: Library of America, 1984), p. 270.

4. Thomas Paine, *Collected Writings* (New York: Library of America, 1995), pp. 685 ("GIFT OF REASON"), 703 ("power, wisdom, and benignity"), 712 ("the God in whom we believe"), 716 ("moral character of Christ"), 825 ("pure and simple deism," "purpose of despotic governments"). A good start on analyzing Paine's religious thinking is Edward H. Davidson and William J. Scheick, *Paine, Scripture, and Authority: The Age of Reason as Religious and Political Idea* (Bethlehem, PA: Lehigh Univ. Press, 1994). But no one has put Paine's radical republicanism in full relation to his religious convictions. For him as for Jefferson, republicanism without religion was inconceivable. The Library of America volume of his *Collected Writings,* edited by Eric Foner, omits all of Paine's post–*Age of Reason* religious writings. By contrast, Philip S. Foner included 170 pages of those post-1795 "theological dissertations" in his edition of *The*

Complete Writings of Thomas Paine (New York: Citadel Press, 1945), vol. 2. Eric Foner's *Tom Paine and Revolutionary America* (New York: Oxford Univ. Press, 1976) does note (pp. 258–59) that "in the last years of his life Paine devoted most of his energies to religious writings." If Paine had a "modern cast of mind," as Foner concludes (p. 270), it was a modernism premised on belief in God, not just, as Foner suggests, on Paine's "rationalism and faith in human nature." Paine was a nineteenth-century-style secular-religionist, not a twentieth-century-style secularist.

5. Jefferson to Priestley, Apr. 9, Apr. 24, 1803, in Adams, ed., *Jefferson's Extracts from the Gospels*, pp. 327–28, 336–37 (the Apr. 9 letter is also in Jefferson, *Writings,* pp. 1120–22). Eugene R. Sheridan provides a useful account of the political and religious forces at work on Jefferson in 1803 in his Introduction to *Jefferson's Extracts*, pp. 21–22.

6. Jefferson to Rush, Apr. 21, 1803, in Adams, ed., *Jefferson's Extracts*, pp. 329, 331 (also in Jefferson, *Writings*, pp. 1122–23).

7. Jefferson, "Syllabus of an Estimate of the merit of the doctrines of Jesus, compared with those of others," in Adams, ed., *Jefferson's Extracts*, pp. 332–34 (also in Jefferson, *Writings*, pp. 1123–26).

8. Rush to Jefferson, Aug. 29, 1804, Priestley to Jefferson, May 7, 1803, in Adams, ed., *Jefferson's Extracts*, p. 341. Rush's own Commonplace Book, the journal he kept from 1792 to 1813, is the best introduction to his religious thinking, and a marvelous resource on the cultural and political events of his time. It is included in George W. Corner, ed., *The Autobiography of Benjamin Rush* (Princeton: Princeton Univ. Press, 1948).

9. Jefferson to Charles Thomson, Jan. 9, 1816, in Adams, ed., *Jefferson's Extracts*, p. 365 (also in Jefferson, *Writings*, pp. 1372–74). Scholars have recently reconstructed the 1804 "Philosophy of Jesus" (the original copy disappeared after Jefferson's death), thanks to the availability of the actual cut-up Bibles that Jefferson used to compile it. The "wee little book" of 1804, as Jefferson described it to Thomson in 1816, was, like the later "Life and Morals of Jesus," nothing but a resequencing of actual gospel passages; neither work contained any commentary by Jefferson himself. The resurrected "Philosophy of Jesus" is in Adams, ed., *Jefferson's Extracts*, pp. 55–105.

10. Jefferson to William Short, Aug. 4, 1820, in Adams, ed., *Jefferson's Extracts*, p. 397 (also in Jefferson, *Writings*, pp. 1435–40).

11. Jefferson to William Short, Apr. 13, 1820 ("ignorance" . . . "imposture"), Jefferson to John Adams, Oct. 12, 1813, in Adams, ed., *Jefferson's Extracts*, pp. 391, 352 (letter to Adams also in Jefferson, *Writings*, pp. 1300–1304). E. P. Sanders argues for seeing the historical Jesus as primarily an eschatological prophet in *The Historical Figure of Jesus* (1993; New York: Penguin, 1995).

12. Jefferson to James Fishback, Sept. 27, 1809, in Adams, ed., *Jefferson's Extracts*, p. 343.

13. Jefferson to Vine Utley, Mar. 21, 1819, Miles King to Jefferson, Aug. 20, 1814, Jefferson to King, Sept. 26, 1814, in Adams, ed., *Jefferson's Extracts*, pp. 38 n. 129, 360–61. The most incisive discussion of Jefferson's religious beliefs is Paul Conkin's "The Religious Pilgrimage of Thomas Jefferson," in *Jeffersonian*

Legacies, ed. Peter S. Onuf (Charlottesville: Univ. Press of Virginia, 1993), pp. 19–49. Also useful as overviews are Edwin S. Gaustad, *Sworn on the Altar of God: A Religious Biography of Thomas Jefferson* (Grand Rapids: Eerdmans, 1996), and Charles B. Sanford, *The Religious Life of Thomas Jefferson* (Charlottesville: Univ. Press of Virginia, 1984).

14. Roosevelt quoted in Eric Foner, *Tom Paine and Revolutionary America,* p. 270. On the 1904 publication of "The Jefferson Bible," see Austin Matlack Courtenay, "The Jefferson Bible," *Methodist Review* 54 (Apr. 1905): 308–14. Merrill D. Peterson discusses the vagaries of Jefferson's religious reputation in *The Jefferson Image in the American Mind* (New York: Oxford Univ. Press, 1960), pp. 301–04.

15. John Hayward, *The Religious Creeds and Statistics of Every Christian Denomination in the United States* (Boston: self-published, 1836); James D. Knowles, review of Hayward, *Christian Review* 2 (June 1837): 195–209. Hayward and Knowles agree that Methodists and Baptists were underestimated, since new congregations were springing up too fast for Methodist officials or Baptist associations to count them, and since denominational statistics excluded splinter groups. It was even harder to measure the adherents, since virtually the entire American population, according to Knowles, chose some religious affiliation, even if they were not active participants. "There are a few meetings of infidels, in some of the large cities; and a small number of deists and atheists are scattered over the country. But it is everywhere considered disreputable to be opposed to religion, and hence the whole population, with very trifling exceptions, are connected, as occasional adherents, at least, with some one of the religious denominations" (p. 205). Hayward guessed that there were perhaps 30,000 "infidels and atheists" in the United States. The Protestant quest for original purity is a major theme of Paul Conkin, *American Originals: Homemade Varieties of Christianity* (Chapel Hill: Univ. of North Carolina Press, 1997), a cogent survey of the major new American denominations of the nineteenth century. On the Methodists, Baptists, and other mainline churches in the same period, see Conkin's excellent companion volume, *The Uneasy Center: Reformed Christianity in Antebellum America* (Chapel Hill: Univ. of North Carolina, 1995).

16. Mordechai Noah, lecture on "The Restoration of the Jews" at the Broadway Tabernacle, Oct. 28, 1844, reporter's summary from the *New York Express,* reprinted in *The Presbyterian,* Nov. 9, 1844, p. 177. Jonathan Sarna, *Jacksonian Jew: The Two Worlds of Mordechai Noah* (New York: Holmes and Meier, 1981), is the best account of Noah's career. In seeing the arrest and execution of Christ as a joint Jewish-Roman action, Noah anticipated the contemporary scholarly consensus, according to which the Jewish leadership quite likely sought the death of Jesus, with the active concurrence of Pontius Pilate. The Jewish leadership would have sought the death of Jesus not because he had blasphemed but because he posed a threat of political disorder. Caiaphas and other Jewish leaders would have had no need to pressure a reluctant Pontius Pilate to crucify Christ. Pilate quite likely was either happy to comply or untroubled by one more in a long line of crucifixions. The Christian communities

that produced the Gospels had a strong interest in exculpating the Romans retroactively. As E. P. Sanders put it, "the stories of Pilate's reluctance and weakness of will are best explained as Christian propaganda; they are a kind of excuse for Pilate's action which reduces the conflict between the Christian movement and Roman authority." *The Historical Figure of Jesus*, p. 274.

17. "Memoirs of the Life, Religious Experience, Ministerial Travel and Labors of Mrs. Zilpha Elaw, an American Female of Colour" (London: self-published, 1846), reprinted in William L. Andrews, ed., *Sisters of the Spirit: Three Black Women's Autobiographies of the Nineteenth Century* (Bloomington: Indiana Univ. Press, 1986), pp. 55–57, 60. See also Catherine Brekus, *Strangers and Pilgrims: Female Preaching in America, 1740–1845* (Chapel Hill: Univ. of North Carolina Press, 1998), pp. 181–86.

18. Garth M. Rosell and Richard A. G. Dupuis, eds., *The Memoirs of Charles G. Finney: The Complete Restored Text* (1875; Grand Rapids: Academie Books, 1989), pp. 9–10, 12. See also Charles E. Hambrick-Stowe, *Charles G. Finney and the Spirit of American Evangelicalism* (Grand Rapids: Eerdmans, 1996), chap. 1.

19. Rosell and Dupuis, eds., *Memoirs of Charles G. Finney*, pp. 18–19, 21–24.

20. Joseph Smith, "History, 1832," in Dean C. Jessee, ed., *The Personal Writings of Joseph Smith* (Salt Lake City: Deseret Book, 1984), pp. 5–6. See also Richard L. Bushman, *Joseph Smith and the Beginnings of Mormonism* (Urbana: Univ. of Illinois Press, 1984), chap. 2. The Mormon tradition diverges from all other Christian groups in asserting that faithful human beings can aspire to the status of "gods." Greek and Russian Orthodox theology goes further than Roman Catholicism or Protestantism in stressing the faithful Christian's likeness to Christ—an insistence that has the effect of de-emphasizing, like the Mormon tradition, the persistent power of sin. On the other hand, the Orthodox do even more than many Catholics and Protestants (and, *a fortiori*, more than the Mormons) to proclaim the kingly power and sovereignty of Christ. See Catherine Albanese, "Nontraditional Religions," in *Encyclopedia of the United States in the Twentieth Century*, vol. 4, ed. Stanley I. Kutler (New York: Scribner, 1996), pp. 1546–47.

21. Smith, "History, 1832," in Jessee, ed., *Personal Writings of Joseph Smith*, pp. 7–8. The ministry of Jesus in America is described in 3 Nephi, chaps. 11ff., of the Book of Mormon. In *Awash in a Sea of Faith: Christianizing the American People* (Cambridge: Harvard Univ. Press, 1990), pp. 245–46, Jon Butler discusses the miracles claimed by Smith and his followers between 1830 and 1835. On the contested history of the Book of Mormon, inside and outside the LDS Church, consult Richard N. Ostling and Joan K. Ostling, *Mormon America: The Power and the Promise* (San Francisco: HarperSanFrancisco, 1999), chap. 16.

22. Thomas R. Gray, *The Confessions of Nat Turner* (Baltimore: Thomas R. Gray, 1831), pp. 7, 9–11. The debate over the authenticity of the words attributed by Gray to Turner is well summarized in Mary Kemp Davis, *Nat Turner Before the Bar of Judgment: Fictional Treatment of the Southampton Slave Insurrection* (Baton Rouge: Louisiana State Univ. Press, 1999), chap. 2. She rightly concludes that there is no reason to doubt the basic accuracy of Gray's transcription.

23. Ellin Kelly and Annabelle Melville, eds., *Elizabeth Seton: Selected Writings* (New York: Paulist Press, 1987), pp. 26, 64, 167.

24. William Ellery Channing, "Unitarian Christianity" (1819), in David Robinson, ed., *William Ellery Channing: Selected Writings* (New York: Paulist Press, 1985), p. 81.

25. Paul Conkin surveys the complexities of Unitarian history and doctrine in *American Originals*. On the Arianism of Unitarianism's leading light in the 1820s, see William Henry Channing's one-volume abridged biography of his father, *The Life of William Ellery Channing* (1880; Hicksville, NY: Regina Press, 1975), p. 274.

26. Channing's "Unitarian Christianity" begins with a lengthy argument for the use of reason in Bible-reading and notes the kinship of skepticism and Christian anti-rationalism.

27. Channing, "Unitarian Christianity," pp. 79, 81, 85. The early nineteenth-century Unitarians, led by Joseph Buckminster and Andrews Norton, made an enthusiastic if ultimately restrained embrace of the new German historical criticism of the Bible. Jerry Wayne Brown, *The Rise of Biblical Criticism in America, 1800–1870* (Middletown, CT: Wesleyan Univ. Press, 1969), shows how limited the reach of such criticism was in the United States until the very end of the century. Channing, for one, had little interest in it.

28. Channing, "The Evidences of Revealed Religion" (1821), in Robinson, ed., *William Ellery Channing*, pp. 134–35.

29. Channing, "The Evidences of Revealed Religion," p. 137.

30. William Adam, "The Moral Character of Christ," *Christian Examiner* 39 (Sept. 1845): 236.

31. Alvan Lamson, *On the Doctrine of Two Natures in Jesus Christ* (Boston: Bowles and Dearborn, 1828), pp. 15–16.

32. Emerson Sermon V, in Albert J. von Frank, ed., *The Sermons of Ralph Waldo Emerson* (Columbia: Univ. of Missouri Press, 1989), vol. 1, pp. 85–90 [hereafter *Sermons*]. Wesley T. Mott provides fascinating biographical context for this sermon, which Emerson preached twelve times between June 1827 and July 1828, in "'Christ Crucified': Christology, Identity, and Emerson's Sermon No. 5," in Joel Myerson, ed., *Emerson Centenary Essays* (Carbondale: Southern Illinois Univ. Press, 1982), pp. 17–40.

33. Emerson Sermon V, in *Sermons*, 1:86–87, 91. A good starting point on Emerson's cultural influence is Mary Kupiec Cayton's *Emerson's Emergence: Self and Society in the Transformation of New England* (Chapel Hill: Univ. of North Carolina Press, 1989). His personal stature as a cultural sage grew despite the often hostile response leading reviewers accorded to some of his famous essays. See Joel Myerson, ed., *Emerson and Thoreau: The Contemporary Reviews* (Cambridge, UK: Cambridge Univ. Press, 1992). Emerson's edgy but still spiritual radicalism is one secret to his influence over many nineteenth-century northern Protestants, who were always drawn to novel quests for purity; another is his startling command of the English language, a talent prized by southern and northern Protestants steeped in Shakespeare and the King James Bible.

34. Alfred R. Ferguson, ed., *The Journals and Miscellaneous Notebooks of Ralph Waldo Emerson,* vol. 4 (Cambridge: Harvard Univ. Press, 1964), pp. 27, 309 [hereafter *Journals*]. Emerson continued preaching in various churches through the 1830s, but he held no pastorates. The original version of Emerson's "Lord's Supper" sermon, as read to his Second Church congregation on Sept. 9, 1832, is reprinted in *Sermons,* 4:185–94. A revised version, done by Emerson himself with an eye to publication, appears in Joel Porte, ed., *Ralph Waldo Emerson: Essays and Lectures* (New York: Library of America, 1983), pp. 1129–40. This sermon of Emerson's was the only one published during his lifetime (in 1876 in Octavius Brooks Frothingham's *Transcendentalism in New England*).

35. Emerson, *Journals,* 5:459; Emerson, "An Address Delivered before the Senior Class in Divinity College," in Porte, ed., *Ralph Waldo Emerson: Essays and Lectures,* pp. 80–81, 83, 88. Among the many interesting treatments of the Divinity School Address, Carol Johnston's discussion is noteworthy: "The Underlying Structure of the Divinity School Address: Emerson as Jeremiah," in *Studies in the American Renaissance, 1980,* ed. Joel Myerson (Boston: Twayne, 1980), pp. 41–49. The Unitarians did not take Emerson's aspersions lying down. Henry Ware, Jr., Emerson's predecessor at Second Church, Boston, had been taking his iconoclastic tendencies to task since the early 1830s, and responded to the Divinity School Address with a sermon on "The Personality of the Deity," published in *Sermons by Henry Ware, Jr.,* vol. 1 (Boston: James Munroe, 1847), pp. 26–39.

36. Emerson, *Journals,* 5:306, 7:255. Emerson used the 1837 passage on immortality in his essay "The Oversoul," published in 1841. (Porte, ed., *Ralph Waldo Emerson: Essays and Lectures,* p. 393.) He repeated the observation in a journal entry of the mid-1840s: "It is strange that Jesus is esteemed by mankind the bringer of the doctrine of immortality. He is never once weak or sentimental: he never preaches the personal immortality; whilst Plato & Cicero had both allowed themselves to overstep the stern limits of the Spirit & gratify the people with that picture." Emerson, *Journal,* 9:106. Emerson used that passage in his essay on "Immortality," published thirty years later in his *Letters and Social Aims* (1875; Boston: Houghton-Mifflin, 1888), p. 330.

37. Emerson to Elizabeth Palmer Peabody, 1835, in Ralph L. Rusk, ed., *The Letters of Ralph Waldo Emerson,* vol. 1 (New York: Columbia Univ. Press, 1939), p. 451; Emerson to Lidian Emerson, Feb. 18, 1855, in Rusk, ed., *Letters of Ralph Waldo Emerson,* 4:493.

38. Emerson, *Journal,* 7:104, 348; 8:337. Emerson repeated this last reflection on Socrates and Confucius in 1839 in his public lecture on "Duty." Robert E. Spiller and Wallace E. Williams, eds., *The Early Lectures of Ralph Waldo Emerson,* vol. 3 (Cambridge: Harvard Univ. Press, 1972), p. 144.

39. Emerson, *Journal,* 5:5; Emerson, "Circles," in Porte, ed., *Ralph Waldo Emerson: Essays and Lectures,* pp. 409, 411, 414.

40. Emerson, *Journal,* 5:253; Emerson, "Circles," p. 413.

41. Emerson, *Journal,* 9:395 ("secular personalities"), 7:255 ("cold denying irreligious"). Emerson used the verb "Christizes," not the adjective "Chris-

tized" (*Journal*, 3:287). He frequently used the adjective "Christianized," so it is possible that "Christized" was a hastily penned misspelling, or else a typo in the published edition of his journal. George Kateb's *Emerson and Self-Reliance* (Thousand Oaks, CA: Sage, 1995) is an explicitly non-religious reading of Emerson, but Kateb does much more to illuminate Emerson's religious faith than most treatments of Emerson's "religion" do. Among the many noteworthy works on Emerson's religion, I have profited especially from Susan L. Roberson, *Emerson in His Sermons: A Man-Made Self* (Columbia: Univ. of Missouri Press, 1995), Christopher Lasch, *The True and Only Heaven: Progress and Its Critics* (New York: Norton, 1994), Gary Richard Hall, "Emerson and the Bible: Transcendentalism as Scriptural Interpretation and Revision," Ph.D. diss., UCLA, 1989, David Robinson, *Apostle of Culture: Emerson as Preacher and Lecturer* (Philadelphia: Univ. of Pennsylvania Press, 1982), Sue Kelsey Tester, "Ralph Waldo Emerson's Sermons: A Critical Introduction," Ph.D. diss., Boston University, 1978, and Edward Wagenknecht, *Ralph Waldo Emerson: Portrait of a Balanced Soul* (New York: Oxford Univ. Press, 1974).

42. Emerson, *Journal*, 5:5; Porte, ed., *Ralph Waldo Emerson: Essays and Lectures*, pp. 271–72. Emerson's secular heroes included a wide array of world philosophers, artists, and writers, but in light of his praise of Jesus as being akin to a "writer" who established the "conventions" by which all later original creators "composed," it is worth noting that when pressed to identify the two greatest geniuses of all time, he picked Jesus and Shakespeare: "I told [Bronson] Alcott that my First Class stood for today perhaps thus: Phidias, Jesus, [Michel]Angelo, Shakespeare; or, if I must sift more sternly still, Jesus & Shakespeare were two men of genius." Emerson, *Journal*, 7:284–85.

43. Emerson, *Journal*, 3:287. Emerson anticipated the anti-Christian strictures of Nietzsche's *Antichrist*, published posthumously in 1902. Nietzsche was deeply marked by his reading of Emerson. The first edition of Nietzsche's *Gay Science*, published in 1882, opened with an epigraph from Emerson.

44. Emerson in his manuscript "Encyclopedia," in Rusk, ed., *The Letters of Ralph Waldo Emerson*, 2:166; Emerson, *Journals*, 5:5, 362.

CHAPTER FIVE

1. Nathan Bangs, "Is It Right?" *Christian Advocate*, Dec. 5, 1834, quoted in Charles Elliott, *History of the Great Secession from the Methodist Episcopal Church in the Year 1845* (Cincinnati: Swormstedt and Poe, 1855), p. 98; Shipley W. Willson et al., "Appeal to the Members of the New England and New Hampshire Conferences of the Methodist Episcopal Church," Dec. 19, 1834, in Elliott, *History*, pp. 862 ("meek and lowly Jesus"), 863 (1784 Discipline), 878 ("God and bleeding humanity"). See also Donald G. Mathews's excellent study *Slavery and Methodism: A Chapter in American Morality, 1780–1845* (Princeton: Princeton Univ. Press, 1965).

2. Angelina E. Grimké, *Appeal to Christian Women of the South* (New York: New York Anti-Slavery Society, 1836), pp. 13–14.

3. On the early days of American biblical criticism, consult Jerry Wayne Brown, *The Rise of Biblical Criticism in America, 1800–1870: The New England Scholars* (Middletown, CT: Wesleyan Univ. Press, 1969).

4. Grimké, *Appeal to Christian Women of the South*, p. 28.

5. "Narrative of the Life of Frederick Douglass," in *Frederick Douglass, Autobiographies* (1845; New York: Library of America, 1994), p. 5 (Garrison), p. 97 ("meek and lowly"), p. 99 ("bind heavy burdens"). The Puritans may have preferred the Geneva Bible, but even they made frequent reference to the King James Version. By the eighteenth century the King James Bible was becoming the American Protestant Bible and hence, given the small numbers of non-Protestants in the English colonies, the American Bible. Its influence on American letters in the nineteenth and twentieth centuries was incalculably large. Cf. the fine overview by Paul C. Gutjahr in *An American Bible: A History of the Good Book in the United States, 1777–1880* (Stanford: Stanford Univ. Press, 1999).

6. Garrison to Elizabeth Pease, July 2, 1842, in Walter M. Merrill, ed., *The Letters of William Lloyd Garrison*, vol. 3 (Cambridge: Harvard Univ. Press, 1973), p. 90.

7. Garrison to Elizabeth Pease, July 2, 1842, in Merrill, *Letters*, 3:89; Garrison, "Reply to the Blasphemous Charge of a False Accuser," *The Liberator*, May 24, 1850, reprinted in Merrill, *Letters*, 4:19; Garrison, "Letter to the Editor of the Boston Transcript," *The Liberator*, May 31, 1850, reprinted in Merrill, *Letters*, 4:27.

8. Garrison to Elizabeth Pease, June 20, 1849, in Merrill, *Letters*, 3:634.

9. Garrison to Theobald Mathew, Sept. 28, 1849, in Merrill, *Letters*, 3:663; Garrison to the editor of "The Christian Witness," *The Liberator*, Dec. 4, 1846, reprinted in Merrill, *Letters*, 3:456–57.

10. Devereux Jarratt quoted in Douglas Ambrose, "Of Stations and Relations: Proslavery Christianity in Early National Virginia," in *Religion and the Antebellum Debate over Slavery*, ed. John R. McKivigan and Mitchell Snay (Athens: Univ. of Georgia Press, 1998), pp. 42–44.

11. James H. Thornwell, "The Rights and Duties of Masters," in *"God Ordained This War": Sermons on the Sectional Crisis, 1830–1865*, ed. David B. Chesebrough (Columbia: Univ. of South Carolina Press, 1991), pp. 188–89.

12. Catharine E. Beecher, *Essay on Slavery and Abolitionism* (Philadelphia: Henry Perkins, 1837), pp. 46, 146, 151.

13. Angelina Grimké, *Letters to Catharine Beecher* (Boston: Isaac Knapp, 1838), pp. 30, 33.

14. Grimké, *Letters to Catharine Beecher*, p. 118, *Appeal to Christian Women of the South*, p. 19.

15. Beecher, *Essay on Slavery and Abolitionism*, pp. 100–102, 128, 151.

16. Harriet Beecher Stowe, *Uncle Tom's Cabin: or, Life Among the Lowly* (1852; New York: Norton, 1994), pp. 314, 77, 43–44.

17. Stowe, *Uncle Tom's Cabin*, pp. 156, 421 (reprinted excerpt from *The Key to Uncle Tom's Cabin*).

18. Stowe, *Uncle Tom's Cabin*, pp. 224, 227.

19. Stowe, *Footsteps of the Master* (New York: J. B. Ford, 1877), p. 70.

20. Martin Delany to Frederick Douglass, Mar. 22, 1853, in *Frederick Douglass' Paper*, Apr. 1, 1853 (available at the *"Uncle Tom's Cabin* and American Culture" Web site); Donald G. Mathews, *Religion in the Old South* (Chicago: Univ. of Chicago Press, 1977), pp. 230–36. Mathews's book is required reading for anyone who wishes to understand slave religion. His fifth chapter, "The Trumpet Sounds within-a My Soul," is in my view the best overview of slave Christianity in print. Other indispensable works in the phenomenal outpouring of post–Civil Rights movement literature on black religion under slavery are Albert J. Raboteau, *Slave Religion: The "Invisible Institution" in the Antebellum South* (New York: Oxford Univ. Press, 1978), Eugene D. Genovese, *Roll, Jordan, Roll: The World the Slaves Made* (New York: Knopf, 1974), Lawrence W. Levine, *Black Culture and Black Consciousness: Afro American Folk Thought from Slavery to Freedom* (New York: Oxford Univ. Press, 1977), and Mechal Sobel, *Trabelin' On: The Slave Journey to an AfroBaptist Faith* (Westport, CT: Greenwood Press, 1979). Among the many recent works with special bearing on Jesus in antebellum black culture see, for example, Eddie S. Glaude, Jr., *Exodus! Religion, Race, and Nation in Early Nineteenth-Century Black America* (Chicago: Univ. of Chicago Press, 2000), Jon F. Sensbach, *A Separate Canaan: The Making of an AfroMoravian World in North Carolina, 1763–1840* (Chapel Hill: Univ. of North Carolina Press, 1998), and Sylvia R. Frey and Betty Wood, *Come Shouting to Zion: African American Protestantism in the American South and British Caribbean to 1830* (Chapel Hill: Univ. of North Carolina Press, 1998). A single chapter (eight) of Marvin L. Michael Kay and Lorin Lee Cary, *Slavery in North Carolina, 1748–1775* (Chapel Hill: Univ. of North Carolina Press, 1995), lays essential foundation for understanding antebellum black religion.

21. Sojourner Truth [and Olive Gilbert], *Narrative of Sojourner Truth*, in *Slave Narratives* (New York: Library of America, 2000), pp. 610–12.

22. Truth, *Narrative of Sojourner Truth*, pp. 615–16.

23. Truth, *Narrative of Sojourner Truth*, pp. 616–18.

24. Truth, *Narrative of Sojourner Truth*, pp. 650–51, 646. The best book on Truth's career (including the production of the *Narrative*) is Nell Irvin Painter, *Sojourner Truth: A Life, A Symbol* (New York: Norton, 1996). Rural encampments dotted the East Coast in October 1844. See, for example, the account in the Philadelphia weekly newspaper *The Presbyterian* describing the tents put up around the city: "Millerism," Oct. 26, 1844, p. 170. A week before the end, two hundred people gathered at the "Second Advent" chapel in Philadelphia for the purpose of ritual feet-washing. "The Excitement on Millerism," *Christian Observer* (also a Presbyterian paper), Oct. 18, 1844, p. 166. The essential starting point on the Millerites is Ronald L. Numbers and Jonathan M. Butler, eds., *The Disappointed: Millerism and Millenarianism of the Nineteenth Century*, 2nd ed. (Knoxville: Univ. of Tennessee Press, 1993).

25. Isaac T. Hecker, *The Church and the Age* (New York: Catholic Book Exchange, 1896), p. 260, quoted in Ann Taves, *The Household of Faith: Roman Catholic Devotions in Mid-Nineteenth Century America* (Notre Dame: Univ. of Notre Dame Press, 1986), p. 48.

26. The figures are from Edwin Scott Gaustad and Philip L. Barlow, *New Historical Atlas of Religion in America* (New York: Oxford Univ. Press, 2001), pp. 54, 157–58.

27. Theodore Parker quoted in Octavius Brooks Frothingham, *Theodore Parker: A Biography* (Boston: James R. Osgood, 1874), p. 473, and in Michael Fellman, "Theodore Parker and the Abolitionist Role in the 1850s," *Journal of American History* 61 (Dec. 1974): 676–77.

28. Parker quoted in Frothingham, *Theodore Parker,* pp. 194–97.

29. William Ellery Channing, *Dr. Channing's Discourse Preached at the Dedication of the Second Congregational Unitarian Church, New York,* Dec. 7, 1826 (New York: Second Congregational Church, 1827), pp. 13–14, 16–18.

30. On nineteenth-century American Catholic devotions, I have relied on Taves, *Household of Faith.* By the 1950s "saying the Rosary" had evolved into a single Apostle's Creed followed by a succession of Our Fathers, Hail Marys, and Glory Be to the Fathers. "How to Say the Rosary," *St. Joseph Sunday Missal* (New York: Catholic Book Publishing Company, 1957), p. 461.

31. I follow Ann Taves's description of Holy Family Church, which has recently been restored in all its statue-packed nineteenth-century glory. Taves, *Household of Faith,* pp. 120–25.

32. "Significant Sign," *The Presbyterian,* Aug. 17, 1844, p. 130. Another Presbyterian periodical in Philadelphia remarked that the Catholic campaign to "suppress" the reading of Scripture in the schools was part of a "universal crusade against the Bible" led by the pope. The pope "is afraid of the Bible—when it is placed in the hands of the people." "The Conflict against the Bible," *Christian Observer,* Dec. 20, 1844, p. 202. Michael Feldberg gives a good summary of the Protestant-Catholic altercation in *The Philadelphia Riots of 1844: A Study of Ethnic Conflict* (Westport, CT: Greenwood Press, 1975).

33. "Symbolical Religion," *The Presbyterian,* Aug. 17, 1844, p. 130. Ryan K. Smith, "The Cross: Church Symbol and Contest in Nineteenth-Century America," *Church History* 70 (Dec. 2001): 705–34, is an excellent discussion of the spread of the Latin cross to the Protestant churches.

34. Parker, "The Transient and the Permanent in Christianity," in Conrad Wright, ed., *Three Prophets of Religious Liberalism: Channing, Emerson, Parker* (Boston: Beacon Press, 1961), pp. 114, 133, 142, and "The Relation of Jesus to His Age" (1844), in Parker, *The Transient and the Permanent in Christianity* (Boston: American Unitarian Association, 1907), p. 56. "The Transient and the Permanent" sermon was available for purchase less than a month after it was delivered. "A Sermon on Slavery," delivered several months earlier, was not put on sale until 1843. "If there is a crime in the land known to us," it said, "and we do not protest against it to the extent of our ability, we are partners of that crime." Quoted in Chesebrough, ed., *"God Ordained This War,"* p. 332.

35. Parker, review of Strauss, *Das Leben Jesu, Christian Examiner* 28 (July 1840): 273–317.

36. Parker, "The Transient and the Permanent in Christianity," p. 140.

37. Henry F. May noted the surprisingly "modern" character of Parker's social critique in *Protestant Churches and Industrial America* (1949; New York: Harper and Row, 1967), p. 32.

38. William H. Furness, *Two Discourses* (Philadelphia: J. Crissy, 1845), pp. 13–14.

39. The starting point for thinking about the appeal of Catholicism among antebellum Protestants—including those who converted and those who did not—is Jenny Franchot's *Roads to Rome: The Antebellum Protestant Encounter with Catholicism* (Berkeley: Univ. of California Press, 1994).

40. Orestes A. Brownson, "A Sermon on the New Birth," *The Gospel Advocate and Impartial Investigator*, Aug. 16, 1828, reprinted in Patrick W. Carey, ed., *The Early Works of Orestes A. Brownson*, vol. 1 (Milwaukee: Marquette Univ. Press, 2000), pp. 140, 146–47.

41. Theodore Parker quoted in Dean Grodzins, *American Heretic: Theodore Parker and Transcendentalism* (Chapel Hill: Univ. of North Carolina Press, 2002), p. 412; Brownson, "Christianity and Reform," *Unitarian*, Jan. 1834, reprinted in Carey, ed., *Early Works*, 2:300; Brownson, "The Present State of Society," *Democratic Review*, July 1843, reprinted in Russell Kirk, ed., *Orestes Brownson: Selected Essays* (Chicago: Henry Regnery, 1955), pp. 54–55, 57; Brownson, "Free Labor," *Boston Quarterly Review* 3 (1840): 370.

42. Brownson, "The Transcendental Road to Rome," *Brownson's Review* 1 (Jan. 1856), 94–95.

43. Brownson, "The Mediatorial Life of Jesus," in Henry F. Brownson, ed., *The Works of Orestes A. Brownson*, vol. 4 (1842; New York: AMS Press, 1966), pp. 157, 159, 161–62; Parker quoted in Grodzins, *American Heretic*, p. 411.

44. Brownson to Hecker, Aug. 2, 1844, Joseph F. Gower and Richard M. Leliaert, eds., *The Brownson-Hecker Correspondence* (Notre Dame: Univ. of Notre Dame Press, 1979), p. 109.

45. Henry David Thoreau, *A Week on the Concord and Merrimack Rivers* (1849; New York: Library of America, 1985), pp. 59, 62. Thomas Tweed discusses Thoreau's interest in Buddhism in *The American Encounter with Buddhism, 1844–1912: Victorian Culture and the Limits of Dissent* (Bloomington: Indiana Univ. Press, 1992), p. xix.

46. Thoreau, *A Week on the Concord and Merrimack Rivers*, pp. 55, 60, 63, 116.

47. Thoreau, "Walking" in *Thoreau: Collected Essays and Poems* (1862; New York: Library of America, 2001), p. 254; Michael West, *Transcendental Word-Play* (Athens: Ohio Univ. Press, 2000), pp. 436–37 (on the Bible in *Walden*).

48. Thoreau, "A Plea for Captain John Brown," in *Collected Essays and Poems* (New York: Library of America, 2001), pp. 403, 407–08, 414–15.

49. Emerson quoted in Ralph L. Rusk, *The Life of Ralph Waldo Emerson* (New York: Scribner, 1949, p. 402; Thoreau, "A Plea for Captain John Brown," in *Collected Essays and Poems* (New York: Library of America, 2001), p. 416. Emerson took the gallows/cross comparison from Mattie Griffith, a reformer whom he described as "a brilliant young lady from Kentucky." She had told him that "if Brown is hung, the gallows will be as sacred as the cross." Emerson, *Journals and Miscellaneous Notebooks of Ralph Waldo Emerson*, vol. 14 (Cambridge:

Harvard Univ. Press, 1978), p. 333. Charles Joyner's "'Guilty of Holiest Crime': The Passion of John Brown," in Paul Finkelman, ed., *His Soul Goes Marching On: Responses to John Brown and the Harpers Ferry Raid* (Charlottesville: Univ. Press of Virginia, 1995), passim, gives a fine assessment of the Brown-Christ connection.

50. John Brown letters to his wife, to his friend E. B., and to the Charlestown *Independent Democrat*, all cited in Oswald Villard, *John Brown, 1800–1859: A Biography Fifty Years After* (Boston: Houghton Mifflin, 1911), pp. 537, 539, 545.

51. Excerpt from Garrison's Boston speech, and Garrison to James Redpath, Dec. 1, 1860, reprinted in Merrill, *Letters*, 4:604, 703–04. C. Vann Woodward's elegant assault on Thoreau and his fellow abolitionists as "fellow travelers" of the "wily old revolutionist" Brown rightly questions their dubious subordination of means to ends. But Woodward fails to evoke the particular urgency of the political and cultural situation as they experienced it in 1859. They thought that freedom was threatened on all sides and that Brown, thanks to his prophetic vision, uniquely registered the nature of the emergency. "John Brown's Private War" (1952), in *The Burden of Southern History*, 3rd ed. (Baton Rouge: Louisiana State Univ. Press, 1993), p. 51. The most curious aspect of Garrison's execution-eve address is its assertion of moral equivalency between Nat Turner's killing of fifty-five civilians and George Washington's military campaign. Even John Brown's irregulars at Harpers Ferry (though not at Pottawatomie) sought out military targets.

52. Warren H. Cudworth sermon, in *Sermons Preached in Boston on the Death of Abraham Lincoln* (Boston: J. E. Tilton, 1865), p. 201; Garfield and Crane quoted in Lloyd Lewis, *Myths After Lincoln* (1929; New York: Reader's Club, 1941), pp. 98, 95.

53. "Handbill on Religion" (1846), reprinted in Michael P. Johnson, ed., *Abraham Lincoln, Slavery, and the Civil War: Selected Writings and Speeches* (Boston: Bedford/St. Martin's, 2001), p. 36; A. L. Stone sermon, in *Sermons Preached in Boston*, p. 352. Allen Guelzo documents Lincoln's lukewarm Christian commitment in his brilliant *Abraham Lincoln: Redeemer President* (Grand Rapids: Eerdmans, 2000). Don E. and Virginia Fehrenbacher, *Recollected Words of Abraham Lincoln* (Stanford: Stanford Univ. Press, 1996) is the indispensable source on all of the apocryphal sayings attributed to him after his death.

54. On the religious significance of the Second Inaugural Address, see Ronald C. White, Jr., *Lincoln's Greatest Speech: The Second Inaugural* (New York: Simon and Schuster, 2002), and on the Gettysburg Address, consult Garry Wills's remarkable *Lincoln at Gettysburg: the Words That Remade America* (New York: Simon and Schuster, 1992).

55. "C.," "A Novel Sabbath in Charleston," *Independent*, Apr. 27, 1865, p. 3; Henry Ward Beecher, "Narrative of the Trip to South Carolina," *Independent*, May 11, 1865, p. 2. Stephen Elliott and Henry Wharton quoted in Charles Reagan Wilson, *Baptized in Blood: The Religion of the Lost Cause, 1865–1920* (Athens: Univ. of Georgia Press, 1980). The best recent work in postbellum southern religious history puts Jesus at the center of cross-racial and cross-national experiences. Consult, for example, Paul Harvey, *Redeeming the South:*

Religious Cultures and Racial Identities among Southern Baptists, 1865–1925 (Chapel Hill: Univ. of North Carolina Press, 1997), and James T. Campbell, *Songs of Zion: The African Methodist Episcopal Church in the United States and South Africa* (New York: Oxford Univ. Press, 1995).

56. Jacquelyn Dowd Hall, *Revolt Against Chivalry: Jessie Daniel Ames and the Women's Campaign Against Lynching*, rev. ed. (New York: Columbia Univ. Press, 1993), gives an excellent brief summary of the history of lynching, pp. 130–36. Brendan I. Koerner, "Why Does the Ku Klux Klan Burn Crosses?" *Slate*, Dec. 17, 2002 (http://slate.msn.com/id/2075584/), claims cross-burning as intimidation began in 1915, and Wyn Craig Wade, in *The Fiery Cross: The Ku Klux Klan in America* (New York: Simon and Schuster, 1987), p. 146, agrees that "burning crosses had never been part of the Reconstruction Ku-Klux." In "The Southern Rite of Human Sacrifice," *Journal of Southern Religion* 3 (2000), online at http://jsr.as.wvu.edu, Donald Mathews examines lynching in relation to the cross-cultural practice of ritual sacrifice.

CHAPTER SIX

1. I explore the secular and religious dimensions of nineteenth-century American love experiences in "New Baptized: The Culture of Love in America, 1830s to 1950s," in Susan Mizruchi, ed., *Religion and Cultural Studies* (Princeton: Princeton Univ. Press, 2001), esp. pp. 112–19.

2. My interpretation of liberal Protestantism derives from my encounter with the work of many earlier historians. I especially salute the deans of them all, Henry May and William R. Hutchison, whose main works, *Protestant Churches and Industrial America* (1949; New York: Harper and Row, 1967) and *The Modernist Impulse in American Protestantism* (1976; Durham, NC: Duke Univ. Press, 1992), respectively, are still the places to begin. I summarize my view of liberal Protestantism in the article on that subject in Richard Wightman Fox and James Kloppenberg, eds., *A Companion to American Thought* (Cambridge, MA: Blackwell, 1995), and in "The Culture of Liberal Protestant Progressivism, 1875–1925," *Journal of Interdisciplinary History* 23 (Winter 1993): 639–60.

3. On the Protestant encounter with science in nineteenth-century America, consult the important work of Ronald L. Numbers, *Darwinism Comes to America* (Cambridge: Harvard Univ. Press, 1998). See also Jon H. Roberts, *Darwinism and the Divine in America: Protestant Intellectuals and Organic Evolution, 1859–1900* (Madison, WI: Univ. of Wisconsin Press, 1988).

4. Ronald L. Numbers, *Prophetess of Health: Ellen G. White and the Origins of Seventh-day Adventist Health Reform*, rev. ed. (Knoxville: Univ. of Tennessee Press, 1992), is indispensable for understanding the dialectic of worldliness (reform the cultural practices that make people's bodies sick) and apocalyptic millennialism (the world is doomed) brought together in mid- and late-nineteenth-century Seventh-day Adventism. Paul K. Conkin provides a very helpful summary of the "Apocalyptic Christianity" of the Adventists in *American Originals: Homemade Varieties of Christianity* (Chapel Hill: Univ. of North Carolina Press, 1997), pp. 110–61.

5. George Fitzhugh, *Cannibals All! Or, Slaves Without Masters* (1857; Cambridge: Harvard Univ. Press, 1960), pp. 228–29.

6. I discuss Beecher's slave "auctions" (actually fundraisers to procure the prearranged purchase price of a slave) in my essay "Performing Emancipation," in Steven Mintz et al., eds., *The Problem of Evil: Slavery, Race, and the Ambiguities of Reform* (Amherst: Univ. of Massachusetts Press, forthcoming).

7. David Swing, "The Decline of Theology," *Chicago Tribune*, May 11, 1874, p. 3. William R. Hutchison gives a good summary of Swing's heresy trial in *The Modernist Impulse in American Protestantism*, pp. 58–68.

8. Henry Ward Beecher, *Yale Lectures on Preaching*, 3 vols. in 1 (New York: Ford, Howard, and Hulbert, 1889), vol. 1 (1872), pp. 261–62, vol. 2 (1873), p. 237, vol. 3 (1874), pp. 104–05. On Taylor and Lyman Beecher, see Douglas A. Sweeney, *Nathaniel Taylor, New Haven Theology, and the Legacy of Jonathan Edwards* (New York: Oxford Univ. Press, 2003), pp. 46–47 and passim.

9. Horace Bushnell, *God in Christ* (Hartford: Brown and Parsons, 1849), p. 82.

10. Beecher, *Yale Lectures on Preaching*, vol. 1 (1872), pp. 3, 7, vol. 3 (1874), p. 145. My book *Trials of Intimacy: Love and Loss in the Beecher-Tilton Scandal* (Chicago: Univ. of Chicago Press, 1999) examines the explosive outcome of Beecher's preaching of love at Plymouth Church from the 1840s to the 1870.

11. Henry Ward Beecher, *The Life of Jesus, the Christ* (New York: J. B. Ford, 1871), pp. 184, 187, 194.

12. Daniel Walker Howe offers an excellent introduction to Bushnell's thought (noting the adumbration of Freud) in "The Social Science of Horace Bushnell," *Journal of American History* 70 (Sept. 1983): 305–22.

13. "A Christmas Sermon" in 1844 (apparently by William Furness, the Philadelphia Unitarian) claimed that Christmas was growing in favor as "the festival of childhood," but the preacher was plainly struggling to persuade his congregation to adopt what he granted was an imported German custom. He urged them to at least consider "the planting of the Christmas tree in your homes, . . . with the figure of the Christ-child hovering over its top." Sprague Pamphlet Collection, American Antiquarian Society, pp. 2, 4.

14. Horace Bushnell, *The Character of Jesus* (1860; New York: Scribner, 1902), pp. 10–11, 15–16.

15. Beecher, *The Life of Jesus*, pp. 52–53.

16. Charles Hodge, "God in Christ," *Princeton Review*, 1849, in Hodge, *Essays and Reviews* (1857; New York: Garland, 1987), pp. 433–71.

17. Hodge, "God in Christ," pp. 448–49.

18. Bushnell, *God in Christ*, p. 94.

19. Bushnell to ?, Feb. 14, 1860, in Mary Bushnell Cheney, ed., *Life and Letters of Horace Bushnell* (1880; New York: Arno Press, 1969), pp. 435–36. The literary critic Harold Bloom's inspired screed exposing "the American religion" as a "Gnostic" quest for a self-worshiping transcendence of all limits is very similar to Hodge's interpretation of Bushnell's "spiritual inebriation." But just as Hodge misses the counterbalancing insistence on "sacrifice" in Bushnell's thought and preaching, Bloom misses the countervailing emphasis on self-

denying social transformation in mainstream American religion. Bloom, *The American Religion: The Emergence of the Post-Christian Nation* (New York: Simon and Schuster, 1992).

20. Beecher, *The Life of Jesus*, pp. 36–37.

21. Beecher, *Yale Lectures on Preaching*, vol. 1 (1872), pp. 3, 110–11.

22. Quimby manuscript of 1863 quoted in Horatio W. Dresser, *Health and the Inner Life* (New York: G. P. Putnam's Sons, 1906), pp. 37, 39, 34–35. Among the books on mind-cure and New Thought, Dresser's later book *A History of the New Thought Movement* (New York: Thomas Y. Crowell, 1919), Beryl Satter's, *Each Mind a Kingdom: American Women, Sexual Purity, and the New Thought Movement, 1875–1920* (Berkeley: Univ. of California Press, 1999), Gail Thain Parker's, *Mind Cure in New England: From the Civil War to World War I* (Hanover, NH: Univ. Press of New England, 1973), Donald Meyer's, *The Positive Thinkers: A Study of the American Quest for Health, Wealth, and Personal Power from Mary Baker Eddy to Norman Vincent Peale* (Garden City, NY: Doubleday, 1965), and William James's 1902 classic *Varieties of Religious Experience* (Lectures 4 and 5 on "The Religion of Healthy-Mindedness") are especially helpful. On Quimby himself, see Craig James Hazen, *The Village Enlightenment in America: Popular Religion and Science in the Nineteenth Century* (Urbana: Univ. of Illinois Press, 2000), and Ann Taves, *Fits, Trances, and Visions: Experiencing Religion and Explaining Experience from Wesley to James* (Princeton: Princeton Univ. Press, 1999).

23. Warren Felt Evans, *Soul and Body* (Boston: Colby and Rich, 1876), pp. 57–58, 64.

24. Mary Baker Eddy, *Science and Health with Key to the Scriptures* (1875; Boston: The Trustees, 1934), pp. 19, 22, 583, 589. Stephen Gottschalk, *The Emergence of Christian Science in American Religious Life* (Berkeley: Univ. of California Press, 1973), is a very useful analysis of Eddy's reworking of central Christian concepts, such as the atonement.

25. Harold Bloom's insightful discussion of Eddy and other American "Gnostics" in *The American Religion* goes a long way toward restoring them to their proper place in American religious history. For Bloom Eddy shares with Emerson and Joseph Smith (the two greatest religious geniuses America has produced, in Bloom's view) a very unbiblical yearning for an original state of pure knowledge that preceded the creation-fall. But Bloom is needlessly Procrustean in forcing even Emerson into the Gnostic camp, and gleefully antediluvian in seeing Protestant Gnosticism as the "American religion." Wholly aside from the exclusion of Catholics and other non-Protestants, Bloom's omission of Methodists and the neglect of the social-justice impulse in American religion is startling. Taves, *Fits, Trances, and Visions*, is an excellent corrective to Bloom since it takes Calvinism, Methodism, and spiritualism equally seriously as interpenetrating American religious movements.

26. The Presbyterian critic, and Eddy's defense of "Christ and Christmas," are cited in Raymond J. Cunningham, "The Impact of Christian Science on the American Churches, 1880–1910," *American Historical Review* 72 (Apr. 1967): 898–99. Many late-nineteenth-century printings of *Science and Health* used the

pronouns "she" and "her" for God. In the first edition of 1875, Eddy said that God was "better rendered as feminine." It appears that Eddy never referred to Jesus himself as embodying feminine and masculine traits. In the case of Jesus Eddy was preoccupied with establishing his jointly material and immaterial character. "Major Revisions of Science and Health," official Web site of the Mary Baker Eddy Library for the Betterment of Humanity.

27. Eddy, *Science and Health*, p. 313. Apocalyptic religions in America— Seventh-day Adventists, Jehovah's Witnesses, Latter-day Saints—tend to be "materialist," seeing spirit as necessarily embodied. Some liberal Christians, like Thomas Jefferson, have been materialists too. Jefferson scorned Plato, one of Emerson's main heroes. But liberal Christianity as a whole has tended to the spiritualist side, the extreme case being the virtually Gnostic Christian Scientists. See Paul Conkin's discussion of apocalyptic Christianity in *American Originals*, pp. 110–61.

28. Ralph Waldo Trine, *In Tune with the Infinite; or, Fullness of Peace, Power, and Plenty* (1897; London: George Bell, 1905), pp. 167–69. Eddy's visit to Emerson is described in Gottschalk, *The Emergence of Christian Science*, p. 88.

29. Trine, *In Tune with the Infinite*, pp. 199, 167; Emerson, "Fate," in *Ralph Waldo Emerson: Essays and Lectures*, ed. Joel Porte (New York: Library of America, 1983), p. 947. Emerson thus did Jefferson one better: the president had praised Jesus for being the first to see that the sin lay not in the act, but in the antecedent thought. For Emerson the flaw lay not in the thought, but in the prior animal impulse. Twentieth-century positive thinkers included many secularists like Dale Carnegie, many religionists like Norman Vincent Peale and Robert Schuller, but very few secular-religionists like Trine, who remained devoted to Jesus while avoiding the churches.

30. Ralph Waldo Emerson, "Experience," in *Essays: First and Second Series* (New York: Library of America, 1990), p. 244.

31. Henry Ward Beecher, "The New Birth," *The Sermons of Henry Ward Beecher*, 6th series (New York: J. B. Ford, 1871), pp. 448–50.

32. Lyman Abbott, *Reminiscences* (Boston: Houghton-Mifflin, 1915), p. 440.

33. Washington Gladden, *Reminiscences* (Boston: Houghton-Mifflin, 1909), pp. 36, 63, 252, 254.

34. Gladden, *Reminiscences*, pp. 298–99, 306–07.

35. Peter J. Thuesen, *In Discordance with the Scriptures: American Protestant Battles over Translating the Bible* (New York: Oxford Univ. Press, 1999), pp. 55–56; Abbott, *Reminiscences*, p. 447.

36. Gladden, *Reminiscences*, pp. 260–62, 322–23. The "higher" criticism launched in Germany in the early part of the century had very little influence in the United States until after the Civil War, and even then it was limited to a tiny cohort of American scholars. This critical outlook approached the Bible, like any other cultural text, as the product of historically contingent social forces. Most higher critics still regarded the Bible as inspired by God. Its status as revealed truth was a question of faith, not of science. Faith and reason each had its proper sphere. Faith could not be invoked to prove, for example, that

Christ's disciple John had actually penned every word of the fourth gospel, or that Jesus had in fact been born in Bethlehem rather than Nazareth. Reason, meanwhile, was powerless to disprove divine inspiration. If God wished to communicate himself through Scripture, he could do so through a very human process of multiple authors and narrative embellishment just as easily as he could through single-author inerrancy. On the higher and lower criticism, see Thuesen, *In Discordance with the Scriptures*, pp. 44–46.

37. Gerald D. McDonald, "In His Steps—All-Time Best Seller," in *In His Steps: The Seventieth Anniversary Commemorative Edition* (Topeka: Shawnee County Historical Society, 1967), pp. 1–6. I thank my colleague Tom Cox for alerting me to this edition, which reproduces the 150 lantern slides of the "picture play."

38. Charles M. Sheldon, *In His Steps* (1896; Uhrichsville, OH: Barbour, 1993), pp. 16, 148. A very helpful book on Jesus in fiction is Theodore Ziolkowski, *Fictional Transfigurations of Jesus* (Princeton: Princeton Univ. Press, 1972).

39. Sheldon, *In His Steps*, pp. 88, 224.

40. Sheldon, *In His Steps*, pp. 78, 89.

41. Sandra S. Sizer, *Gospel Hymns and Social Religion* (Philadelphia: Temple Univ. Press, 1978), is an important source on church music in the development of social Christianity. Two essential works that illuminate the significance of song especially in popular evangelization in the nineteenth century are Nathan O. Hatch, *The Democratization of American Christianity* (New Haven: Yale Univ. Press, 1989) and Karen B. Westerfield Tucker, *American Methodist Worship* (New York: Oxford Univ. Press, 2001).

42. O. B. Frothingham, "The Drift Period in Theology," *Christian Examiner* 79 (July 1865): 20; "The New Birth of Jesus," *The Radical* 2 (Feb. 1867): 330. An able biography of Frothingham is J. Wade Caruthers, *Octavius Brooks Frothingham, Gentle Radical* (University, AL: Univ. of Alabama Press, 1977). A compelling example of the fallen-away Christian attributing his departure from the church to Jesus himself is Theodore Tilton, editor of the New York *Independent* in the 1860s, whose spiritual travails I assess in *Trials of Intimacy*, pp. 224–28. I adapt the image of Jesus as a cushion for fallen-away Christians from Thomas Haskell's pitch-perfect description of the idea of hegemony as "a feather pillow, perfect for catching falling Marxists." Haskell derived the phrase, ironically, from its original religious use by Erasmus Darwin (grandfather of Charles), who saw Unitarianism as a cushion for falling Christians. Haskell, "Convention and Hegemonic Interest in the Debate over Antislavery," *American Historical Review* 92 (Oct. 1987), reprinted in Thomas Bender, ed., *The Anti-Slavery Debate* (Berkeley: Univ. of California Press, 1993), p. 206.

43. Frothingham, "The Drift Period in Theology," pp. 11–12; "Christ the Spirit," *Christian Examiner* 73 (Nov. 1862): 332. Frothingham's explicit criticism of Bushnell is in his extraordinarily probing review of Ernest Renan's *Vie de Jésus, Christian Examiner* 75 (Nov. 1863): 337–38. Frothingham listed the exemplary virtues of Jesus in "The New Birth of Jesus," p. 330.

44. Frothingham, "The Drift Period in Theology," pp. 20–22.

45. Frothingham, "The Drift Period in Theology," p. 23; "The New Birth of Jesus," pp. 326, 330–31. Frothingham did not subject Strauss's *Leben Jesu* to the same lengthy treatment he accorded Renan's *Vie de Jésus* (see n. 43, above). But his occasional critical comments on Strauss are extremely insightful, as in "The Evangelist's Debt to the Critic," *Christian Examiner* 76 (May 1864): pp. 383–85. He observes that when Strauss calls gospel accounts "mythic," he is not calling them untrue. He is simply asserting that the gospel writers were not writing historical (and certainly not biographical) truths about Jesus. They were creating spiritual and poetic truths about Jesus. But, added Frothingham, Strauss lacked the literary skill and spiritual sensitivity to show how and why the gospel stories were true to the gospel writers, and to believers ever since. On Strauss and Baur, consult the authoritative discussion by Colin Brown, *Jesus in European Protestant Thought, 1778–1860* (Durham, NC: Labyrinth Press, 1985), pp. 183–219.

46. Frothingham, "The New Birth of Jesus," p. 330; "Address of Mrs. Elizabeth Cady Stanton," "Hearing of the Woman Suffrage Association before the Committee on the Judiciary" (1892), p. 4 (copy of reprint in author's possession, thanks to Kathi Kern). Stanton's address, later entitled "Solitude of Self," is frequently anthologized in an abridged version that leaves out her crucial mention of Jesus. The complete version of her remarks is available on-line at www.pbs.org/stantonanthony/resources.

47. Elizabeth Cady Stanton, *The Woman's Bible*, vol. 2 (New York: European Publishing Co., 1898), pp. 116–17, 120–21; reprint ed., Boston: Northeastern Univ. Press, 1993. Cullen Murphy provides a fine account of the production of *The Woman's Bible* in "The Gospel According to Eve," *American Heritage*, Sept. 1998, pp. 67–74.

48. Jane Addams, *Twenty Years at Hull House* (1910; New York: Signet, 1960), pp. 96–97, 270.

49. Addams, *Twenty Years at Hull House*, p. 94.

50. Eugene Debs, "Jesus, the Supreme Leader," *The Coming Nation*, new series, 1 (Feb. 1914): 2; Debs, "An Appeal to the Working Class," *The Toiler*, Feb. 7, 1902, quoted in Harold W. Currie, "The Religious Views of Eugene V. Debs," *Mid-America* 54 (July 1972): 149 (Currie's article is reprinted as chap. 8 of his *Eugene V. Debs* [Boston: G. K. Hall, 1976]); "Bouck White's Great Book," *The Coming Nation*, new series, 1 (May 1913): p. 16; Bouck White, *The Call of the Carpenter* (Garden City, NY: Doubleday, Page, 1912), pp. xxi–xxii. White made no effort to show that his tiny sample of working-class testimonials to Jesus accurately represented workers as a whole.

51. White, *The Call of the Carpenter*, p. 351.

52. Ray Ginger, *Altgeld's America: The Lincoln Ideal Versus Changing Realities* (1958; Chicago: Quadrangle, 1965), p. 235 (Stead); Bruce C. Nelson, "Revival and Upheaval: Religion, Irreligion, and Chicago's Working Class in 1886," *Journal of Social History* 25 (Winter 1991): 237–38 (Baptist minister); Clark D. Halker, *For Democracy, Workers, and God: Labor, Song-Poems, and Labor Protest,*

1865–1895 (Urbana: Univ. of Illinois Press, 1991), pp. 142, 188 n. 14 (Iron Molders and Knights of Labor).

53. *The Coming Nation* cover portrait of Jesus appeared on Apr. 5, 1913. Bouck White's "Why Did Jesus Commend Confiscation?" came out on Apr. 26.

54. Halker, *For Democracy, Workers, and God*, pp. 143–45. Anti-clerical radicals in the labor movement sometimes went beyond devotion to a secularized Jesus and expressed religious convictions in their song-poems. Anarchist Dyer Lum, for example, wrote "On the Way to Jericho" along with testimonials to the Haymarket martyrs. (Halker, pp. 140–41.)

55. W. E. B. Du Bois, "The Church and the Negro," *The Crisis*, Dec. 1913, p. 291. (See also Chapter Eight, n. 11, below.)

56. Debs, "How I Became a Socialist," *New York Comrade*, Apr. 1902, in *Debs: His Life, Writings, and Speeches* (Girard, KS: The Appeal to Reason, 1908), p. 80. In "John Brown: History's Greatest Hero," *Appeal to Reason*, Nov. 23, 1907 (also reprinted in *Debs: His Life, Writings, and Speeches* and later anthologies of Debs's work), he listed the sequence of historical martyrs who preceded him. He also quoted Thoreau's remark that Brown had been crucified like Christ. Nick Salvatore's *Eugene V. Debs: Citizen and Socialist* (Urbana: Univ. of Illinois Press, 1982), p. 312, notes the Hofmann reproduction on the walls of Debs's jail cells. The image is in Folder 9, Box 2, of the David Fulton Karsner Papers at the New York Public Library. Salvatore is excellent throughout his book on the Christ-centered vision of Debs—who apparently had no religious upbringing—and of much of the American industrial working class (e.g., pp. 155, 237, 310–11, 316–17). He makes the point that Debs's disciples kept reminding him of his destiny as another crucified lamb, thus reinforcing his chosen self-conception.

57. We know a great deal about the nineteenth- and twentieth-century American Protestant shift on using images of Christ, thanks to the path-breaking research of art historian David Morgan. Much of what follows draws on his *Protestants and Pictures: Religion, Visual Culture, and the Age of American Mass Production* (New York: Oxford Univ. Press, 1999), chap. 8 ("The Devotional Likeness of Christ"). See also the astonishing array of visual and material manifestations of Christ in Colleen McDannell, *Material Christianity: Religion and Popular Culture in America* (New Haven: Yale Univ. Press, 1995).

58. Beecher, *The Life of Jesus, the Christ*, pp. iv–v.

59. Beecher, *The Life of Jesus, the Christ*, pp. 135, 143.

60. Doris M. Alexander, "The Passion Play in America," *American Quarterly* 11 (Fall 1959): 353–54.

61. Alexander, "The Passion Play in America," p. 358. A splendid account of Morse's travails and of the Passion Play as a commercial entertainment from the era of lantern slides to the age of film is Charles Musser's "Passions and the Passion Play: Theatre, Film, and Religion in America, 1880–1900," *Film History* 5 (1993): 419–56 (a truncated version, minus vital tables and remarkable early photographs, is reprinted in Francis G. Couvares, ed., *Movie Censorship and American Culture* (Washington: Smithsonian Institution Press, 1996).

62. F. Holland Day, "Opening Address, A New School of American Photography" (1900), in Verna Posever Curtis and Jan Van Nimmen, eds., *F. Holland Day: Selected Texts and Bibliography* (New York: G. K. Hall, 1995), p. 88–89. The biography by Estelle Jussim, *Slave to Beauty: The Eccentric Life and Controversial Career of F. Holland Day: Photographer, Publisher, Aesthete* (Boston: David R. Godine, 1981), is remarkably rich and insightful, but inexplicably peremptory in judging the outdoor crucifixion photographs "exceedingly bad art and worse photography" (p. 135).

63. Washington Gladden, "Christianity and Aestheticism," *Andover Review* 1 (Jan. 1884): 23. The photographer Guglielmo Marconi photographed a crucified "Christ" sometime between 1865 and 1870. Nissan N. Perez's *Corpus Christi: Les représentations du Christ en photographie, 1855–2002* (Jerusalem: Israel Museum, 2002) contains both Harrison's "Infant Savior Bearing the Cross" (p. 39) and Marconi's untitled image (p. 72). The best short introduction to Day's "sacred" work in its Anglo-American context is Allen Ellenzweig, *The Homoerotic Photograph: Male Images from Durieu/Delacroix to Mapplethorpe* (New York: Columbia Univ. Press, 1992), pp. 47–64. On Nietzsche in relation to Emerson, and on the reception in America of Nietzsche (himself often depicted in Europe and America as a post-Christian suffering servant), I draw on the extensive knowledge, based on archival research in Germany, of Jennifer Ratner-Rosenhagen of the University of Miami.

64. "Sacred Art and the Camera," *Photogram*, Apr. 1899, p. 98, quoted in Jussim, *Slave to Beauty*, p. 127.

65. On the comparison between Eakins's 1882 painting and Day's 1898 photography—both accused of disrespect for their sacred subject because they did not sufficiently uplift and inspire—see James Crump, "Suffering the Ideal," in *F. Holland Day: Suffering the Ideal* (Santa Fe: Twin Palms, 1995), p. 138, n. 112.

66. Frank Samuel Child, *The Friendship of Jesus* (New York: Baker and Taylor, 1894), pp. 38–39; R. Warren Conant, *The Virility of Christ: A New View* (Chicago: The Author, 1915), pp. 29–30. John Higham's classic essay on "The Reorientation of American Culture in the 1890s" (1965), reprinted in his *Hanging Together: Unity and Diversity in American Culture* (New Haven: Yale Univ. Press, 2001), pp. 173–97, is a fine survey of the frenzy for physical ardor in the *fin-de-siécle* United States.

67. "Foreword," *YMCA Association Hymn Book* (1907), and "Men Are Wanted," *Manly Songs for Christian Men* (1910), both quoted in Clifford Putney, *Muscular Christianity: Manhood and Sports in Protestant America, 1880–1920* (Cambridge: Harvard Univ. Press, 2001), pp. 96–97. The gendered character of the Social Gospel, first treated in Janet Forsythe Fishburn, *The Fatherhood of God and the Victorian Family: The Social Gospel in America* (Philadelphia: Fortress, 1981), has been reexamined in Wendy J. Deichmann Edwards and Carolyn De Swarte Gifford, eds., *Gender and the Social Gospel* (Urbana: Univ. of Illinois Press, 2003).

68. "In the Garden" is available, with melody, at www.cyberhymnal.org.

CHAPTER SEVEN

1. Fosdick quoted in Robert Moats Miller, *Harry Emerson Fosdick: Preacher, Pastor, Prophet* (New York: Oxford Univ. Press, 1985), p. 60. Fosdick urged that no picture house in Montclair be allowed to present "trashy vaudeville," and that every movie theater be required to be "so well lighted that it would be possible to read with comfort or recognize the face of one's friends across the hall" (p. 61).

2. Charles Musser, *Before the Nickelodeon: Edwin S. Porter and the Edison Manufacturing Company* (Berkeley: Univ. of California Press, 1991), pp. 121–26, 132. Musser rightly stresses the role of slide shows in readying "respectable" audiences for the era of film, but another reason for their approval of cinema was their gradual accommodation to the theater in the early twentieth century. Protestant "progressive" reformers legitimized the theater by mounting a well-publicized attack on its excesses. I put this development in the context of the liberal Protestant endorsement of commercial amusements generally in "The Discipline of Amusement," in William Taylor, ed., *Inventing Times Square: Commerce and Culture at the Crossroads of the World* (New York: Oxford Univ. Press, 1991), pp. 83–98. In *Selling the Old-Time Religion: American Fundamentalists and Mass Culture, 1920–1940* (Athens: Univ. of Georgia Press, 2001), Douglas Carl Adams argues that conservative Christians continued to assail the theater in the early twentieth century, while frequently accepting cinema. He does not examine their response to Jesus films. But their eager appropriation of film for evangelical purposes (combined with their predictable rejection of immoral visual spectacles on film or stage—a reaction fully shared by liberals) suggests they had no objection *per se* to visualizing Christ.

3. "The 'Passion Play" Given Here in Boston," *Boston Herald*, Jan. 4, 1898, p. 6, reprinted in Charles Musser, *Edison Motion Pictures, 1890–1900: An Annotated Filmography* (Washington, D.C.: Smithsonian Institution Press, 1997), pp. 370–71. Christ's "Passion" is technically limited to the period he spent in Jerusalem between the Last Supper and the crucifixion. But "Passion Plays" roamed widely through the earlier life and ministry as well.

4. *New York Dramatic Mirror* review, Oct. 23, 1912 ("almost too ghastly"), and *Moving Picture World* review, Oct. 26, 1912 ("chaste decorum"), both reprinted in Anthony Slide, *Selected Film Criticism, 1912–1920* (Metuchen, NJ: Scarecrow Press, 1982), pp. 97, 100. Patrick G. Loughney, "The First American Film Spectacular," *Quarterly Journal of the Library of Congress* 40 (Winter 1983): 57–69, gives a fine discussion of the film's production and shrewdly notes the details of the scourging and nailing to the cross.

5. *From the Manger to the Cross*, paired with the Pathé Frères' *Life and Passion of Jesus Christ* (1905), is available on a 2003 DVD from Image Entertainment. Loughney, "The First American Film Spectacular," p. 69, notes that this restoration varies slightly in its editing from the original, but not in any way that affects the depiction of the character it identifies as "Jesus, the Man."

6. Lyman Abbott, "The Manliness of Christ," *Outlook*, Dec. 9, 1893, p. 1084. The other quotations are from the film's captions. Charles Musser notes

Thomas Dixon's lectures on Jesus in "Passions and the Passion Play: Theatre, Film, and Religion in America, 1880–1900," *Film History* 5 (1993): 444, 447.

7. Quotations are from the film's captions. As *Intolerance* neared completion, Griffith was accused of intolerance himself by Jewish critics of the film's anti-Semitism. The first cut apparently had Jewish authorities nailing Jesus to the cross themselves. Griffith reshot the scene with Roman soldiers doing the job. Patricia Erens, *The Jew in American Cinema* (Bloomington: Indiana Univ. Press, 1984), p. 72.

8. *New York Times* review, Apr. 20, 1927, p. 2, reprinted in *The New York Times Film Reviews*, vol. 1 (New York: New York Times, 1970), p. 360; Donald Hayne, ed., *The Autobiography of Cecil B. DeMille* (Englewood Cliffs, NJ: Prentice-Hall, 1959), p. 276.

9. Erens, *The Jew in American Cinema*, p. 72.

10. Hayne, ed., *The Autobiography of Cecil B. DeMille*, p. 282. Joseph Klausner observed that according to Josephus and Philo, Pilate was no coward but a "cruel and tyrannical . . . 'man of blood.'" Moreover, "all the stories of Pilate's opposition to the crucifixion of Jesus are wholly unhistorical, emanating from the end of the first Christian century." Klausner concluded that "the Jews, as a nation, were far less guilty of the death of Jesus than the Greeks, as a nation, were guilty of the death of Socrates; but who now would think of avenging the blood of Socrates the Greek upon his countrymen, the present Greek race?" *Jesus of Nazareth* (New York: Macmillan, 1925), p. 348.

11. An excellent entry point into the vast literature on "orality and literacy" in relation to religious experiences of the Word is William A. Graham, *Beyond the Written Word: Oral Aspects of Scripture in the History of Religion* (Cambridge: Cambridge Univ. Press, 1987). See also Leigh Eric Schmidt's brilliantly innovative *Hearing Things: Religion, Illusion, and the American Enlightenment* (Cambridge: Harvard Univ. Press, 2000).

12. *Variety* review of *King of Kings*, Apr. 20, 1927, p. 15, reprinted in *Variety Film Reviews, 1926–1929*, vol. 3 (New York: Garland, 1983), n.p.

13. Bruce Barton, *The Man Nobody Knows: A Discovery of the Real Jesus* (Indianapolis: Bobbs-Merrill, 1925), pp. 140, 143. The Book of the Month Club rated *The Man Nobody Knows* as the number-one best-seller of 1926. Frank Luther Mott, *Golden Multitudes: The Story of Best Sellers in the United States* (New York: R. R. Bowker, 1947), p. 330. An indispensable introduction to the Bartons, father and son, is T. J. Jackson Lears, "From Salvation to Self-Realization: Advertising and the Therapeutic Roots of the Consumer Culture, 1880–1930," in his and my collection *The Culture of Consumption: Critical Essays in American History: 1880–1980* (New York: Pantheon, 1983), pp. 30–38.

14. "Booming Religion as a Business Proposition," *Christian Century*, May 21, 1925, p. 658; Barton, *Man Nobody Knows*, pp. 181, 186, and final page of Preface.

15. In my essay "Experience and Explanation in Twentieth-Century American Religious History," in *New Directions in American Religious History*, ed. Harry S. Stout and D. G. Hart (New York: Oxford, 1997), pp. 409–10, I note that even the most culturally conscious liberal lives of Jesus, such as Shirley Case's

Jesus: A New Biography (Chicago: Univ. of Chicago Press, 1927), fall unconsciously into the liberal exaltation of deliberative, open-ended, open-minded selfhood. As Henry J. Cadbury pointed out in his trenchant *The Peril of Modernizing Jesus* (New York: Macmillan, 1937), there was no reason to assume liberality rather than impetuousness combined with steely obedience to his Father's wishes, hardly signs of the emancipated, modern self. Jesus could still be the Son of God even if his human consciousness (like ours) was culturally embedded in his own time. Jack Miles, in his magnificent *Christ: A Crisis in the Life of God* (New York: Knopf, 2001), considers the question whether Christ's death, as configured in the gospels, was a form of suicide (pp. 160–78).

16. Barton, *Man Nobody Knows,* p. 162 (italics in original); Gottschall and Gaebelein quoted (and Bryan discussed) in Abrams, *Selling the Old-Time Religion,* p. 45; "Booming Religion as a Business Proposition," p. 658.

17. "Booming Religion as a Business Proposition," p. 658; Barton, *Man Nobody Knows,* pp. 121, 168, 177–78, and penultimate page of Preface.

18. "Jesus as Efficiency Expert," *Christian Century,* July 2, 1925, pp. 851–52. This editorial is unsigned, but Niebuhr wrote it.

19. I give a detailed treatment of Niebuhr's transition from "idealism" to "realism," and of his influence over a generation of liberal Protestants from the 1930s to the 1960s, in *Reinhold Niebuhr: A Biography* (1985; Ithaca, NY: Cornell Univ. Press, 1995). The 1995 edition has a new Afterword and Bibliography.

20. Walter Rauschenbusch, *Christianity and the Social Crisis* (1907; New York: Harper and Row, 1964), p. 305.

21. Lyman Abbott, "Did Jesus Christ Teach Non-Resistance?" *Outlook,* Nov. 10, 1915, pp. 596–97; Abbott, "Resist Not Evil: The Pacifist Doctrine and Its Fallacy," *Outlook,* Mar. 21, 1917, p. 501; Theodore Roosevelt, *Fear God and Take Your Own Part* (1916), quoted in Clifford Putney, *Muscular Christianity: Manhood and Sports in Protestant America, 1880–1920* (Cambridge: Harvard Univ. Press, 2001), p. 172.

22. Walter Rauschenbusch, "Dr. Rauschenbusch on the War," *Christian Century,* Aug. 1, 1918, p. 13; Harry Emerson Fosdick quoted in Robert Moats Miller, *Harry Emerson Fosdick, Preacher, Pastor, Prophet* (New York: Oxford Univ. Press, 1985), pp. 497–98. I treat Niebuhr's wartime zeal in chap. 3 of *Reinhold Niebuhr.* The pacifist position was outlined by John Haynes Holmes, "Was Jesus a Non-Resistant?" *North American Review* 202 (Dec. 1915): 879–87.

23. Reinhold Niebuhr, "Wanted: A Christian Morality," *Christian Century,* Feb. 15, 1923, pp. 202–03; Niebuhr, "Jesus as a Radical," *Student World,* July 1928, pp. 294–95; Niebuhr, "The Ethic of Jesus and the Social Problem," *Religion in Life,* Spring 1932, reprinted in D. B. Robertson, ed., *Love and Justice: Selections from the Shorter Writings of Reinhold Niebuhr* (Philadelphia: Westminster Press, 1957), p. 33; Niebuhr, *An Interpretation of Christian Ethics* (1935; New York: Seabury Press, 1979), p. 37. On Harry Ward's extension of Methodist "perfectionism" from individual holiness to social transformation, consult David Nelson Duke, *In the Trenches with Jesus and Marx: Harry F. Ward and the Struggle for Social Justice* (Tuscaloosa: Univ. of Alabama Press, 2003).

24. I treat Niebuhr's own relation to the "personal work" of evangelism in *Reinhold Niebuhr*, pp. 81–82.

25. Garry Wills, *Under God: Religion and American Politics* (New York: Simon and Schuster, 1990). The standard sources on the conservative evangelical movement before Billy Graham are at last, thankfully, too numerous to list. Good places to start are Joel A. Carpenter, *Revive Us Again: The Reawakening of American Fundamentalism* (New York: Oxford Univ. Press, 1997), Margaret L. Bendroth, *Fundamentalism and Gender, 1875 to the Present* (New Haven: Yale Univ. Press, 1993), and George M. Marsden, *Fundamentalism and American Culture: The Shaping of Twentieth-Century Evangelicalism, 1870–1925* (New York: Oxford Univ. Press, 1980).

26. On twentieth-century American de-Christianization and the assimilation of Jews into American intellectual life, the indispensable resource is the work of David A. Hollinger, beginning with his "Jewish Intellectuals and the De-Christianization of American Public Culture in the Twentieth Century," in his collection *Science, Jews, and Secular Culture: Studies in Mid-Twentieth-Century American Intellectual History* (Princeton: Princeton Univ. Press, 1996), pp. 17–41.

27. Mark Silk analyzes the rise of the twentieth-century concept of "the Judeo-Christian tradition" in "Notes on the Judeo-Christian Tradition in America," *American Quarterly* 36 (Spring 1984): 65–85. Masses of Catholics and Protestants, black and white, continued to disdain actual Jews even as the idea of a Judeo-Christian tradition took root in northern American culture. Masses of Protestants and Jews, meanwhile, held Catholics under continuing suspicion of secret disloyalty to American democracy—of preference for autocracy in general and the Vatican in particular—into the 1960s. See John T. McGreevy's important *Catholicism and American Freedom: A History* (New York: Norton, 2003), esp. chaps. 6–7.

28. Stephen Wise to Richard W. Montague, Dec. 21, 1925, in Carl Hermann Voss, ed., *Stephen S. Wise: Servant of the People* (Philadelphia: Jewish Publication Society, 5729/1969), p. 132; Rabbi Joseph Krauskopf, *A Rabbi's Impressions of the Oberammergau Passion Play* (Philadelphia: Rayner, 1901), p. 12.

29. Very helpful interpretations of the apocalyptic frame of mind in modern America are offered by Timothy D. Weber, *Living in the Shadow of the Second Coming: American Premillennialism, 1875–1925* (New York: Oxford Univ. Press, 1979), and Paul Boyer, *When Time Shall Be No More: Prophecy Belief in Modern American Culture* (Cambridge: Harvard Univ. Press, 1992).

30. Reinhold Niebuhr, "Why I Am Not a Christian," *Christian Century*, Dec. 15, 1927, p. 1482. Niebuhr's title was ironic. Niebuhr signaled his detachment from evangelicalism by putting the phrase "give their hearts to Jesus" in quotation marks, as if it were a locution favored by some alien tribe. On Carl Henry and the neo-fundamentalist Fuller Seminary, see George M. Marsden's important study *Reforming Fundamentalism: Fuller Seminary and the New Evangelicalism* (Grand Rapids: Eerdmans, 1987).

31. Machen and Fosdick quoted in Miller, *Harry Emerson Fosdick*, pp. 114–15.

32. D. G. Hart's excellent study *Defending the Faith: J. Gresham Machen and the Crisis of Conservative Protestantism in Modern America* (Baltimore: Johns Hopkins Univ. Press, 1994) establishes the line of demarcation between the popular fundamentalism of Presbyterians such as Carl McIntire and the "confessional" fundamentalism of Machen. Both McIntire and Machen deprecated "liberalism," but Machen dissented from McIntire's quest to make America a "Christian nation."

33. J. Gresham Machen, *Christianity and Liberalism* (1923; Grand Rapids: Eerdmans, 1985), pp. 81, 84, 91–94, 96, 103, 115.

34. Harry Emerson Fosdick, *The Living of These Days* (New York: Harper & Sons, 1956), pp. 35–36, 48, 66. I discuss Fosdick's and other liberals' "lived experience" of Jesus in "Experience and Explanation in Twentieth-Century American Religious History," in *New Directions in American Religious History*, ed. Harry S. Stout and D. G. Hart (New York: Oxford Univ. Press, 1997), pp. 405–10.

35. Machen, *Christianity and Liberalism*, p. 65; H. Richard Niebuhr, "Inconsistency of the Majority," *The World Tomorrow*, Jan. 18, 1934, p. 44. Reinhold Niebuhr took an additional page from J. Gresham Machen when he dismissed Harry Emerson Fosdick's liberal Christianity in "How Adventurous Is Dr. Fosdick?" a review of Fosdick's essay collection *Adventurous Religion* in *Christian Century*, Jan. 6, 1927, pp. 17–18.

36. The remarkable Phoebe Palmer is examined in Charles Edward White's *The Beauty of Holiness: Phoebe Palmer as Theologian, Revivalist, Feminist, and Humanitarian* (Grand Rapids: Zondervan, 1986) and in Thomas C. Oden, ed., *Phoebe Palmer: Selected Writings* (New York: Paulist Press, 1988).

37. Walter Rauschenbusch, "Speaking in Tongues—What Was It?" *The Watchman* 78 (Sept. 30, 1897): 10. The now-standard work on early-twentieth-century American Pentecostalism is Grant Wacker, *Heaven Below: Early Pentecostals and American Culture* (Cambridge: Harvard Univ. Press, 2001). Thirteen issues of Seymour's newsletter *The Apostolic Faith* (Sept. 1906 to May 1908) are available online at www.dunamai.com.

38. "The Same Old Way," *Apostolic Faith*, Sept. 1906, p. 3.

39. *Apostolic Faith*, Sept. 1906, p. 2.

40. "Spanish Receive the Pentecost" and "Shall We Reject Jesus' Last Words?" *Apostolic Faith*, Oct. 1906, pp. 3–4.

41. "A Message Concerning His Coming," *Apostolic Faith*, Oct. 1906, p. 3.

42. "Weird Babel of Tongues," *Los Angeles Daily Times*, Apr. 18, 1906, p. 1, quoted in Vinson Synan, "William Seymour," *Christian History*, Winter 2000, p. 18; "A Know-So Salvation," *Apostolic Faith*, Oct. 1906, p. 2.

43. Reinhold Niebuhr, *Leaves from the Notebook of a Tamed Cynic* (Chicago: Willett, Clark, and Colby, 1929), pp. 103–05; McPherson lyrics quoted in Edith L. Blumhofer, *Aimee Semple McPherson: Everybody's Sister* (Grand Rapids: Eerdmans, 1993), p. 228. I am indebted to Blumhofer's excellent book for my account of McPherson's ministry and its Los Angeles context. We still badly need a full study of Los Angeles Protestantism from 1900 to 1950, treating Pentecostal and fundamentalist developments in relation to Hollywood-driven

mass culture. Blumhofer's work will be an important foundation for that study, as will George Marsden's *Reforming Fundamentalism*.

44. Albert Dod comments (in *The Biblical Repertory and Theological Review*, Oct. 1835) quoted in William G. McLoughlin, Jr., *Billy Graham: Revivalist in a Secular Age* (New York: Ronald Press, 1960), p. 16. McPherson kept her altar calls "old-fashioned." Some other twentieth-century revivalists, notably Billy Graham, allowed those who came forward to retire to a private room for their profession of faith. She insisted on getting "sinners to accept Christ personally in public" because "Christ took a public stand for us." McPherson, *The Story of My Life* (Los Angeles: Echo Park Evangelistic Association, 1951), p. 199.

45. Aimee Semple McPherson, "A Certain Man Went Down," *This Is That: Personal Experiences, Sermons, and Writings* (Los Angeles: Echo Park Evangelistic Association, 1923), p. 634.

46. Shelton Bissell, "Vaudeville at Angelus Temple," *Outlook*, May 23, 1928, p. 126.

47. Aimee Semple McPherson, *The Story of My Life* (Waco, TX: Word Books, 1973), p. 234. This version of her autobiography is a complete rewriting of the "memorial" edition published in 1951. The new edition provides no inkling of who produced the revision.

48. McPherson, "They Have Taken Away My Lord," *This Is That*, pp. 764–67. A brief audiotape of McPherson's preaching is available in the "Lost and Found Sound" archive at www.npr.org. It is long enough to convey a good sense of her melodramatic style.

49. McPherson, *The Story of My Life* (1951), p. 234.

CHAPTER EIGHT

1. John Pollock, *Billy Graham: The Authorized Biography* (1956; Grand Rapids, MI: Zondervan, 1957). On Graham's return crusade in Los Angeles in 1963, over 130,000 people attended the final session at the L.A. Coliseum.

2. *Los Angeles Daily News*, Sept. 30, 1949, quoted in William Martin, "Billy Graham," *Christian History*, Winter 2000, p. 14; Curtis Mitchell, *God in the Garden: The Story of the Billy Graham New York Crusade* (Garden City, NY: Doubleday, 1957), p. 108.

3. Mitchell, *God in the Garden*, pp. 155–57. Fundamentalists and liberals alike criticized Graham's shrewdly centrist move of getting liberal as well as traditionalist sponsors for the crusade. Presbyterian fundamentalist Carl McIntire was incensed at all the mingling with the modernists, while dean-of-the-liberals Reinhold Niebuhr was disturbed that the Protestant Council of the City of New York had officially endorsed the crusade. Graham, *Just As I Am: The Autobiography of Billy Graham* (San Francisco: HarperSanFrancisco, 1997), pp. 302–03 (on McIntire), "Graham Sermon in Garden on TV," *New York Times*, June 2, 1957, p. 38 (on Niebuhr).

4. Mitchell, *God in the Garden*, pp. 133, 158–59.

5. Pollock, *Billy Graham*, pp. 259–60; Mitchell, *God in the Garden*, p. 134–35.

6. "Editorial Notes," *Christianity and Crisis*, June 27, 1955, p. 82; Reinhold Niebuhr to Theodore Gill, June 20, 1956, Reinhold Niebuhr Papers, Box 16, Li-

brary of Congress; Niebuhr in *Life,* quoted in Pollock, *Billy Graham,* p. 177; Niebuhr, "A Proposal for Billy Graham," *Christian Century,* Aug. 8, 1956, reprinted in D. B. Robertson, *Love and Justice: the Shorter Writings of Reinhold Niebuhr* (Philadelphia: Westminster, 1957), pp. 154–55, 158. On Graham's response to Niebuhr's criticism, compare John Pollock's 1957 *Billy Graham,* which (pp. 177–78) archly defends the revivalist against Niebuhr's charges, with his later *Billy Graham: Evangelist to the World* (New York: Harper and Row, 1979), p. 157, in which Graham is quoted as saying, "I thought about it a great deal. He [Niebuhr] influenced me, and I began to take a stronger stand." Graham's own autobiography *Just As I Am,* p. 301, notes Niebuhr's view that Graham subordinated "social concern" to "evangelism," but says nothing about his having been influenced by Niebuhr. Instead he criticizes Niebuhr for allegedly refusing to meet with him during the New York crusade.

7. Niebuhr, "The Billy Graham Campaign," *Messenger,* June 4, 1957, p. 5 ("Graham honestly believes"); Niebuhr, "Literalism, Individualism, and Billy Graham," *Christian Century,* May 23, 1956, reprinted in D. B. Robertson, ed., *Essays in Applied Christianity* (New York: Meridian, 1959), pp. 128, 130.

8. Niebuhr, "Literalism, Individualism, and Billy Graham," p. 129 ("even the most devoted Christians"); Henry P. Van Dusen, "Billy Graham" (letter to the editor), *Christianity and Crisis,* Apr. 2, 1956, p. 40; Mitchell, *God in the Garden,* p. 161. "Nixon, Billy Graham Target Jews on Tape," *St. Petersburg Times,* Mar. 2, 2002, gives substantial excerpts from Graham's taped Feb. 1, 1972, conversation with Richard Nixon, along with his apology for his statements about the Jews (available online at TampaBay.com). Graham did more than nod politely at President Nixon's fulminations about supposed Jewish control of major media outlets. Graham announced that while many Jews "swarm around me and are friendly to me" because of his support for Israel, "they don't know how I really feel about what they're doing to this country." Graham told Nixon that if he got reelected, "we might be able to do something" about the "stranglehold" Jews exercised over the media. "They're the ones putting out the pornographic stuff," Graham claimed. In his 2002 apology, Graham said, "I deeply regret" the comments, which "do not reflect my views."

9. To begin to fathom the power of Jesus in twentieth-century African American culture, I suggest starting with a range of short accounts: Richard Wright's text and the accompanying federal government photos in *12,000,000 Black Voices* (New York: Viking, 1941), Albert J. Raboteau's treatment of James Baldwin's *Go Tell It On the Mountain* in *A Fire in the Bones: Reflections on African-American Religious History* (Boston: Beacon, 1995), chap. 8, and Michael Eric Dyson's account of black preachers (including Aretha Franklin's father C. L. Franklin) in "What's Derrida Got to Do with Jesus?" in Marjorie Garber and Rebecca L. Walkowitz, eds., *One Nation Under God? Religion and American Culture* (New York: Routledge, 1999), pp. 76–97). Then return to the masterwork, W. E. B Du Bois, *The Souls of Black Folk* (1903).

10. Booker T. Washington, "A Speech Before the Unitarian Club of Boston" (1888) and "A Speech Before the National Unitarian Association (1894)," in

Louis R. Harlan, ed., *The Booker T. Washington Papers* (Urbana: Univ. of Illinois Press, 1972), vol. 2, p. 505, vol. 3, pp. 477–78.

11. W. E. B. Du Bois, "The Church," *The Crisis,* Apr. 1916, p. 302; "Good Will Toward Men," *The Crisis,* Dec. 1910, p. 16; "The Church and the Negro," *The Crisis,* Dec. 1913, pp. 290–91. On Du Bois's own Christian practice and subsequent disbelief, consult David Levering Lewis, *W. E. B. Du Bois: Biography of a Race: 1868–1919* (New York: Henry Holt, 1993), esp. pp. 48–50, 312–13. Du Bois published an eminently forgettable short story on lynching, entitled "Jesus Christ in Waco" (1920). Compare it to his gripping and biting story "Of the Coming of John" (chap. 13 of *Souls of Black Folk*) and to his one-page nonfictional *cri de coeur* "Lynchings" (1932). "Jesus Christ in Waco" and "Lynchings" are reprinted in Lewis's *W. E. B. Du Bois: A Reader* (New York: Henry Holt, 1995), pp. 478–79, 495–502.

12. Marcus Garvey, "Speech," Sept. 4, 1921, and "Christmas Message" (1921), in Robert A. Hill, ed., *The Marcus Garvey and Universal Negro Improvement Association Papers* (Berkeley: Univ. of California Press, 1985), vol. 4, pp. 25, 310.

13. Martin Luther King, Jr., quoted in David J. Garrow, *Bearing the Cross: Martin Luther King, Jr., and the Southern Christian Leadership Conference* (New York: William Morrow, 1986), p. 428; Garvey, "Speech," Mar. 26, 1921, *Garvey Papers,* 3:283; Garvey, "Speech," Dec. 25, 1927, *Garvey Papers,* 7:71. Garvey was not the first to suggest that Jesus was not white; Native American writer and preacher William Apess made the same claim in 1833. But few Americans made any reference at all in print to Christ's color before the twentieth century. Even Garvey seems to have pressed the color question more assiduously when he was in Jamaica than when he was in the United States. Apess took Jesus as "colored" because he thought all Jews were colored. But Jesus, he added, showed no interest in skin color. Barry O'Connell, ed., *On Our Own Ground: The Complete Writings of William Apess, A Pequot* (Amherst: University of Massachusetts Press, 1992), p. 158.

14. Martin Luther King, Jr., "I Have a Dream," in *A Call To Conscience: The Landmark Speeches of Dr. Martin Luther King, Jr.,* ed. Clayborne Carson and Kris Shepard (New York: Warner Books, 2001), pp. 84–87. The Revised Standard Version of Amos 5:24 has "justice roll down like waters, and righteousness like an ever-flowing stream," while the King James Version has "judgment run down as waters, and righteousness as a mighty stream." In his preaching and speaking King sometimes used the KJV's "mighty," but he always used the RSV's "justice."

15. King on Niebuhr and Gandhi, quoted in Clayborne Carson, ed., *The Autobiography of Martin Luther King, Jr.* (New York: Warner Books, 1998), pp. 26–27.

16. King, "Loving Your Enemies," sermon preached at Dexter Avenue Baptist Church, Montgomery, Alabama, Nov. 17, 1957, in Clayborne Carson and Peter Holloran, eds., *A Knock at Midnight: Inspiration from the Great Sermons of Reverend Martin Luther King, Jr.* (New York: Warner Books, 1998), pp. 41–49.

17. King, "I've Been to the Mountaintop," in Carson and Shepard, eds., *A Call To Conscience*, pp. 217–23.

18. Dorothy Day, "Martin Luther King," "'What Do the Simple Folk Do?'" and "Holy Obedience," in *By Little and By Little: The Selected Writings of Dorothy Day* (New York: Knopf, 1983), pp. 168–79, 339–40.

19. Day, *The Long Loneliness* (1952; New York: Image Books, 1959), pp. 57–58; Day, *By Little and By Little*, p. 168.

20. Day, "Room for Christ," and "We Go on Record," in *By Little and By Little*, pp. 95, 317.

21. Day, "The Pearl of Great Price," in *By Little and By Little*, pp. 112, 114; Day quoted (on the diamond) in Jim Forest, *Love Is the Measure: A Biography of Dorothy Day*, rev. ed. (Maryknoll, NY: Orbis Books, 1994), p. 67.

22. The last two paragraphs are adapted from my discussion of Day in "New Baptized: The Culture of Love in America, 1830s–1950s," in *Religion and Cultural Studies*, ed. Susan L. Mizruchi (Princeton: Princeton Univ. Press, 2001), pp. 133–34.

23. Francine du Plessix Gray, *Divine Disobedience: Profiles in Catholic Radicalism* (1970; New York: Vintage Books, 1971), pp. 56–57; Daniel Berrigan, *No Bars to Manhood* (Garden City, NY: Doubleday, 1970), pp. 61–62, 64. See also Philip Berrigan, *Fighting the Lamb's War: Skirmishes with the American Empire: The Autobiography of Philip Berrigan* (Monroe, ME: Common Courage Press, 1996), p. 98: "Jesus was an activist, not a monk. He lived among the poor. He drove the money-changers from the temple, criticized the rich and powerful, ridiculed government officials. He would not have remained in a monastery while his own government was slaughtering the Vietnamese."

24. David Tracy, *The Analogical Imagination: Christian Theology and the Culture of Pluralism* (New York: Crossroad, 1981), pp. 322–23. The post–Vatican II reorientation of official Catholic theology to emphasize the church's primary allegiance to Christ is well expressed in the *Catechism of the Catholic Church* (New York: Doubleday, 1995). An impassioned Catholic rebuff to the liberal Protestant quest for the "historical Jesus" is Luke Timothy Johnson, *The Real Jesus: The Misguided Quest for the Historical Jesus and the Truth of the Traditional Gospels* (San Francisco: HarperSanFrancisco, 1996). On Dorothy Day in relation to several significant Catholic writers—Thomas Merton, Flannery O'Connor, and Walker Percy—see the excellent book by Paul Elie, *The Life You Save May Be Your Own: An American Pilgrimage* (New York: Farrar, Straus, Giroux, 2003). John T. McGreevy's *Catholicism and American Freedom: A History* (New York: Norton, 2003) is a fine introduction to John A. Ryan, John Courtney Murray, and much else besides. New work is emerging on "Mexican Traditions in U.S. Catholicism," as Timothy Matovina and Gary Riebe-Estrella subtitle their breakthrough collection *Horizons of the Sacred* (Ithaca: Cornell Univ. Press, 2002). Along with the fascinating documents collected in Timothy Matovina and Gerald E. Poyo, eds., *¡Presente! U.S. Latino Catholics from Colonial Origins to the Present* (Maryknoll, NY: Orbis Books, 2000), it affirms the persistence of traditional views of Jesus throughout American history while establishing the diversity of cultural practices around Christ.

25. For visual evidence of the change in Catholic church interiors, consult the "before" and "after" photographs of St. Donatus Church (Brooten, Minnesota) in Colleen McDannell, *Material Christianity: Religion and Popular Culture in America* (New Haven: Yale Univ. Press, 1995), p. 172.

26. David Morgan, *Visual Piety: A History and Theory of Popular Religious Images* (Berkeley: Univ. of California Press, 1998), p. 181.

27. Morgan, *Visual Piety*, pp. 57, 157, 194. Sojourner Truth saw Jesus as a mediator to whom she could turn for aid in communicating with the Father, but it never occurred to her to visualize him with an image. She brought him to mind in words and narrative.

28. The review of "King of Kings" in the evangelical *Christianity Today* (founded by Billy Graham in 1955) noted the film's insistence on blaming the Romans as much as the Jews for the crucifixion of Jesus, but implied that such a goal was an unjustifiable imposition of "racial purpose" on the script. The review also criticized Jeffrey Hunter's Jesus as "effeminate and unconvincing" in his uniform "sincerity." James Daane, "King of Kings," *Christianity Today*, Oct. 27, 1961, p. 28. Harold Lindsell, the magazine's reviewer for "The Greatest Story Ever Told" (Feb. 26, 1965, p. 52), applauded it as "more than a humanistic production; [its] Jesus Christ is the Son of God and Saviour of the world." But he faulted the film for omitting the annunciation, the presentation of Jesus at the Temple, his appearance in the temple when he was twelve, the transfiguration, the parables, and the Olivet discourse.

29. "Comment on Jesus Spurs a Radio Ban Against the Beatles," *New York Times*, Aug. 5, 1966, p. 20; "Lennon of Beatles Sorry for Making Remark on Jesus," *New York Times*, Aug. 12, 1966, p. 38.

30. *Superstar* offered a Jesus who, in his status as a celebrity, seemed humanly persuasive to evangelicals as well as liberals like James Wall, who reviewed the film enthusiastically in the *Christian Century* (Sept. 5, 1973). Evangelicals just wanted divinity to redeem humanity at the finale. Reviewing the play in *Christianity Today*, Lutheran seminary student Gilbert Meilaender, Jr., said it delivered a compellingly human Jesus but failed at conveying his transcendence. It made no effort to join the apparent defeat of the human Jesus with the ultimate victory of the divine Jesus. "The New Paganism," Sept. 24, 1971, p. 4. *Jesus Christ Superstar* lyrics are available at www.members.tripol. com/~JCSKelly/lyrics2.html.

31. Aljean Harmetz, "7,500 Picket Universal Over Movie About Jesus," *New York Times*, Aug. 12, 1988, p. C4; Harmetz, "'The Last Temptation of Christ' Opens to Protests but Good Sales," *New York Times*, Aug. 13, 1988, p. 11; Andrew Greeley, "Blasphemy or Artistry?" *New York Times*, Aug. 14, 1988, pp. B1, B22; David Tracy, "Letter to the Editor," *New York Times*, Sept. 3, 1988, p. A22. A probing letter on the same page from David Cameron, "a Bible-believing, evangelical" Christian, rightly noted that protesting evangelicals were missing the orthodox heart of the film: this human Jesus claimed to be the divine Christ.

32. "A Holy Furor," *Time*, Aug. 15, 1988, p. 35 (on "most" conservatives turning down Universal's invitation to attend special showings of *Last Tempta-*

tion); Aljean Harmetz, "Turning 'Last Temptation' Into a Hit," *New York Times*, Aug. 24, 1988, p. C15. See also Harmetz, "'Last Temptation' Sets a Record as Pickets Decline," Aug. 15, 1988, p. C14. The super-heated debate over Gibson's film picked up steam with Peter Boyer's "The Jesus War," *New Yorker*, Sept. 15, 2003, pp. 58–71. Unlike Scorsese, Gibson barred potential naysayers from early showings. Much of the battle over the film is archived at www.beliefnet.org and www.christianitytoday.com.

33. In a 1991 interview Serrano described himself as "a former Catholic" still "drawn to Christ" and producing "religious art." Coco Fusco, "Shooting the Klan: An Interview with Andrew Serrano, *High Performance*, Fall 1991, reprinted in *The Citizen as Artist*, ed. Linda Frye Burnham and Steven Durland (Gardiner, NY: Critical Press, 1998), available online at www.communityarts.net. *High Performance* noted that the prices for Serrano's work rose after the public controversy over "Piss Christ" in 1989, but also pointed out the heavy price the artist paid in antagonism and threats received. In the same exhibit with Renée Cox's "Yo Mama's Last Supper" at the Brooklyn Museum in early 2001 was a photo of a topless female torso crucified on a cross. European photographers displayed photos of fully nude female crucifixions beginning in the 1880s. See Nissan N. Perez, *Corpus Christi: Les représentations du Christ en photographie, 1855–2002* (Jerusalem: The Israel Museum, 2002).

34. "Ethanol Issue Stirs Pot at Lively Republican Debate," *Des Moines Register*, Dec. 14, 1999, p. 1.

35. James Carroll, "Which Christ is Bush's Model?" *Boston Globe*, Dec. 21, 1999, p. A31; Maureen Dowd, "Playing the Jesus Card," *New York Times*, Dec. 15, 1999, p. A31; Richard L. Berke, "Religion Center Stage in Presidential Race," *New York Times*, Dec. 15, 1999, p. A18. Howard Fineman gives an insightful assessment of Bush's faith in "Bush and God," *Newsweek*, Mar. 10, 2003, pp. 22–30. In his book *The Bush Dyslexicon* (New York: Norton, 2001), p. 111, cultural critic Mark Crispin Miller concurs with Carroll: "No thoughtful Christian could be happy with [Bush's] answer, since Jesus was definitely not a 'political philosopher or thinker.'" Yet in recent times Quakers, Mennonites, and other pacifists have made extensive use of Jesus as a political thinker.

36. The "Jesus Day" proclamation is available online at TomPaine.com. On Jefferson's and Madison's objections to official supports for religious belief, see John T. Noonan Jr., *The Lustre of Our Country: the American Experience of Religious Freedom* (Berkeley: Univ. of California Press, 1998), pt. 1.

37. In his autobiography, Billy Graham asserts that Martin Luther King, Jr., explicitly told him to stay out of King's direct-action campaigns. "You stay in the stadiums, Billy," he has King saying, "because you will have far more impact on the white establishment there than you would if you marched in the streets. Besides that, you have a constituency that will listen to you, especially among white people, who may not listen so much to me. . . . If a leader gets too far out in front of his people, they will lose sight of him and not follow him any longer." *Just As I Am* (San Francisco: HarperSanFrancisco, 1997), p. 426. Though it is hard to imagine King turning down an offer from Graham to join the Selma March, or opposing stronger statements from Graham about the

gospel demand for justice, King surely valued his immediate access to Graham (a confirmed opponent of racial discrimination) and Graham's immediate access to presidents of both parties. In 1984 Graham in turn criticized Jerry Falwell (a strong supporter of Ronald Reagan) and Jesse Jackson (a candidate for the Democratic nomination) for politicizing the gospel. Ari L. Goldman, "Graham Say Clerics 'Went Too Far' in '84 Races," *New York Times,* Jan. 3, 1985, p. B7.

38. Danny Hakim, "A Group Links Fuel Economy to Religion," *New York Times,* Nov. 19, 2002, p. C1; Hakim, "Now, Add God to the List of Enemies of the S.U.V.," *New York Times,* Nov. 24, 2002, p. D3.

39. Nicholas D. Kristof, "God On Their Side," *New York Times,* Sept. 27, 2003, p. A27; "Following God Abroad," *New York Times,* May 21, 2002, p. A21.

40. Lauren F. Winner, "T. D. Jakes Feels Your Pain," *Christianity Today,* Feb. 7, 2000, pp. 53–59. Winner cites Boston preacher Eugene Rivers's concern that Jakes is disproportionately interested in "promoting black middle-class consumerism. He is not offering black Christians a developed sense of biblical justice, like we got from King. The prophetic dimension of biblical faith is absent from Jakes' teaching" (p. 56).

41. Michael Farrell, Janet McKenzie, and Sister Wendy Beckett quoted in "Jesus 2000," *National Catholic Reporter,* Dec. 24, 1999, pp. 2, 7; Peter De Firis quoted in Pamela Schaeffer and John L. Allen, Jr., "Jesus 2000," *National Catholic Reporter* online edition, Dec. 24, 1999.

42. I thank Dimitar Kambourov, a Bulgarian professor of literature, for clarifying the *kataphatic* and *apophatic* approaches to iconic representation (corresponding to what I call "positive" and "negative" paths).

43. "Alabama Panel Ousts Judge Over Ten Commandments," *New York Times,* Nov. 14, 2003, p. A12.

44. H. Richard Niebuhr, *The Kingdom of God in America* (1937; New York: Harper, 1959), p. 193. Paul Tillich was the greatest liberal Protestant theologian of twentieth-century America, and he self-consciously embraced the idea of religion as therapeutic empowerment. Among the many American thinkers and believers whom I have had to leave out of this book, Tillich represents one of the most egregious omissions. For my penance I offer a reminiscence. When I was in college, students religious and secular carried dog-eared copies of his book *The Courage to Be* around campus. (Published by Yale University Press in 1952, it was in its eighth printing when I entered college a decade later.) Tillich was an erudite Christian thinker, even if one who from the Niebuhr brothers' perspective was by the 1950s wrongly fixated on human psychological development and self-creation. In February 1965, I attended a Saturday gathering of undergraduates invited to converse with Tillich in Santa Barbara. He was physically frail less than a year before his death, but his intense eyes and august bearing were intimidating. For a nineteen-year-old California Catholic like me, his Europeanness conveyed instant authority. I finally managed to emit a question in Tillich's direction, but I made the mistake of asking him whether the "myth" of the resurrection was essential to his view of Christianity. He shifted in his throne-like chair twenty feet in front of me, glanced momentarily in my direction, then commenced his sonorous and lengthily

dialectical answer by correcting me. His first words, uttered in a thick German accent, have been engraved in my brain for almost forty years: "Zee resoorekshun eez note a meet, eet eez a shtoree."

45. H. Richard Niebuhr, "The Anachronism of Jonathan Edwards," in William Stacy Johnson, ed., *Theology, History, and Culture* (1958; New Haven: Yale Univ. Press, 1996), pp. 127–30, 132. My summary is adapted from my discussion of Niebuhr in "The Culture of Love in America, 1830s–1950s," in Susan L. Mizruchi, ed., *Religion and Cultural Studies* (Princeton: Princeton Univ. Press, 2001), pp. 130–32.

46. H. Richard Niebuhr, *Christ and Culture* (1951; San Francisco: HarperSanFrancisco, 1996), pp. 68–71, 76.

47. Niebuhr, *Christ and Culture,* pp. 104, 109.

48. William James, "On a Certain Blindness in Human Beings," in James, *Writings, 1878–1899* (New York: Library of America, 1992), p. 860 (last paragraph of essay).

49. James, "On a Certain Blindness in Human Beings," p. 847 (paragraph 21 of essay).

50. Robert Kinloch Massie, "Called to Something New," a sermon preached for the baptism of Oliver Sargent Fox at St. James's Episcopal Church, Cambridge, Nov. 2, 2003, sermon typescript, p. 4 (in author's possession).

51. "8 Compelling Reasons Why: Christ Is Coming Very Soon!" advertisement in the *Los Angeles Times,* Nov. 7, 2003, p. B13. On the history of end-time thinking in America, see Paul Boyer, *When Time Shall Be No More: Prophecy Belief in Modern American Culture* (Cambridge: Harvard Univ. Press, 1992). To catch the flavor of apocalyptic thinking, read the phenomenal 1970 best-seller *The Late Great Planet Earth,* by Hal Lindsey. Four years after it was published, four million copies were in print.

52. ABC *Primetime Monday,* "Jesus, Mary, and Da Vinci," Nov. 3, 2003. Telling critiques of Brown's historical theorizing are found in Margaret M. Mitchell, "Cracking the Da Vinci Code," *Sightings* (the online journal of the Martin Marty Center at the University of Chicago Divinity School), Sept. 24, 2003, and Bruce Boucher, "Does 'The Da Vinci Code' Crack Leonardo?" *New York Times,* Aug. 3, 2003, p. B26.

53. On Mary Magdalene, the essential starting point is now the just-released *Gospel of Mary Magdala: Jesus and the First Woman Apostle* by Karen L. King (Santa Rosa, CA: Polebridge Press, 2003). See also the landmark work of two decades ago, Elisabeth Schüssler Fiorenza, *In Memory of Her: A Feminist Theological Reconstruction of Christian Origins* (1983; New York: Crossroad, 1987), along with the several important books by Elaine Pagels on early Christianity, including *The Gnostic Gospels* (New York: Random House, 1979) and *Beyond Belief: The Secret Gospel of Thomas* (New York: Random House, 2003).

EPILOGUE

1. Mother Marie de l'Incarnation, "Of the Life and Death of Mother Marie de St. Joseph," *Jesuit Relations,* 38:109–17.

ACKNOWLEDGMENTS

Hail to all the librarians, who preserve and deliver the documents. The staff of the American Antiquarian Society (AAS) was my staff and support during a Mellon Fellowship year in 2000–2001. Gigi Barnhill, Nancy Burkett, Joanne Chaison, Ellen Dunlap, John Hench, Marie Lamoureux, Caroline Sloat, and Laura Wasowicz repeatedly came up with ideas as well as materials. I learned in researching this book why historians of colonial America and of the early-nineteenth-century United States cannot do without the AAS. In addition to the excellence of the collection and the wisdom of the staff, an international stream of historians passes through all year long. Fellow-fellow Cathy Corman introduced me to the thorny field of European-Indian contact, where this history begins. I was also the recipient of a National Endowment for the Humanities Summer Stipend and several University of Southern California research grants that permitted travel to other libraries, especially Harvard University's Widener and Divinity School collections.

My agent and friend Jill Kneerim is master of the gentle tweak. This book owes a great deal to the critical eye she cast upon its earliest textual manifestations, as it does to her patience and interest ever since. She got me to HarperSanFrancisco, where John Loudon, Kris Ashley, Terri Leonard, Roger Freet, and Mark Tauber have exhibited enthusiasm for the topic along with care for the product. I especially appreciate their eagerness to include color as well as black-and-white images. I can only marvel at the skill of my copyeditor,

Kathy Reigstad, who knows the English language better than I knew it could be known.

Many friends and colleagues have helped me sharpen or broaden my ideas. My thanks to Joyce Appleby, Casey Blake, Cheryl Boots, Paul Boyer, Jeannie Cooper Carson, David Brion Davis, Maia Davis, Jeanne Follansbee-Quinn, Tom Fox, Marie Griffith, David Hall, David Hollinger, James Johnson, Paula Kane, James Kloppenberg, Jackson Lears, John McGreevy, Lydia Moland, Robert Orsi, Jennifer Ratner-Rosenhagen, Dana Robert, Leigh Schmidt, John Staudenmeier, Robert Westbrook, and Christopher Wilson.

Elizabeth Battelle Clark and I spent a number of Sundays in the mid-1990s hunting through the Boston area for an Episcopal church that combined singing, preaching, and the sacraments with a keen sense of women's equality. She taught me a lot over many years about American religious history, and she showed me how deep the love of Jesus can run.

Conversations with Steve Prothero, my former colleague at Boston University and my present co-inquirer into the history of Jesus in America, always confirmed the fascination of this topic. We could never quite believe how little had been written directly about it, despite the mushrooming appeal of American religious history. We kept our projects separate, but benefited enormously from our common interest in the overlapping secular and religious uses of Jesus in America. His *American Jesus: How the Son of God Became a National Icon* (New York: Farrar, Straus, Giroux) will appear shortly before this book does.

Kathi Kern went far out of her way to supply me with historical and contemporary images of Jesus. Udo Hebel of the University of Regensburg set up talks for me in Halle and Munich as well as Regensburg. Jennifer Ratner-Rosenhagen accompanied me on my tour of Germany, and she and Ulrich Rosenhagen introduced me to some of the complexities of Jesus in the land of Luther. Alexis McCrossen organized a lecture for me at Southern Methodist University in Dallas and took me on Sunday morning to the Potter's

House to hear T. D. Jakes. Ellen Skerrett arranged a day-long tour of secular and religious sites in Chicago: most notably, for the subject of this book, Jane Addams's Hull House and the magnificently restored Holy Family Church. Ellen gave me a new feel for the intersecting immigrant cultures of Chicago, where Jesus took on an astonishing range of identities. I also wish to thank audiences at the American Antiquarian Society, the University of California at Irvine, the University of Rochester, and the University of Southern California for their critical questions and comments. I am grateful to Jack Miles, dean of all cultural interpreters of Jesus, for commenting on the paper I gave at USC.

Cathy Corman, David Hall, Peter Mancall, and Vanessa Schwartz read chapters of the manuscript on subjects about which they know a lot more than I do, and gave me generous leads and suggestions. Cathy Corman, Jeanne Follansbee-Quinn, Christopher Fox, Jonathan Hansen, and Lori Kenschaft took on the Promethean job of reading and commenting on the whole manuscript. I thank them for their devotion to that work and even more for their honesty.

To those readers who find typos or other mistakes that eluded my efforts to stamp them out: I would appreciate your sending corrections to me at rfox@usc.edu.

Elizabeth, thank you for these three things and more: for the subtitle; for thinking this book through with me, start to finish; for teaching me what Emily Dickinson meant when she wrote, "The brain is just the weight of God / For, lift them, pound for pound, / And they will differ, if they do, / As syllable from sound."

Late in life my father liked to imagine he would write a book about Jesus. He had the enthusiasm but lacked the obsessive gene that produces books. This volume is far from the kind of book he would have written about Jesus, but he is ultimately responsible for it. While pondering his impact on me, and hence on this book, I came across the letter William James wrote to his father from Europe in 1882, as Henry James, Sr., lay ill in Massachusetts, approaching death. "In that mysterious gulf of the past into which the present soon will fall and go back and back," William wrote, "yours is still for me the central figure. All my intellectual life I derive from you; and though we have often seemed at odds in the expression thereof, I'm sure there's a harmony somewhere, and that our strivings will combine. What my debt to you is goes beyond all my power of estimating—so early, so penetrating and so constant has been the influence." William's letter didn't arrive in time for his father to read it, but he didn't need to read it to know what was in his son's heart. Nor does my father need to read this book to know where it comes from, or to know that it's for him.

POSTSCRIPT TO THE PAPERBACK
EDITION OF JESUS IN AMERICA

When I finished this book on Christmas Day 2003 the prerelease furor over Mel Gibson's *The Passion of the Christ* was reaching its peak. No one foresaw the gargantuan commercial success that would greet the film two months later. But the frenzied atmosphere already suggested that in his guise as an American cultural hero Jesus was primed for yet another rebirth. In the sixteenth and seventeenth centuries Christ had received his first American incarnations as the conqueror, healer, martyr, and civilizer. In the eighteenth century he had been reborn as the "personal savior" eager to befriend those who came to him in faith. In the nineteenth and twentieth centuries he had been hoisted aloft by anti-slavery and pro-slavery forces, defenders of labor and capital, and assorted visionaries preaching doom, justice, or tranquility. The most creative Jesus innovators—secular and religious—had created new images of Christ to help change American society but also to promote authentic loyalty to Jesus. At the start of the twenty-first century Mel Gibson showed once again that Jesus is always ripe for a new birth as social advocate and religious symbol.*

---

* The main text of this book has been revised in three places to accommodate the release in February 2004 of *The Passion of the Christ*: pp. 26–27, 382–83, and 461 (n. 32). A number of other passages have been silently amended to correct minor factual errors or to improve expression. My thanks to those who suggested the changes.

Late-twentieth-century "culture wars" over abortion, evolution, multiculturalism, women's rights, and homosexuality had already forged an alliance between Protestant and Catholic conservatives, who had overcome their religious differences to defend "traditional values." Until Mel Gibson came along, no one had tried to revive a very traditional Catholic Jesus—the brutalized suffering servant—to represent this new Protestant-Catholic, anti-liberal gathering. Gibson made it happen. He showed that Catholic and Protestant conservatives could join hands around a visual image of Jesus that Protestants of all persuasions had earlier reviled. They had abhorred it because it came not from the Bible but from the medieval Stations of the Cross: the bleeding savior dragging himself up the hill to Calvary, comforted only by the presence of such Catholic favorites as the Virgin Mary, Veronica, and Simon of Cyrene (see p. 4). Evangelical Protestant conservatives embraced *The Passion of the Christ* because they could use the power of Hollywood—in the person of megastar Mel Gibson—to vanquish the "Hollywood" secular humanism they detested, and to recharge the faith of their churches. The Catholic Gibson permitted Protestant evangelicals to revive revivalism for the electronic age.

At a prerelease screening of *The Passion of the Christ* in Indianapolis on February 5, 2004, for the Christian Booksellers Association, Gibson's publicity director explained how the alliance began. Rebuffed by Hollywood studios, Gibson had feared in 2003 that his nearly completed film might never be distributed. So he flew to Colorado Springs to meet about one hundred evangelical Protestant leaders gathered at the headquarters of Focus on the Family. Those leaders, representing many denominations, realized that Gibson's hat-in-hands visit offered a once-in-a-lifetime chance for evangelical revival and outreach. Their enthusiasm went beyond opportunism. They promised Gibson they would pack their congregations into cineplexes because he embodied their deepest animating belief: a man long lost to God (by his own well-publicized report) had now been found. The new birth in Christ, spelled out in the third chapter of John's Gospel, had rescued one more sinner. Gibson had risen in evangelical Protestants' eyes by offering them his celebrity, endorsing their battle for a reborn America, and reaffirming Christ as his redeemer.

Gibson made it somewhat easier for Protestants to embrace his Catholic Jesus by making clear how thoroughly the present-day ethos of the official Catholic Church disgusted him. *The Passion of the Christ* celebrates the traditional piety in which he and most other middle-aged Catholics grew up. Gibson, at forty-nine, is a youngster among those diehards who give their loyalty not to contemporary Catholicism, but to the old Church that cherished the Latin Mass and the venerable prayers dwelling on the wounds of Christ and his saints. Just as Dan Brown's imagined Catholic Church in *The Da Vinci Code* suppressed the real story of Mary Magdalene's marriage to Jesus, and of their child, Sarah, so Gibson's modern Church covered up the extreme physical suffering of the crucified Lord and replaced it with the easygoing amiability of a liberal, nonjudgmental Jesus. This is the Jesus satirized flawlessly in Kevin Smith's 1999 film *Dogma,* in which George Carlin (playing Roman Catholic Cardinal "Ignatius Glick") unveils the Catholic Church's new "Buddy Christ"—a flashy marketing icon who winks, grins, and pumps a hearty thumbs-up.

Gibson's *Passion* appeals to many conservatives across the religious spectrum because he reaffirms the sacrificial, redemptive death of Jesus rather than dwelling on his life as teacher, preacher, or reformer. Unlike Martin Scorsese's Jesus in *The Last Temptation of Christ* or Tim Rice's in *Jesus Christ Superstar,* Gibson's savior reveals no individual or social aspirations at all. He inhabits a human body but expresses no ordinary human desires or befuddlements. *The Passion of the Christ* retaliates against the liberal bent of both earlier films, in which Jesus experiences a full range of adult emotions. In those earlier depictions he suffers severe psychic turmoil and turns to Judas and Mary Magdalene for companionship and friendship. Gibson reverts to the old Catholic preference for a diabolical Judas, a redeemed-prostitute Mary Magdalene sitting piously in the shadows, and a holy mother with whom Christ maintains his single deep emotional tie. This Jesus exhibits no adult confusion or disarray. For Gibson, who has spoken eloquently about his own battles with adult addiction and disorientation, Jesus offers preemptive victory over both afflictions.

What a shame that Gibson did not make his Jesus film, and play Jesus himself, in 1990. That was the year when, at the age of thirty-four (roughly the age of Jesus at the Passion), he actually starred as Hamlet in Franco Zeffirelli's film of Shakespeare's tragedy. Atop Elsinore Castle in Act One, Gibson shows how he could have played a riveting Gethsemane scene. The distraught Hamlet is trying to grapple with his father's overwhelming absence and ghostly presence. Gibson lets a range of filial emotions color and contort his face: the young boy terrorized by abandonment, the adolescent son in turmoil over losing his adult model, and the grown man plagued by indecision about how to avenge his father's murder. The Gibson of 1990 knew how to depict the mental anguish of a human Jesus disheartened and adrift in the garden.

Sadly, in his zeal to expunge the liberal, human Christ of Scorsese and Rice, Gibson missed the chance to counter centuries of Passion Play anti-Semitism. Scorsese had pointed the way forward with his screen vision of an august, respectable Caiaphas. This Caiaphas decides to push for the death of Jesus but does so without villainy or hypocrisy. He is driven by understandable loyalty to the Jewish tradition, in which a person cannot get away with claiming to be God. Instead, Gibson returns to the example of Cecil B. De-Mille, depicting Caiaphas as a malicious evildoer and portraying the Jewish crowd as a swarming mass calling vindictively for the death of Christ (see pp. 315–16 on DeMille). Asked by Abraham Foxman of the Anti-Defamation League and others to remove from his film the so-called blood curse of Matthew 27:25—where "all the [Jewish] people" shout to Pilate, "His blood be on us, and on our children"—Gibson responded with a partial concession: he removed the English subtitle of the curse while keeping the Aramaic version on the soundtrack. But he reverted to DeMille's precedent by conducting Jesus to his end through the venal machinations of Caiaphas, who persuades a reluctant, conscience-stricken Pilate to crucify Christ.

Gibson's decision to whitewash the character of Pilate and make Caiaphas the bad guy is especially noteworthy since it flies in the face of explicit instructions from the Vatican: in light of centuries-old Christian attacks on Jews—attacks partly traceable to Passion Play stereotypes—Catholics must eliminate long-standard anti-Semitic depictions. Gibson flouts those restrictions with a string of egregious fictions, some of them derived from the decidedly postbiblical meditations of the nineteenth-century German nun Anne Catherine Emmerich, author of *The Dolorous Passion of Our Lord Jesus Christ* (1833). Among his most egregious moves is Gibson's putting a scowling Caiaphas at Calvary itself, where he walks beneath the cross and winces at Jesus. Another is Gibson's portraying members of the Jewish guard as tossing Jesus—whom they are leading from Gethsemane to his nighttime rendezvous with Jewish officials—off a footbridge so that he dangles by his chains.

True, Gibson's Roman soldiers inflict far more pain on Jesus than the Jewish guard, both in the scourging scene and at the crucifixion. The Roman ogres at the scourging deliver a devastating (and wholly nonbiblical) sequence of horrendous lashings, in which Christ's flesh is not just gashed, but literally ripped from his back. When Roman soldiers begin crucifying him on Calvary, they overturn the horizontal cross on the ground so that Jesus hangs, face to the dirt, from the nails in his hands and feet. Gibson certainly did emphasize Roman brutality, thanks to his uncanny knack—amply demonstrated in his earlier film *Braveheart* (1995)—for devising new ways to show old weapons piercing human flesh. He has also made clear that he considers everyone, then and now, responsible for the death of Christ, and that he harbors no anti-Semitic beliefs or intentions. In *The Passion of the Christ* he claims to be imagining scenes that accord with the overall sense of the gospels, which certainly do contain many passages critical of "the Jews" and their role in the death of Jesus. But neither Gibson nor anyone else can legitimately appeal to the authority of particular gospel passages unless he approaches them with the aid of modern scholarship, a support that Gibson has rejected. And the issue of anti-Semitism in the film can be settled only by examining his actual screen choices, not by debating his conscious intentions or beliefs. *The Passion of the Christ* exaggerates the responsibility and villainy of Caiaphas and minimizes the responsibility and (historically documented) maliciousness of Pontius Pilate. Good intentions offer no defense against the condemnation that these decisions deserve in the wake of the twentieth-century events and research underlying current Vatican guidelines.

Some readers of this book have told me they think it lacks a "big picture" backdrop for the parade of individual stories that populate its pages. In my view the individual voices constitute the big picture in their own right, along with the recurrent themes and motifs that the stories carry forward across centuries: the imitation of Christ, the new birth, the Ten Virgins and the Good Samaritan, the quest for pure origins and ever-new departures, the power of sin and routine versus the promise of redemption and empowerment, the necessity and the danger of making images, verbal or visual, of Christ. The drama of Jesus in America lies in his durability and his adaptability. Old incarnations of Christ may be buried for decades or centuries, but as Mel Gibson makes abundantly clear, they are never quite dead. Whatever one may think of *The Passion of the Christ*, one must signal the genius of a twenty-first-century filmmaker capable of reviving the seventeenth-century vision of Jean de Brébeuf.

For those formed, as Gibson and I were, before the era of the Second Vatican Council, Brébeuf's sense of Jesus as a limp, tortured body given up for God—a savior put on earth to be imitated in life and death—posed a provocative and fearsome challenge. Would we be ready to endure physical suffering with the equanimity evidenced by Jesus? Would we know, at the end, how to follow his lead? Brébeuf and his fellow Jesuits hoped they would have the opportunity to find out. This book begins with my individual childhood voice, and ends with my teenaged recollection of Michael Peterson, who I suspect confronted Brébeuf's test when he met his own end. My story and Michael's illustrate the book's central contention: Jesus has been plowed into American history as a momentous cultural force because so many Americans for so many centuries have experienced such decisive encounters with him. My goal has been to hear those voices, the secular ones as much as the religious ones, and to register their passion as well as their diversity.

Venice, California
January 2005

INDEX